THE CORROSION OF MEDICINE

Can the Profession Reclaim Its Moral Legacy?

John Geyman, MD

Common Courage Press   Monroe, Maine

Copyright 2008 © by John Geyman

All rights reserved
Cover design by Bruce Conway
Interior graphics by Bruce Conway
back cover by Erica Bjerning
author photo Joseph (Bill) Reynolds, M.D.

paper 13-digit ISBN: 978-1-56751-384-4
10-digit ISBN: 1-56751-384-0

Library of Congress Cataloging-in-Publication Data is available from
publisher on request.

Common Courage Press
P.O. Box 702
121 Red Barn Road
Monroe, ME 04951

207-525-0900
fax: 207-525-3068

www.commoncouragepress.com
info@commoncouragepress.com

Printed in Canada
First printing

DEDICATION

For the hundreds of thousands of physicians and health professionals struggling to retain their idealism and professionalism against the tide of commercialism and market forces, and for the many millions of our patients. Their future—and ours—depends on working together to reform the health care system.

CONTENTS

Tables and Figures

ACKNOWLEDGMENTS

The support and encouragement of many colleagues have made this book possible. I am indebted to these colleagues for their constructive comments and suggestions through their peer review of selected chapters:

- Howard Brody, MD, PhD, Director, Institute for the Medical Humanities, University of Texas Medical Branch, Galveston

- Richard Deyo, MD, MPH, Professor of Medicine and Co-Director of the Center for Cost and Outcome Research, University of Washington, Seattle

- Larry Green, MD, Robert Graham Center for Policy Studies in Family Practice and Primary Care, Washington, D.C.

- Albert Jonsen, PhD, bioethicist and former Chairman of the Department of Medical History and Ethics at the University of Washington, Seattle

- Ida Hellander, MD, Executive Director of Physicians for a National Health Program (PNHP), Chicago

- Don McCanne, MD, past President of Physicians for a National Health Program and PNHP Senior Health Policy Fellow

- Fitzhugh Mullan, MD, Professor of Medicine and Health Policy at the George Washington University, Washington, D.C.

- Charles North, MD, Clinical Director, Albuquerque Service Unit, Indian Health Service

- John Nyman, PhD, Professor of Health Services Research and Policy, University of Minnesota

- William Phillips, MD, MPH, Clinical Professor of Family Medicine, University of Washington, Seattle

- Jack Rodnick, MD, Professor and former Chairman, Department of Family and Community Medicine, University of California, San Francisco

- Roger Rosenblatt, MD, MPH, Professor of Family Medicine, University of Washington, Seattle

- John Saultz, Professor and Chairman, Department of Family Medicine, Oregon Health and Science University

- Joseph Scherger, MD, MPH, Professor of Family and Preventive Medicine, University of California San Diego

Many sources of reference materials were especially helpful as this project progressed, especially reports from the Kaiser Family Foundation, the Commonwealth Fund, Public Citizen, the National Academy of Social Insurance, the Medicare Rights Center, the Medicare Payment Advisory Commission (MEDPAC), the Centers for Medicare-Medicaid Services (CMS), and the General Accounting Office (GAO). Thanks are also due to the many publishers and journals which granted permission to reprint or adapt materials as extensively cited throughout the book.

As with my previous books, Virginia Gessner, my administrative assistant for over 30 years, skillfully converted handwritten manuscript through many drafts to final copy. Bruce Conway of Illumina Publishing, Friday Harbor, Washington, created the cover design and all graphics.

Finally, I am grateful to Greg Bates, President of Common Courage Press for his encouragement and editorial expertise throughout the project. His insightful suggestions have made this a better book. And most important of all, this book could not have been completed without the support of Gene, my lovely wife and soulmate of 51 years. It is now even possible that she will see me reduce the stacks and clean up my home office.

Fix the System with Medicare for All

By Marcia Angell

The following is an article I wrote for the Boston Globe *(January 29, 2007). In it I make the case that the only way to provide universal health care at a cost we can afford is to expand the Medicare program to cover everyone. What I didn't address in that short piece is the need for physicians to change their behavior. As public demand grows for thoroughgoing reform of our disastrous system, physicians must play a constructive role. No reform can work if they continue to be part of the problem, not the solution. It is for this reason that I am enthusiastic about Dr. Geyman's fine new book. He shows clearly that physicians are central to any health system, and offers a powerful argument that they need to reclaim their moral commitment to put patients' needs first.*

The greatest source of insecurity for many Americans is the soaring cost of health care. Leaving jobs can mean losing health insurance, and even when insurance is offered, many workers turn it down because they can't afford their growing share of the premiums.

Businesses are having trouble, too. Those that provide good health benefits see more of their revenues siphoned off by the health insurance industry, with a resulting loss of competitiveness (General Motors spends far more on health benefits than Toyota).

Insurance is not the same thing as health care—not by a long shot. Private insurers maximize profits mainly by limiting benefits or by not covering people with health problems. The United States is the only advanced country in the world with a health care system based on avoiding sick people.

It's not surprising, then, that health care reform is at the top of the political agenda. Most current proposals de-couple health benefits from employment and encourage individuals to buy their own insurance. The fact that they were ever coupled is a historical accident; there is no logical reason for it. Yet, employment-based insurance has been the only practical option for people not old enough for Medicare or poor enough for Medicaid, since the individual insurance market is notoriously treacherous.

In his State of the Union address, President Bush proposed tax deductions for individuals who venture into that market and buy insurance on their own. Family premiums above $15,000 and single premiums above $7,500 would be taxed. This is a gesture, not a plan. It is just one more example of the conceit, shared by many on the right, that nearly any problem can be solved by jiggering the tax code. In fact, many of the uninsured don't pay taxes at all, and many more would find their small tax relief greatly outweighed by the price of insurance.

More serious proposals are coming from the states, with Massachusetts in the lead. These aim for universal coverage by requiring uninsured individuals to purchase health insurance, under pain of—you guessed it—tax penalties, with state subsidies for the poor and near poor. In Massachusetts, there will be a token contribution by employers who don't provide health benefits, but most of the cost will be borne by individuals. A new state agency, the Commonwealth Health Insurance Connector, is charged with seeing that insurers offer adequate benefit packages at reasonable premiums.

Though well-intentioned, plans like these all have the same fatal flaw: They offer no workable mechanism to control costs, mainly because they leave the private insurance industry in place. Yet, soaring costs are the fundamental problem; lack of coverage follows from that. Already the Massachusetts Connector is having difficulty holding premiums down to the levels forecast when the plan was enacted. Even if they are held down at the start, there is little to stop insurers from raising them afterward, shrinking benefits, or both. It will take a large and costly bureaucracy to ride herd on all the ways to game this system. Perhaps the biggest risk is that failure will give universal care a bad name, just as the failure of the Clinton plan did 13 years ago. (That plan, too, made the mistake of giving the private insurance industry a central role.)

We need to change the system completely and get the insurance industry, as well as employers, out of it. Private insurance companies offer little of value, yet skim off 15 to 25 percent of the health care dollar for profits and overhead. It would make much more sense to extend Medicare to everyone. That could be done gradually by dropping the eligibility age a decade at a time, while phasing out the insurance companies. The loss of insurance jobs would probably be more than offset by job gains in other industries no longer saddled with health costs.

Medicare is not perfect, but its problems are readily fixed. It is far more efficient than private insurance, with overhead of less than 4 percent, and since it is administered by a single public agency, controlling costs would be possible. Unlike private insurers, it cannot select whom to cover or deny care to those who need it most.

It is time to stop tinkering at the margins. Medicare for all is the only reform that has a prayer of providing universal coverage while containing costs.

Dr. Marcia Angell is a senior lecturer at Harvard Medical School and former editor-in-chief of the *New England Journal of Medicine.*

PREFACE

"in the context of the problems that now beset medicine, there will be few answers without development of bold new ways of thinking about the relationships between physicians and patients and between the profession and the industry of medicine."

Troyan Brennan,
Professor of Health Policy and Management
at Harvard University's School of Public Health.[1]

We all know that the health care "system" in the U.S. is not just in disarray, but broken. Daily reports in the media tell us about the growing number of uninsured and underinsured; the increasing problems of access, cost, and quality; corporate mergers and fraud in what has become an enormous medical-industrial complex. A sea change has occurred over the past 30 years, which has taken the medical profession and health care from a cottage industry to a complex and chaotic industry largely driven by business goals of profitability and financial bottom lines, an agenda increasingly driven by the needs of investors. Health care has been reduced to a commodity for sale on an open market. Long-established traditions of public service and professionalism have been compromised by this transformation, and the nation's safety net of providers and facilities is now being stressed to the breaking point.

A growing body of literature over the last ten years has called attention to a wide range of conflicts of interest between many physicians and industry, a decline in public trust of the medical profession, decrease in physicians' clinical autonomy, and demoralization within the profession. A number of excellent books have recently been published addressing one or another aspect of these problems, including *Medicine, Money & Morals*: *Physicians' Conflicts of Interest* (Marc Rodwin, 1993),[2] *Some Choice: Law, Medicine and the Market* (George Annas, 1998),[3] *The Truth about the Drug Companies: How They Deceive Us and What We Can Do About It* (Marcia Angell, 2004),[4] *Overdo$ed America: The Broken Promise of American Medicine* (John Abramson, 2004),[5] and *On The Take: How Medicine's Complicity with Big Business Can Endanger Your Health* (Jerome Kassirer, 2005).[6]

As these problems worsen, we hear a myriad of ideas to "fix" the system. Most are incremental proposals aimed to serve the interests of the private marketplace, especially by shifting more costs to patients and their families ("consumers" in today's jargon). Largely missing from the public debate are more fundamental questions, such as what are the goals of medicine and whose interests should the health care system serve?

A Colloquium on Commercialism in Medicine was held in San Francisco in 2005, involving leading bioethicists from around the country and sponsored by the Program in Medicine and Human Values at California Pacific Medical Center. In his closing remarks, Dr. William Andereck, a Co-Director of that program, made the case for a close look at money and medicine:

> *"There is no issue of such central social and existential importance about which there exists more hypocrisy and anxious confusion than the question of our relation to money. In the modern commodified world, the money factor enters into nearly every corner and pocket of human life, and to speak frankly and openly about it remains what has been called "the last great taboo." It is just this "last taboo" that now lies close to the heart of the crisis in medicine. Is the influence of money eroding the quality and the very meaning of the practice of medicine? If so, to what extent? And why? And what must be done to ameliorate the situation? How to maintain the primacy of the values and ideals that have traditionally defined medicine as a calling and profession in the face of the increasing pressures of commercialism?"[7]*

To answer these vital questions, we need to understand the history of how we got here. We need to assess how far we have slid from our ethical heritage as a profession. And we need to consider how our profession can reclaim its moral legacy and lead toward reform of our failing health care system. My goal here is not to denigrate my profession or its organizations, but to better understand the changes which have occurred over the last 50 years. I have always felt medicine to be a noble calling with a proud tradition of service, and would enter our profession just as enthusiastically today as when starting medical school 50 years ago.

Why does medicine's moral legacy matter? Many assume that in this richest country in the world those without insurance will somehow receive necessary health care. After all, we have Medicare, Medicaid, and other safety net programs, together with hospitals, physicians, and other health professionals providing charity care. Unfortunately, however, many millions of Americans go without basic health services. The costs of care have become increasingly unaffordable for at least one-half of the U.S. population. The Institute of Medicine has found that 8 million uninsured people with chronic disease have increased morbidity and worse outcomes, that 18,000 Americans die prematurely every year, and that the costs of diminished health and shorter life spans amounts to between $65 and $130 billion each year.[8] So how should the medical profession deal with this medical and moral crisis?

My perspective is that of a family physician who started practice in 1963, just two years before the passage of Medicare and Medicaid. With 13 years in rural practice and over 25 years in academic family medicine, together with 30 years as editor of national family practice journals, I have had an opportunity to witness first-hand a major change of commercialization of health care. Medicine for me has been a fulfilling and challenging career, a blend between art and science, and a privilege to take part in the lives of patients and their families and on occasion to make a difference. Moreover, as a matter of further disclosure, I am neither a socialist nor a revolutionary but a lifelong Republican until recent years (now an Independent). But I have come to believe, on the basis of evidence presented throughout this book, that the deregulated private health care marketplace often puts profits ahead of patient care, and that incremental "reforms" of the market cannot resolve system problems of access, cost, quality, and equity. I have also come to believe that a single-payer system of national health insurance (NHI or Medicare for All), coupled with a private delivery system, is the only hope for lasting health care reform in this country. Of all reform alternatives before us, NHI will best serve the public interest while also allowing the medical profession to concentrate on its primary purpose—service through patient care—with less distractions from the many conflicts of interest which pervade today's market-based system. The accompanying editorial by Dr. Marcia Angell, former Editor of the *New England Journal of Medicine,* provides a succinct and compelling case for this kind of fundamental reform.

This is a logical sequel to my previous books on health care. The first *Health Care in America: Can Our Ailing System Be Healed?* dealt with the overall health care system,[8] followed by *The Corporate Transformation of Health Care: Can The Public Interest Still Be Served?,*[9] *Falling Through The Safety Net: Americans Without Health Insurance,*[10] and most recently, *Shredding the Social Contract: The Privatization of Medicare.*[11] To complete this picture comes this fifth book, focusing on the renewal of the ethics of the medical profession and its social contract. I am neither an ethicist nor an economist, but a physician who has been involved on the front lines of this debate, a witness and a participant in the ethical choices described here.

In this effort, I will draw from a rich literature base in medical history, ethics, health economics, and health policy. The book is organized in four parts. Part I provides historical background for medicine as a moral enterprise, rise of the medical industrial complex, and commercialization of the health care system. Part II describes the new medical marketplace and the impacts of the business ethic on health care. Part III examines how, and to what extent, the medical profession has been complicit with these changes. Part IV reconsiders the goals of medicine and ways in which the profession can renew itself in the public interest and lead toward health care reform. Since physicians play a central role throughout the health care system and order almost all services provided by health care professionals, this discussion has everything to do with future directions of the entire health care system.

I write for physicians (including residents and medical students in training); other health professionals; policy makers; legislators; business and labor groups; citizens' reform groups, and others involved in planning, financing, delivery, or evaluation of health care services. The book should also be of interest to many lay readers concerned about depersonalization of health care in an increasingly unaffordable, bureaucratic and chaotic system.

The changes which are described in this book have been gradual but cumulative, perhaps too slow for many physicians to recognize the full implications of these changes. Recall the example of the proverbial frog in a tank of water—as the water is very slowly brought to boil, the frog accommodates to the rising temperature without realizing any change until it is too late. The changes described in these chapters show how ineffective the medical profession has been in resisting the tide of commercialization of health care and how the business "ethic" of the marketplace threatens the soul of medicine. We cannot escape the growing evidence that our health care system is imploding in our time and that the medical profession so far has been a marginal force in leading toward lasting health care reform. It is long overdue for the profession to reassert its traditional principles and values and to reclaim its moral legacy, and I hope that this book will be a nudge in that direction.

John P. Geyman, MD

PART I

HISTORICAL BACKGROUND

CHAPTER 1

MEDICINE AS A MORAL ENTERPRISE: A LEGACY OF PROMETHEAN GIFTS

"Medicine is at heart a moral enterprise and those who practice it are de facto members of a moral community. We can accept or repudiate that fact, but we cannot ignore it or absolve ourselves of the moral consequences of our choice. We are not a guild, business, trade union, or a political party. If the care of the sick is increasingly treated as a commodity, an investment opportunity, a bureaucrat's power trip, or a political trading chip; the profession bears part of the responsibility."[1]

Edmund Pellegrino, MD
Physician, ethicist and moral philosopher

In past times the medical profession was the dominant force in determining the way in which health care is delivered in America. Those times have long since past, and the profession now finds itself in a crossfire of competing interests and with a much reduced role in shaping health care policy. Its traditional professional ethics are under assault as the system around it has largely adopted a business ethic maximizing profit over service. The profession has also seen a decline in its public trust in recent decades and its moral credibility is being called into question. In order to better understand and deal with what has become a moral crisis in medicine, historical perspective is useful. To see where we are, and where we are headed, history shows that while our technology may be new, and the pace of living may be faster, the dilemmas we face are ancient.

MEDICINE AS A MORAL COMMUNITY

The basic aspects of illness have remained the same over thousands of years regardless of geography or culture. Illness and disease place the sick person in a vulnerable situation needing help without regard to time or place, and raise a threat to the sick individual's personhood.

Medicine as a learned profession has established a long and often noble tradition over many centuries which embraces the well being of the patient as the raison d'être for medicine. Alex Comfort, English physician, gerontologist and writer best known for his 1972 book *The Joy of Sex*, had this to say on the subject over 50 years ago:[2]

> *"It happens that the branch of science in which I was trained, medicine, is the only branch which not only has such a unified ethic but has had it for almost 6,000 years. The idea of the human responsibility of the doctor has been present since medicine was indistinguishable from magic."*

Edmund Pellegrino, a leading medical ethicist at Georgetown University's Center for Clinical Bioethics, has identified four special characteristics of the medical profession which impart moral status to physicians and their profession:[3]

1. *vulnerability and inequality*—when illness strikes, the sick person frequently becomes anxious and fearful, often losing personal freedom and functional capabilities. He or she is then dependent on a caregiver's knowledge and skill to regain health. In the course of treatment, the physician has an obligation to protect the patient from exploitation.

2. *the nature of medical decisions*—the physician's recommendations must go beyond technical expertise in diagnosis and treatment to include respect for the patient's right of self-determination. The physician must render care consistent with the patient's moral values, with the patient's well being the overarching goal in the physician-patient relationship.[4]

3. *the characteristics of medical knowledge*—in the course of medical education, society entrusts physicians with medical knowledge for the care of the sick, thereby requiring a reciprocal responsibility by the profession to make that knowledge available, accessible and scientifically correct.

4. *moral complicity*—since the physician writes almost all the orders that other physicians or health professionals carry out, physicians hold non-transferable responsibility for the patient's well being; if physicians knowingly allow their patients to be exploited or otherwise adversely affected, they are morally complicit in those outcomes unless they try to protect the patient's interests.

All of these dimensions of the physician-patient relationship impose a moral obligation on the physician to act in the best interests of the patient.

There are countless examples of physicians' dedication to the best interests of their patients, as illustrated by these three examples. Several hundred years before Christ, the teachings of Hippocrates (c. 460–377 B.C.) in Greece emphasized the need for physicians to suppress their self-interest in the care of patients.[5] Aristotle (384-322 B.C.) focused on the virtues of the physician to protect the patient's interest, also objecting to the direct linkage of fees to medical practice.[6] During the second century A.D., Galen of Pergamum, a leading physician and philosopher of his time, admonished that *"The physician should be contemptuous of money, interested in his work, self-controlled, and just. Once he is possessed of these basic virtues, he will have all others at his command as well."*[7]

Physicians in more recent times were often of the educated privileged class who were able to bring a sense of noblesse oblige to their patients. Sir William Osler (1849-1919) was the best-known physician in the English-speaking world at the turn of the 20th Century as a diagnostician, clinician and medical educator. Despite his phenomenal success, however, Osler was not independently wealthy in his early years, and throughout his life held that charity was essential to the practice of medicine:

> *"As the practice of medicine is not a business and can never be one, the education of the heart—the moral side of the man—must keep pace with the education of the head. Our fellow creatures cannot be dealt with as man deals in corn and coal; "the human heart by which we live" must control our professional relations."*[8]

And further:

> *"The profession of medicine is distinguished from all others by its singular beneficence. It alone does the work of charity in a Jovian and God-like way, dispensing with free hand truly Promethean gifts."*[9]

There were many times in the history of medicine when members of the profession rose to heroic proportions through self-sacrifice. A good example is the dedicated commitment shown by the apothecaries in England more than 400 years ago. In the early 1600s they were originally general shopkeepers compounding over-the-counter prescriptions. They earned public acceptance to care for the sick during the plague pandemic of 1665, when many physicians fled the community along with their more affluent patients. Because of their continued commitment to patient care and despite the opposition of the Royal College of Physicians in London, they later became fully recognized as general practitioners, with their medical roles and training requirements well established by law.[10]

MEDICAL ETHICS OVER CENTURIES

A series of codes of medical ethics have been promulgated within the medical profession for more than 2,000 years, illustrated by oaths taken by new physicians joining the profession. In the process of "pro-fessing" the oath, the new physician joins the moral community of medicine, united by service beyond self-interest and reflecting such virtues as honesty, compassion, and fidelity to trust.[11] Reviewing how the oaths have changed through history provides an intriguing roadmap to the development of ethical issues, suggesting that some of today's hot battles may be supplanted in importance by new concerns, while others retain a timeless quality.[12]

The Hippocratic Oath is so famous, I am reluctant to repeat it here. Yet a close reading reveals an incredible grasp of the moral dilemmas we face today—from abortion to physician assisted suicide, from sexual abuse to doctor/patient confidentiality, today's dilemmas play out in the shadow of his thinking.

I swear by Apollo Physician and Asclepius and Hygieia and Panaceia and all the gods and goddesses, making them my witnesses, that I will fulfill according to my ability and judgment this oath and this covenant:

To hold him who has taught me this art, as equal to my patients and to live my life in partnership with him, and if he is in need of money to give him a share of mine, and to regard his offspring as equal to my brothers in male lineage and to teach them this art—if they desire to learn it—without fee and covenant; to give a share of precepts and oral instruction and all the other learning to my sons and to the sons of him who has instructed me and to pupils who have signed the covenant and have taken an oath according to the medical law, but to no one else.

I will apply dietetic measures for the benefit of the sick according to my ability and judgment; I will keep them from harm and injustices.

I will neither give a deadly drug to anybody if asked for it, nor will I make a suggestion to this effect. Similarly I will not give to a woman an abortive remedy. In purity and holiness I will guard my life and my art.

I will not use the knife, not even on sufferers from stone, but will withdraw in favor of such men as are engaged in this work.

Whatever houses I may visit, I will come for the benefit of the sick, remaining free of all intentional injustice, of all mischief and in particular of sexual relations with both female and male persons, be they free or slaves.

What I may see or hear in the course of the treatment or even outside of the treatment in regard to the life of men, which on no account one must spread abroad, I will keep to myself holding such things shameful to be spoken about.

If I fulfill this oath and do not violate it, may it be granted to me to enjoy life and art, being honored with fame among all men for all time to come; if I transgress it and swear falsely, may the opposite of all this be my lot.

Translated from the Greek by Edelstein[13]

Another grasp of the dilemmas from a different place and time comes from Maimonides (1135-1204), a physician who was the most important Jewish philosopher of the Middle Ages.

"The eternal providence has appointed me to watch over the life and health of Thy creatures. May the love for my art actuate me at all time; may neither avarice nor miserliness, nor thirst for glory or for a great reputation engage my mind; for the enemies of truth and philanthropy could easily deceive me and make me forgetful of my lofty aim of doing good to Thy children.

May I never see in the patient anything but a fellow creature in pain.

Grant me the strength, time and opportunity always to correct what I have acquired, always to extend its domain, for knowledge is immense and the spirit of man can extend indefinitely to enrich itself daily with new requirements.

Today he can discover his errors of yesterday and tomorrow he can obtain a new light on what he thinks himself sure of today. Oh, God, Thou has appointed me to watch over the life and death of Thy creatures; here am I ready for my vocation and now I turn until my calling."

The Physician's Oath has been taken by physicians in many countries around the world since the mid-20th-Century. It was adopted by the General Assembly of the World Medical Association, Geneva, Switzerland, in September 1948 and amended by the 22nd World Medical Assembly, Sydney, Australia, in August 1968.

At the time of being admitted as a member of the medical profession:

- *I solemnly pledge myself to consecrate my life to the service of humanity;*
- *I will give to my teachers the respect and gratitude which is their due;*
- *I will practice my profession with conscience and dignity; the health of my patient will be my first consideration;*
- *I will maintain by all the means in my power, the honor and the noble traditions of the medical profession; my colleagues will be my brothers;*
- *I will not permit considerations of religion, nationality, race, party politics or social standing to intervene between my duty and my patient;*
- *I will maintain the utmost respect for human life from the time of conception, even under threat, I will not use my medical knowledge contrary to the laws of humanity;*
- *I make these promises solemnly, freely and upon my honor.*

The Hippocratic Oath was revised and updated in 1964 by Louis Lasagna, Academic Dean at Tufts University's School of Medicine, in this form:

- *I swear to fulfill, to the best of my ability and judgment, this covenant:*
- *I will respect the hard-won scientific gains of those physicians in whose steps I walk, and gladly share such knowledge as is mine*

with those who are to follow.

- *I will apply, for the benefit of the sick, all measures which are required, avoiding those twin traps of overtreatment and therapeutic nihilism.*

- *I will remember that there is art to medicine as well as science, and that warmth, sympathy, and understanding may outweigh the surgeon's knife or the chemist's drug.*

- *I will not be ashamed to say "I know not," nor will I fail to call in my colleagues when the skills of another are needed for a patient's recovery.*

- *I will respect the privacy of my patients, for their problems are not disclosed to me that the world may know. Most especially must I tread with care in matters of life and death. If it is given me to save a life, all thanks. But it may also be within my power to take a life; this awesome responsibility must be faced with great humbleness and awareness of my own frailty. Above all, I must not play at God.*

- *I will remember that I do not treat a fever chart, a cancerous growth, but a sick human being, whose illness may affect the person's family and economic stability. My responsibility includes these related problems, if I am to care adequately for the sick.*

- *I will prevent disease whenever I can, for prevention is preferable to cure.*

- *I will remember that I remain a member of society, with special obligations to my fellow human beings, those sound of mind and body as well as the infirm.*

- *If I do not violate this oath, may I enjoy life and art, respected while I live and remembered with affection thereafter. May I always act so as to preserve the finest traditions of my calling and may I long experience the joy of healing those who seek my help.*

There is a common theme of beneficence running through all of these oaths which transcend culture, religion, and historical time. There is also an underlying theme, perhaps unique to the medical profession, not just "be kind" but also an explicit obligation of philanthropy: Physicians are charged with helping, not just avoiding immoral choices. Non-Christian physicians in the ancient world and Middle Ages, including Egyptian, Hebrew, Muslim, Indian, and Chinese, espoused similar ethical precepts binding them together in the moral community of medicine.[14]

Today nearly all U.S. medical schools administer some kind of oath at their annual commencement exercises for new graduates. However, there are many variations from one school to another as they struggle to make their oaths more relevant to today's world.[15] A 1993 study showed that only 14 percent of U.S. and Canadian medical schools invoked a deity in these oaths, while the great majority of others omitted reference to two especially controversial issues of our times—abortion and physician assisted suicide.[16] Another long discarded provision of the original Hippocratic oath—"never to use the knife, not even on sufferers from the stone" was discarded long ago as modern surgery became widely practiced.

There can be no question that oaths professed by medical professionals today need to be further updated to become more relevant to ethical issues in our complex, commercially oriented market based system with myriad new opportunities for financial conflicts of interest among physicians. Many critics now consider the Hippocratic oath irrelevant to our times and view it as the "Hippocritic" oath. We also need to recognize that these oaths are ethically problematic as ceremonial proclamations by physicians without input from the public or enough specificity to provide concrete ethical guidance.[17] Although these oaths continue to be powerful reminders to physicians of their legacy to work for a higher good than their own self-interest, they may have little bearing on how many physicians behave in everyday practice. What happens to a medical student, a physician, and a profession that makes choices antithetical to these values? It is a major goal of this book to show how the medical industrial complex operates, and how varied physicians' conflicts of interest have become.

As Dr. Albert Jonsen, bioethicist and former chairperson of the University of Washington's Department of Medical History and Ethics, makes clear in his excellent book *A Short History of Medical Ethics,* medical ethics has a long and complex history in both Western and Eastern cultures. Although certain themes emerge over that history, there have been marked variations from time to time and from one culture to another. Most earlier writings on medical ethics were written by physicians themselves without input from others outside of medicine. Ambiguity permeates many ethical pronouncements, and the field does not lend itself to simplification. Jonsen identifies three different domains of medical ethics—*decorum* (i.e., outward behavior displaying inner virtues, such as respectfulness), *deontology* (referring to duty or obligations of what physicians ought to do), and *politic ethics* (i.e., principles and values which contribute to success of the medical profession itself).[18] Politic ethics has gained importance in more recent years as medical practice has become more commercialized. As Jonsen observes:

> *"The politic ethics of the profession is intrinsically ambiguous: it can refer either to the expedient, self-serving adaptation of the profession to public expectations or to the internalized morality of practitioners who really believe that, as physicians, they are held to a high standard of public accountability for their professional behavior."*[19]

An important change in medical ethics has taken place since the 1960s with the development of *bioethics*. During a time of moral questioning and introspection over such issues as civil rights, racism (e.g., the Tuskegee syphilis experiments among blacks), and the Vietnam War, it became acknowledged that the many moral questions in medicine require the input of other disciplines outside of medicine, such as philosophy, theology, sociology, and the law. New concepts became part of the medical ethics lexicon (such as autonomy of patients and social justice), new questions were asked about the goals of medicine and the role of medical technology, and many established ethical principles of medicine were reformulated. The U.S. Congress established the National Commission for the Protection of Human Subjects of Biomedical and Behavioral Research in 1974, which was followed in the late 1970s by the President's Commission for the Study of Ethical Problems in Medicine and Biomedical and Behavioral Research. Institutional Review Boards (IRBs) were soon established in research institutions to monitor research and protect the rights of human subjects, and multidisciplinary discussion of ethical issues became the rule. Over the last 40 years, bioethics has become firmly established as an essential adjunct to medical practice and health policy.[20]

There are some interesting parallels between the ethics in business and in medical practice. In business there are four principal parties: customers, owners/investors, employees, and communities. Business is about the delicate balance between competing interests; when one gains the upper hand, others may lose. So too in medicine, where the major interests are patients, owners, employees (including most physicians today), and communities (which may involve both regulation of the industry and a focus on public health issues). All of these practices have competing and overlapping interests. Each has financial and other needs that compete with the needs of other groups, and these play out through the interaction and struggle between the groups.

MEDICINE'S "STRUCTURAL PARADOX"

From time immemorial, there has always been a tension among physicians between altruistic service to patients and entrepreneurial self-interest. Given the special skills of physicians and the urgency of need for care of illness by patients, there have always been many opportunities for physicians to exploit this role at their patients' expense. Jonsen has called this tension the "structural paradox" of the medical profession.[21]

Jonsen and other bioethicists recognize that physicians' altruism and self-interest are not mutually exclusive. On the one hand, there is an obvious need for medical practice to be grounded on sound business practices and business *per se* is not inherently unethical. In addition, Lawrence McCullough, Professor of Medicine and Medical Ethics at Baylor College of Medicine, reminds us that there are many areas of legitimate self-interest that physicians deserve, such as sufficient time to study, reflect and learn; fulfillment of obligations to family and friends; and pursuit of other meaningful balancing activities in their lives.[22] On the other hand, the professional roles of physicians as healers and moral agents require them to put the interests and needs of their patients above their own self-interest.

Public anger over high physician fees has surfaced on many occasions and places over the years, long predating current anger over costs of health care.[23] In this country, an editorialist in the 1850s, reacting to rapid increases in physician fees, warned that

> "if they go on for thirty more years at the rate they have been— the whole community will be little better than slaves of the medical profession."[24]

One medical historian reported that almost all physicians in Virginia charged exorbitant fees during the 17th Century, with average medical bills in York County nearly equaling a laborer's annual income.[25] The colony

of Virginia even passed legislation in 1639 limiting the size of physicians'
fees, expressing concern over the vulnerable position of the sick poor.[26]

In a recent paper on commercialism and professionalism in American
medicine, Dr. Larry Churchill, well-known bioethicist at Vanderbilt
University, describes the power of money in today's health care system as
"hegemony," a word derived from the Greek term for dominance of one
city-state or country over another. Equally applicable to health care, he
makes a convincing case that money and the market-based system have
had a corrupting influence on medical practice, education, and research. Of
further concern, he observes

> *"What is less discussed, through arguably more important, is
> the commercialization of the sensibility of physicians, that is, the way
> in which money tends to dominate not only the measures of "good
> practice" from an organizational viewpoint, reducing them to industrial
> efficiency and profitability, but the way money tends to dominate other
> measures of professional self-understanding and satisfaction."[27]*

As we shall see in the next chapter, American medicine was transformed
over the 20th Century from a cottage industry with a small business,
professional service ethos, to the corporate ethos of a market-based system
dominated by the business "ethic" of profitability. In this transformation,
physicians have been faced with many potential conflict of interest situations.
In the fee-for-service arena, where physicians can augment their income
by providing unnecessary services, Marc Rodwin, Professor at Suffolk
University Law School and author of the 1993 book *Medicine, Money and
Morals: Physicians' Conflicts of Interest*, has identified these common ways
in which physicians can "game the system," often without knowledge of
their colleagues or patients:[28]

1. Paying and receiving kickbacks for referrals.
2. Income earned by doctors for referring patients to medical
   facilities in which they invest (physician self-referral).
3. Income earned by doctors for dispensing drugs, selling medical
   products, and performing ancillary medical services.
4. Payments made by hospitals to doctors to purchase physicians'
   medical practices.
5. Payments made by hospitals to doctors to recruit and bond

physicians.

6.   Gifts given to doctors by medical suppliers.

In the managed care arena, physicians are paid predetermined "capitation" rates based upon the number of patients in their care regardless of what services are actually provided to covered patients. This arrangement raises other conflict-of-interest situations whereby physicians are rewarded by providing *less* care and saving their employers money. These are some of those ways by which physicians can gain income by restricting care:[29]

1.   Hospital incentive pools that return money to primary care physicians when rates and duration of hospitalization are kept down

2.   Specialty pools that return unused referral fees to primary care physicians

3.   Capitation rates for primary care and specialist physicians above costs of their care

4.   End-of-year bonus programs, when costs come in below pre-defined targets regardless of patients' needs.

Physicians now find themselves in a clinical environment with less autonomy and privacy than in traditional practice of earlier times. Jonsen describes this new environment in these graphic terms:

> "The encounter between patient and physician is no longer a private place. It is a cubicle with open walls, surrounded by a crowd of managers, regulators, financiers, producers and lawyers required to manage the flow of money that makes that encounter possible. All of them can look into the encounter and see opportunities for profit or economy. All would like to have a say in how the encounter goes—from the time consumed by it, to the drugs prescribed in it, to the costing out of each of its elements."[30]

PROFESSIONAL ETHICS vs. THE BUSINESS ETHIC: WHICH WILL PREVAIL?

In an address to the New York Academy of Medicine in 1990, Pellegrino pointed out the central dilemma facing medicine as a choice between two opposing moral orders, "one based in the primacy of our ethical obligations to the sick, the other to the primacy of self-interest and the marketplace."[31] The basic, unavoidable question facing the profession, now even more than then, is whether medicine should revise its ethical codes to the ethos of a commercialized marketplace, legitimating self-interest over beneficence[32] or does the profession need to rebuild its legacy of morality-based ethics of service.[33] That is the central question of this book, and as we will see in later chapters, the business ethic of making money as a primary goal has already taken such firm hold on health care that it remains an open question how the profession will respond.

CHAPTER 2

THE RISE OF THE MEDICAL INDUSTRIAL COMPLEX: A SEA CHANGE IN HEALTH CARE

"The rise of a corporate ethos in medical care is already one of the most significant consequences of the changing structure of medical care. It permeates voluntary hospitals, government agencies, and academic thoughts as well as profit-making medical care organizations. Those who talked about "health care planning" in the 1970s now talk about "health care marketing." Everywhere one sees the growth of a kind of marketing mentality in health care. And, indeed, business school graduates are displacing graduates of public health schools, hospital administrators, and even doctors in the top echelons of medical care organizations. The organizational culture of medicine used to be dominated by the ideals of professionalism and voluntarism, which softened the underlying acquisitive activity. The restraint exercised by those ideals now grows weaker. The "health center" of one era is the "profit center" of the next."

Paul Starr
Author of *The Social Transformation of American Medicine: The Rise of a Sovereign Profession and the Making of a Vast Industry*[1]

The above observation by Paul Starr, well-known sociologist at Princeton University who has written one of the most widely acclaimed books on American medicine, was made 25 years ago. It was accurate then and the trends he described are now firmly entrenched in U.S. health care. A sea change has occurred, so that most people now just assume "that's how it is." Markets completely dominate health care, which has now become just another commodity on the open market. Unfortunately, however, as we will see in later chapters, markets in health care do not function as they do elsewhere in the economy, especially with respect to competition and setting of prices.

How did the medical industrial complex gain control of our health care and more than 16 percent of our GDP? What are the political dynamics underlying this revolution? What exactly are the differences between for-profit and not-for-profit services? Finally, how has the medical industrial complex shifted power relationships within the health care system and changed the medical profession itself? These questions drive our discussion in this chapter. In later chapters, we will consider whether patients are better off as a result of these changes.

RISE OF THE MEDICAL-INDUSTRIAL COMPLEX

In his landmark article in 1980, Arnold Relman, an internist and then Editor of *The New England Journal of Medicine*, coined the term "medical-industrial complex" to describe the growing network of for-profit corporations infiltrating the U.S. health care system. This term harkened back to the "military-industrial complex" which Dwight Eisenhower warned us about in the 1950s. Relman warned us that this new medical-industrial complex would "create the problems of overuse and fragmentation of services, overemphasis on technology, and "cream skimming" and it may also exercise undue influence on national health policy."[2] Three years later, the Institute of Medicine (IOM) raised these disturbing and provocative questions about investor-owned corporate health care.[3]

> *"Does the development of for-profit medical care represent a change in the goals pursued by medical professionals and institutions, or is it only a change in the methods by which the traditional goals of service are pursued? Does the growth in for-profit health care represent a decline in the ideals that morally anchored a powerful profession and facilitated necessary patient trust, or does it embody a more honest acknowledgment of realities that have always been present? Or is it a neutral development?"*

A critical turning point in the development of the medical industrial complex came in 1965 with the inauguration of Medicare and Medicaid. Opposed and feared by organized medicine at the time as the potential precursor of socialized medicine, these two public programs ironically hastened the arrival and dominance of corporate health care. Prior to Medicare and Medicaid, most care was either not-for-profit or nominally for-profit. Medicare and Medicaid opened up new opportunities for corporate investment throughout the health care system. By 1998, for-profit corporate ownership was predominant in health maintenance organizations (HMOs) (64%), nursing homes (70%), home care programs (70%), and dialysis centers (85%).[4] These two programs contributed to the growth in corporate health care by allowing corporate takeover of hospitals, nursing homes, rehabilitation centers, home care, clinical laboratories, the drug, medical device and medical supply industries, and the insurance industry.

As corporate health care took off in America, investor-owned facilities and services grew rapidly in hospital chains, emergency rooms, nursing homes, home care, clinical laboratories, dialysis centers, mental health, and health screening programs. Wall Street soon became enamored of profits in health care; in 1979 the net earnings of health care corporations increased by 30 to 35 percent.[5] The U. S. health care industry's corporate profit after taxes increased by more than 100-fold between 1965 and 1990, at a pace almost 20 times greater than profits for all U.S. corporations.[6] Medicare accounted for more than one-half of the revenue for many hospitals by the mid-1980s, while dialysis centers were almost entirely dependent on Medicare and Medicaid funding.[7] The largest investor-owned hospital chain, Hospital Corporation of America (HCA), headquartered in Nashville, Tennessee, is the world's largest hospital company with 190 hospitals and 90 freestanding surgery centers in 23 states, England and Switzerland; according to its Web site it had revenues of over $23 billion in 2005.

Table 2.1 lists the 12 largest publicly held health care corporations in the world. Nine of these 12 are American, including 3 of the 6 largest.[8]

The growth of corporate health care here and abroad is part of similar trends in many other fields, and is aided by laissez faire economic policies and world trade agreements over the last 25 years. The U.S. has played a strong role in the creation of new international institutions in recent years, including the World Trade Organization (WTO), founded in 1995, the General Agreement on Trade in Services (GATS), the World Bank, and the International Monetary Fund (IMF). Corporations embrace globalization as an opportunity to pursue a common market and capital source while avoiding many market restraints previously imposed by national governments. World trade agreements are conducted in secret and frequently bypass laws and regulations of any given country. These world trade agreements emphasize deregulated market approaches to global markets, with privatization of such services as health care, prescription drugs and insurance.[9-11] As a result of these policies, the corporation has emerged as the dominant player on the world's economic stage, even surpassing all but the largest nation-states in size, scope, and power.[12]

As described so well in William Finnegan's 2003 article *The Economics*

TABLE 2.1

THE WORLD's 12 LARGEST PUBLICLY-HELD HEALTH CARE CORPORATIONS 2002

Rank among all World's Corporations, 2002	COMPANY (Country)	MARKET VALUE (in millions U.S. $)
1.	General Electric (U.S.)	$245,254
5.	Pfizer (U.S.)	$179,624
6.	Johnson & Johnson (U.S.)	$160,906
12.	Glaxo-Smith Kline (U.K.)	$117,178
14.	Novartis (Switzerland)	$111,371
15.	Merck (U.S.)	$102,828
36.	Abbott Laboratories (U.S.)	$63,116
38.	Eli Lilly (U.S.)	$62,173
46.	Amgen (U.S.)	$53,300
47.	AstraZeneca (U.K.)	$52,432
49.	Medtronic (U.S.)	$51,171
51.	Pharmacia (U.S.)	$50,163

Source: The global giants: amid market pain, U.S. companies hold greater sway. *Wall Street Journal*, October 14, 2002:R1O.

of Empire (also the author of *Cold New World*), the core tenets of "free trade" in the new global economy include deregulation, privatization, "openness" (to foreign investment and imports), lower taxes, and unrestricted movement of capital. As such, pursuit of these goals under the mantra of market fundamentalism becomes a major part of Empire America since so many of the largest global corporations are American. One by-product of these changes in this country has been the downsizing of our work force as more corporations outsource skilled jobs overseas, leaving lower-level, often non-union jobs behind (e.g., Wal-Mart). Between 1980 and 1995, for example, the total assets of the 100 largest multinational corporations increased by seven-fold while their direct employment dropped by 8 percent. One example of how corporate interests influence health care is the favored treatment of the pharmaceutical industry by government's protection of drug manufacturers' patents of AIDS drugs even as the AIDS epidemic worsens around the world.[13]

James Robertson of the University of California Berkeley, a leading health economist, has described the impacts of these changes on U.S. health care in this way.[14]

> *"In the waning decades of the twentieth century, the basic structures of the health care system began to lose their uniqueness and came to resemble those in the mainstream of the economy. Insurance plans and hospital chains were the first to adopt corporate strategies and structures, integrating vertically and horizontally, seeking economies of scale and scope, financing growth through the stock and bond markets, and competing ever more aggressively on price and service. The tumult of change initially appeared to be passing the physician by, with solo practice and fee-for-service payment remaining the dominant forms of organization and payment. But suddenly in the 1990s the storm of change broke upon the profession, sweeping away the illusion of continuity along with unquestioned clinical autonomy, unconstrained practice income, and unparalleled cultural authority. Now the medical marketplace is a maelstrom of primary care and multi-specialty medical groups, independent practice associations and single-specialty networks, physician practice management firms and physician-hospital systems, open-access provider panels and tightly integrated prepaid plans. The emerging forms of physician organization vary across geographic regions, influenced by local demographics, economics, and politics. But the change convulsing health care is national in scope, with turbulence everywhere replacing stability, innovation replacing inertia, and risk replacing security."*

FOR-PROFIT OR NOT-FOR PROFIT: IS THERE A DIFFERENCE?

Many of the corporations now forming the infrastructure of the health care system are for-profit and investor-owned. The figure for general hospitals is misleading on the low side since many for-profit hospital chains also own and manage many clinical laboratories, rehabilitation, long-term care, and psychiatric services.[15]

In 1986, the Institute of Medicine released a report of a study of for-profit enterprise in health care. Their report noted basic differences in purpose, mission, values, and operations based on type of ownership, as shown in Table 2.2.[16] Although some of these distinctions have blurred somewhat in recent years as not-for-profits compete with for-profits, these general distinctions still hold true today.

The first major difference between for-profits and their not-for-profit counterparts is their higher administrative costs and, of course, profit margins. The insurance industry offers a striking example of these differences. The overhead of not-for-profit Blue Cross plans averages about 16 percent, compared to 20 percent for commercial carriers, 26 percent for investor-owned Blues, and only 3 percent for Medicare.[17] The compensation of Chief Executive Officers (CEOs) of U.S. HMOs in 2003 provides insight into extraordinary profits that are being taken from the health care enterprise and skimmed away from direct patient care (Table 2.3).[18] These levels of CEO compensation, of course, are more the norm in corporate America today than not. Indeed, we are living in the Second Gilded Age. The average CEO's compensation in the U.S. now is 475 times greater than the average worker's salary, compared to an 11-fold difference in Japan, 20-fold in Canada, and 22-fold in Britain. Aggregate CEO compensation of the S & P 500 companies increased by 39 percent between 2003 and 2004.[19] By comparison, the average CEO compensation in 1978 in the U.S. was 40 times the median worker income.[20]

But even more troubling is the stock income, often taken illegally, by CEOs through backdating manipulations of stock options. The case of Dr. Bill McGuire, pulmonologist turned United Healthcare CEO, is the most egregious example so far in the backdating scandal. After receiving more than $2 billion in total compensation over his 15-year term as CEO (mostly through stock options), he was fired in late 2006 when the Board of Directors concluded that he had financial ties to the head of the company's compensation committee and that the timing of backdating was fraudulent. United Healthcare's stock soared by more than 50-fold during his term in office, with much of that increase benefitting executives at the expense of patients, health care providers, and investors.[21] A recent in-depth article in the *Wall Street Journal* identified many other corporate CEOs taking very

TABLE 2.2

Common Distinctions Between For-Profit And Not-For Profit Organizations

For-Profit	Not-for-Profit
Corporations owned by investors	Corporations without owners or owned by "members"
Can distribute some proportion of profits (net revenues less expenses) to owners	Cannot distribute surplus (net revenues less expenses) to those who control the organization
Pay property, sales, income taxes	
Sources of capital include:	Generally exempt from taxes
a. Equity capital from investors	Sources of capital include:
b. Debt	a. Charitable contributions
c. Retained earnings (including depreciation and deferred taxes)	b. Debt
d. Return-on-equity payments from third-party payers (e.g., Medicare)	c. Retained earnings (including depreciation
Management ultimately accountable to stockholders	
	Management accountable to voluntary, often self-perpetuating boards
Purpose: Has legal obligation to enhance the wealth of shareholders within the boundaries of law; does so by providing services	**Purpose**: Has legal obligation to fulfill a stated mission (provide services, teaching, research, etc.); must maintain economic viability to do so
Revenues derived from sale of services	Revenues derived from sale of services and from charitable contributions
Mission: Usually stated in terms of growth, efficiency, and quality	
Mission and structure can result in more streamlined decision making and implementation of major decisions	**Mission**: Often stated in terms of charity, quality, and community service, but may also pursue growth
	Mission and diverse constituencies often complicate decision making and implementation

SOURCE: Reprinted with permission from: Gray B.E. (ed). *For-profit enterprise in health care: Supplementary statement on for-profit enterprise in health care*. Washington, D.C.: National Academy Press, 1986.

large stock option packages through other kinds of manipulations of their prices and value.[22]

A 2003 study compared the performance over 20 years of for-profit and not-for-profit institutions in terms of access, quality, and cost-effectiveness. A total of 149 studies were reviewed for six types of institutions—hospitals,

TABLE 2.3

HMO CEO'S Compensation, 2003

Executive	Firm	Total Pay
Larry Glasscock	Anthem	$50.9 mil
William McGuire	United Healthcare	$30.0 mil
Leonard Schaefer	Wellpoint	$27.4 mil
John Rowe	Aetna	$16.2 mil
Allen Wise	Coventry	$14.6 mil
Howard Phanstiel	Pacificare	$10.2 mil
Jay Gellert	Health Net	$7.9 mil

SOURCE: Graef Crystal October 8, 2004 and Physicians for a National Health Care Program, Chicago, IL.

HMOs, nursing homes, psychiatric hospitals, hospices, and dialysis centers. The results were overwhelmingly clear. Not-for-profit institutions performed better in 88 studies (59 percent), 43 studies (29 percent) found little differences, and 18 studies (12 percent) showed better performance in for-profit institutions.[23] The differences were especially striking for psychiatric hospitals, with only one of 17 studies finding that for-profit facilities were better.[24]

Three brief examples from the hospital industry show how marked the differences are between for-profits and not-for-profits in terms of mission, values, and practices. Each shows a pattern of drastic cutting of costs, such as for nursing positions and services, and excessive billing for services. HCA, the nation's largest investor-owned hospital chain, took over Good Samaritan Health System in San Jose, California, a not-for-profit in 1996. In the aftermath of that takeover, nursing positions were cut, overnight housekeeping was eliminated, quality of care suffered, and charity care was reduced. After HCA took over another hospital in Florida, emergency care (a financial loser) was eliminated, requiring a 45-minute drive to the nearest emergency room during the resort town's busy season.[25] As the second largest investor-owned hospital chain, Tenet has hospitals in California that mark up their operating room charges by more than 800 percent and charge more than 12-times as much for chest x-rays (two views) than public hospitals.[26,27]

These kinds of differences, as we will soon see in later chapters, are pervasive throughout the health care industry, whether hospitals, HMOs, the drug and medical device industry, or insurance industry. The typical defense by the for-profits is that they are a business, need to be efficient, and pay taxes, while not-for-profits are exempt from taxes. Those defending for-profit health care do have a point: it is different from not-for-profit care. But tax exemption plays a minor role if any. In fact, corporate taxes as a share of the nation's tax revenues fell from 28 percent to 11.8 percent between the mid-1950s and mid-1990s,[28] and a GAO study in 1995 concluded that a majority of corporations, both foreign and U.S. controlled, were paying *no* U.S. income tax.[29] Rather, the overarching difference is that for-profits serve different master-investors, whose only measuring stick is profit. The result is a striking ideological gulf between the missions of for-profit and not-for-profit health care. This is most clearly embodied in these opposing perspectives:[30]

> *"Do we have an obligation to provide health care for everybody? Where do we draw the line? Is any fast-food restaurant obligated to feed everyone who shows up?"*

Richard Scott, co-founder, chairman,
C.E.O. and president,
Columbia/HCA Healthcare Corporation

> *"Making fat profits on hospitals at the expense of the poor and the sick may not be a prison offense in this country. What is a crime is the galloping privatization of the nation's health resources and the rise of a competitive health care system that has less and less to do with health and access to care and everything to do with money."*

California Representative Pete Stark
Member of the House Ways and Means health subcommittee

The point is well taken that private enterprise is not designed to take care of everyone who shows up. But necessary health care is hardly a discretionary product which should be available only to those with the ability to pay their full costs. We therefore need a different system to assure universal access to affordable health care, as will be discussed in the last chapter. The debate comes down to the question of whether we should have a health care system that assures care of everyone, or not? This becomes a matter of values—are we all in this together or is everyone on his or her own?

In his excellent article examining these issues in the hospital industry, Robert Kuttner, Co-Editor of *The American Prospect* and well-known health care analyst, stated in dire terms the trend that is destroying not-for-profit care.[31]

> *"Columbia/HCA insists that medicine is a business, and increasingly imposes its rules on the competitive game. If nonprofits are to retain their claim to fiscal and moral difference, they will need not only to match the chains lawyer for lawyer, ad for ad, market strategy for market strategy, and cost saving for cost saving, but also to be clearer about their own mission. And society, through better regulation and disclosure, will need to fashion clearer ground rules—or cede them to the market."*

SOME DRIVERS OF CORPORATE HEALTH CARE

Given the favorable economic and regulatory climate over the last 25 to 30 years, a massive corporate health care complex has grown rapidly, driven by various factors, including aggressive marketing by providers and suppliers of services, increasing intensity of services, the impact of new technologies, aging of the population with increasing prevalence of chronic disease, and a considerable amount of unnecessary care in a system of excess capacity. Three major drivers of this new "system" have been especially important in this transformational change—medicalization of preventive and therapeutic services, the growth of new technologies, and effective promotion leading to increased demand for services, whether necessary or not.

Medicalization

The boundaries of health care have been continuously expanded in recent decades. *Sociomedical-cultural* changes can be gradual and subtle, but often lead to medicalizing of a natural processes, such as substitution of infant bottle-feeding for breast feeding[32] and the rapid growth of aesthetic medicine for cosmetic skin care.[33] *New technologies* can obviously medicalize natural processes, such as the introduction of fetal monitoring, which led to more aggressive management of labor and a marked increase in the rate of Caesarian sections with little evidence of improved outcomes. *New diagnostic tools* have further added to boundary expansion of health care; MRI scanning can now find "abnormalities" in completely asymptomatic people and label them as unexpected "problems"; one study found that one-half of young adults have lumbar disk bulge without back pain,[34] while another showed knee "abnormalities" in one quarter of asymptomatic young adults.[35] *Changing definitions of existing diseases* also plays a major role in medicalizing our lives. When hypercholesterolemia was redefined from threshold levels of total cholesterol from 240 mg/dl to 200 mg/dl, disease prevalence increased by 86 percent.[36] *Definition of new diseases* is still another powerful boundary expander of health care; obvious examples are the blockbuster drug Viagra for erectile dysfunction and the current effort by the pharmaceutical industry to widely define and treat female sexual dysfunction.[37]

The *political process* is still another less obvious but powerful factor in the increasing medicalization of society and the shape of our health care system. The connections between corporate health care stakeholders and government have become closely intertwined in recent decades through lobbying, deregulation, and a revolving door of leadership between government, regulators, and industry, as will be discussed in Chapter 6. State legislators frequently get involved in regulation of medical practice, such as mandatory school screening of children for scoliosis mandated in 26 states without evidence of effectiveness.[38,39]

Growth of Technology

New technologies have been continuously reshaping U.S. health care and accelerating its costs since World War II. Almost all of today's techniques of diagnosis and treatment were unknown in 1950.[40] New non-invasive diagnostic procedures have come on line in waves since 1975, including ultrasound, computed tomography (CT) scanning, and magnetic resonance imaging (MRI). They have been joined by a host of new therapeutic procedures, such as LASIK eye surgery, organ transplantation, joint replacements, and endovascular stent-graft systems. Other emerging technologies that will likely reshape health care in the next 15 or 20 years include robotic surgery; genetic profiling for targeting drugs; genetic diagnosis and therapy; and culturing and grafting of human cells.[41] The rapidity of these changes is shown by the growing workload of the Food and Drug Administration (FDA). In 2002, for example, the FDA approved 89 new drugs and biologic agents, 172 new indications of use, and over 4,000 new or improved medical devices.[42]

The growth of new technologies is a double-edged sword. There is no question that technological advances have greatly broadened the capabilities of modern medicine for more effective diagnosis and treatment of disease. But many of these new technologies are not curative of disease, instead may only delay death (e.g., heart transplants); Lewis Thomas, one of the country's best known analysts of medical progress, labeled them "halfway technologies."[43] Technology development also leads to an arms race in expensive and lucrative procedures which raise critical issues of priorities and equity within our system. When resources are limited, as they are in the real world, how do we decide between providing heart transplants, which benefit only a few people with marginal outcomes, and public health or preventive measures which can benefit millions? As will be discussed in later chapters, there is a clear need for better management in a more accountable system to answer such questions.

Promotion and Increasing Demand

The above drivers of corporate health care are further multiplied by vigorous promotion of products and procedures by providers and suppliers. Direct-to-consumer advertising of drugs and procedures has been a large marketing strategy, and has recently been joined by direct-to-consumer advertising of surgical procedures (e.g., for joint replacement). Some of these marketing practices are so subtle as to not be recognized as advertising by the public, such as payments by drug companies to pharmacies to send letters to patients promoting their drug and "health newsletters" as point-of-purchase ads wrapped into warning labels given to patients picking up their prescriptions.[44] These ads typically hype the benefits of the product while downplaying the risks. Bioethicists point out that the movement toward patient autonomy in recent years coincides beautifully with corporate interests to sell their products.[45] These trends go way beyond national borders. Iona Heath, a general practitioner in London, recently called attention to the huge profits that can be gained by aggressive marketing of health products and procedures to relatively healthy people:

> *"Global capitalist hegemony is opening up the whole arena of*

human health for the pursuit of profit, trading on human fear in an explicit and calculated manner. People living in the wealthy countries of the world are now living healthier and longer lives than ever before. Only a minority are sick, and so the profit to be made by convincing the healthy majority of the immediacy of threats to their health and the need to take action to avert or minimize these threats. "[46]

POWER SHIFTS IN HEALTH CARE

A massive change in the circumstances of clinical practice has taken place in the U.S. over the last 40 years, so that then and now are radically different. For the first two-thirds of the 20th Century, American medicine was a cottage industry with a professional service ethos. Physicians were in solo or group practice, with their services reimbursed on fee-for-service, indemnity insurance, or out-of-pocket payments.[47] Patients without insurance were typically cared for on a sliding scale or charity basis. Fast forward to today's world, and we find that the traditional dyadic physician-patient relationship has been drastically altered. In his book *Balancing Act: The New Medical Ethics of Medicine's New Economics*, E. Haavi Morreim, Professor in the Department of Human Values and Ethics at the University of Tennessee, has offered us this overview of these drastic changes in medical practice:[48]

> *"Insurers, governments, private corporations, and institutional providers now generally determine which technologies will be developed, and how quickly; which technologies will be locally available, and to whom; what level of funding will be available for which interventions for what kinds of patients; what sorts of incentives will limit and direct physicians' and patients' choices; which sorts of medical practice will, and will not, be attractive for physicians to enter; and what sorts of health care will, and will not, be attractive for patients to accept."*

Eliot Friedson, Professor Emeritus of Sociology at New York University, has identified these changes in the physician-patient relationship and the environment of medical practice:[49]

- Public and private health insurance has destroyed the direct economic relationship between physician and patient. Patients and physicians now rely primarily on insurers to pay for care.

- The proliferation of elaborate technologies and specializations has diffused the responsibility for providing care through a host of personnel. Responsibility has become embedded in a *system* rather than concentrated in the hands of one physician.

- The patient's record is no longer the virtual private property of the individual physician. It now circulates among a number of therapeutic and clerical personnel as well as to central insuring agencies and is theoretically available for the patient's scrutiny.

- Medicine has lost much of its control over the information available to consumers and faces a more suspicious public.

- Physicians now depend for their income on government agencies, large corporate employers, and health insurance companies, and must usually accept the economic terms offered by those organizations.

- An increasing number of physicians work for a salary or on a capitation basis in circumstances organized and financed by large for-profit organizations.

- Physicians are becoming divided into clinical practitioners, on the one hand, and managers or owners of practice organizations, on the other.

Instead of the medical profession, the dominant players controlling the landscape of medical practice today are the insurers, HMOs, hospitals, employers, and to a lesser extent the government through its public programs. There is no single party responsible or accountable for the overall health care "system," and competition is intense among the major players in the medical marketplace. In other parts of the economy, competition might be expected to lower prices and increase value to the consumer. But this is usually not the case for health care, where the top priority among many owners and providers of services is to maximize net income, often at the expense of patients. Insurers want to enroll healthier and lower-risk patients while charging premiums that assure high returns to shareholders. Drug and medical device companies have wide latitude to set their own prices, with the interests of shareholders trumping affordability of their products by patients. The business ethic of market forces has become the driving ethos in our health care system. While market forces have always been present in medicine, the difference now is the pervasive influence of large corporations as owners and providers of health care services. Dr. Larry Churchill, a well-known ethicist at Vanderbilt University, offers this perspective on the new corporate ethos:

> *"While there were some health care corporations in the past, they were typically businesses owned by medical groups or nonprofit organizations that were governed by boards of local citizens and were community oriented. While not always altruistic in their aims, these organizations were often responsive to local needs. The new health care corporation has a Wall Street orientation and is responsive to markets [illegible] and mergers. The new corporate providers are also far more skilled than the cottage industry entrepreneurs at advertising and selling their services, cutting costs, and shaping the way their customers think not only about the services they offer but about the economic arrangements that undergird their profitability."*[50]

Where do all of these changes leave the medical profession? Internally, it has been weakened and fragmented among its growing number of specialty and subspecialty organizations. Membership in the American Medical Association (AMA) now includes less than 30 percent of the nation's 800,000 plus physicians; its roster dropped by 20 percent between 1993 and 2004.[51] Medicine lacks a clear political voice or consensus over health policy. The profession has been moved to the sidelines in the health policy debate as other more powerful stakeholders take center stage, as illustrated by the exclusion of organized medicine from the planning of the flawed Clinton Health Plan in 1993-1994. Many policymakers and the public have come to see medicine as just another self-interest party. Our profession also finds itself in a difficult negotiating position since there are so many conflicts and stakeholders external to medicine. Even if medicine were to have a unified political stance, there are too many stakeholders for effective negotiation. Dr. Rosemary Stevens, Professor of History and Sociology of Science at the University of Pennsylvania, sums up medicine's predicament today in this way:

> *"Notwithstanding its direct stake in many health policy questions and its perennial ranking near the top of political contributors, organized medicine has become conspicuous politically by its marginality among a cacophony of players, demoted from center stage and seen as just*

another self-interested player."[52]

We are told every day that the very self-interest of the parties will drive the market to promote better efficiencies and value through competition, and that market dynamics will "fix" any system problems if we just stand back and let the market work. We have now had several decades of marketplace medicine to test that claim, a focus of later chapters. Can the unfettered market ever solve our growing health care crisis?

CHAPTER 3

MEDICINE AND MARKETS: WHAT'S THE PROBLEM?

"The market metaphor leads us to think about medicine in already-familiar ways: emphasis is placed on efficiency, profit maximization, customer satisfaction, ability to pay, planning, entrepreneurship, and competitive models. The ideology of medicine is displaced by the ideology of the marketplace. Trust is replaced by caveat emptor. There is no place for the poor and uninsured in the market model. Business ethics supplants medical ethics as the practice of medicine becomes corporatized. Hospitals become cost centers. Nonprofit medical organizations tend to be corrupted by adopting the values of their for-profit competitors. A management degree becomes as important as a medical degree. Public institutions, by definition, cannot compete in the for-profit arena, and risk demise, second-class status, or privatization."

George J. Annas, JD, MPH *Bu*
Some Choice: Law, Medicine, and the Market[1]

The above observation by George Annas, a leading bioethicist and Professor of Law and Medicine at Boston University gives us an insightful summary of problems with the market metaphor in health care. Yet the idea that 'unfettered markets,' if they are allowed to work their magic, assure efficiency and value through competition has become so engrained in our society over the last 30 years as to become a meme (i.e., a self-replicating idea that is promulgated without regard to its merits until it becomes by constant repetition, part of our language and culture.) We are assured at every turn that the competitive marketplace is fair and efficient. If that is true elsewhere in the economy, why not also in health care?

This chapter undertakes four goals: (1) to describe briefly the market ideology in health care; (2) to show some of the many ways how markets do not work in health care; (3) to consider the adverse effects of a deregulated health care market on patients and the system; and (4) to illustrate how the market distorts medical practice itself.

IDEOLOGY OF MARKETS IN HEALTH CARE

Proponents of markets in health care, first through "managed care" and more recently through "managed competition" have promised us decreased cost, improved efficiency, less waste and improved quality through competition and greater choice. This message is delivered incessantly through a wide range of media. The National Center for Policy Analysis (NCPA) provides a good example. Founded in 1983 and based in Dallas, Texas, it describes itself as a non-profit nonpartisan public policy research organization, but its single-minded goal is to "develop and promote private alternatives to government regulation and control, solving problems by relying on the strength of the competitive, entrepreneurial private sector." It disseminates its message and results of "research" through press releases, television appearances, talk shows, op-ed pieces and guest editorials.[2] Its claims about the problems of publicly financed health insurance[3] have been rebutted elsewhere.[4] A typical recent example of market ideology in health care, written by senior fellows at the Hoover Institution, another conservative think tank, put forward these assurances:[5]

> *"Greater reliance on individual choice and free markets are the solutions to what ails our health care system—a handful of policy changes that harness the power of markets for health services have the potential to give patients and their physicians more control over health-care choices, create more health insurance options, lower health costs, reduce the number of uninsured persons—and give workers a pay increase to boot."*

Consumer choice has become a central mantra of market ideology, with the often-unfounded claim that government funded insurance reduces choice by comparison. Another basic tenet is based on a theory of "moral hazard," which for 40 years has been accepted by most economists. The theory holds that insured individuals will overuse health care services and make choices without any thought to cost unless they are constrained by enough cost-sharing such as co-payments and deductibles (i.e., constraints that would entice them to spend resources wisely because they have a stake in conserving them).[6]

Is the logic of patients conserving services and resources when they pay a portion of the cost upfront true? In an excellent recent book on the subject, *The Theory of Demand for Health Insurance*, Dr. John Nyman, a health economist at the University of Minnesota, exposes the flaws of the moral-hazard based conventional theory of insurance and proposes a new theory of insurance which recognizes the adverse impacts of excessive cost-sharing on access to health care.[7]

Meanwhile, we are surrounded by a new language of health care. Private insurers talk about "covered lives" and "medical losses" as they market their plans. Advertising is targeted to low-risk groups, known within the industry as "revenue bodies." The goal is to increase market share and maximize profits for the plans and their shareholders. In order to meet the expectations of investors for sustained growth of profits, corporations pursue strategies of "de-marketing," whereby unprofitable (sick) patients are disenrolled or forced to pay unaffordable premium increases. All of this is just the logic of the market as it develops health care as a business.[8]

WHY MARKETS DON'T WORK IN HEALTH CARE

Despite the long-held view by many economists and proponents of a market-based health care system, there are many reasons why markets don't work as they do in other parts of the economy, such as automobiles or housing. Here are some of the more important reasons.

1. The health care system is driven by acute illness as patients seek care for urgent or semi-urgent problems. They do not generally have the time or means to compare prices or options of facility and provider. They usually don't have reliable information about price and quality of health services[9] and their choices are limited to what is available within their community. In addition, there are large subsets of the population, including many elderly, frail, chronically ill, disabled, and those with literacy or language barriers, who have limited ability to shop for their health care. This is a far cry from what proponents call "individual choice" that the market provides, as if someone were shopping for a traditional consumer good such as a TV or car. With health care, in many situations the consumer must buy; with a TV, buying or not buying, or even buying the wrong one, is of limited consequence.

2. Health care is a complex and personal process with endless variations based on the circumstances of care. It is not a linear

activity amenable to industrialization. The industrial model of efficiency in delivering episodic services is not well suited to the reality of the dominance of chronic illness and often multi-system disease.[10]

3. To an even greater extent than other markets, such as for automobiles or computers, there are less checks and balances or comparative information available to assure patients that health care services are necessary or useful. Many services, procedures and products that are brought to the health care marketplace are of dubious or unproven value (e.g., "phen-fen" diet drugs, full-body CT scanning, Botox for cosmetic care) or even potentially hazardous (Vioxx, for example).

4. Much of the vaunted "competition" in today's health care marketplace is over profits and how best to exclude unprofitable patients. Thus private insurers pursue medical underwriting and "experience rating," whereby premiums are based upon the costs of care being consumed by enrollees. Insurers know that plans are not profitable when two-thirds of enrollees make a significant claim during the year.[11] Julian Tudor Hart, experienced general practitioner and health services analyst in the United Kingdom, has coined the term "inverse care law" to describe the reality that the sickest people in greatest need are always the least profitable and worst served when markets control the system.[12] We also know that 5 percent of people are responsible for 50 percent of health care spending each year, while 10 percent account for 72 percent of spending.[13] Insurers and HMOs that disenroll patients are therefore just making good business decisions, though not in the best interests of patients. Their goal is simple: evade or shake off those 5 to 10 percent and focus on insuring those who make fewer claims.

5. When private insurers "cherry pick" the market by selectively covering healthier and more affluent enrollees, they shift costs of sicker individuals to a smaller higher-risk pool to be borne by public programs (i.e., Medicare, Medicaid, SCHIP). Federal and state governments already under fund these public programs.

If the private sector's practice of cost shifting onto the public sector is carried far enough, resources for the care of the sickest populations cease to be available and can lead to a "death spiral" of public programs. Professor Arthur Schafer, bioethicist and Director of the Centre for Professional and Applied Ethics at the University of Manitoba, offers this perspective on cost-shifting:[14]

> *"What all of these market-oriented schemes have in common is that they shift health-care financing away from larger segments of the population, thereby pooling financial risk, toward more risk for the individual.*
>
> *When the risks of ill-health are assigned to individuals, then those with higher incomes are able to purchase the standard of care they desire, without having to pay, through higher taxes, for a similar standard for the rest of the community. In such a market-oriented health system, individual self-reliance replaces social solidarity."*

6. It has been estimated that a market population of about 400,000 is required to enable any real competition between hospitals or HMOs. With less densely populated areas, the market is simply not big enough to support enough businesses to foster competition between them. However, one-third of Americans live in areas with populations less than 400,000 and there are four states today with populations less than 660,000.[15] Moreover, even where population density could potentially foster competition, consolidation among providers in large metropolitan areas often restricts choice and competition as monopolies take over. In El Paso, Texas, for example, nearly 80 percent of hospital beds in the community are controlled by the two largest hospital chains in the country, HCA and Tenet.[16]

If the above reasons are not sufficiently persuasive that the claimed efficiencies, added value, and cost savings of markets through competition are not grounded in evidence, the actual track record of the deregulated health care marketplace answers any remaining doubts.

• Many studies of the performance of for-profit investor-owned facilities have confirmed higher costs and lower quality compared to their not-for-profit counterparts. Table 3.1 summarizes the findings of these studies.[17] Figure 3.1 reveals the extent of unnecessary care for five common surgical procedures, according to a 2002 report by the Commonwealth Fund.

• After a nine-year study of 12 major health care markets, the landmark Community Tracking Study, carried out by the non-partisan policy research organization, Center for Studying Health System Change, found widespread and deep skepticism that markets can improve efficiency and quality of health care delivery. Periodic interviews were conducted in 60 communities with 60,000 households and 12,000 physicians, as well as with employers and insurers. Four major barriers to efficiency were found: (1) providers' market power; (2) absence of potentially efficient provider systems; (3) employers' inability to push the system toward efficiency and quality; and (4) insufficient health plan competition.[32]

• The claims of private Medicare HMOs mirror the promises of the rest of the industry: better care at a lower price thanks to efficiency and competition driven by the desire to make a profit. But the reality is far different: government subsidies are needed to make that profit, and even with the help, private companies withdraw from the market because those profits aren't high enough. Between 1998 and 2000, they were paid 13 percent more than Original Medicare but still many withdrew from the market and 2.4 million seniors had to find alternative coverage and often other health care providers.[33] Medicare Advantage, the successor to Medicare + Choice plans, makes the same claims, but there is no reason to believe it can make them good, even with generous government subsidies. Payments to Medicare Advantage plans averaged 12.4 percent more than costs in traditional Medicare in 2005,[34] and payments were 11 percent higher in 2006 with high-cost counties receiving payments (standardized for health risk) almost twice as high as low-cost counties.[35]

• Although Part D of the Medicare Prescription Drug, Improvement, and Modernization Act of 2003 (MMA) was intended to provide

TABLE 3.1

Investor-owned care: Comparative examples versus not-for-profit care

Hospitals	Costs 3 to 13 percent higher, with higher overhead, fewer nurses, and death rates 6 to 7 percent higher [18-23]
HMOs	Higher overhead (25 to 33 percent for some of the largest HMOs); worse scores on 14 of 14 quality indicators reported to National Committee for Quality Assurance [24-26]
Dialysis Centers	Death rates 30 percent higher, with 26 percent less use of transplants [27, 28]
Nursing Homes	Lower staffing levels and worse quality of care (30 percent committed violations that caused death or life-threatening harm to patients) [29]
Mental Health Centers	Medicare expelled 80 programs after investigations found that 91 percent of claims were fraudulent [30]; for-profit behavioral health companies impose restrictive barriers and limits to care (e.g., premature discharge from hospitals without adequate outpatient care) [31]

SOURCE: Geyman JP: adapted with permission from the American Board of Family Medicine, Lexington, Kentucky

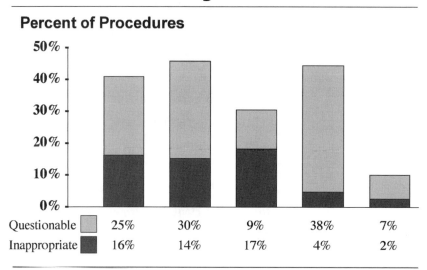

FIGURE 3.1

Unnecessary Procedures

Percent of Procedures

Questionable	25%	30%	9%	38%	7%
Inappropriate	16%	14%	17%	4%	2%

SOURCE: Reprinted with permission from: Commonwealth Fund, Quality of Health Care in the U.S. Chartbook, 2002.

prescription drug coverage to seniors and the disabled, it could hardly have been more inefficient. It did nothing about the key issue—soaring drug prices. Worse, it prevented the very thing that actually can lower prices; the Act prohibited the government from negotiating discounted drug prices for Medicare's 42 million beneficiaries. Such negotiation is well known to be effective as shown by the Veterans Administration. The VA often achieves discounts of more than 40 percent off market prices. Instead private Medicare managed care plans were handed a windfall of about $46 billion over the next 10 years[36] and the drug industry was protected against any price controls. Seniors were given confusing and for many, meager drug benefits, requiring them to sort through up to 50 private plans managing the drug benefit. The Consumers Union has estimated that only 22 percent of projected drug costs over the next 10 years will be covered by the new drug benefit[37] and it was only a matter of months before drug companies raised their drug prices to minimize potential savings under the temporary drug discount cards used in 2004 and 2005.[38] As an example of soaring drug prices helped along by MMAs Part D, Lilly increased its prices in the U.S. by 11 percent in the third quarter of 2006 while its prices fell by 3 percent in Europe and 5 percent in Japan.[39]

- After the Anthrax scare caused by anthrax-laced letters in 2001, which resulted in five deaths, the $5.6 billion national effort Project BioShield was launched by the federal government to expand the nation's stockpile for preparedness against bioterrorism. The top priority was to develop an improved anthrax vaccine. After five years, no new products have been developed and the project is beset with problems, including non-participation of any of the large pharmaceutical companies (too risky and not enough profits), lobbying battles between small competing biotech companies which have never taken a new vaccine to market, and delayed orders of an older vaccine with potentially serious side effects (six deaths from mandatory use in military personnel led to its discontinuation in 2004).[40]

In view of this overwhelming body of evidence disproving the rhetoric about greater efficiencies, value and quality in the for-profit marketplace, Robert Evans, distinguished health economist at the University of British Columbia, contends that "there is in health care no 'private competitive market' of the form described in the economics textbooks, anywhere in the world. There never has been, and inherent characteristics of health and health care make it impossible that there ever could be."[41]

ADVERSE IMPACTS OF MARKETS IN HEALTH CARE

As we have already seen, the U.S. health care system has been transformed over the last 30 to 40 years from a service-oriented industry to a market-based industry driven by the business ethic in pursuit of profits. Our "system" now is based on ability to pay, not human need. Though commonly denied by enthusiasts of markets, we *ration* care in this way. Markets in a deregulated, largely unaccountable "system" decrease access to care for many millions of Americans, increase costs beyond the means of much of the population, and lead to growing inequities and waste. Dr. David

Whiteis of the School of Public and Environmental Affairs at Indiana-Purdue University in Fort Wayne, has shown how growing corporate dominance in U.S. health care has resulted in reduced access to necessary preventive and curative services while putting large disadvantaged populations at risk for disease and social dysfunction in American cities.[42]

A solid primary care base that is widely available to all has been shown by Dr. Barbara Starfield, Professor of Health Policy and Management at the Johns Hopkins Bloomberg School of Public Health, to be the essential underpinning of any nation's health care system. She has found that countries with strong primary care have improved health outcomes, healthier populations, and lower overall health costs.[43] Her comparative study of performance of the primary care base of 11 industrialized countries has found the United States to rank last on all 11 criteria used in the study.[44] Studies in this country likewise show the essential benefits of primary care. Even when income disparities are accounted for, states with more primary care resources have better health outcomes,[45] and hospitalization rates are lower in areas with higher family physician-to-population ratios.[46]

Yet the nation remains underinvested in primary care as resources are diverted to more specialized services, some of which are of dubious value to the health of our population. The previously mentioned Community Tracking Study) has recently found that, in 12 U.S. markets, emergency rooms are being strained to their limits by steadily increasing numbers of patients seeking primary care (for which emergency departments are not designed), including many seriously mentally ill patients. This strain is further aggravated by the reluctance of many specialists to provide on-call services to emergency rooms since they are better reimbursed in other sites, such as ambulatory surgery centers and specialty hospitals.[47] The CTS has also found that access to specialty care for both Medicaid and uninsured patients is declining as safety net programs continue to deteriorate, with average waits of six months for specialty clinic appointments not at all uncommon.[48]

Health care costs continue to rise at two to three times the rate of cost of living increases. They now consume 16.5 percent of the gross domestic product (GDP), a total of $2.16 trillion in 2006, or $7,110 per capita.[49] A recent study by the Centers for Medicare and Medicaid Services (CMS) shows that this spending is driven by new medical treatments, rising prices, and growing utilization of services.[50]

The U.S. spends about double what is spent on health care in other industrialized countries, yet does not receive higher value for that spending. New technologies are brought to market and promoted widely to the public, often without clinical evidence of effectiveness. A good example currently is the wide use of whole body computed tomography (CT) scans, now available at more than 167 centers around the country. Many patients self-refer themselves and pay $700 to $1,500 for an imaging procedure of unproven value and potential harm (radiation equivalent to that received by some of the survivors of the 1945 atomic bombings of Hiroshima and Nagasaki (who had increased risk of cancer thereafter), as well as risks of follow-up care chasing false positives, etc.).[51] Total body scans have been vigorously promoted to the public by radio, television, print media, and the Internet.[52] This situation has led Dr. Donald Berwick, President of the Institute for Healthcare Improvement and a leading expert on quality assurance in medical care, to this comment:[53]

> *"We have a learning disability in this country with respect to the difference between technologies that really do help and technologies that are only adding money to the margins of the companies that make them, without essentially paying their way in value. One of the drivers of low value in health care today is the continuous entrance of new technologies, devices, and drugs that add no value to care."*

It doesn't have to be this way. We have known for years that the prices of prescription drugs are much lower just across the border in Canada (by about 40 percent).[54] But higher prices are the rule elsewhere in health care as well. A recent study of coronary artery bypass graft surgery, for example, found that costs in U.S. hospitals for that procedure are approximately twice those for the same procedure in Canadian hospitals, with little difference in clinical outcome and despite shorter length of stay in U.S. hospitals.[55]

It is clear that we are not getting our money's worth in U.S. health care, by far the most expensive system in the world. Comparative studies document better value, not just in Canada but also in other industrialized countries around the world. A 2000 study by the World Health Organization gave the U.S. an average ranking of 15th out of 25 industrialized countries, using such indicators as disability-adjusted life expectancy, child survival to five years, and social disparities of care.[56]

In our "free-market" system, resources tend to go to where profits can be maximized, thus increasing the disparities and inequities of the overall system. Three examples make the point:

- The national marketing plan of Tenet, the second largest investor-owned hospital chain in the country, focuses on highly reimbursed services in cardiology, orthopedics, and neurology; its hospitals are located in large communities across Southern California, Texas, Louisiana, and South Florida, where reimbursement levels are high and a growing population of baby boomers will need these services.[57]

- Specialty hospitals have usually been located in affluent areas in states without requirements to first obtain a certificate-of-need. They are often physician-owned, at least in part, and focus most commonly on cardiovascular, orthopedic, and neurosurgical procedures. They have yet to demonstrate improved quality over general hospitals, and many purchasers and health plans are concerned that they add to health care costs, cherry pick the patient population, may induce unnecessary services due to physicians' conflicts of interest, and threaten the viability of general hospitals.[58]

- Dr. John Wennberg and his colleagues at the Center for Evaluative Clinical Sciences at Dartmouth Medical School have demonstrated marked geographic variations from one part of the country to another. In 2000, for example, per capita Medicare spending in Manhattan, New York, was $10,550 compared to $4,823 in Portland, Oregon, even after adjusting for age, sex, and race.[59] Higher spending areas have been found to have higher concentrations of specialists, more specialist visits, more hospitalizations, and more use of ICUs *without* any better quality of care than lower spending areas. This is precisely the opposite of what is promised by market advocates. According to market theory, the denser the population the easier it should be for competition to grow, prices to fall and quality to rise. By that theory, Manhattanites should have the least expensive and best care in North America, but they pay more for less or at best the same as in Portland.[60]

An overall comparison between the private market and a publicly run health care program is instructive in terms of market dynamics. The Medicare program, now 40 years old and with 42 million beneficiaries, allows such a comparison. Based upon the experience of privatized Medicare plans since the early 1990s, Table 3.2 displays important differences from traditional Medicare.[61]

MARKET-BASED DISTORTIONS OF MEDICINE

If one were to visit the U.S. from Mars and look over our health care system, one couldn't help but see a large, busy and expensive industry overly focused on cure, widespread emphasis on "half-way" technologies, battling death to the end, and organized more around the interest of providers than patients. Reimbursement policies and patterns shape where resources are allocated, while chronic disease, mental health, long-term care, and home care are relatively neglected compared to the quest for cures over care. In this quest, a large part of the nation's health care resources are spent on "flat-of-the-curve medicine, (i.e., unnecessary services which yield little or no benefit, and may even be harmful), as illustrated by Figure 3.2.[62]

The reductionistic biomedical model still holds sway in the U.S. over the chronic care model. New treatments and diagnostic tests are developed and widely adopted, often with little or no clinical evidence of efficacy or cost-effectiveness and even with the potential for harm (e.g., whole body computed tomography (CT) scans).[63,64] Here are some examples of the extent to which medical services have been shifted by the market from the needs of patients and populations to the interests of stakeholders in the delivery system.

- A 1998 review of the country's quality of care literature found that only 50 percent of people received recommended preventive care, while 30 percent received contraindicated acute care and 20 percent received contraindicated chronic care.[65]

- A 2002 report by the Commonwealth Fund concluded that more than 40 percent of cardiac bypass and angioplasty procedures performed each year are either questionable or inappropriate.[66]

- Back surgery rates are highest in areas where MRIs are most highly reimbursed.[67]

TABLE 3.2

Comparative Features of Privatized and Public Medicare

Privatized Medicare	Original Medicare
Experience-rated eligibility	Universal coverage
Managed competition	Social insurance as earned right
Defined contribution	Defined benefits
Segmented risk pool	Broad risk pool
Market pricing to risk	Administered prices
More volatile access & benefits	More reliable access & benefits
Increased cost sharing	Less cost sharing
Less accountability	Potential for more accountability
Less choice of provider and hospital	More choice of provider & hospital
Less well distributed	Well distributed
Less efficiency, higher overhead	More efficiency, lower overhead

SOURCE: Reprinted with permission from Geyman, J. P., *Shredding the Social Contract: The Privatization of Medicare*, Monroe ME, Common Courage Press, 2006, p206

- A study of all Medicare patients who died of cancer in 1996 and one of twenty cancer deaths in California that year found that one in four patients received chemotherapy in their last three months of life, and that the cancer's responsiveness to treatment did not influence whether or not chemotherapy was received.[68]

- Another study of hospitalized patients over 80 years of age found that 70 percent of patients wanted comfort care rather than prolonging of life; nevertheless, 63 percent received at least one life-sustaining treatment before they died, including ICU

FIGURE 3.2

The Law of Diminishing Returns

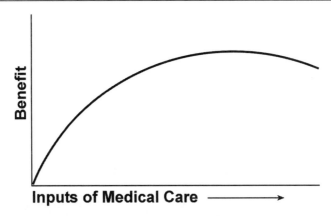

The first unit of input provides substantial benefits (imagine the first physician in a community), while additional units provide declining additional benefits (imagine the thousandth physician). Eventually, increasing inputs lead to no additional benefit (the "flat of the curve"). At some point, in theory, additional inputs lead to harm.

SOURCE: Reprinted with permission from Fisher ES, Welch HG. Avoiding the unintended consequences of growth in medical care: How might more be worse? JAMA. 1999;281:446-453.

admission, respirator care, surgery, and renal dialysis[69]

- Still another study of Medicare patients in their last six months of life found that high-spending, resource-rich areas of the country involved more physician visits, more tests and procedures, and more days in the hospital, but without any improvements in outcomes, and in some cases worse outcomes.[70]

- Even though percutaneous gastrostomy (PEG) tubes are known to be generally ineffective in prolonging life or preventing aspiration, and may lead to use of physical restraints, such tubes were placed in one of three patients with Alzheimer's dementia in 1995.[71]

Returning to values and whether health care is more than just another commodity for sale in an unfettered market, this observation by Drs. Steffie

Woolhandler and David Himmelstein at Harvard Medical School cuts to the heart of the issue:[72]

> "the most serious problems with such care is that it embodies a new value system that severs the communal roots and Samaritan traditions of hospitals, makes doctors and nurses the instruments of investors, and views patients as commodities. In nonprofit settings, avarice vies with beneficence for the soul of medicine; investor ownership marks the triumph of greed. A fiscal conundrum constrains altruism on the part of nonprofit hospitals: No money, no mission. With for-profit hospitals, the money is the mission; form follows profit – health care is too precious, intimate, and corruptible to entrust to the market."

CONCLUDING COMMENT

The U.S. health care system is clearly in trouble. "Managed care" of the 1980s and 1990s has been discredited, and "managed competition" has succeeded it. Both are really only managed costs, not care, and both are ineffective in containing runaway costs of health care. Markets have long been hailed as "the American way," but we are seeing a disturbing downside of the open market in health care. It is now of interest to turn our attention to what has happened to public health in these times of change.

CHAPTER 4

PUBLIC HEALTH:
FROM PARTNER TO
NEGLECTED STEPCHILD OF MEDICINE

Although the profession was closely involved with public health in its earlier history, the last 90 years in the U.S. have seen increasing distance between medicine and public health. Most physicians have little interest, training, or expertise in public health or population-based medicine. Their focus, and that of the health care system itself, is oriented primarily to the care of individual patients.[1] As the gap between medicine and public health has widened, so too have disparities in access and outcomes of care. This is not surprising since it has long been recognized that public health measures have improved the health of populations far more than medical care of individuals.[2] Indeed, medical care in excess doses can be harmful, as studies of variations in medical care have shown.[3,4]

This chapter addresses two goals: (1) to briefly review some historical markers in the relationship between medicine and public health in the U.S.; and (2) to consider changing needs and challenges to the health care system.

MEDICINE AND PUBLIC HEALTH:
SOME HISTORICAL BENCHMARKS

Medicine and public health have shared common goals, especially concerning the promotion of health and prevention of disease or injury. Each has its own target focus—the individual patient/family for medicine, a community or population for public health. Both fields are involved with prevention of disease in one of two ways:

- *primary prevention*: efforts to prevent the occurrence of a disease or injury, such as immunizations against infectious diseases

- *secondary prevention:* early detection of a disease process and intervention to reverse or lessen the progression of disease (egs., exercise stress testing for coronary artery disease, mammography for breast cancer)[5]

Despite some similarity of goals, however, the two fields take quite different approaches to their mission. Concerning the prevention of chronic disease, for example, the medical model works to identify high-risk individuals and offer them individual help, such as through screening for hypertension and counseling about diet, exercise, and smoking cessation. The public health model attempts to reduce disease in the population as a whole by such means as mass education campaigns, labeling of foods, environmental protection, and taxation of tobacco to make it less affordable.[6]

While medical practice has a long history dating back over 2,500 years, the field of public health has a much shorter history of about 200 years. The relationship between medicine and public health has varied greatly over the last two centuries in the U.S. During the 19th Century and early years of the 20th Century, the two fields worked well together in the primary prevention of disease, and were especially effective in reducing the incidence of many infectious diseases. Public health measures were responsible in large part for the dramatic decline in infectious disease, which Dr. Milton Terris, an internationally known epidemiologist, has termed the first epidemiological revolution. The bacterial and viral causes of these diseases were brought under control by such measures as water purification and pasteurization of milk. These two public health measures have been credited as the main reasons for a sharp decline of mortality from gastroenteritis and reduction in infant mortality rates.[7,8] Between 1900 and 1940, public health measures led to a 97 percent reduction in the death rate from typhoid fever, 92 percent for infectious diarrhea, and 77 percent for tuberculosis.[9]

Medicine and public health began to diverge in the early 20th Century. With the support of the Rockefeller Foundation, independent schools of public health sprung up around the country after 1916. These schools strengthened the education and science of public health by bringing together such disciplines as sanitary engineering, nutrition, biostatistics, epidemiology, and other relevant fields. Although the new public health schools led to many advances in public health, their emergence had a downside as well. Many scholars have argued that their development contributed to a growing gap between the worlds of medicine and public health, with clinical medicine shifting its focus away from prevention to curative care of acute disease of individuals while preventive medicine and public health were de-emphasized in medical education.[10]

In what Terris has called the second epidemiological revolution, early detection and treatment of chronic disease has received increased emphasis by both medicine and public health since 1950. While some of these efforts have been quite effective (e.g., Pap smears in reducing the incidence of cancer of the cervix), most approaches to secondary prevention, such as periodic physical examinations and multiphasic screening, have yielded only modest gains compared to primary prevention.[11] Indeed most of the gains which have been achieved have been due to the interventions of public health, especially population-based efforts to reduce smoking, encourage exercise, and lower serum cholesterol levels through lower-fat diets. Between 1950 and 1987, for example, age-adjusted mortality rates for coronary heart disease dropped by almost one-half due much more to smoking cessation and diet than to such medical advances as coronary care units and cardiac bypass surgery.[12,13] Between 1965 and 1993, the age-adjusted percentage of current smokers in the U.S. dropped from 52 percent to 28 percent for men and from 34 percent to 23 percent for women; these reductions in smoking have been estimated to have prevented 3 million deaths between 1964 and 2000.[14,15] The Centers for Disease Control and Prevention (CDC) have reported that the 20th century brought a 30-year extension of life expectancy for Americans, with 25 of those years attributable to the ten public health achievements listed in Table 4.1.[16]

The paths of medicine and public health have diverged in the post-World War II era to their present status of functional separation (many would call it *dysfunctional* separation, with little coordination or communication between the two fields). Table 4.2 lists the three major stages over the last 200 years in the relationship between medicine and public health in the U.S., as framed by the Committee on Medicine and Public Health of the New York Academy of Medicine.[17]

The considerable conceptual gulf between medicine and public health in recent years is illustrated by this statement by Dr. Norman Levinsky twenty-some years ago in the *New England Journal of Medicine*: "physicians are required to do everything that they believe may benefit each patient, without regard to costs or other societal considerations."[18] Most practicing physicians, especially in the non-primary care specialties, focus mainly on the care of their individual patients with little regard for public health considerations.

Recent decades have seen the relationship between medicine and

TABLE 4.1

Ten Public Health Achievements, 1900-1999

• Vaccination

• Motor vehicle safety

• Safer workplaces

• Control of infectious diseases

• Decline in deaths from coronary heart disease and stroke

• Safer and healthier foods

• Healthier mothers and babies

• Family planning

• Fluoridation of drinking water

• Recognition of tobacco use as a health hazard

SOURCE: Reprinted with permission from: The Institute for the Future. Health and Health Care 2010: The Forecast, the Challenge (2nd Ed). San Francisco: Jossey-Bass, 2003:167.

public health become one of competition more than collaboration. Both the public and private sectors provide direct medical services to lower-income and poor populations. With the passage of Medicaid and Medicare in 1965, private physicians often found themselves competing with local public health agencies for these reimbursements. Ironically, that legislation allowed the private sector to siphon off most of that income, leaving public health agencies with the burden of providing medical care for the poor with inadequate support of its infrastructure.[19] By 1995, only 3 percent of the nation's $1 trillion expenditure on health care was being allocated to government public health activities targeting prevention of disease.[20]

Public health in recent years has become an overburdened, underfunded

TABLE 4.2

Stages of Relations Between Public Health and Medicine

Period	Public Health	Medicine
Pre 20th century era of infectious disease: Cooperation	Focus on prevention: sanitary engineering, environmental hygiene, quarantine	Focus on treatment: direct patient care within comprehensive framework
Early 20th century era of bacteriology: Professionalization	Establishment of targeted disease control; Rockefeller Foundation report creates science-based schools of public health	Establishment of the biomedical model of disease, Flexner Report leading to standard science-based medical education
Post World War II era of biomedical paradigm: Functional separation	Focus on behavioral risk factors, development of publicly funded medical safety net (Medicaid/Medicare)	Pursuit of biological mechanisms of heart disease, cancer, and stroke, success with pharmacology, diagnostics, therapeutic procedures

SOURCE: Reprinted with permission from: The Institute for the Future. Health and Health Care 2010: The Forecast, the Challenge (2nd Ed). San Francisco: Jossey-Bass, 2003:166.

stepchild of medicine in the U.S. A 1988 report by the Institute of Medicine concluded that "this nation has lost sight of its public health goals and has allowed the system of public health activities to fall into disarray."[21] Managed care has further increased the functional gulf between medicine and public health, exposing their conflicting goals—managed care organizations viewing individuals as "covered lives" with an emphasis on risk avoidance, while public health agencies are focused on identification and treatment of risk of communities and populations.[22] The Institute of Medicine revisited these issues several years ago. Its 2002 report still found the country's public health enterprise in disarray, pointed out the responsibilities and roles of key partners with the public health system (e.g., academia, medical care system, community organizations, and private industry), and called for increased funding for infrastructure and research relevant to the health of the public.[23]

CHANGING NEEDS AND
CHALLENGES FOR HEALTH CARE

The needs facing the U.S. health care system today are entirely different from those a century ago when public health was in its heyday of the first epidemiological revolution. Figure 4.1 reveals a marked shift in leading causes of death in the U.S. from 1900 to 1999, with heart disease, cancer and stroke displacing infectious diseases as the major problems over that period.[24] Dramatic increases in life expectancy over the last century have led to important epidemiological transitions. At the time of its 25th Anniversary Symposium in 1995, the Institute of Medicine identified three generations of diseases as shown in Table 4.3. We are now in the second generation of diseases, primarily involving cardiovascular, cancer, and degenerative diseases of adults, with a third generation of diseases on the immediate horizon.[25]

It is paradoxical that, despite the many remarkable advances in medical technology in the care of acute illness, the U.S. is now confronting new threats, including environmental and infectious disease, chronic disease, and threats related to bioterrorism, that will again require strong public health interventions so useful in the last century. The anthrax scare of several years ago and the current spread of avian flu around the world are good examples of these new threats. A recent report on the nation's public health infrastructure noted that "the vigor and effectiveness of population-oriented health agencies continue to be important factors in the nation's health because some of the twentieth-century threats to health have returned or persist, and emerging threats will require similar prevention strategies of these same agencies."[26, 27]

Globalization has led to fundamental changes in trade, finance, the environment, crime, terrorism, and health care.[28] A 1997 report by the Institute

FIGURE 4.1

Changes in the Causes of Death
1900 - 1999

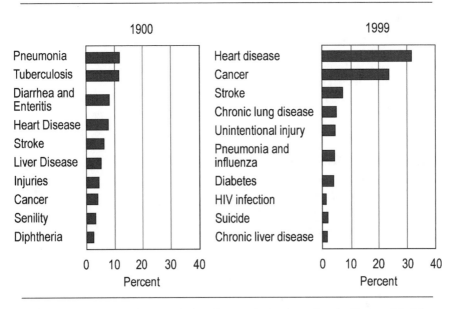

SOURCE: Reprinted with permission from: The Institute for the Future. Health and Health Care 2010: The Forecast, the Challenge (2nd Ed). San Francisco: Jossey-Bass, 2003:167.

of Medicine concluded that "distinctions between domestic and international health problems are losing their usefulness and are often misleading."[29] The international transfer of health risks now confronts all countries around the world,[30] much as it has in past centuries. The Black Death of 1347 was a direct result of international trade, and caused the deaths of one-third of the European population. Today, the growth of worldwide air travel provides means of transmission of a wide variety of communicable diseases with the speed of jet travel shorter than their incubation periods.[31] Meanwhile, the arsenal of terrorism now includes chemical and biological weapons.[32]

In order to improve its relatively poor performance in access and outcomes of care compared to most other industrialized countries, the U.S. needs to reform its health care system to provide universal access, strengthen its primary care infrastructure, and develop an effective partnership between medicine and public health. The focus of this reform must necessarily be the

TABLE 4.3

Epidemiologic Transitions

First Generation of Diseases
  Common Childhood Infections
  Malnutrition
  Reproductive Risks

Second Generation of Diseases
  Cardiovascular
  Oncotic
  Degenerative

Third Generation of Diseases
  Environmental Threats
    Air, water, chemical
    Ozone depletion, global warming
  New/Emerging Infections
    HIV/AIDS, Ebola virus, plague
    Tuberculosis, dengue, cholera
  Sociobehavioral Pathologies
    Violence
    Drug abuse
    Mental and psychosocial illness

SOURCE: Reprinted with permission from: Institute of Medicine. *2020 Vision: Health in the 21st Century.* Washington, D.C.: National Academy Press, 1996:19.

entire population of the country. Improving the health of the public will face severe limitations if many millions of Americans lack access to care, and if essential preventive and public health interventions remain underfunded and neglected. The present market-based system selects out patients by ability to pay, leaving lower-income and sicker patients to an underfunded and fraying public safety net of facilities and providers. But more affluent insured Americans will find themselves as vulnerable as their lower-income and uninsured counterparts when trauma and burn centers have closed due to lack of funding or when a newly drug-resistant infectious disease spreads throughout the entire population without regard to socioeconomic groups.

The Katrina disaster, both before and after the hurricane struck, is a good example of how poorly prepared the nation's health care system is prepared to deal with natural disasters or acts of bioterrorism. The stark images of Hurricane Katrina shocked Americans and many others around the world that such a disaster can occur in this country despite credible warnings in advance and the (bungled) efforts of government to respond to the crisis. Pictures of floodwaters putting most of New Orleans under water, of floating corpses, and of bodies wrapped in white sheets in the chapel of Tenet's Memorial Hospital—all looked like a war zone in some third world country rather than the United States of America. Communication and coordination between public and private relief efforts were poor. At least 154 patients died in hospitals or nursing homes, which were not completely evacuated until five days after the storm hit.[33] The most vulnerable in the community were often the last to be evacuated. Despite the heroic efforts of many doctors, nurses, and relief workers across the city, almost 1,000 people died and nearly half a million were left homeless, perhaps the largest number in the United States since the Civil War.

Katrina also made clear that New Orleans has been a tale of two cities, sharply divided along income, class, and racial lines, in much the same way as the overall health care system is divided, especially along income lines. The driest areas of the city, such as the French Quarter and the Garden District, are 90 percent white, while the worst flooding occurred in overwhelmingly black areas with high levels of poverty and unemployment.[34] Katrina exposed for all to see the staggering gaps in our society between the advantaged and the disadvantaged, as well as the incompetence and neglect of an inadequate government response. In the aftermath of Katrina, the federal government did little to reduce socioeconomic disparities within the displaced population. It waived prevailing wage laws on the Gulf Coast to allow contractors to cut wages to workers and offered Medicaid waivers to states whereby refugees would be given only the health benefits they'd be entitled to in their home states;[35] in Louisiana, families of three cannot earn more than $174 a month (about 14 percent of the Federal poverty level) in order to qualify for Medicaid.[36] More than three months after the hurricane, New Orleans' Charity Hospital, a main source of health care for poor and lower-income residents and the only level I trauma center for the entire Gulf Coast region,[37] was still devastated and only partly functional, having furloughed over 2,500 employees.[38] Seven months after the hurricane,

Charity reopened its trauma center at a temporary location in a suburban hospital pending its return to its University Hospital campus, but the area's entire health care system was devastated by the storm. Only about one-quarter of an estimated 1,500 active physicians who were practicing in three New Orleans area-parishes had returned seven months later, and critical shortages are still being experienced in primary care, hospital, mental health and long-term care services.[39]

As health care professionals, educators, and policymakers reassess the needs and challenges of U.S. health care after 9/11, the anthrax scare, and Katrina, these are some of the problems facing them.

- Many policymakers have failed to recognize that the major determinants of individual and population health lie beyond medical care, including socioeconomic and environmental circumstances and behavioral factors; there has been a lack of political will to reverse deterioration of the nation's public health system.[40]

- The pubic health infrastructure is chronically underfunded and taken for granted at both state and federal levels; funding for prevention and population-based services accounts for only a small fraction of health spending, estimated to be about 1 percent at the state level[41] and less than 5 percent at the federal level.[42]

- There is a functional gulf and lack of adequate communication between physicians and public health professionals; (e.g., little or no communication concerning immunization records in a community); a declining number of physicians have had any training in public health; a CDC study in October 2001 found that only two-thirds of county health agencies had Internet connectivity,[43] while a 1999 study revealed that 78 percent of public health administrators lacked formal public health training.[44]

- Before 9/11, less than 5,000 physicians in the entire country had received training in bioterrorism,[45] a 2003 report of a national study found that only 21 percent of U.S. physicians feel prepared to deal with bioterrorism, though 80 percent are willing to undergo such training.[46]

- Market forces in U.S. health care have failed to meet today's threats to health of the public; three examples are the closure of emergency rooms by some hospitals in order to avoid the care of uninsured patients;[47] the underinvestment by pharmaceutical manufacturers in new vaccines or drugs for infectious diseases most prevalent in the third world which pose a growing potential threat in this country;[48] and the unhindered marketing of "junk" foods to children by the food industry which has led to marked increases in prevalence of obesity and diabetes in American children.[49]

We will now turn to Part II to see how the marketplace really works, looking first much more closely at the practices of ten major players in the medical industrial complex, including health insurers, managed care organizations, hospitals, dialysis centers, nursing homes, and the drug and medical device industries.

PART II

THE BUSINESS ETHOS AND MARKET-DRIVEN HEALTH CARE

CHAPTER 5

INSIDE THE MEDICAL ARMS RACE: WINNERS AND LOSERS

"In America, the overreliance on market logic and market institutions is ruining the health care system. Market enthusiasts fail to tabulate all the costs of relying on market forces to allocate health care—the fragmentation, opportunism, asset rearranging, overhead, underinvestment in public health, and the assault on norms of service and altruism. They assume either a degree of self-regulation that the health markets cannot generate, or farsighted public supervision that contradicts the rest of their world view. Health care now consumes fully one-seventh of our entire national income. There is no realm of our mixed economy where markets yield more perverse results."

Robert Kuttner
Everything for Sale:
The Virtues and Limits of Markets[1]

"Markets are designed to facilitate the free exchange of goods and services among willing participants, but are not capable, on their own, of taking care of collective needs. Nor are they competent to ensure social justice. These "public goods" can only be provided by a political process."

George Soros
Businessman and philanthropist
The Bubble of American Supremacy[2]

Today's medical marketplace is complex, now deeply entrenched in pursuit of the business ethic, with many everyday practices going on without awareness of consumers (patients and their families). This chapter asks the question "Whom does this system now serve?" We will briefly address two related questions in order to answer this question: (1) how do the major players in the market operate? and (2) to what extent does the corporate ethos respond to its social responsibilities? These questions illuminate the structure in which moral choices are made by the medical profession, showing the limits of what is possible within its current framework.

EIGHT MAJOR PLAYERS IN THE MARKETPLACE

Health Insurers

The private health insurance industry in the U.S. is a massive administrative enterprise spread across some 1,300 companies with an administrative workforce 10 to 25 times larger than that of Canadian provincial plans.[3] The industry accounts for more than $300 billion in health care spending by employers each year.[4] There are about 50,000 brokers, agents, and consultants across the country who sell health insurance plans to employers and charge commissions up to 20 percent of the total cost of their plans.[5] What regulations that are in place are mainly at the state level, and are relatively ineffective in assuring value in benefits or cost containment for their enrollees. This is because insurance regulations vary widely from one state to another, and health insurers frequently base their operations in permissive states, even while conducting business in other states. Collectively, health insurers fragment the market so much that the basic purpose of insurance—providing financial security through broad risk pools—is defeated. Consolidation throughout the industry is leading to even less competition in costs as premiums continue to escalate at double-digit rates, generally for less coverage.

This history of health insurance shows a disturbing trend away from ethical practices. In early years, insurers practiced what they called guaranteed issue and community rating (providing the same coverage for the same premium throughout the entire covered community without regard to individual risk). This has been replaced by medical underwriting and "experience rating," a practice by which insurers avoid coverage of high-risk groups and raise premiums based upon illnesses experienced by enrollees. Once considered unethical, these practices became the industry norm after 1970.[6]

The trend within the industry is toward for-profit investor-ownership. Thus even Blue Cross, which pioneered health insurance as a not-for-profit company since about 1930, now has more than one-quarter of its enrollees across the country insured by the largest of all insurers, investor-owned Wellpoint (which recently acquired Anthem).[7] In the aftermath of its acquisition of Anthem, California-based Wellpoint increased its quarterly net income by $640 million, more than two and a half times over the previous quarter, planned an average rate increase of 16.7 percent for employers in 2006,[8] and reassured investors that it was committed to a 15 percent return for 2006.[9]

Health insurers, especially the for-profits, maximize their profits by avoiding coverage of higher-risk people. It is well known that 5 percent of people account for 50 percent of all health care costs, 10 percent for 72 percent, and 20 percent for 90 percent.[10] These people are easily excluded by medical underwriting. Three large insurers in California (Blue Shield of California, PacifiCare Health Systems, Inc., and Health Net Inc.,) exclude entire categories of occupations as too risky to cover, (e.g., roofers, pro-athletes, dockworkers, and firefighters), even if they are in good health and can afford coverage.[11] Many insurers also practice re-underwriting on an annual basis in order to control its "medical loss" ratio (i.e., lower its payments for direct patient care). As an example, one large insurer, American Medical Security Group, Inc., routinely raises its premiums by 37 percent at the time of annual renewal for its least healthy enrollees or those with claims, while also imposing other across-the-board increases.[12] The top seven U.S. health insurers took in a combined net profit of $10 billion in 2005, triple their profits five years earlier, largely as a result of raising their premiums well above health care costs.[13]

Other deceptive practices commonly used within the health insurance industry include "bait and switch" (e.g., addition of restrictive new policies in fine print after enrollment, such as new surcharges for top-tier hospitals or new co-payments for cancer radiation treatment),[14] cancellation of unprofitable policies,[15] use of non-profit associations as false fronts for their own for-profit marketing activities,[16] refusal to reimburse hospitals for previously authorized health care services,[17] and automatic reductions of physician reimbursement.[18]

The country is now immersed in the "consumer-directed health care" (CDHC) era, a misleading term since it is directed more by corporate industry than by consumers. Private insurers are rolling out a wide selection of new policies, most of which offering incomplete coverage, but all with hopes to find profitable niches in the market. Here are some examples of this new trend.

- High-deductible health insurance (HDHI) plans accompanying health savings accounts (HSAs), with minimum deductibles of $1,000 for an individual and $2,000 for a family; together with coinsurance at a typical level of 20 percent for hospital and physician costs; deductibles in HDHI plans can range up to $10,000 even without preventive services and drugs being counted against the deductible.[19]

• AARP has partnered with UnitedHealthcare to market a plan aimed at people between 50 and 64 years of age that would pay less than $8,000 toward a cardiac bypass procedure, hardly enough to qualify as an "insurance policy."[20]

• Other limited benefit plans now being offered to employees of WalMart Stores, Inc., and McDonald Corporation cap annual benefits at only $1,000.[21]

• Short-term policies are being marketed to healthy young people, which exclude any pre-existing conditions and offer no continuing protection.[22]

These kinds of policies masquerade as protection against the costs of major illness or accidents, but are a bonanza for the insurance industry even as it decreases the rolls of the uninsured by increasing the ranks of the underinsured. Dr. Don McCanne, Senior Health Policy Fellow for Chicago-based Physicians for a National Health Program (PNHP) summarizes these current trends this way:[23]

"Private health plans have ratcheted down rates for providers, wringing that sponge dry. They have pushed up premiums for employers and other purchasers to the maximum tolerated. That leaves only the patient as the source of increased health plan net revenues. By reducing benefits and increasing cost sharing, the insurers are able to create a "price point" that may appear to be affordable for moderate and low income individuals, but it purchases a Swiss cheese product that is marketed in yet smaller and smaller packages. And it can only get worse. The tragedy is that most proposals for reform continue to use these evolving plans in the health care marketplace as the basis for reform. What good does it do to have "universal" coverage if the plans fail to make health care affordable for the individual with significant health care needs?"

The investor-owned Blue Cross of California has been a trendsetter for these new kinds of insurance products, which take so much from our health care dollar while providing limited financial security to enrollees. It increased its profit margins from about 15 percent to more than 20 percent in recent years, and its medical loss ratio (what is paid out for patient care) has remained below 80 percent for the last five years.[24] By way of comparison, not-for-profit Kaiser in California spent 96 percent of every premium dollar on patient care in 2000, as compared to only 76 percent of investor-owned Blue Cross premium dollars in that year.[25] A recent study of the costs of health insurance in California showed that sales, marketing, billing and other administrative tasks account for about 22 percent of private insurance premiums.[26] Figure 5.1 compares overhead costs among private insurers in the U.S. by type of carrier.

FIGURE 5.1

Private Insurer's High Overhead
Investor Owned Plans are the Worst

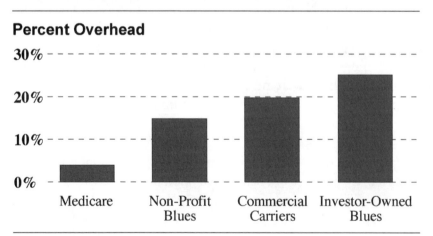

SOURCE: Reprinted with permission from S. Woolhandler and
D. U. Himmelstein, The National Health Program Slide-show Guide, Center for
National Health Program Studies, Cambridge, Mass., 2000.

Managed Care Organizations

Managed care plans include health maintenance organizations (HMOs) and preferred provider organizations (PPOs). The early HMOs date back to the 1940s and 1950s as not-for-profit staff-model organizations that have pioneered delivery of cost-effective preventive services and quality of care to large populations for many years (e.g., Kaiser Permanente and Group Health Cooperative). However, two-thirds of managed care organizations (MCOs) are now for-profit and investor-owned, and the drive toward profits in many of the for-profits has trumped quality of care and fair business practices in many instances. For-profit MCOs typically have higher administrative costs, spend less on direct patient care, and have worse quality of care than their not-for-profit counterparts. Figure 5.2 quantifies the differences between for-profit and not-for-profit HMOs in a 1998 study of 76 plans. The results of lowering the medical expense ratio (that spent on patient care) while raising administrative costs (including profits) are predictable— lower quality of care.[27] A 1999 national study found that investor-owned HMOs scored worse than their not-for-profit counterparts on all 14 quality indicators reported to the National Committee for Quality Assurance (e.g., a 27 percent lower rate of eye examinations for enrollees with diabetes.)[28] Another 1998 national study compared assessments by affiliated physicians in not-for-profit, more local managed care plans with for-profit multistate corporate plans. Physicians were much more likely to report deceptive and exploitative practices, as well as less trustworthiness in investor-owned plans.[29]

Investor-owned HMOs became discredited during the 1990s for a wide range of deceptive practices and conflicts of interest between their business ethic and service to enrollees. These have included false advertising,[30] undertreatment and denial of services;[31] disenrollment of sick enrollees,[32] gag rules on physicians,[33] hiding performance data,[34] and outright fraud.[35] A public, legislative, and political backlash ensued (e.g., by 1997 over 1,000 legislative bills were introduced in 39 states in an effort to rein in the excesses of managed care plans).[36]

In the aftermath of the 1990s, HMOs were forced to relax some of their restrictions and moderate their business practices. In many parts of the country, the emphasis has shifted toward preferred provider organizations (PPOs). Less regulated than HMOs and more flexible in design, PPOs are

FIGURE 5.2

Medical & Administrative Expense Ratios for 76 Plans

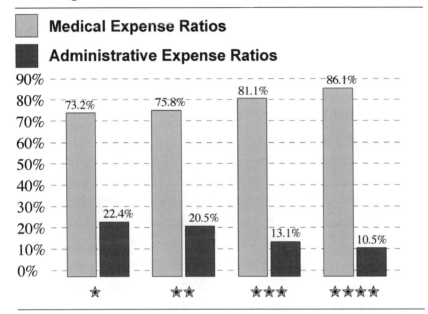

A comparison of medical expense ratios and administrative expense ratios for the 76 plans in the sample, averaged across the four quality categories.

SOURCE: Reprinted with permission from: Born P. & Geckler C. HMO quality and financial performance: Is there a connection? J Health Care Finance 24(2):69, 1998.

looser-knit than HMOs, with networks of physicians who agree to discounted fee-for-service reimbursement. About a dozen national managed care companies control nearly one-half of the HMO-PPO industries in the U.S.; in one-half of states, one insurer controls about one-third of the HMO/PPO market.[37] There is therefore less competition in the managed care market than one might expect. The common pattern in managed care continues to be to gain market share by offering attractive premiums (at least at first), restrict benefits, and increase cost-sharing with enrollees.

Despite a widespread backlash to managed care organizations in the 1990s, particularly those that are investor-owned,[38-40] fairness and accountability remain issues today, as illustrated by these examples:

- A 2003 report found that Medicaid HMOs in New Jersey have been rejecting 17 to 30 percent of claims for hospital stays.[41]

- Amerigroup, a Virginia-based managed care program which operated Medicaid plans in Illinois, was found by federal prosecutors to be guilty of systematically avoiding coverage of pregnant women and others with health problems in an effort to maximize its profits; damages of $144 million were assessed, with an additional $200 million being sought for filing 18,000 false claims with the state.[42]

- After grabbing the largest market share of the new Medicare Part D prescription drug benefit by offering low initial premiums, Humana increased its premiums for its least expensive option by an average of 60 percent for 2007 in a classic "bait and switch" move with average increases of 466 percent in seven states.[43]

- A 2006 report found that a growing number of California managed care plans, including Blue Shield of California, are now outsourcing non-emergency care of 20,000 California workers to Mexico, where costs are 40 to 50 percent lower.[44]

- Every year there are more than 250,000 appeals filed by enrollees in private HMOs over contractual and medical necessity disputes; however, the for-profit HMO industry has persistently lobbied against patient bills of rights legislation in Congress, effectively killing such legislation for the last several years.[45]

Hospitals

Though imposing by their numbers and importance, U.S. hospitals are struggling to survive and continue what for many have been traditional social roles that do not pay their way, such as charity care, health professions education, emergency care, and such labor-intensive and underreimbursed services as trauma centers, burn centers and neonatal intensive care units. The hospital industry is involved in its biggest building boom in 50 years. Most new hospitals are being located in affluent suburbs, while one in six public safety net hospitals were forced to close between 1991 and 2002.[46] Only about 11 percent of the nation's 5,764 hospitals are investor-owned, but the large investor-owned hospital chains multiply exponentially their influence on the system through ownership of many clinical laboratories, ambulatory surgery centers, rehabilitation, long-term care, and psychiatric services.[47] The January-February 2006, issue of *Health Affairs* was devoted to the now critical issue as to whether, and how, the social mission and safety net functions of our hospitals can be preserved. This question became even more pressing with the 2006 buyout of HCA, the largest investor-owned hospital chain in the country, by three private equity firms on Wall Street. The $31.6 billion buyout became the largest leveraged buyout in U.S. history.[48]

The two biggest forces challenging the future of U.S. hospitals are the threats to cross-subsidies by which hospitals have supported their money-losing services and the growing trend for physicians to move their patients to freestanding ambulatory care centers, specialty hospitals, and other facilities in which they have a financial ownership.[49,50] Hospitals have depended on cost shifting to support vital money-losing services, as illustrated in Figure 5.3. Thus, in 2002, private payers were paying about 120 percent of hospital charges, which made up for shortfalls of Medicare and Medicaid payments as well as uncompensated care.[51] It becomes obvious, as this cost-shift hydraulic works, how vulnerable under-compensated services become when private and public payers squeeze down their payments (as they are) and when investor-owned ambulatory surgery centers and specialty hospitals skim off the most lucrative patients from general hospitals without having to maintain their own emergency departments.

The specialty hospital issue is an especially troubling one, about which public policy is still undecided. There is considerable evidence already that they cherry pick the most profitable patients and provide less uncompensated care.[52,53] The specialty hospital industry lobbies strongly on its behalf through its trade group, the San Diego-based American Surgical Hospital Association.[54] The Community Tracking Study (CTS) recently reported on purchasers' views on 9 specialty hospitals in three sites of the study; they concluded that "specialty hospitals are contributing to a medical arms race that is driving up costs without demonstrating clear quality advantages."[55] The American Hospital Association (AHA) and the Federation of American Hospitals (FAH), which together represent almost all hospitals in the country,

FIGURE 5.3

The Cost-Shift Payment Hydraulic
As of 2002

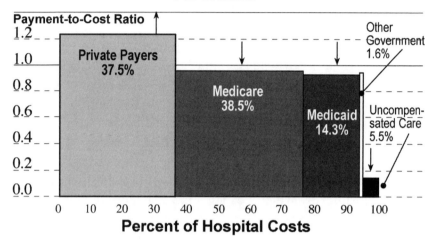

NOTE: The bold ruling line at 1.0 represents costs and payments in balance.

SOURCE: Reprinted with permission from: Dobson A., Da Venzo J & Sen N.
The cost-shift payment hydraulic: Foundation, history, and implications. Health
Aff(Millwood) 25(1):24, 2006.

have taken strong positions against specialty hospitals.[56] The American
Medical Association (AMA) has yet to take a position on the issue and
Medicare has twice extended its moratorium on building of new specialty
hospitals.

Pharmaceutical Industry

The investor-owned drug industry has been the most profitable of all
other industries in the U.S. for many years. In 2000, for example, despite
a recession, the top 10 U.S. drug companies increased their profits by
33 percent while the overall profits of Fortune 500 companies fell by 53
percent.[57] Profit margins in the industry in 2004 averaged 18 percent, with
Merck & Company leading the way at 25 percent.[58]

The most important reason for these extraordinarily high profits is
the drug industry's pricing policies. The industry tells us that it costs $800
million to bring a new drug to market, and threatens loss of innovation if

their prices, the highest in the world, are not held up. This is disingenuous on many counts—a study by Public Citizen puts this cost closer to $110 million and notes that more than one-half of studies involved in discovery and development of new drugs are funded at taxpayers expense by the National Institutes of Health (NIH).[59] Drug development conjures up visions of miracles, but 85 to 90 percent of new drugs are "me-too" drugs providing no important benefits over existing drugs.[60] Research and development (R&D) costs in 1998 accounted for just over one-third of the U.S. drug industry's marketing and administrative costs in that year.[61] Despite lower (regulated) drug prices abroad, a number of other countries spend more on drug R and D than the U.S., still profit from drug sales, and discover innovative new drugs proportionately with the U.S.[62]

While drug manufacturers enjoy many government protections (e.g., 17-year patent protection from competitors, generous tax policies, and freedom to set their own prices), the industry lobbies persistently and successfully at state and federal levels to retain and enhance these privileges. The industry hired 675 different lobbyists in 2002 (seven for every U.S. senator and more than one for every member of Congress), who were able to fend off price controls in the Medicare Prescription Drug, Improvement, and Modernization Act of 2003 (MMA).[63] Industry lobbyists appear to have been successful in extending monopolies of drug manufacturers and their prices as part of the Central American Free Trade Agreement (CAFTA),[64] and are actively engaged in defeating cost containment legislation in all 50 states.[65]

Many of the practices by the U.S. drug industry do not stand the light of day as it games the system to gain profits. Here is a partial list illustrating this point:

- false and misleading advertising which hypes the claimed benefits and downplays their risks[66]

- contractual restrictions on what insurers, hospitals, and other health facilities can tell physicians about certain drugs[67]

- delayed or inaccurate reporting of risks and adverse outcomes[68]

- gaming the system to extend patents and monopolies beyond 17 years or blocking other competitors from acquiring patents[69]

- gaming prices of AIDS drugs by quintupling prices of an older

AIDS drug, thereby forcing patients to drop competitors' drugs in favor or one manufacturer's newer drug[70]

• commissioning ghost writers to write articles promoting drugs without regard to their risks [71]

• publishing favorable research results while suppressing publication of negative results[72]

• attempting to harass, intimidate or discredit investigators who conduct unfavorable studies (e.g., a study showing that Synthroid was no more effective than less expensive competing drugs[73]

• manipulating the process of practice guideline development for marketing purposes[74]

• sharing non-public scientific data with selected Wall Street analysts while requiring them not to share the information[75]

• purchasing physician-specific prescribing data, often without physicians' knowledge, compiled by investor-owned intermediary companies and combined with physician profiles purchased from the AMAs Masterfile, for use by sales representatives for marketing purposes[76]

• recurrent prosecutions for outright fraud (e.g., GlaxoSmithKline paid $70 million in 2006 to settle suits against it by individuals, health plans and six states over fraudulently inflated prices of drugs purchased by federal health care programs[77]; Pfizer paid $430 million in 2004 to settle lawsuits involving marketing Neurontin for unapproved uses;[78] in 2007, Lilly agreed to pay up to $500 million to settle 18,000 lawsuits from patients who developed diabetes or other conditions after taking Zyprexa, which Lilly promoted for off-label uses while downplaying its risks;[79] Medco Health, the largest U.S. pharmacy benefit manager, agreed in 2006 to pay $155 million to settle fraud allegations, including kickbacks to insurers in exchange for business, switching prescriptions without physicians' consent, and canceling or destroying prescriptions to avoid penalties[80]

Medical Device Industry

This is a much bigger industry than one might think, with some 6,000 U.S. medical device companies bringing to market over 8,000 new products every year. These range from cardiac pacemakers, coronary stents, and implantable defibrillators to hip and knee replacements, lasers, and respiratory/patient monitoring equipment. The industry is dominated by very large health care corporations, including Medtronic, Inc. and Boston Scientific. The largest 2 percent of U.S. companies accounted for almost one-half of industry sales in 2001. Wall Street analysts carefully track the progress of FDA approval decisions as well as decisions by CMS for Medicare reimbursement. The industry is about as profitable as the drug industry while spending less on R & D.[81]

The medical device industry shares with the drug industry almost a free hand in setting prices for its products. For example, a recent survey of 100 U.S. hospitals found that the prices charged to hospitals for hip and knee replacements has been increasing by 8 percent a year in recent years; the prices for hip prostheses have ranged from $2,000 to $9,000 each.[82]

About one-half of medical devices are considered low-risk and are exempt from any regulation whatsoever. The others are subject to some review by the FDA, but this is a relatively corporate friendly process, as we will see in more detail in Chapter 7. That there is a risk of real hazards and adverse outcomes is indicated by the recall of more than 1,000 medical devices each year.[83]

These examples, unfortunately all too common, show that the unrestrained mission to make money by major corporations, together with lobbying and political chicanery, can trump manufacturers' responsibilities to patients.

- Many defective Bjork-Shiley heart valves were manufactured by Pfizer in its Caribbean factory. Although they were known to be subject to rupture due to poor welds and despite the written protests of their developer, Dr. Viking Bjork, they were marketed worldwide. After 800 valve fractures and 500 deaths, the company paid civil penalties in order to avoid criminal charges, then lobbied its trade group, the Health Industries Manufacturers Association (HIMA) to make efforts to ban all lawsuits against manufacturers of body parts. This was nearly successful when the Republican

Senate leader slipped such a provision into a bill; fortunately, it was killed after it was discovered.[84]

• Boston Scientific bought Guidant in 2006 for a total of about $27 billion. Together, they now have a No. 1 market position for coronary stents and No. 2 position for implantable pacemakers.[85] Guidant introduced an implantable heart device (Prism 2 DR) in 1999 that malfunctioned in more than one-third of patients over the next 19 months. The company failed to report to the FDA that this resulted in emergency surgery for 57 patients and 12 deaths. The device was finally recalled in 2001, and in 2003 the company agreed to a settlement of $92.4 million in criminal and civil penalties.[86,87] That same Guidant later delayed reporting of known short-circuits in some of its implantable cardiac defibrillators and continued to market the device (about $10,000 each) without informing physicians or patients about the risk of failure.[88,89] In early January, 2006, the FDA sent a warning letter to the company stating that further actions the agency might take "include, but are not limited to seizing your product inventory, obtaining a court injunction against further marketing of the product, or assessing civil money penalties."[90]

Dialysis Centers

Dialysis may seem like a straightforward procedure, not as prone to harm through the marketplace that is seen in the insurance, drug, and medical device industries. Yet a close review reveals serious problems here as well. The dialysis industry in the U.S. is 85 percent for-profit and investor-owned. Fresenius Medical Care North America (FMCNA) is by far the dominant company in this country, with over 1,000 dialysis clinics providing treatment to more than 75,000 people with chronic kidney failure. FMCNA was formed when the world's largest provider of dialysis products and services for patients with end-stage-renal disease, German-based Frensenius Medical Care AG, acquired National Medical Care (NMC) in 1996. According to its own Website, FMCNA is thriving, expecting growth in net income of 12 to 15 percent in 2005.[91]

Investor-owned dialysis services have not fared well by quality measures by comparisons to their not-for-profit counterparts. A 2002 study found their death rates to be 30 percent higher, with 26 percent fewer referrals for transplants, compared to not-for-profit dialysis centers.[92,93] For-profit dialysis centers have been found to be 55 percent more likely to use short dialysis periods, thereby decreasing survival but increasing profits. NMC manufactured dialyzers, labeled them for single use in only one patient, but then often reused them in their own centers, with savings of about $130 million a year through reuse of dialyzers which should have been discarded.[94] Following prosecution by the government for these kinds of practices, Frensenius pleaded guilty to charges of conspiracy and fraud, and paid $486 million in fines and settlements to the government in 2000.[95]

Nursing Homes

About two-thirds of the nation's nursing homes are for-profit and investor owned. But since the majority of reimbursement for nursing home care is from Medicaid, which has been continuously cut back in recent years, there are limited opportunities for profits these days without cutting corners on care. Not surprisingly, for-profit nursing homes have been found to cut nurse and nurses' aide positions and other expenses in their efforts to sustain their profits in a poorly reimbursed industry. A 2001 national study of U.S. nursing homes was done by Dr. Charlene Harrington and co-investigators from the Department of Social and Behavioral Sciences at the University of California San Francisco School of Nursing and the Center for National Health Care Studies at Cambridge Hospital and Harvard Medical School. With the intent to assess whether or not investor ownership of nursing homes compromises the quality of care, they studied almost 14,000 facilities. They found that investor-owned nursing homes had lower nurse staffing and worse quality of care. One quarter of nursing homes even had such deficiencies that some patients were either harmed or put at risk for serious injury or death. The authors of this study came to this conclusion:

"Nursing homes care for many people too frail, too sick, too poor, and too powerless to choose or even protest their care. We believe it unwise to entrust such vulnerable patients to profit-seeking firms."[96]

A series run by the *St. Louis Post Dispatch* in 2002 entitled "Neglected to Death" called attention to the scandalous condition of nursing homes in the U.S. Although there is a consensus among experts that 4.5 hours of nursing care are required every day to provide proper care to a nursing home patient, only one state (Alaska) exceeded this minimal level. It is difficult to recruit and retain staff in nursing homes, given the low salaries and difficult working hours day and night. Regulators are underfunded and penalties, when imposed, are minimal. For example, penalties for causing a preventable death can be as little as $250.[97] This bad situation is sure to become even worse for the 1.6 million people in nursing homes in view of the President's 2007 budget proposal calling for freezing nursing home reimbursement at their present levels. A 2006 study by *Consumer Reports* found that not-for-profit nursing homes provide almost an hour of additional nursing care per resident each day and almost twice as much care from registered nurses compared to their for-profit counterparts.[98] There can be little question that this difference is largely due to for-profit nursing homes cutting costs below levels needed to provide quality care, for the same reasons as for-profit dialysis centers reuse single-use dialyzers. In each case, the mission to serve investors trumps service to patients.

Medical Supply Industry

Another enormous industry that operates below the radar screen of public awareness is the medical supply industry. It is dominated in the U.S. by two large for-profit firms, Novation and Premier. They act as middlemen for about one-half of the country's not-for-profit hospitals. Each company uses the market power of more than 1,500 hospitals to negotiate the best prices for medical supplies, ranging from pharmaceuticals to pacemakers, syringes, and beds. But how these prices are negotiated is murky, and the industry has drawn scrutiny by regulators and Congressional committees for kickbacks and other illegal practices.

The basic conflict of interest is that these buying groups are financed by the companies that sell their products, not by the hospitals that buy them. Companies pay Novation and Premier hundreds of millions of dollars every year as a percentage of their sales to hospitals; the higher the hospitals' spending, the more the middlemen companies make from the suppliers.[99] Full accounting of these arrangements is generally not available to hospitals, and there is evidence of profiteering along the way through padding of salaries, expenses, and CEO compensation. For example, it was reported in 2002 that Premier's spending had increased by 84 percent over a previous three-year period, including increases of 53 percent in salaries and benefits over just two years earlier.[100] More recently, the Connecticut attorney general completed a two-year investigation of the little-known Healthcare Research and Development Institute (HRDI), which provides access to hospital executives for suppliers of medical devices and other services. HDRI agreed to pay a $150,000 fine after it was found that vendors were paying health care executives up to $50,000 to attend two private consulting sessions a year with hospital officials at such resorts as the Broadmoor.[101]

Novation, as the largest purchasing firm in the country, pools the purchasing volume of 2,200 hospitals, as well as thousands of nursing homes, clinics, and physicians' practices. It has been under investigation for unscrupulous business practices since 2004.[102]

CORPORATE SOCIAL RESPONSIBILITY: IS IT FOR REAL?

The foregoing discussion documents the extent to which conflicts of interest throughout the health care system serve investor-owned corporations at the expense of the public. Recognizing growing public concern over exorbitant CEO compensation and corporate scandals, a new coalition, Business for Social Responsibility (BSR), was established during the 1990s. Many Fortune 500 companies have joined this coalition since then, including General Electric, General Motors, Hewlett-Packard, Procter & Gamble, GlaxoSmithKline, Johnson & Johnson, Pfizer, and Wal-Mart.

According to its Web site, BSR is a global organization that "helps member companies achieve success in ways that respect ethical values, communities, and the environment. BSR provides information tools, training, and advisory services to make corporate social responsibility an integral part of business operations and strategies."[103] It is a laudable mission, and some of its member companies are initiating new socially responsive initiatives in their communities, including such activities as providing skill development and retraining programs for their workers, as well as efforts to help the homeless and renovate low-income housing.[104] This goal could not be more opposite than this philosophy expressed by that leading economic guru of market capitalism, Nobel laureate Milton Friedman, over 40 years ago:[105]

"Few trends could so thoroughly undermine the very foundations

of our free society as the acceptance by corporate officials of a social responsibility other than to make as much money for their shareholders as possible."

As much as this new direction being espoused by BSR is needed, indeed long overdue, it remains to be seen whether actual corporate behavior will match the rhetoric. These examples of major corporations involved in health care do not yet provide much reason for optimism.

- After facing billion dollar lawsuits during the 1990s for smoking-related claims, the tobacco industry agreed to a 25-year $200 billion settlement with the states, including a provision to stop marketing cigarettes to children.[106] Yet studies have shown that the major tobacco companies have not abided by that requirement.[107] R.J. Reynolds, maker of Camel cigarettes, is now promoting new flavored brands targeting young smokers which have a hidden plastic pellet placed in the cigarette filter; little is known about the health risks of these products, public health officials have not been informed of these new flavored technologies, and the flavored pellet is concealed from the consumer.[108]

- Philip Morris joined British American Tobacco (BAT), the world's second largest tobacco corporation, and Japan Tobacco in developing an international voluntary code for marketing the Global Reporting Initiative (GRI). Among its requirements, GRI called for accurate information about risks and outcomes of smoking. After much foot dragging, the first "social responsibility report" of BAT omitted information on adverse effects of smoking, and was regarded by many critics as artful PR and deception.[109]

- After getting its "sweetheart deal" in the 2003 Medicare drug legislation (MMA), including full protection of its pricing prerogatives, drug companies battle any efforts to expand drug discount programs for low-income people; for example, the industry spent $72 million to defeat a 2005 initiative in California which would have extended discounts to lower-income Californians.[110] Another strategy used by the drug industry is to finance charity organizations which can then turn around and pay co-payments for expensive drugs which many insured people cannot afford; drug companies not only receive profits from these sales, but can also deduct their charitable contributions from their taxes. [111]

- While the drug industry chases profits from blockbuster drugs (as is just good business), it sets prices at, or way beyond, what the market can bear (e.g., Genentech plans to charge about $100,000 per year of use of its new drug, Avastin, for colon cancer[112;] its second-quarter profits in 2006 rose by 79 percent, largely from sales of this drug.[113] Meanwhile, the drug industry avoids low profit-margin vaccines and antibiotics which are essential to health of the public; in 2004, for example, the U.S. was dependent for its supply of flu vaccine on a single French-owned plant in Pennsylvania.[114]

- General Electric, the largest corporation in the world and manufacturer of medical diagnostic equipment and robotics, has led the way in outsourcing of U.S. jobs to gain drastic reductions in labor costs abroad (e.g., its workers in Mexico are paid less than two dollars a day, without benefits).[115] Outsourcing has become big business in health care, with 7 to 10 percent of medical transcription now being done overseas, together with software development, customer service and call centers, back-office accounting and product development, and offshore teleradiology.[116] Although GE has taken some socially responsive initiatives, such as helping with early childhood education and helping the poor and disadvantaged minorities,[117] it tripled its net income while cutting its workforce by one-quarter through outsourcing,[118] has opposed any examination of its business operations by its own network program, NBC News,[119] and has joined with allied corporate partners in the Business Roundtable and other business groups to fight any efforts by the states to limit outsourcing.[120]

- Wal-Mart, the world's biggest retailer and the country's largest private employer, despite annual sales of some $245 billion in 2002, skimps on health care benefits for its own workers (Table 5.1), despite its national PR campaign to represent itself as a

TABLE 5.1

Wal-Mart: Rich Company, Poor Health Care

- America's largest private employer - 1.4 million workers

- Annual profit = $7 billion; Walton's net worth = $102 billion

- Average wages about $7.50 per hour/$15,000 per year

- 38 percent of employees are covered by company health plan vs. 68% at other large firms

- Wal-Mart Plan has $1,000 deductible, pays 80 percent after that, excludes coverage for vaccines, etc.

- In Georgia, 10,261 children of Wal-Mart employees are enrolled in SCHIP - one for every four Wal-Mart employees, far more than other retailers-1/16 of all SCHIP enrollees are WAL-MART workers' children.

SOURCE: Woolhandler S. & Himmelstein D.U. 2005 Slide Set. Physicians for a National Health Program, Chicago, IL.

good employer with happy employees. The Maryland Legislature passed a law in early 2006 requiring all companies with more than 10,000 employees to spend at least 8 percent of their payrolls on health insurance or else pay the difference into a state Medicaid fund. Wal-Mart, below the 8 percent level, bitterly fought this bill, which nevertheless was passed over the Governor's veto.[121] In a major effort to remake its image, Wal-Mart has hired Edelman, the largest U.S. public relations firm, to promote itself as a positive social force. The anti-union Wal-Mart, one of the world's largest companies with 6,700 stores and $312 billion in sales in 2005, now has a massive PR campaign underway, including a new "grass-roots" organization, Working Families for Wal-Mart, funded by the company and staffed by Edelman operatives.[122]

- In 2002, the CEO of Bristol-Myers Squibb was paid $74.9

million plus stock options valued at another $76 million.[123] In 2004, salaries and the values of unexercised stock options totaled about $48 million for the CEO at Merck, $43 million for Pfizer's CEO, and $40 million for Johnson & Johnson's CEO.[124] How can we view these levels of compensation, especially as drugs become increasingly unaffordable, as anything but corporate greed?

As we see from the above, corporate social responsibility is still not much of a reality. Competition among corporations for investor dollars appears to be a root cause of unethical and criminal behavior of corporate interests in the health care marketplace. These practices are far more widespread than a few bad apples in management. Charles Derber, Professor of Sociology at Boston College and author of the excellent book *Corporation Nation: How Corporations Are Taking Over Our Lives and What We Can Do About It*, offers this perspective on the subject:

> *"Only a larger social movement, in concert with current corporate advocates, can move a meaningful corporate-responsibility agenda from the fringes of the business world to its cutting edge. The corporate-responsibility movement should not be abandoned. But it should be redefined and absorbed within a new, authentic populism."*[125]

If the interests of patients and their families are to be protected within our complex health care marketplace, we cannot rely upon the voluntary actions of corporate interests. More effective regulation of the market will be required. Here is how Robert Kuttner sums up the problem with markets:

> *"No matter how hard the enthusiasts of the new corporation try to infer social values from the logic of competition itself, markets remain fundamentally amoral; values need to be found elsewhere—and then imposed on corporations lest they overrun everything that we hold dear."*[126]

It is clear that the public interest is being overrun by private stakeholders in the medical industrial complex. In the next chapter we will examine what human costs are involved by allowing these stakeholders to dominate the marketplace and dictate health policy.

CHAPTER 6

MARKET TIERS AND PATIENTS' TEARS: THE HUMAN COSTS OF AN UNFETTERED MARKET

> *"Market capitalism will have the same inefficient, exploitative outcome as Soviet Communism if the ownership of resources becomes concentrated in the hands of fewer and fewer large corporations; and if economic business decisions come to be made by those relatively few individuals who own and/or operate large concentrated corporations."*

Dr. Friedrich A. Hayek,
the *American Economic Review* 1946,[1] Professor of Social and Moral Sciences, University of Chicago, (1950-1962)

One might think that the above statement by Dr. Hayek, internationally acclaimed economist, neuroscientist and Nobel laureate in Economics in 1974, was that of a radical, but the opposite in the case. As the author of a classic 1944 book, *The Road to Serfdom*, Dr. Hayek was actually a leading light for conservatives. The 50th Anniversary edition of this book in 1994 featured an introduction by Milton Friedman, who as we saw in the last chapter, had little use for corporate social responsibility. So even as a conservative economist, Hayek had serious concerns that unrestrained markets could go too far.

We have already seen how our health care market place works, and how the sick are being exploited in today's market-based health care "system." Relentless increases in costs are pricing health care beyond the reach of tens of millions of ordinary Americans. As health care costs continue to rise at rates well above cost-of-living increases, we are seeing increased tiering (i.e., levels or strata) of coverage and benefits among Americans. Higher-income families have access to any and all services while lower-income families have difficulty gaining access to even the most basic health care services. With containment of prices and costs nowhere on the horizon, we need to ask where this runaway train is going.

This chapter will attempt to answer that question by asking three related questions: (1) can the current trend toward consumer-directed health care (CDHC) rein in health care inflation and waste in the system?; (2) to what

extent are tiered health care services limiting access to care?; and (3) what
is the human cost of tiering in health care?

CONSUMER-DIRECTED HEALTH CARE: ANOTHER ILLUSION OF "REFORM"

It stands to reason that the costs of health care will go up each year
if only on the basis of our expanding and aging population. However,
the continued cost increases in U.S. health care are way beyond those
adjustments. They far exceed cost-of-living increases, and represent the
dominant problem which has resisted all efforts to manage costs over the
years. The list of failed attempts is now long, including diagnostic related
groups (DRGs), managed care, and utilization management. Stakeholders
in our increasingly expensive health care system are now serving up other
incremental hopes for cost containment, including disease management,
wide adoption of electronic information systems, tiering of benefits, and
consumer-directed health care (CDHC). As we will see in later chapters,
however, none of these approaches are likely to slow down this runaway
train, pushed along as it is by the kinds of drivers discussed in Chapter 2.

A look at the big financial picture is daunting. Total health care spending
increased by 7.9 percent in 2004 compared to a rise in the Consumer Price
Index (CPI) of 3.3 percent in that year.[2] Home care for the elderly has become
especially costly—Medicare spending for home care skyrocketed by 19.3
percent in 2004.[3] Medicare, Medicaid, and Social Security account for 43
percent of the federal budget today, costing the federal government about
$3 billion a day.[4] We now have an almost $300 billion federal deficit not
including the Iraq war and Katrina hurricane relief, and the budget deficit
is expected by the Congressional Budget Office to exceed $300 billion a
year for much of the next decade.[5] Most state budgets are also strained to
their limits. While carrying a very large debt load of $288 billion, they are
under pressure from rising Medicaid costs; many states have shortfalls in
their funding of public employee pension plans, which could threaten their
credit-worthiness.[6]

The intensity of the political battle over how to constrain these runaway
costs is indicated by the House of Representatives' budget deficit package
passed in early 2006 by the slimmest of margins, 216-214, with Vice
President Cheney casting the deciding vote. Over the five-year period ending

in 2010, the bill will cut $6.4 billion in Medicare spending (including higher premiums and freezing payments to home health care providers) and reduce federal spending on Medicaid by $4.8 billion (by increasing co-payments and cutting payments for prescription drugs).[7]

The problem with all these attempts to constrain health care costs is that they are efforts at the margins, and fail to address the main causes of health care inflation. Our massive private health insurance bureaucracy consumes 31 percent of every health care dollar.[8] Pharmaceutical and medical device manufacturers bring to market billion-dollar products without regard to their cost-effectiveness, and then set their prices to what the market will bear. Some reports have estimated that up to one-third of all health care services are either unnecessary or of little value and a 1998 study by Rand and UCLA investigators found that 30 percent of acute care provided in the U.S. is actually *contraindicated*, often even hazardous. We have excess capacity of the system (at least in more affluent and higher-reimbursed parts of the country) which profit from patient demand, whether necessary or not.[11] Ironically enough, areas of excess capacity and higher reimbursement actually provide *lower* quality of care than in areas with lower reimbursement, as has been so well documented by researchers at Dartmouth Medical School.[12]

None of our cost-containment initiatives to date address these important drivers of inflation, rather they merely shift the burden of who pays. The common denominator of nearly all current health care policies in this era of consumer directed health care is to shift more costs to consumers themselves. As we saw in the last chapter, employers are shifting to defined contribution instead of defined benefit plans (*if* they cover their employees at all) while cutting or eliminating pensions and health care benefits [13,14] Insurers are promoting more bare-bones policies which provide little or no protection against accident or major illness. Medicare and Medicaid are requiring higher premiums or co-payments.

The centerpiece of the current push by the Bush Administration and conservative legislators is the health savings account (HSA), coupled with high-deductible health insurance (HDHI) plans. We saw in the last chapter how scant some of these policies are and how high the deductibles can run (eg.,up to $10,000). These plans give the insurance industry another bonanza as they skim off the healthiest Americans and provide them with an illusion of being insured. The perverse result is adverse selection whereby the healthy join low-risk pools of people that insurance companies can profit from and leave higher-risk enrollees to public programs (if they qualify), or to swell the ranks of the uninsured.

The consequences for individuals and their families of these plans can be devastating. Already, we know that medical bills account for about one-half of all bankruptcies, and that three-quarters of those filing for bankruptcy were employed and insured whey they fell ill.[15] As HDHI plans become more widespread, we can expect to see many more Americans face bankruptcy from medical debt. With these underinsurance plans, they are just one accident or major illness away from financial disaster. In a recent interview, Bruce Bodaken, CEO of Blue Shield of California, envisions low-cost policies costing about $50 a month that can provide about six physician visits, three hospital days, and generic drug coverage with a limit. He concedes the limits of such coverage—"you'd obviously burn through that very quickly if you had a chronic illness," but maintains that "it would cover about 90 percent of what the uninsured need."[16]

HSAs are tax-preferred savings accounts, into which individuals, their employers (or both) can contribute on a tax-deductible basis up to $2,850 for an individual or $5,650 for a family each year.[17] Qualifying HDHI plans must have deductibles of at least $1,050 for individuals or $2,100 for a family.[18]

HSAs are being touted by their proponents as a strategy for cost containment by making consumers more prudent in their choices of health care, and also as a way to make health insurance more affordable for the uninsured. Both claims are unrealistic, for these reasons:[19]

- The 10 percent of the population which incurs 72 percent of all health care spending generally have such acute and or chronic illnesses that they are not able to "shop around" for the best prices; comparative prices are usually not available; urgency to access providers often precludes such shopping, and cognitive or language barriers are formidable barriers for many patients. Moreover, physicians typically play a larger role in deciding among providers, facilities, and treatment options, while the restrictions placed upon patients by managed care organizations further limit enrollees' choices.

- Individual consumers have no clout to influence provider prices;

the uninsured are generally billed undiscounted prices, often two or more times higher than what the insured pay[20]

- Since lower-income people tend to delay or skip necessary care if they can't afford the full bill, their health care expenses are often higher because they present for care with more advanced, or otherwise preventable disease.[21]

- The Tax Policy Center estimates that 95 percent of all health care spending from insured households exceeds HSA deductibles, leaving little incentive to bargain hunt after reaching their deductibles.[22]

- Lower-income people and those with chronic illness are not likely to find HSAs affordable or useful; according to the Kaiser Family Foundation, 38 percent of American families earn less than $25,000 a year, with 23 percent of families earning between $25,000 and $50,000 a year;[23] most lower-income families have little left to put money aside in an HSA after paying for housing, food and other basic necessities.

- Any tax savings would not make much difference in allowing lower-income people to buy health insurance (eg., a dollar put in an HSA saves 35 cents for an individual in the 35 percent tax bracket, but only 10 cents for someone in the 10 percent bracket).

- The General Accounting Office (GAO) has already shown that most enrollees in the new HDHI/HSA option in the Federal Employees Health Benefits Program (FEHBP) are higher-income people[24] In essence then, while HSAs confer tax benefits on more affluent individuals, they have little to do with cost containment.

Despite their problems, HSAs are the darlings of Wall Street (which gets to manage potentially vast new sums of money), the government (which can shift more of its public entitlement responsibilities to consumers), and employers (who can decrease their contributions to their employees' health care). A 2006 report found that employer health plans across the country will cut their average annual premiums for their employees' family coverage from $8,167 to $6,245 for HDHI coverage with accompanying HSAs.[25]

TIERING WITHIN THE SYSTEM

Another increasingly common strategy intended to place more responsibility on consumers to make cost-conscious health purchasing choices is the concept of tiering of coverage and benefits. This option now cuts across many parts of the system from insurance plans to hospitals and prescription drugs.

The most important tier in our system, of course, is that between the uninsured and insured. This big difference in access to care is not much improved, however, by many of the *underinsurance* plans being marketed to the public, especially to younger and healthier people. As we saw in the last chapter, these include HDHI plans with deductibles up to $10,000,[26] limited benefit plans with caps at only $1,000 (e.g., Wal-Mart, McDonalds),[27] and short-term policies excluding all pre-existing conditions.[28]

Many choices are now available to consumers for hospital and health plan services. Tiers can cover most hospital services but usually exclude emergency services. Blue Shield of California, for example, assigns facilities with average costs (weighted for inpatient and outpatient services) that are consistently above the average for their regional and teaching status group to an "affiliate" low co-payment tier (85 percent of contracted hospitals) with the remaining 15 percent in a high co-payment "choice" tier.[29] In the Boston area, where higher-cost large academic medical centers (AMCs) dominate the market, the Tufts plan encourages enrollees to use lower-cost community hospitals whenever possible (the "core" tier), with AMCs in the higher-cost "premium" tier.[30]

Tiering is also applied to other services as well. Specialty hospitals cater to more affluent patients and typically avoid their share of the uninsured.[31] Tiering may be extended to ambulatory surgery centers, radiation and chemotherapy centers, and substance abuse services. Boutique or "concierge" practices are another example where an "upper tier" of more affluent patients is selected by physicians for comprehensive continuity of care.[32] Physician visits are now tiered to many plans, with patients paying larger co-payments to see a specialist than to see a primary care physician. And of course, another very common example of tiering today involves prescription drugs. Patients typically pay less for off-patent generic drugs than for an on-patent brand-name drug, less for on-formulary drugs compared to those off formulary, and less if a prescription is filled by a mail-order house than by a retail pharmacy.[33]

There is considerable controversy about the effects of tiering on both patients as well as the system. Tom Prisilac, CEO of Cedars-Sinai Medical Center in Los Angeles (in a high-cost tier) worries about adverse impacts on AMCs which are heavily involved in medical education, research and uncompensated care. He also contends that tiering cannot contain costs, which are driven by factors other than consumer choice, such as advancing technology, specialist-based practice patterns, costs of drugs, and competition for profit.[34] James Robinson, Professor of Health Economics at the School of Public Health, University of California, Berkeley, likewise has doubts that tiering will be very effective as a cost-containment strategy.[35]

There is no question but that current tiering trends negatively impact lower-income and sicker individuals and their families. As co-payments increase, a 2002 study found that one-half of chronically ill patients with household incomes less than $50,000 a year postponed or skipped physician visits.[36]

TEARS FOR A GROWING POPULATION

Tiering and related policies of CDHC are leading to more tears among not just lower-income people, but the middle class as well. As is obvious, unrelenting inflation of health care costs leads to decreased access to necessary care, reduced quality of care, and worse outcomes. These deteriorating trends have produced two crises—growing unaffordability of care and a shredding safety net. The two crises exacerbate each other: as health care becomes less affordable, the safety net is further strained. As it deteriorates, more people delay or avoid necessary care, and the cost of the care rises.

Unaffordability of Health Care:
Health Security Under Siege

A 2002 national survey by the Kaiser Family Foundation found that 60 percent of families earning less than $50,000 a year had problems paying their medical bills.[37] With a median annual family income of about $41,000, U.S. households are spending almost 14 percent of disposable income on servicing their debts, and median household debt is now more than $100,000.[38] Families earning annual incomes of less than about 300 percent of the federal poverty level (FPL) ($58,050 was 300 percent of the FPL in 2005 for a family of four), account for about one-half of the non-elderly U.S. population.[39] Many of these families find it difficult to gain access to medical care and still pay for other basic necessities—rent, mortgage payments, transportation, and food.[40] There are now more than 46 million Americans without health insurance, and two-thirds of these have cost-related barriers to physician visits, prescription drugs, and necessary care.[41] Further, 56 percent of the uninsured are ineligible for public safety net programs but can't afford coverage.[42]

There is widespread consensus that America is now in the midst of its second Gilded Age. Income inequality has become wider than at any previous time in the country's history. The wealthiest 1 percent of Americans now own more wealth than the bottom 90 percent of the U.S. population.[43] At the low end, the federal minimum wage has been frozen at $5.15 an hour since 1996, despite many legislative efforts to increase it. Between 1980 and 2004, real wages in manufacturing fell by 1 percent while the real incomes of the richest 1 percent rose by 135 percent.[44] The compensation of corporate CEOs grew from 40 times the median U.S. income in 1978 to 500 times that income in 2000.[45]

The middle class is being squeezed from all sides by adverse trends, including corporate downsizing of the U.S. workforce, outsourcing of jobs overseas, and stagnant wages not keeping up with the cost of living. The number of middle-class jobs has dropped since 2000, and most new jobs are low-income.[46] In their excellent 2003 book, *The Two-Income Trap: Why Middle-Class Mothers and Fathers Are Going Broke*, Elizabeth Warren and Amelia Warren Tyagi, report that the average two-income middle-class family today has *less* discretionary income than average one-income families in 1970.[47] Median family income even dropped by $1,500 a year between 2000 and 2003.[48] A 2006 study found that median household debt has soared in recent years while income has remained flat (Figure 6.1).[49] American households spent $42 billion more than they earned in 2005—for the first time since 1933 during the Great Depression.[50]

Deteriorating Safety Net

Meanwhile, as wages stagnate for middle-class Americans, household debt increases, and prices of health care exceed cost-of-living increases, the nation's safety net continues to fall apart. What safety net we have is a

FIGURE 6.1

Real Median Houshold Net Worth, Debt and Income, in 2000 Dollars

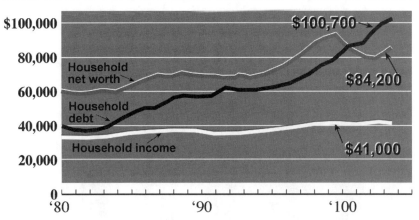

Consumers seized on low interest rates to buy new homes and refinance old home loans. Households debt outpaced wealth as income remained flat.

SOURCE: Reprinted with permission from: Henderson N. Greenspan's mixed legacy: America prospered during the Fed chiefs tenure, but built up massive debt. *Washington Post National Weekly Edition*. January 30February 5, 2006, p 6.

loosely woven patchwork of mostly public programs, including community health centers, local health departments, urgent care clinics, and emergency rooms reimbursed mainly by Medicaid, Medicare, and SCHIP. Collectively they are underfunded, with low reimbursement levels threatening the viability of facilities and the participation of physicians and other providers. Figure 6.2 shows wide disparities in federal per-capita funding for various public programs, with the Indian Health Service (IHS) most seriously underfunded.[51]

With the exception of community health centers, which have received modest funding increases in recent years, annual funding cutbacks are the rule. Faced with rapidly increased costs of Medicaid (up 63 percent in the last five years to over $300 billion nationally), the National Governors Association in 2005 pushed for more flexibility in their efforts to rein in state spending on Medicaid, including tighter eligibility criteria, increased cost sharing, and cutting benefits.[52] In the 774-page Budget Deficit Reduction Act

FIGURE 6.2

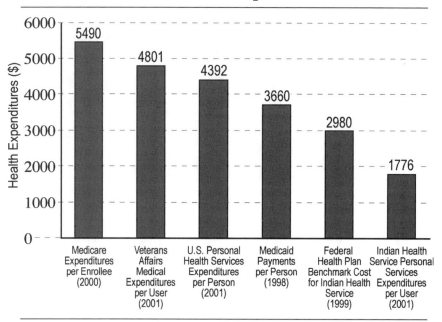

Comparative Per-Capita Federal Health Care Expenditures

Data from the Indian Health Service

SOURCE: Reprinted with permission from: Roubideaux Y. Beyond Red Lake-The persistent crisis in American Indian health care. N Engl J Med 353(18):1882, 2005.

passed by Congress in early 2006, states are permitted to impose premiums and co-payments as high as 10 percent of a medical service, a level certain to have a profound impact on low-income individuals and families.[53] States are also given more latitude to set their own eligibility requirements and benefit packages. Missouri has already decreased its eligibility threshold for a family of three to qualify for Medicaid to an annual income of only $3,504 (only 22 percent of federal poverty level).[54] Many states have made draconian cuts in Medicaid enrollments, while cutting back such benefits as dental, vision, and mental health services. Utah even eliminated Medicaid coverage of hospital and specialty care.[55] California, which already has the lowest physician reimbursement rate of all 50 states in its Medi-Cal program, has made a further cut of 5 percent in 2006, and only one-half of providers accepted Medi-Cal patients before the latest cut.[56]

The bottom line of all these cutbacks is that "savings" are achieved by federal and state governments by reducing essential services for the most vulnerable among us. Shortly after the Deficit Reduction Act was passed by Congress, the Congressional Budget Office (CBO) concluded that "about 80 percent of the savings from higher cost-sharing would be due to decreased use of services."[57] Critics point to the inequities of these budget cuts, particularly in view of the failure by conservative legislators to enact other much larger ways to reduce the deficit, such as repeal of tax cuts benefiting the affluent, permitting the government to negotiate discounts of drug prices for the new Medicare drug benefit, and eliminating over payment subsidies to private Medicare Advantage plans.[58]

Community health centers (CHCs) deserve special mention. While they are exemplary in terms of accessible and culturally sensitive care to underserved populations, they remain underfunded and underequipped to realize the hopes of the Administration to seriously impact the nation's uninsured rate or racial and ethnic disparities in health care. For example, in 2004, when the average annual per capita health care costs were $5,600 only $36 was allocated for each uninsured person receiving care in a community health center.[59] At that time, CHCs provided care for only 20 percent of the country's underserved and 10 percent of the uninsured.[60] Nor are emergency rooms likely to fill the gap. One might expect that they might be crowded with visits by the uninsured, but studies have shown the opposite. A 2004 national study by the Community Tracking Study Household Survey found that 85 percent of ER visits were by people with health insurance, and that one-quarter of people without a regular source of primary care were less likely to make an emergency visit than those with a primary care physician, at least in part to avoid higher charges of emergency room services.[61]

Adverse Impacts of Cost-Sharing and CDHC

The above two trends come together as a "perfect storm" builds in U.S. health care. Here are some of the major ways in which increased cost-sharing of CDHC negatively impacts patients, their families, and the system itself.

1.   The ranks of the uninsured and underinsured grow.

There is a large and growing gap between those that can afford
health insurance and eligibility for Medicaid. In Oregon, for
example, within a year after "modest" premiums and co-payments
were imposed, one-half of Medicaid patients disenrolled due to
these costs, and three-quarters of them became uninsured.[62] In
Rhode Island, new premiums ranging from $43 to $58 per month,
based on income, resulted in nearly one in five families with
incomes above 150 percent of poverty being disenrolled within
three months due to non-payment of premiums.[63] As insurers
sharpen their medical underwriting and avoid sick enrollees (or
charge them unaffordable premiums), and as employers reduce
their contributions to their employees' health plans, more people
cannot afford health insurance. In addition, just being able to
afford health insurance has little to do with being able to afford
out-of-pocket costs of care, especially as bare-bones insurance
plans multiply. A 2005 report from the California HealthCare
Foundation found, for example, that the premium for Blue Cross
or Blue Shield plans with limited benefits and higher cost-sharing
would be 66 percent (not a typo!) of the entire income of minimal
wage employees; for employees with median wages, the median
premium was 14 percent (PPO) and 17 percent (HMO) of wages.[64]
Most experts believe that out-of-pocket health care spending over
10 percent of annual income raises significant barriers to health
care access for most people.

**2.   The uninsured and underinsured delay, avoid, or other-
wise cannot gain access to necessary care.**

There is an extensive literature over many years documenting this
fact. Proponents of cost sharing argue that patients overutilize
health care unnecessarily, especially if insured. The problem with
this theory (effectively rebutted by Dr. John Nyman in his new
theory of insurance),[65] is that necessary and beneficial medical care
is delayed or avoided, including preventive care. What may seem

to higher-income people to be "small" increases in co-payments can have large impacts on lower-income patients' use of health care. Several examples illustrate the point. After introduction of cost-sharing to an annual maximum of $200, a large study of 55,000 low-income people in Quebec, Canada, found that use of essential drugs dropped by 15 percent, emergency room visits doubled, and adverse events (hospitalizations, nursing home admissions, and mortality) also doubled.[66] A 2004 Rand study found that doubling co-payments for prescription drugs, resulted in reduction by one-quarter in overall days supplied for anti-hypertensives, antidepressants, and antidiabetic drugs.[67] A 2005 report from the Center for Studying Health System Change found that the uninsured are as likely as insured to perceive need for care, but only half as likely to get care.[68] A 2005 study of uninsured patients found that only one-quarter of them were offered follow-up clinic appointments for urgent problems even after they offered to pay $20 and arrange payments of the balance.[69]

3.   **The uninsured and underinsured have
                  worse clinical outcomes**

In her 2003 testimony to a Congressional Subcommittee, Patricia Neuman, Director of the Kaiser Medicare Policy Project, called attention to the "triple jeopardy" for elderly and disabled people with modest incomes—(1) unlikely to have supplemental insurance to cover cost-sharing requirements; (2) with lower incomes, more likely to be in poorer health and need more medical care; and (3) will have worse outcomes if they don't get additional medical care.[70] That same summary applies to younger people as well.

The Institute of Medicine's (IOM) Committee on the Consequences of Uninsurance has produced a series of important reports documenting worse outcomes, including less preventive care; higher rates of premature death from heart disease, cancer, and other chronic diseases; less care for mental illness; and higher risk of disability among the uninsured compared to their insured counterparts.[71] The IOM's 2003 report calculated that the aggregate, annualized cost of the diminished health and shorter life spans of Americans is between $65 and $130 billion for each year of health insurance foregone, that 8 million uninsured people with chronic disease have increased morbidity and worse outcomes, and that 18,000 Americans die prematurely each year.[72]

4.   **Gaps persist, even increase, in quality of care due to racial ethnic, and income disparities.**

Despite a national goal to reduce or eliminate health disparities by 2010, these gaps persist, and in the case of Hispanics, are increasing. Figure 6.3 shows the latest figures as revealed in the most recent National Healthcare Disparities Report. Compared to a previous report, the gap has widened for 58 percent of Hispanics. A striking finding is that 85 percent of people earning less than the federal poverty level are receiving poorer quality of care compared to high-income people (those 400 percent or more above the federal poverty level—more than $77,400 for a family of four in 2005).[73]

5.   **Medical debt and bankruptcies now increasingly common for the middle class.**

Median household debt outstanding has jumped by 80 percent in the U.S. since 1990.[74] A 2005 report found that about one-half of two million Americans filing for bankruptcy in 2001 did so as a result of medical bills. Three-quarters of those declaring bankruptcy were middle-class and insured; more than one-half had at least some college education. The average out-of-pocket costs since the start of the illness leading to bankruptcy was $11,854. Since 1981, the risk of medical bankruptcy has increased by 2,200 percent. While COBRA (Consolidated Omnibus Budget Reconciliation Act of 1985) is intended to provide continued health insurance coverage after loss of a job, its premiums are

FIGURE 6.3

Gaps Persist in the Quality of Care Received by Various Demographic Groups

Quality of Care

By selected groups who experienced better, same or poorer quality of care compared with reference group.

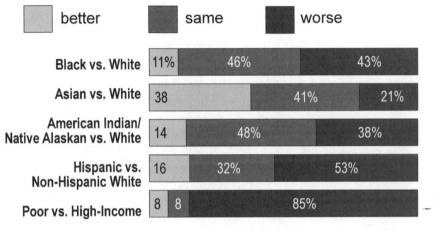

- ☐ better
- ■ same
- ■ worse

	better	same	worse
Black vs. White	11%	46%	43%
Asian vs. White	38	41%	21%
American Indian/ Native Alaskan vs. White	14	48%	38%
Hispanic vs. Non-Hispanic White	16	32%	53%
Poor vs. High-Income	8	8	85%

— bigged ∆: income

Poor: family income less than 100% of federal poverty level. High-income: family income
400% or more over federal poverty level.
NOTE: Some categories do not add to 100% because of rounding.

SOURCE: Reprinted with permission from: Kaufman M. & Stein R. Whats Ailing Us? Health Care costs rise to a record 16 percent of nation's economic output. *Washington Post National Weekly Edition,* January 16-22, 2006:p21

often more than $10,000 a year and only one in four workers who lose their jobs can afford continued coverage.[75,76] Since the classic 2005 bankruptcy study by Harvard researchers, the insurance industry commissioned and funded a rebuttal to that study, claiming that most of those filing for bankruptcy were not middle-class and not bankrupted by illness.[77] The Harvard group effectively discredited this attack, showing, for example, that the insurance industry relied on debtors' incomes just before filing for bankruptcy, thereby creating the impression that those filing were not middle class. But measuring income at this point ignores the starting point before the medical and financial troubles began, and disingenuously picks up the story when those filing for bankruptcy had already lost jobs or small businesses because of illness.[78]

6.   **Cost-sharing raises little income, just shifts costs and decreases necessary health care services**

As we have seen, despite the claims and beliefs by advocates of moral hazard, imprudent choices by patients are hardly a main factor driving health care inflation. There are many other more powerful cost drivers in play. Whatever cost "savings" are gained by increased cost sharing is achieved by limiting necessary services.[79] A 2006 special report on Medicaid by the Pew Center on the States drew this conclusion:

> *"In the final analysis, as much as cuts in Medicaid may seem like real savings for the states and federal government, the bills for uncompensated health care don't go away. They're paid by average Americans and by a variety of state and federal programs. The illusion of real savings comes because those expenses don't flow through just one program and aren't easily tracked."* [80]

CONCLUDING COMMENT

As it is clear from the foregoing, consumer-directed health care (CDHC) has little chance to contain run-away health care costs. It merely shifts more costs to individuals. That cost-shift results in growing tiers of unaffordability, further straining public safety net programs. As the nation's safety net further deteriorates, we are seeing more barriers to access, more inequities, and worse outcomes of care. Despite the depth of these problems, there is a fix, as we shall see in Chapter 11. For now, however, let's turn to the question of how this irrational and unaccountable system ever got this way, and how it is perpetuated despite its growing departure from the public interest.

CHAPTER 7

WHERE ARE MARKET FORCES TAKING US? AND WHY AREN'T THEY SELF-CORRECTING?

"... in Washington at the moment we have a government owned and operated by a rapacious oligarchy that seeks to privatize—i.e., appropriate or destroy—the public infrastructure (schools, roads, air, water, power plants, bridges, levees, hospitals, forests, broadcast frequencies, wetlands, bids) that provides the country with the foundations of its common enterprise."

Lewis Lapham, Editor of *Harper's Magazine*[1]

" I don't want to abolish government. I simply want to reduce it to the size where I can drag it into the bathroom and drown it in the bathtub."

Grover Norquist, president of Americans for Tax Reform
in 2001 on NPR's *Morning Edition*[2]

The above two polar opposite views illustrate an intense and ongoing political battle across a wide divide of opinion about the proper role of government. Lapham speaks from the liberal end of the spectrum, making what may seem to some an unsupported claim about the agenda of powerful interests in this country. Yet Norquist from the right confirms Lapham's worst fears, making the objective clear—destroy the common good.

It does strain credibility, but how in this most affluent country in the world, which prides itself on its innovation and egalitarian values, could such an obviously broken health care system persist? Are its problems unique and insoluble? What are the forces that perpetuate our broken system, even as it gets worse? Complicated questions, but it seems to me that the following reasons largely account for the continued failure of incremental "reforms" to get a handle on this unaccountable system.

Blind Worship of Markets

As we saw in Chapter 3, our society has been engulfed over at least 30 years by an ideology that the "free market" will fix any of our problems, if we just give it room to work its magic. The claim of market superiority to any other approach has been repeated so often, and in so many ways, as to become a meme (i.e., part of our language and culture). In a recent article in *Harper's Magazine*, Gordon Bigelow, author of *Fiction, Famine, and the Rise of Economics in Victorian Britain and Ireland*, observes that U. S. policy debate, both in Congress and in the press, proceeds today as if the neoclassical theory of the free market were incontrovertible; endorsed by science and ordained by God." As he further notes, however, "free markets don't promote public virtue, they promote private interest."[3]

We have been told to worship markets as the answer to any policy question, including in health care. Markets are touted as being "the American way," a guarantor of greater efficiency and value through competition. This message has been picked up and disseminated by the media with very little critical analysis. We have seen a proliferation of private think tanks in this country over the last 30 years, mostly on the conservative end of the political spectrum, such as the Heritage Foundation and the American Enterprise Institute for Public Policy Research. Most are well funded, produce studies and reports favoring their own interests, and press the case for competitive open markets. They permeate the media through press releases, their web sites, television, talk radio, guest editorials and Op-Ed pieces in major newspapers. They lobby actively at all levels of government, and some of their "white papers" are even released by members of Congress.[4,5]

In Chapter 3, we reviewed a number of well-documented ways in which markets fail to function in a freely competitive way in health care and how the "free" market is in fact a set of rules to favor more powerful interests over others. Yet, despite these obvious failures, the drumbeat of the virtues of markets still goes on, an incredible disconnect from reality. Two recent examples bring the point home. The private option Medicare HMOs of the 1990s (Medicare + Choice) were discredited by their track record as a way to provide added value or cost savings for Medicare beneficiaries. With government subsidies, they cost more than traditional Medicare. Yet their successors, Medicare Advantage (MA) programs, were established in the 2003 Medicare bill and are being promoted by conservative policymakers and legislators in open denial of M + C shortcomings.[6] MA programs are also more costly than traditional Medicare, and are dependent upon subsidies for their existence. Despite the recommendations of the Medicare Payment Advisory Commission (MedPAC) to vary payments by risk adjustment and to stop subsidies of private Medicare plans, conservative legislators continue to protect MA programs from loss of their overpayments well above the costs of traditional fee-for-service Medicare.[7,8]

Another jarring example of how the marketplace doesn't serve the public interest is the failure of our vaunted pharmaceutical industry to assure a reliable supply of flu vaccine, when in 2004 we were dependent on a single-French owned plant in Pennsylvania for our nation's supply.[9] Efficient business principles call for avoidance of excess inventory. However, when applied to preparedness for major health care needs, such as a pandemic flu outbreak, efficient markets fail to protect the public. As director of the Center for Infectious Disease Research and Policy at the University of Minnesota, Dr. Michael Osterholm notes that our economy favors just-in-time delivery with no surge capacity, leaving us vulnerable to acute shortages of critical products to deal with crises, such as vaccines, syringes, and ventilators. A recent report by the Trust for America's Health, a public health advocacy group based in Washington, D.C.,estimates that 40 percent of the states lack enough backup medical supplies to deal with a pandemic flu or other major disease outbreak.[10]

Deregulation and Corporate-Friendly Regulation

We have had an extended period of deregulation in this country since about 1980, when free market principles were reasserted in a new era of a global economy. Taxes were reduced for the rich, corporations were allowed more flexibility to merge and downsize their workforces, and corporations were given new subsidies and tax breaks.[11] The trend has been to limit the funding and capability of regulatory agencies and curtail new legislation while developing a "cooperative" relationship with industry. Free trade in a global economy has given a further boost to the deregulation trend. The U.S. has played a leading role in the development of the World Trade Organization (WTO) and other new institutions of globalization. As a result, more than one-half of the 100 largest "economies" in the world are now corporations, not countries; nine of the twelve largest health care corporations in the world are U.S. corporations.[12] WTO governance is mostly a process of closed-door negotiations, and its rules often supercede the laws or regulations of any given country.[13]

The Food and Drug Administration (FDA) provides an interesting example of how corporate-friendly the regulatory process has become. The agency dates back almost 100 years, having been established after the Pure Food and Drug Act was passed in 1906. Its first director, Harvey Wiley, presciently recognized the special challenges to this agency as early as 1930:

> *"There is a distinct tendency to put regulations and rules for the enforcement of the law into the hands of the industries engaged in food and drug activities. I consider this one of the most pernicious threats to pure food and drugs."*[14]

The FDA has an enormous job—it is responsible for the safety and efficacy of most food products and all human and veterinary drugs, biologic products, medical devices, cosmetics, and products emitting radiation that are sold in the U.S. Collectively, these products account for about 20 percent of consumer spending, estimated at about $1.5 trillion every year.[15] The FDA employs about 10,000 people, and has a budget of $1.7 billion, less than 2 percent of that of the Department of Agriculture.[16]

The last 15 years have seen four pieces of federal legislation, which in each case have weakened the regulatory role of the FDA:

- Prescription Drug User Fee Act of 1992, intended to shorten the time lag in review of drug applications by increasing FDA funding from the industry it is regulating.[17]

- Dietary Supplement Health and Education Act of 1994, which authorized regulation of manufacturing practices, but liberalized labeling and marketing and minimized requirements for review of dietary supplements.[18]

- Food and Drug Administration Modernization Act of 1997, which reauthorized user fees from the drug industry, exempted more low-risk medical devices from pre-market notification requirements, authorized manufacturers of drugs and medical devices to disseminate information about off label uses, and set up a pilot program for private sector review of device pre-market notifications.[19]

- Medical Device legislation of 2002, whereby manufacturers partially fund safety reviews and are authorized to hire private contractors to inspect manufacturing facilities and review some devices for approval.[20]

All of these changes have built in more conflicts of interest between regulators and the regulated. User fees from the drug industry account for about one-half of the FDA's budget for review of marketing applications, thereby making the FDA reliant on the hand it regulates.[21] Industry keeps pressing the FDA for faster approvals and less oversight, and the FDA is held hostage to industry for much of its funding. Here are just some of the many ways in which this Faustian bargain has left the fox in the hen house and the public inadequately protected.

- A 1998 study by Public Citizen found that FDA physician reviewers had opposed the approval of 27 drugs that were approved over the previous three years.[22]

- The percentage of new drugs approved between 1997 and 2000, which were later withdrawn from the market for safety reasons, increased by more than threefold compared to the period from 1993 to 1996.[23]

- At least seven of the thirteen drugs removed from the market since 1997 were approved over the objections of FDA safety reviewers, who either warned of serious potential risks or refused to sign official approval letters.[24]

- The Government Accountability Office (GAO) criticized the FDAs rejection decision for the morning after pill (Plan B) in 2005, following approval recommendations by FDA staff and a 23 to 4 vote for approval by an independent advisory committee.[25]

- 10 of 32 members of an FDA advisory committee considering withdrawal from the market of Vioxx and Bextra had conflicts of interest with drug companies; their 10 votes carried the day in voting to keep those drugs on the market.[26]

- A recent study by Public Citizen's Health Research Group found that 28 percent of FDA advisory committee members and temporary voting members had at least one conflict of interest with industry between 2001 and 2004; almost one-quarter of contracts or grants between advisors and companies exceeded $100,000.[27]

- The GAO has found a number of occasions when physicians were precluded from presenting adverse drug information at FDA Advisory Committee meetings and have even received harassing telephone calls from industry.[28]

- Ephedra, though a drug, has been a popular as a dietary supplement and heavily advertised product as a way to achieve weight loss, increased energy, and improved athletic performance[29]; despite receiving over 16,000 reports suggesting possible links to strokes, cardiac arrhythmias, and psychotic episodes (with 100 deaths) and again ignoring the calls by the AMA and other professional organizations to ban ephedra products, the FDA responded by requiring nothing more than warning labels until it was finally forced to ban its use after 155 deaths had occurred from its use.[30]

- Under pressure from the manufacturer of AneuRx, a stent graft for abdominal aortic aneurysm, the FDA toned down its safety warnings of the device, against the findings of investigators.[31]

- Since FDA regulations on advertising were relaxed in 1997, direct-to-consumer advertising (DTCA) has increased by almost 150 percent; though frequently misleading, typically hyping claims and downplaying side effects, the FDA is way behind the curve in regulating this important area, with a staff of only 40 people to review 30,000 ads and promotions each year.[32,33]

- Meanwhile in the wake of all these scandals, the number of warning letters issued by the FDA to drug companies, medical device manufacturers, and others dropped by 54 percent from 2000 to 2005.[34]

Following scathing criticism of the FDA in recent years for its handling of such products as Vioxx, Paxil, and ephedra, the agency is trying to toughen up some of its regulatory activities. As an example, it is now requiring more "blackbox" labels for higher-risk drugs over the protests of industry (which is concerned about scaring patients and slowing sales).[35] But the long-term problem remains—it is still in bed with industry (by design of Congress and industry advocates) more than is healthy for the public, and many basic issues remain unaddressed, all opposed by industry. These unaddressed issues include: the use of cost-effectiveness as a criterion for drug or device approval; requiring new drug applications to demonstrate benefit over competitor drugs, not just placebo; reviewing new applications of dietary supplements for safety; requiring manufacturers to share data on adverse events; and taking an active role in allowing importation of less expensive drugs from overseas when their safety can be assured. Meanwhile, however, the FDA is underfunded, under-authorized by Congress for these larger public health roles, and still lacks teeth as a regulatory agency (egs. it does not have the authority to levy civil penalties for violations of its regulations, to subpoena industry records in order to investigate suspected problems, or to require mandatory drug recalls not undertaken voluntarily by manufacturers).[36]

Business Ethic Trumps Professional Service Ethic

As health care services have become just another commodity for sale on the open market, the gap between the business and professional service ethic has been exposed with all its hazards and inequities. In so many instances, what serves corporate and shareholder interests (i.e., profits) is diametrically opposed to the interests, even safety of patients and their families. We have seen a number of examples of this ethical gap in earlier chapters. Here are just a few to remind us of the problem.

- mass marketing of products, with hyped claims but without evidence of safety or clinical effectiveness, (e.g., many dietary supplements, full-body screening CT scans).

- continued marketing of unsafe products, using deceptive advertising, even when their risks are known (e.g., Vioxx by Merck,[37] implantable cardiac defibrillators by Guidant[38]).

- corrosion of research by such practices as suppression of unfavorable research results,[39] paying physicians for lending their names to biased ghostwritten articles,[40] marketing activities disguised as science,[41] and intimidation of investigators conducting studies with unfavorable results.[42]

- corporate greed; how else can we regard annual compensation levels of CEOs in the drug and insurance industries in excess of $90 to $100 million or more a year, of corporate CEOs earning 475 times median salaries, of CEOs who "cook the books" earning twice as much as honest CEOs,[43] or of the accumulation of $1.78 billion in unexercised stock options by the end of 2005 by the CEO of UnitedHealthcare, who was recently forced out in an options backdating scandal.[44]

• outright fraud, there are many examples of huge settlements involving large and well-known health care corporations, representing all parts of the system, including Blue Cross,[45] HCA,[46] Tenet (formerly National Medical Enterprises),[47] HealthSouth,[48] Guidant,[49] TAP Pharmaceutical Products, Inc.,[50] and Pfizer.[51]

Economic and Political Power of Corporate Stakeholders

Whether we realize it or not, we now have a corporate ruling class— an oligarchy—with a few corporations spanning the globe with enormous economic and political power, often beyond accountability to their own governments. The U.S. is home to 60 of the world's top 100 public investor-owned companies, led by General Electric, Microsoft, Wal-Mart, ExxonMobile, and Pfizer.[52] U.S. corporations are closely interconnected with government, and they enjoy a broad range of government-sanctioned favors, including direct government subsidies and tax breaks. In our system of "corporate welfare," corporate taxes as a share of the country's tax revenues, dropped from 28 percent in the mid-1950s, to less than 12 percent in the mid-1990s.[53] A 1995 GAO report found that a majority of corporations, both U.S. and foreign, were paying no U.S. income tax.[54]

Corporate interests maintain close connections with policymakers and legislators at both state and national levels, using their economic power and political connections to shape policy, often behind the scenes. These are some of the ways that they promote their own interests.

1. Use of the media. Large corporations, of course own or otherwise control many of the large media organizations, to the extent that their role in influencing legislation has been called the "fourth branch of government." Alan Murray of the *Wall Street Journal* considers the large media conglomerates, such as General Electric and AOL Time Warner, the most powerful lobby in Washington.[55] One example of corporate media clout is the misrepresentation by NBC News of the issues surrounding Oregon's Initiative 23 for single-payer universal coverage in 2002, which played an active role in defeating the measure without any disclosure that General

Electric, as owner of the news network, is heavily invested in the insurance and health care industries.[56]

2. Conservative think tanks. Some of the most influential think tanks representing the neo-conservative movement are the Heritage Foundation, the American Enterprise Institute, the Cato Institute, the American Economics Institute for Public Policy Research, and the Business Roundtable. The latter includes the CEOs of about 200 of the nation's largest corporations, collectively accounting for about one-half of the U.S. GDP.[57] The Roundtable promotes its sponsors' political agendas through commissioned studies, white papers, editorials, television commentaries, and news releases.[58] Predictably, for example, the Heritage Foundation and Cato Institute both advocate for HSAs and privatization of Medicare and Medicaid.[59]

3. Use of non-profit front groups. Not-for-profit, tax-exempt organizations are not required to disclose their funding sources. Corporate interests often establish and fund such organizations under misleading names which suggest their working in the public interest. Examples include Citizens for Better Medicare (a drug industry front group which opposed price controls of prescription drugs under Medicare)[60] and the Center for Patient Advocacy, through which the North American Spine Society lobbied Congress to eliminate funding for the Agency for Health Care Policy and Research (AHCPR) after the Agency published guidelines favoring conservative management of back pain over surgical approaches.[61]

4. Lobbying of government. We saw in Chapter 5 how effectively the drug industry lobbied legislators to protect its interests in the runup to passage in 2003 of the Medicare Prescription Drug, Improvement, and Modernization Act. Lobbying has become an enormous and lucrative industry all its own, especially at the national level. In the first six months of 2005, U.S. corporations and interest groups spent $1.16 billion to lobby Congress and the Administration. The lobbying business has grown by almost 10 percent a year since 1999, a rate to more than double in size every

decade. The biggest expenditures in early 2005 were by AARP (especially to defeat Social Security privatization) and General Electric (lobbying on tax policy and asbestos litigation overhaul).[62] There is a new trend in the lobbying business toward dual roles whereby lobbyists also serve as principle campaign fund-raisers for legislators they are trying to persuade.[63]

The 2003 Medicare law, now called the Medicare Middleman Multiplication Act by Paul Krugman,[64] has prompted a goldrush among lobbyists. The health industry spent $325 million in 2004, more than any other sector, led by drug companies and hospitals. Hundreds of billions of dollars are at stake as a myriad of rules are made and revised. The extent to which lobbyists have joined the mainstream in policy making is suggested by two subtle linguistic changes. Lobbyists and trade associations, once considered special interests, are now seen as "stakeholders," while "expanding coverage" now refers more to Medicare coverage and reimbursement policies than to expanding health insurance coverage.[65] The wide spectrum of lobbying activity by major corporations is illustrated by Pfizer's numbers in 2004 (Table 7.1).[66]

Despite the recent Jack Abramoff political corruption scandal and current efforts in Congress to "reform" lobbying practices, the lobbying industry is certain to keep growing, partly as a First Amendment "right" and also because it provides such a big bang for a buck. A $1.6 million lobbying investment by 60 major corporations, including Pfizer, Hewlett-Packard and Altria, saved these companies over $100 billion in taxes when the tax rate on foreign earnings was reduced from 30 percent to 5 percent. One Washington-based lobbying firm has provided a return on investment to its clients of better than 100 to 1.[67]

At the state level as well, there are extensive intertwined connections between legislators and business interests, most of which are invisible. According to the Center for Public Integrity, 28 percent of the 7,400 state legislators across the country sit on a committee that regulates one of their personal business interests;

TABLE 7.1

Pfizer by the Numbers

- $52.5 billion - sales in 2004
- 9.8 – market share in 2004 (as of Dec 2004)
- $11.4 billion – profit in 2004
- More than 150 – countries in which Pfizer products are sold
- $16.90 billion – money spent on marketing and administration in 2004
- $7.68 billion – money spent on research and development in 2004
- 28 – agencies lobbied since 1998
- $43.52 million – money spent on lobbying since 1998
- $5.66 million – money spent on lobbying in 2004
- 41 – lobbying firms used since 1998
- 83 – lobbyists used since 1998
- 25 – companies and organizations who have spent more on federal lobbying since 1998

Compiled by Emily McNeill
SOURCE: *The Public I* Investigative Journalism in the Public Interest 11(4) July 2005, p 5.

nearly one in five of lawmakers who are required by law to disclose their personal financial interests have ties to companies that are registered to lobby their state legislature.[68]

5. Revolving doors. There is a fast-moving revolving door between corporate management, government (including staff), and lobbying by which corporate interests are protected and moved forward. According to a 2005 report by the Center for Public Integrity,

almost 250 former members of Congress and agency heads are active lobbyists and more than 2,000 lobbyists previously worked in senior government positions.[69] A 2004 investigation by the *Denver Post* found over 100 high-level officials in the Bush Administration who had formerly worked as lobbyists, lawyers, or company executives; at least 20 of them were former advocates-turned-regulators who helped their agencies write or shape regulatory and other corporate-friendly policies.[70] That lobbying is a bipartisan sport is shown in Figure 7.1 for the proportion of departing members of Congress in both parties who became federal lobbyists.[71] The move to Washington's K Street, the federal lobbying strip, is no surprise, since top government officials can command employment packages as lobbyists upward of $2 million a year while the going rate for Capitol Hill staffers turned lobbyists is now about $300,000 a year.[72]

Three examples illustrate how perverse the conflicts-of-interest are through the freewheeling revolving door.

- As a Republican Congressman from Louisiana, Rep. Billy Tauzin chaired the U.S. House committee that crafted the Medicare drug bill in 2003 (MMA), generous as it is to the pharmaceutical and insurance industries. In 2004, within months after the law was enacted, he became president and CEO of PhRMA, the drug industry's powerful trade group. He is also one of the top lobbyists in Washington, reportedly with a salary in the $2 million a year range, as he continues to lobby against price controls of drugs or importation of drugs from Canada or other countries.[73]

- Thomas Scully, then CEO of the Federation of American Hospitals, a trade group for for-profit hospitals, was involved in large settlements for Medicare fraud by its biggest member, HCA; then he went through the revolving door and served as head of CMS and pushed for privatization of Medicare while helping to shape the 2003 Medicare law; while still heading CMS, he negotiated a high-paying position with a legal firm serving drug

FIGURE 7.1

Percentage of Departing Members of Congress Who Became Federal Lobbyists, 1998-2004 (By Year of Departure)

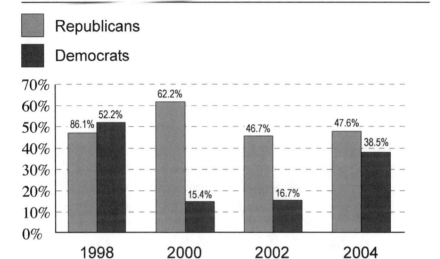

CONGRESSIONAL REVOLVING DOOR, ILLUSTRATED. Since 2000, with the White House and both houses of Congress in Republican hands, departing Republican members of Congress have had an advantage over Democrats in seeking well-paid lobbying work.

SOURCE: Reprinted with permission from: Guldin B. How to earn millions after Congress: Become a lobbyist and cash in. Public *Citizen News*July/August 2005, p 7.

industry clients.[74]

• As an aide to Republican members of the House Ways and Means Committee, John McManus helped to draft the Medicare drug bill of 2003 while receiving $620,000 in consulting fees from PhRMA, Merck and other companies; he later formed his own lobbying firm.[75]

6. Hidden conflicts of interest. Many of the above revolving door circumstances present obvious conflicts of interest. Others,

however, are much less obvious, or altogether hidden. The AARP is an interesting case in point. Against the interests of many of its members, AARP's support played a crucial role in passage of the 2003 Medicare bill, which calls for privatizing Medicare through Medicare Advantage, promotion of HSAs, and prohibits the government from negotiating the price of drugs (the main problem in the beginning!) After the bill was passed and many seniors became unhappy over the bill (60,000 AARP members resigned from the organization), many questioned the AARP's credibility as an advocacy organization for seniors. It turns out that about 60 percent of AARP's income comes from sales of insurance policies, sales of its membership list, and related activities.[76] More recently, the AARP has been found to have another conflict of interest with private industry. AARP sold its name to UnitedHealthcare, a big player in the private Part D prescription drug benefit for Medicare. When seniors search Google to get information from AARP on the drug benefit, they are met with a Web site created by UnitedHealthcare, which pays for it to be the first entry on Google. Thus AARP is paid for inconspicuously recommending one among dozens of private plans.[77]

Starving the Beast: The Attack on Government Programs

Privatization of government programs has been an increasing trend in the U.S., especially since 1980 during years of predominant Republican control of government. To the extent that programs are privatized, the role of government in promoting the collective good is reduced, as is accountability for cost, value, and efficiency of these programs. As we have just seen, corporate and business interests are a constant presence in the halls of power, seeking to promote their interests and expand private markets at government expense.

Medicare serves as a good case in point for privatization. A year after the Republicans gained control of the executive branch and both houses of Congress in 1994, they brought a bill forward to convert Medicare from an entitlement program to one managed by the private sector, thereby reducing the obligation of government. Newt Gingrich, then Speaker of the House, proclaimed "If we solve the Medicare program, I think we will govern for a generation."[78] At around the same time, Gingrich gave a speech to the Blue Cross/Blue Shield Association about government-run Medicare:[79]

"We don't get rid of it in round one because we don't think that politically smart, and we don't think that's the right way to go through a transition. But we believe it's going to wither on the vine because we think people are going to leave it voluntarily."

The insurance industry has found a bonanza, since Medicare was enacted in 1965, as intermediaries between hospitals and the government. Physicians and other providers have gained new sources of revenue, particularly in higher-reimbursement parts of the country. Many private interests continue to exploit Medicare by seeking a larger share as a private market while at the same time lobbying to "save the program from future bankruptcy" by killing it as a 40-year social contract between the government and the elderly and disabled. Even as these private stakeholders raise the spectre of future bankruptcy, they fight against potential cost-containment of reforms of Medicare, such as eliminating special subsidies and overpayments to private plans or allowing the government to negotiate discounted drug prices. As we have seen earlier, the 2003 Medicare law continues the push toward privatization through such programs as Medicare Advantage and HSAs.

As Patricia Williams observes in a recent issue of *The Nation*:

"To Republicans, 'privatization' no longer means cost-cutting efficiency. These days, the federal government has been diminished as a public entity, re-emerging instead as a wholly owned subsidiary of various private concerns. Public accountability in every area has eroded, as though information about government were a kind of trade secret:"[80]

So what we are now seeing is a successful and ongoing effort to starve the beast, whether the government itself or one of its programs, such as Social Security, Medicare, Medicaid, food stamps, or regulatory agencies. But first, of course, the private stakeholders want to maximize profits as long as tax breaks and subsidies are available. The far right of the political spectrum sees government itself as the problem. Even as it profits from government programs, the far right wants to underfund, limit the capability, and denigrate the role of government. A cynical approach but unfortunately, effective in encouraging more people to question the effectiveness of government when its programs are being starved.

These problems, of course, are not unique to the U.S. Pressures to privatize health care systems are a continued presence in other countries, such as the U.K., Canada, and Australia. But our system is surely the most market-based system in the world.

As a result of the trends discussed in this chapter and as another factor in pushing them along, there has clearly been a societal change from the unity of the World War II era to today's climate of "everyone for himself." The more that privatization goes forward, the more markets divide us and erode the social solidarity and reliability of such programs as Medicare and Medicaid. Kuttner adds this important perspective about solidarity:

"Thus, the politics of a particular health regime is self-reinforcing. An egalitarian system of health care is solidarity building. When everyone is in the same system, the more affluent and sophisticated demand high quality care. And when solidarity values reign, there is also a logic to push outward and downward available services—more comprehensive immunizations, more wellness education, more preventive care. But when basic care is shabby, and it is attractive for the affluent to buy their way out, political support for the universal system dwindles and there is more pressure to divert resources to the individualistic, privatized alternative, diminishing social empathy or solidarity, and reducing support for the public-health approach."[81]

It is interesting to note that, despite the radical differences between the views of Gingrich and Norquist on the right and Lapham and Kuttner on the left, all agree that forces which weaken public programs also reduce pubic support for them, further imperiling their viability.

As health care continues to become unaffordable for an ever-larger part of the population, already serious access and quality of care problems worsen. The question remains, will the medical profession become a powerful collective voice protesting the adverse impacts of our market-based system, or not? This question cuts to an even more sobering questions—to what extent is our profession part of the problem, or part of the solution? We now turn to Part III of this book to consider those questions.

PART III

COMPLICITY OF THE MEDICAL PROFESSION

CHAPTER 8

DOCTORS ON THE TAKE: PERVASIVE, OFTEN HIDDEN PHYSICIAN CONFLICTS OF INTEREST

"The low level which commercial morality has reached in America is deplorable. We have humble God fearing Christian men among us who will stoop to do things for a million dollars that they ought not to be willing to do for less than 2 millions."

Mark Twain, 1902[1]

"Thus the battle in and around the (inevitable) conflicts of interest that arise is a battle for the soul of the institutions in which future physicians are trained, future therapies are discovered, and today's patients are treated. It is a battle we dare not lose."

Julius B. Richmond, MD
Rashi Fein, PhD
*The Health Care Mess: How We Got Into It
and What It Will Take to Get Out*, 2005[2]

"Recent investigations into business methods have unearthed a degree of corruption which is almost incredible to those unacquainted with the conditions and which have been destructive of confidence in the integrity of the modern commercial world. With no intention of self-righteous boasting and no desire of condoning unjustifiable practices, we are proud to believe that the medical profession is freer from graft than any other equal number of men in the ranks of a profession or business. And this is as it should be. The relation of a patient to his physician is a most intimate one, and one in which implicit confidence is the very foundation of the relationship. The patient puts his life and his health unhesitatingly in his physician's hands; he feels that even if his physician lacks skill or needs assistance in an emergency he at least is honest and will do what seems best for the patient's interest. But it would be remarkable, considering the almost universal prevalence of "graft," if some doctor did not abuse this relationship. This he does in the so-called division of fees, a species of graft that we are compelled

to acknowledge does exist, although undoubtedly it is extremely rare. While there is a probability of any of this kind of business going on demands that we give thought to the matter, it is something we can not afford to treat in an ostrich fashion."

Editorial on business methods and professional morals,
Journal of the American Medical Association, March 10, 1906[3]

The foregoing editorial commentary appeared in *The Journal of the American Medical Association* 100 years ago, and is even more relevant today. The big concern in 1906 was on one or another kind of fee splitting, whereby physicians could increase their own income by sharing some of their fees with other physicians who referred their patients to them. Today's complex medical industrial complex presents many more opportunities for physicians to pursue their own self-interest rather than the trust which society and their patients have placed on them. We introduced some common financial conflicts of interest for physicians in fee-for-service and managed care settings in Chapter 1. In Chapter 3 we examined the entrepreneurial behavior of the major industries in health care. Now we will attempt to answer to what extent physicians themselves have been responsible for, or been complicit with, the abuses of the public interest by an ethic of profits over care.

This chapter undertakes two goals: (1) to take a snapshot of physicians' financial conflicts of interest (COIs) across a wide sweep of the health care system, with implications for patient care, education, and research; and (2) to briefly consider what lessons can be gleaned from this profile of physician COIs.

PHYSICIAN CONFLICTS OF INTEREST: A WIDE RANGE OF ETHICAL PROBLEMS

Physicians and the Drug Industry

Virtually all physicians have been involved with drug companies in one way or another, starting in their medical school days. Since physicians are the prescribers for their products, drug companies target physicians throughout their careers as part of their marketing efforts. Industry defends these activities as "educational," but they are really well-developed marketing strategies. The drug industry spent 33 percent of its revenues on "selling and administration" in 2002.[4] Medical students are showered with gifts, ranging from meals and pens to textbooks and pieces of medical equipment. Surveys of residents have found that they receive an average of six gifts from drug companies each year.[5] During their practice years, physicians are besieged by a sales force of almost 90,000 drug representatives ("reps") promoting their drugs—one salesperson for every 4.7 physicians.[6]

The drug industry spends $12 to $15 billion a year on gifts and payments to physicians.[7] These range across a broad spectrum from meals and free travel to payments for attending talks on drugs being promoted or being a "consultant" at promotional symposia at resorts. A 2001 survey by the Kaiser Family Foundation found that 92 percent of physicians received free drug samples and 61 percent were given meals, entertainment tickets, or free travel.[8] Since direct-to-consumer advertising (DTCA) has come under increasing fire and scrutiny in recent years for distortion and false claims, the drug industry has increased its marketing efforts through physicians themselves. Between 1999 and 2004, the number of promotional meetings led by physicians receiving payments from drug companies increased by four-fold. By 2004, 237,000 meetings and talks were held across the country sponsored and supported by drug companies, almost twice as many as those led by company sales reps.[9]

Although these interactions between physicians and industry raise obvious concerns about COIs, there is solid evidence that these marketing strategies pay off for drug companies and the many physicians so involved. Most physicians tend to deny that their prescribing behavior will be influenced by drug company promotions, but there is abundant evidence to the contrary.[10] Physicians have more positive attitudes toward drug reps from whom they receive gifts.[11,12] The rate of prescription for drugs being promoted increases after physicians see drug reps,[13,14] accept samples[15,16] or attend industry supported symposia.[17] Physicians requesting additions to hospital drug formularies are found to have been more likely to have accepted free meals or travel funds from drug companies.[18]

A classic example is an internist, Dr. Joseph Ferguson, writing in *Medical Economics*, describing how to get "lucrative gigs" speaking on behalf of drug companies. A charismatic speaker, he was being paid $100,000 a year from drug companies as a sideline to his practice. How he handles this conflict of interest is instructive; he sees his role as an idealist helping physicians to take better care of his patients.[19]

Here are some examples which reveal how pervasive and perverse financial COIs are between medicine and the drug industry.

- Clinical practice guidelines (CPGs) are intended to provide practicing physicians with unbiased recommendations based upon assessment of current evidence by expert clinicians. A 2002 study, however, revealed extensive COIs between authors of these guidelines and the drug industry. Of 100 authors of 44 CPGs endorsed by North American and European societies on common adult diseases published between 1991 and 1999, 87 percent had some kind of interaction with the drug industry, 59 percent were involved with companies whose drugs were considered in guidelines they authored, with involvement in almost all cases proceeding the guideline creation process; in only 2 percent of instances were disclosures of personal financial relationships made in published guidelines.[20]

- Among 4,000 attendees at the 2001 World Congress of Biological Psychiatry in Berlin, more than one-half were sponsored by drug companies. That sponsorship included business-class airfare, four-star hotel accommodations, and honoraria ranging from $2,000 to $10,000. Sponsored attendees were also made aware that their performance favoring the company's interests could lead to future invitations and larger honoraria. One expert who claimed that Remeron reverses depression in suicidal patients faster than other drugs was receiving $75,000 a year from the company to support his laboratory in Oregon.[21,22]

- TAP Pharmaceuticals manufactures Lupron, a potent gonado-tropin-releasing hormone agonist used in the treatment of prostate cancer. The company marketed their product to urologists by providing them with Lupron either free or at discounted prices while encouraging them to bill Medicare at its average wholesale price, thereby netting the urologists a substantial profit. The company also employed physicians as "consultants," taking them on free trips for educational seminars and giving them educational grants with no strings attached and no work or reports expected. Tipped off by whistle-blowers, the federal government prosecuted the company for illegal kickbacks. TAP settled with the government for $290 million in criminal fines and $585 million in civil penalties.[23,24]

- Neurontin is an anticonvulsant drug with FDA approval only for epilepsy and the pain of patients with shingles. Although marketing for unapproved "off-label" uses is illegal, its manufacturer, Warner-Lambert (acquired by Pfizer in 2000) aggressively marketed the drug for such off-label uses as bipolar disorder and restless leg syndrome. A former professor of neurology received over $300,000 for talks promoting Neurontin between 1994 and 1997. A whistle-blower suit resulted in the company settling with the government for $430 million in criminal and civil charges.[25-27]

- According to the 2003 Annual Report of the Accreditation Council for Continuing Medical Education (ACCME), the drug industry provided about 90 percent of CME funding that year in the U.S.[28] The industry's main agenda for increasing sales and profits has always been quite clear. Drug companies openly acknowledge that they evaluate the market impact of CME expenditures and fund only those likely to be profitable.[29] As part of their funding role, drug companies often play an active part in curriculum design, development of teaching materials, and selection of speakers. In fact, more than 100 for-profit companies have emerged in a new industry called Medical Education and Communication Companies (MECC). They are hired by drug companies to prepare and present CME programs for hospital grand rounds, other sponsors, and freestanding CME programs. Remarkably, some of these MECCs, hired guns as they are, have been approved by the ACCME and authorized to plan the content of CME programs. In so doing, those involved with ACCME have thereby abdicated their responsibility for the continuing education of its members by handing off its professional responsibility to a commercial venture. Arnold Relman, former Editor of *The New England Journal of Medicine* in 2003 had this to say about this growing trend:[30]

> *"The pharmaceutical industry has gone too far. It is assuming a role in continuing medical education (CME) that is inappropriate for an industry with a vested interest in selling prescription drugs. Worse, many medical educational institutions not only allow the industry's encroachments but also welcome and even solicit pharmaceutical company participation in programs that should be the profession's sole responsibility. As a result, CME is now so closely linked with the marketing of pharmaceuticals that its integrity and credibility are being questioned. The problem is not new, but it has recently grown to alarming proportions."*

- Unrestricted educational grants are frequently given by drug companies to medical organizations with no strings attached. According to the Senate Finance Committee, which launched a Congressional investigation of these grants in 2005, 23 drug manufacturers spent $1.47 billion in 2004 on "educational" grants. One example of such a grant paid for an alumni meeting of a medical specialty society involved in off-label use of Propulsid for childhood reflux, which was approved for treatment of reflux only in adults. It seemed clear to congressional investigators that these grants were being given out by drug companies' sales and/or marketing people.[31]

- The situation has gone so far that the AMA developed guidelines for how physicians should relate to the drug industry. Those guidelines were disseminated with funding from—the drug industry![32]

- An entrepreneurial marketplace has developed in recent years to facilitate clinical trials in community settings, especially Phase IV drug trials. These are uncontrolled registry drug trials funded by industry with minimal academic rigor intended to build a large physician and patient following for drugs being marketed. Participating physicians are paid by the sponsor (eg., $500 per patient) for recruiting and following appropriate .patients and making reports to the sponsor of the trial, depending on whether results are favorable which may or may not be published.[33,34]

- COIs between physicians and the drug industry even include the regulatory process for drugs. As we saw in the last chapter, the FDA is dependent on the drug industry for about one-half of its budget for reviewing marketing applications.[35] Furthermore, more than one-half of the experts hired to advise the FDA on drug safety have ties to the drug industry, such as helping a company to develop a drug, serving on an FDA advisory committee, or holding stock in the company which manufacturers drugs being evaluated.[36]

Physicians and the Medical Device Industry

The medical device and diagnostics industry now has a $75 billion market in the U.S.[37] As we saw in Chapter 4, it encompasses a wide range of products, brings to market 8,000 devices each year, is loosely regulated by the FDA for only higher-risk devices, and is about as profitable as the drug industry. It comes as no surprise that device manufacturers seek out physicians to use and promote its devices as a key part of their marketing programs. We find similar COIs for physicians with ties to device makers, with the main difference from the drug industry being the smaller number of physicians involved. Here are five examples which illustrate financial COIs which are largely hidden from hospitals and patients.

- In December, 2005 the *Wall Street Journal* exposed a number of undisclosed COIs regarding research and use of AtriCure, a device for the treatment of atrial fibrillation made by a company with the same name as the device. The device has been rejected by the FDA for this purpose on three occasions. Despite this, the operation has been performed "off-label" at that institution on 1,247 patients. Financial ties between the Cleveland Clinic and AtriCure, Inc. were not disclosed to the patients. The Clinic helped to set up a venture fund and became its largest investor by investing $25 million when the fund was launched in 2001. The Clinic's CEO, Dr. Delos Cosgrove, sat on AtriCure's Board, helped to manage the venture fund, and invested in it himself. He also developed a device for AtriCure which the manufacturer plans to market, and will receive royalties for its use. Medicare reimbursement for the AtriCure procedure is about $25,700. As with many such clinics, the Clinic has an Institutional Review Board (IRB) and conflict-of-interest committee. But they had not been informed initially of financial ties to the manufacturer.[38] After these COIs came to light and after a flurry of negative publicity, the IRB is now being informed about any investments by the Clinic, the Clinic's Board will receive education on COIs and disclosure, and the Clinic has withdrawn from a clinical trial involving AtriCure and "suspended" a program to train surgeons to use the device for atrial fibrillation. Shortly thereafter, the share value of AtriCure, Inc. stock dropped by 22 percent.[39,40]

- Medtronic is the largest medical device manufacturer in the industry, with annual sales of $10 billion. One of its products is a spinal implant used in back fusion surgery. According to the *New York Times*, internal Medtronic documents revealed by a whistle-blower suit showed that it spent at least $50 million in payments to physicians as part of its marketing program between 2001 and 2005. The company frequently paid for physicians to attend "educational" meetings at resorts, with all expenses and entertainment paid. A Wisconsin surgeon who used the device was paid $400,000 a year by Medtronic for a consulting contract requiring only eight days of work. Another surgeon in Virginia was paid almost $100,000 in consulting fees over the first nine months of 2005.[41] The Justice Department accused it of "sham consulting agreements, sham royalty agreements, and lavish trips to desirable locations offered to physicians between 1998 and 2003." Medtronic agreed to a settlement of $40 million in 2006.[42]

- Guidant is one of the leading manufacturers of electrical cardiac pacemakers. It conducts post-marketing surveys of cardiologists who have implanted the device. The *Wall Street Journal* has reported that Guidant pays each of 250 cardiology practices that use the device $8,200 over two years. These payments are made indirectly through survey companies so that the physicians are unaware of the source of the payments.[43]

- The case of Dr. William Overdyke, an assistant professor of orthopedic surgery at Louisiana State University Health Science Center in Shreveport, provides further insight into arrangements often entered into between surgeons and device makers. He was paid $150,000 to $200,000 a year by one manufacturer of a knee prosthesis. When that arrangement ended in 1998, he signed a contract with another company for $175,000 a year to promote the use of another knee prosthesis without ever having used it. When this COI came to light at his institution, he was fined $10,000 for violating the state ethics code, which forbids state employees from doing business with companies with which they have financial ties. Incredibly, a company sales representative was often present in the operating room during surgery, sometimes helping the surgeon to select a specific prosthesis. These sales reps work on commission, often earn several hundred thousand dollars a year, and sometimes pay the surgeon's assistant $200 a case in order to cultivate the surgeon's loyalty to the company and its product.[44]

- Competing manufacturers of implanted cardiac defibrillators court physicians (to use their products) by offering free CME education to learn implantation techniques, often bypassing guidelines for such training established by the leading specialty organization in the field.[45]

Physicians, Hospitals and Other Facilities

The relationships between physicians, hospitals, and other diagnostic and treatment facilities raise ethical questions of perceived, and often actual COIs. Many kinds of undisclosed financial arrangements may influence physicians' clinical judgment, selection of tests, procedures, and facilities. Here are some examples which give some indication of the types and frequency of these COIs, which include ownership and/or investment stakes in facilities and other self-referral arrangements.

Relocation packages for physicians

Hospitals compete for the loyalty of referring physicians, since physicians are the lifeblood of their business. A 2004 survey by Merritt,

Hawkins & Associates, a Texas-based physician search firm, put numbers on this connection. Seven specialties, led by orthopedic surgery at almost $3 million, generate over $2 million a year for hospitals, including revenues from inpatient procedures and net inpatient and outpatient revenue from patients who are referred to the hospital.[46] The Alvarado Hospital Medical Center in San Diego, California illustrates how these relocation packages work. Owned by Tenet HealthCare Corp, the second largest investor-owned hospital chain in the country, Alvarado spent over $10 million on more than 100 relocation packages over a ten-year period, according to U.S. government prosecutors investigating the hospital for bribery. In exchange for referring patients to the hospital, Alvarado allegedly agreed to pay one physician $70,000 for equipment and improvements in office space, $180,000 for office expenses and $132,000 for a one-year "collections guarantee."[47]

Specialty hospitals

Physician-owned specialty hospitals have emerged in the last 15 years in order to get around laws prohibiting physicians from referring their patients to hospitals in which they are invested. Those laws excluded "whole hospitals," assuming any physician investment in typical multi-service general hospitals would be small. So recent years have seen about 100 limited service specialty hospitals established, especially in states without laws requiring certification of the need for a new facility. The American Hospital Association (AHA), representing general full-service community hospitals, has charged that specialty hospitals cherrypick the patients whose conditions lead to treatments that are well reimbursed. That puts at risk general hospitals which maintain a full range of services because they lose the profitable patients who subsidize less profitable patients, including those needing under-reimbursed but essential burn and trauma services. In response to the AHA's concerns, Congress enacted an 18-month ban on new specialty hospitals in 2003. That ban has since been extended, and the future of these hospitals remains unclear.[48]

Proponents of specialty hospitals claim greater efficiency and value for patients. But there is no question that the potential to maximize their income is a major driver of specialty hospitals. As MedPAC has noted, physician-owners can "triple-dip" by receiving income for performing a procedure, sharing in a facility profit, and gaining the value of their investment in the business.[49] Well-reimbursed services that specialty hospitals focus on include procedures in cardiovascular disease, orthopedic surgery, and neurosurgery. They select out patients who are less sick and better insured than their counterparts in community hospitals.[50] A CMS study of referral patterns, based on Medicare claims data for 2003 and site visits to six market areas, found that physicians had a 34 percent ownership share in cardiac hospitals in the study, with the average ownership per physician of 1 percent. Orthopedic and surgical hospitals have aggregate physician ownership of 80 percent, with average shares per physician of 2 percent.[51] MEDPAC found that annual returns often exceeded 20 percent of physicians' initial investment, with an average all-payer margin of 13 percent compared with a 3 to 6 percent margin for community hospitals in the same markets.[52] The profit goal is clearly illustrated by an advertisement to selected physicians by the Austin Surgical Hospital in Texas claiming that a $4 million investment could earn $55 million over six years.[53] Profit motivation is also well illustrated by the Black Hills Surgery Center, a specialty hospital in Rapid City, South Dakota emphasizing neurosurgery and orthopedic surgery, which doubled its rate of surgical procedures in nine years, now has the highest rate for back surgery in the country, and gained its investors over $145 million when it went public in 2004. The founder of Black Hills Surgery Center, Dr. Larry Teuber, received $9 million at that time.[54]

Ambulatory Surgery Centers (ASCs)

Ambulatory surgery centers are designed for same day surgery not requiring admission to a hospital. The first ASC was opened in 1970, and their numbers have expanded rapidly since then. According to their national organization, the Federated Ambulatory Surgery Association, there are now more than 4,200 ASCs across the country. More than 2,500 different procedures are performed in ASCs, totaling over 8 million a year, with the majority in ophthalmology and gastroenterology. Most ASCs are licensed by their states, and most are certified by Medicare. Insurers gain lower costs compared to hospitalizations, while surgeons welcome their convenience and efficiency.[55]

Physicians (mostly surgeons) also welcome their investment potential, and financial COIs again come to the fore. ASCs are privately owned and for-profit. Often a hospital holds a 50 percent interest and physicians hold the rest. Others are entirely physician owned or owned entirely or in part by a development company. Some investor-owned companies own surgery centers, including AmSurg, HCA, and NovaMed Eyecare. The most successful ASCs provide a return profit margins of more than 20 percent, with a middle tier of ASCs returning profits up to 12 percent a year. Physician investors are at risk for running afoul of anti-kickback regulations, and a 2003 article in *Medical Economics* advises physician investors on how best to avoid these, including investing in mutual funds with ASC holdings to preclude any such risks.[56]

Clinical Laboratories

While physicians generally don't have an ownership stake in clinical laboratories, they often add their own charges for laboratory tests sent to outside clinical laboratories. Although a modest charge to cover collection and processing of test results is acceptable and considered ethical by the AMA, overcharging by physicians appears to be common across the country. In order to increase business, many laboratories offer steep discounts to referring physicians and encourage them to bill insurers (who are usually unaware of these discounts) full market prices for the tests. As an example, a laboratory recently promoted its "revenue share" model at a meeting of the American Urological Association, advising the urologists that they could generate up to $35,000 a year by sending their work to that laboratory. Most of these referral arrangements are hidden from public awareness and continue without restraint. An exception is the indictment by a U.S. attorney in Oklahoma of three former executives of a laboratory which charged physicians as little as $2.75 for a PSA test, who later received reimbursement of $25 and more for each test.[57]

Diagnostic/Screening and Imaging Centers

This is a booming area, and many physicians are investing in these kinds of centers which offer such services as endoscopy, bone densitrometry, lithotripsy, CT scanning and positron emission tomography (PET) scanning. A 2004 report from the Community Tracking Study (CTS) found that physicians were actively investing in these centers and services in all 12 markets being tracked. Self-referral and anti-kickback regulations established in the1990s were not restraining physician investment, and both volumes and costs of these services are increasing markedly as a result.[58] Many of these services are unnecessary, but are done because they are "cash cows." Full-body CT scanning, spreading like wildfire across the country, is a good example. It lacks any scientific evidence for value as a screening test in people without symptoms, has the approval of neither the FDA nor the American College of Radiology, yet is promoted by providers for screening purposes for $800 to $1,500 per procedure.[59]

These centers are rife with financial COIs for participating physicians. Scanning centers typically offer sharply discounted prices to referring physicians in exchange for their referrals. A recent whistle-blower suit in Florida, for example, revealed that through a lease-agreement with a referring chiropractor, the imaging center would provide 20 MRIs a month at $400 per scan and 20 contrast MRIs at $850 each; it was estimated that the chiropractor would collect as much as $2,300 from insurers for each contrast MRI. These kinds of lease-agreements were being offered as incentives to orthopedic surgeons, neurologists, and others. Another strategy used by the imaging center to generate referrals was to appoint referring physicians as "medical directors" with little or no expectation of work.[60] In order to skirt anti-kickback laws when physicians are themselves invested in these centers, some imaging companies even go so far as to provide lease terms whereby the referring physician temporarily rents the center's facilities and employees during the time of each scan![61]

There can be no question but that these financial arrangements lead to gross overuse of unnecessary services. A 1990 study found that referring physicians with an interest in imaging facilities ordered about four-times more examinations for the same medical problems as their colleagues without such an interest; as a result of more frequent testing and higher charges, their average charge per episode of care was 4.4 to 7.5 times higher than average charges for patients of referring physicians without a financial stake in the centers.[62]

Other Facilities

This pattern of overutilization and profiteering is much the same in other kinds of facilities as well. A 1992 study of radiation therapy facilities in Florida found that almost one-half of radiation therapy centers at that time were joint ventures with physicians, and that the frequency and costs of radiation therapy treatments in Florida were 40 to 60 percent higher than in the rest of the U.S. Joint venture facilities avoided underserved areas and radiation physicians spent 18 percent less time with patients over the course of their treatment than in non-joint venture facilities.[63] A 1995 study of physician-owned physical therapy clinics found clear-cut evidence of physician-induced demand. Physician-owned clinics treated patients for 50 percent more visits than did their independent counterparts; three factors were identified as inducing demand—increases in physician density, decreases in population density, and increases in the total number of owners.[64]

Physicians, Research and Academic Medical Centers (AMCs)

One might think that universities and their academic medical centers might be somewhat insulated from the COIs abounding in the everyday world of medicine in the commercial marketplace. But that expectation is unfortunately, not grounded in reality. Universities and their AMCs have been engulfed in recent decades with many COIs involving both their faculties and institutions themselves. The excellent recent book, *Universities in the Marketplace: The Commercialization of Higher Education,* by Derek Bok, former President of Harvard University and Dean of the Harvard Law School, attests to the wide range of COIs to which academic institutions can fall prey. As he observes:

> *"I worry that commercialization may be changing the nature of academic institutions in ways we will come to regret. By trying so hard to acquire more money for their work, universities may compromise values that are essential to the continued confidence and loyalty of faculty, students, alumni, and even the general public."*[65]

This is an especially serious concern, since the stakes of commercialization of AMCs are far higher than in community practice. For it is in AMCs that future generations of physicians are trained, where they form their professional values through faculty mentors, where research is done which later is translated into best practice in communities, and where there is a special responsibility to lead toward improved quality and equity of health care.

Increasingly close relationships between industry and universities have grown exponentially in recent decades as a result of several major factors. In an effort to stimulate economic growth and accelerate technological innovation, the Bayh-Dole Act was passed by Congress in 1980. This Act made available government subsidies to university-industry cooperative ventures to more effectively translate research advances into clinical practice. Universities could own and license patents on discoveries made through publicly funded research and industry could receive tax breaks by investing more in university-based research.[66] By 1990, 200 universities in the U.S. had established technology transfer offices. By the year 2000, the volume of patents licensed to companies had increased by more than ten-fold and universities were earning more than $1 billion in annual royalty and license fees.[67] Biomedical research funding in the U.S. increased from $37.1 billion in 1994 to $94.3 billion in 2003; industry provides twice as much support as the National Institutes for Health (NIH) (57 percent to 28 percent).[68] Universities and their AMCs are chronically underfunded, and medical schools face an increasing challenge to support their educational mission and under-reimbursed clinical activities, especially as their essential role as safety net institutions becomes more stressed. Much as university-industry partnerships would seem to be a win-win situation for both parties, and much as these partnerships have spurred important advances in medical science, there are potential downsides whereby conflicts of interest on both sides may compromise the integrity of research.

Institutional academic industry relationships (IAIRs) can take many forms today, including large research relationships (e.g.,Harvard Medical School and Dupont Company, Yale University and Bristol Meyers, University of California Berkeley and Novartis);[69] gifts to universities from industry (egs., research equipment, endowed chairs, building funds, restricted or unrestricted donations);[70] and various kinds of investments (e.g., separately managed endowments; direct investments in faculty-owned firms or firms sponsoring research).[71,72] A comprehensive study of IAIRs was carried out in four unnamed AMCs (three private, one public; three included a medical school and associated schools of public health, nursing, and allied health fields). These examples from its 2004 report suggest worrisome COIs.[73]

- Several faculty members in one clinical department received between $50,000 and $200,000 a year as consultants to a company, while the department received more than $1 million a year in discretionary funds from the same company; in exchange, faculty physicians helped the company to design research protocols and educate other physicians about the company's products.

- A department chairperson who owned equity in a company got around his institution's ban on faculty serving as principal investigator (P.I.) on research grants in which they have a financial relationship by channeling the funds to young faculty and still retaining supervisory oversight.

- Several institutional officials acknowledged that they served as consultants, scientific advisors, equity holders, and owners of companies that sponsored research being conducted by faculty whom they supervised.

That these well-financed arrangements in academic industry partnerships can become a Faustian bargain is shown by these studies of troubling COIs throughout the research process, starting with decisions as to what kind of research to undertake, research design, and data analysis all the way to publication and dissemination of results. While the financial arrangements between industry, research institutions, and investigators do not necessarily represent COIs, they certainly raise serious concerns about the integrity of the end products of research.

- It is more than likely that the choice of research subject undertaken by investigators and departments will be strongly influenced by industry funding, especially if it is a principal source of research funding.

- A 2003 survey of almost 3,000 faculty members in 121 U.S. medical schools found that almost one-half of all faculty who served on institutional review boards (IRBs) had financial ties to industry as consultants;[74] a 2001 study of five universities by the General Accounting Office (GAO) found lax regulations and procedures for disclosure of financial ties with industry.[75]

- Two high-profile cases illustrate how industry sponsors can distort the results of research studies in their own interest and still have them published in prestigious journals. An article appearing in *The Journal of the American Medical Association* in 2000 falsely represented the safety of Celebrex by omitting six months of trial data.[76] Another article in *The New England Journal of Medicine* in 2000 failed to report some risks of Vioxx; all 13 of the authors of that paper had financial ties to or were employed by its manufacturer, Merck.[77]

- A 2005 survey of 107 medical school research centers found that one-half would allow industry sponsors to draft manuscripts reporting results of studies and limit the role of investigators to suggest revisions.[78,79]

- There are many examples of industry sponsors suppressing publication of unfavorable research findings, such as the experiences of Nancy Olivieri at the University of Toronto concerning a drug for thalassemia major[80] and Betty Dong at the University of California San Francisco concerning her finding that the sponsor's Synthroid was no more effective than less expensive competing drugs.[81] That industry sponsorship plays a large role in outcomes of published studies is more than suggested by Figure 8.1, which includes *no* unfavorable results.[82] A 2003 systematic review of the relationship between industry sponsorship and research quality and outcome found solid evidence of publication bias (avoiding publication of unfavorable results).[83]

- The process of preparing papers for publication is also compromised in other ways. Many research papers are "ghostwritten" by sponsoring companies or writers under contract to for-profit medical communications companies (MCCs); although often not listed in a paper's authorship, ghostwriters may have the final say in a paper's content. Well known lead authors are often invited and paid to "brand" the article; the lead author of a 2003 article on Vioxx recently admitted that he had little to do with the research itself.[84,85] As Editor of a family practice journal, I had personal experience with these kinds of problems on more than one occasion, leading to rejection of major studies "branded" by first authors who were leaders in our field. Another common practice is for authors not to disclose financial COIs to journals reviewing their manuscripts. A 1997 study found only half of one percent of over 60,000 published journal articles included such disclosures, and those appeared in only one-third of the journals examined.[86]

- Although no COIs were disclosed in a 2004 article appearing in *Circulation* updating the National Cholesterol Education Program's (NCEP) recommendations for lowering cholesterol with statin drugs, 8 of the 9 authors were later found to have financial ties to statin manufacturers; one of the authors, a full-

FIGURE 8.1

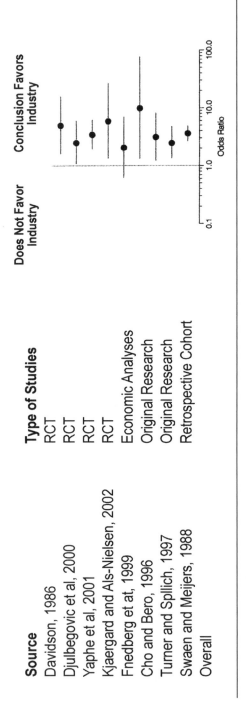

Relation Between Industry Sponsorship and Study Outcome

Source	Type of Studies
Davidson, 1986	RCT
Djulbegovic et al, 2000	RCT
Yaphe et al, 2001	RCT
Kjaergard and Als-Nielsen, 2002	RCT
Fnedberg et at, 1999	Economic Analyses
Cho and Bero, 1996	Original Research
Turner and Spllich, 1997	Original Research
Swaen and Meijers, 1988	Retrospective Cohort
Overall	

OURCE: Reprinted with permission from: Bekelman SE, et al. Scope and impact of financial conflict of interest in biomedical research. JAMA 289:459, 2003.

time employee of the National Heart, Lung and Blood Institute (NHLBI), who supervised the development of these guidelines, had even received $114,000 in consulting fees from statin manufacturers between 2001 and 2003.[87-89]

In a growing trend in recent years, the drug industry has moved much of its research from AMCs to community settings through contracts with commercially oriented research networks. This trend adds further concern that the integrity of research is being compromised by commercial interests, since drug companies can take even greater control of research design, data analysis, and publication of results.[90] A 2005 report issued by the British House of Commons found that about 75 percent of clinical trials that are published by such leading journals as *The Lancet*, the *Journal of the American Medical Association*, and *New England Journal of Medicine* are funded by industry.[91] Only about one-third of industry-supported research is now being carried out in AMCs, with the majority now being conducted in for-profit research networks.[92]

Physicians and Wall Street

As if this wide range of disturbing COIs among physicians were not enough, there is still another especially egregious area of corruption—the increasing links between physicians and Wall Street. A 2005 article by Drs. Eric Topol and David Blumenthal in the *Journal of the American Medical Association* revealed that one of every 10 U.S. physicians is engaged in a formal consultancy arrangement with the investment industry. That number may be even higher among academic physicians involved in research. It is estimated that these relationships have grown by 75-fold over the last 8 years. Several kinds of financial firms seek advice from physicians, including individual stockbrokers and analysts, investment bankers, venture capital firms, and investment firms. Hedge funds, which use such high-risk strategies as betting on a stock to fall, are the biggest players among investment firms. About one-third of hedge fund investments relate especially to publicly traded stocks and derivatives of pharmaceutical, medical device, medical diagnostic, and biotechnology companies.[93]

An entire new industry has emerged to facilitate consultation by physicians to the investment industry. One large company, New York-based Gerson Lehrman Group, was started in 1998 and now has contractual agreements with more than 60,000 physicians and contracts with more than 50 asset management firms.[94,95] Another company, based in Boston, has contractual agreements with over 15,000 research-oriented physicians in a network involving 55 clinical specialties, 21 basic science disciplines, and more than 100 AMCs across the country.[96,97] Physicians are typically paid $300 to $500 an hour for advice and information. The major focus of these "consultations" relates to the conduct, status, and preliminary results of ongoing clinical trials. The intensity of Wall Street's interest in such information is indicated by some stock analysts posing as physicians conducting a trial.[98] A prominent researcher at Cedars-Sinai Comprehensive Cancer Center in Los Angeles is regularly approached by (but rejects) offers of $1,000 or $1,500 to talk to investors for 30 minutes.[99] Some super rich investors pay as much as $1 million a year to "matchmaker" firms to gain access to confidential information from physicians involved in drug research.

A 2005 investigation by the *Seattle Times* found at least 26 cases in which physicians had leaked critical information about their drug research to Wall Street firms. Not only is this practice unethical, it may also be illegal in providing information to facilitate insider trading,[100] is violating contract agreements with drug companies, and seriously compromises randomized drug trials themselves. These kinds of practices have led Arthur Caplan, Director of the Center for Bioethics at the University of Pennsylvania, to this conclusion: "The practice is a moral cesspool. It really just seems to me to be the last straw in the corporatization of American medicine."[101]

LESSONS FROM THESE CONFLICTS-OF-INTEREST

If one was ever unsure that health care in America has become corporatized, the foregoing completely dispels that doubt. Corporate interests have reached into virtually all parts of our health care system, and created an ongoing battle between the business ethic and the professional service ethic. Given this sea change, it is not surprising that physicians' conflicts-of-interest have grown in frequency and types, but what are the consequences? Based on this profile of physician COIs, these lessons stand out.

1.   Conflict of interest is a structural condition, regardless of physicians' actual behavior, which threatens the principles of

medical professionalism.

2. Industry has successfully seduced enough of the medical profession
    to effectively meet its profit goals in what is now one-sixth of the
    nation's economy. Through its gifts and other strategies, it has
    bought both access and collaboration with physicians at all stages
    of their careers in both academic and community settings. We
    have seen how effectively industry's quid pro quo's work.

3. Merging the roles of caregiver and entrepreneur sets up basic
    COIs among physicians, commercializes and distorts the
    physician-patient relationship, and establishes health care services
    as commodities instead of responses serving essential human
    needs.

4. We can no longer assume, or hope, that these wide-ranging COIs
    among physicians involve just "a few bad apples." These ethical
    problems are common, intentional, and are increasingly becoming
    part of the money culture of medicine. We now have reason to be
    skeptical of the integrity of some clinical practice guidelines as
    well as the research and institutions involved in their creation.

5. It appears that physician COIs today are much worse in scope
    and consequences than those of 100 years ago, when they mostly
    involved one or another form of fee splitting.

6. The prevalence of physician COIs is difficult to measure. While
    we now know that they are common, is this profile just the tip of
    the iceberg? It is difficult to know, but it is of serious concern that
    many physicians involved in COIs are well placed as respected
    practitioners, investigators, and academicians, and even leaders in
    their fields. I still have to believe that a large majority of physicians
    in academic and community practice are honest, hardworking,
    and dedicated to their patients' best interests. Moreover, there
    are still many heroes in medicine trying to resist the tide of
    commercialization, including many thousands of physicians
    serving as safety net providers and growing numbers of whistle-
    blowers exposing exploitation of the public interest.

7. The corporatization of medicine has produced a moral and ethical

crisis in medicine. Some have asked whether medicine can be sustained as a profession.[102] The profession does appear to be at a crossroads. Will it be de-professionalized into fragmented groups of well-paid technicians with little influence on health policy, or will the profession pull together to rejuvenate its moral legacy of public service and deal with COIs in its own ranks? That question leads us to the next chapter, where we will consider whether COIs in medicine can be regulated, either within the profession, or by external regulators, if necessary.

CHAPTER 9

WHERE ARE THE REGULATORS, AND IS EFFECTIVE REGULATION POLITICALLY ACHIEVABLE?

We found in the last chapter that conflicts-of-interest (COIs) between physicians and industry are increasingly common, growing in scope and complexity, and now even extend to unethical relationships with Wall Street. These COIs seriously erode the integrity of the physician-patient relationship, may compromise the welfare of patients through a variety of ways from unnecessary procedures to drugs whose testing is tainted, and create distrust of the medical profession by the public. In order to assess the extent to which current regulatory approaches are managing these COIs, this chapter has four goals: (1) to explore the extent and effectiveness of self-regulation by the profession itself; (2) to assess the efforts by industry toward self-regulation; (3) to examine the scope and effectiveness of regulatory activities by federal and state governments; and (4) to consider whether effective regulation of physician COIs is politically achievable.

SELF-REGULATION BY THE PROFESSION

The first question to ask, of course, is how the AMA has dealt with this moral and ethical crisis, which has engulfed our profession in these times. We recall from Chapter 1 that the AMA was formed in 1847 and provided important leadership in reforming medical education and establishing medicine on a firm professional footing. As the largest and oldest of professional organizations in American medicine, the AMA has a well organized Council on Ethical and Judicial Affairs (CEJA), staffed by biomedical ethicists and attorneys, which takes positions on many of these issues. In 1992, for example, the CEJA first issued an opinion on gifts to physicians, holding that such gifts from pharmaceutical and medical device companies should primarily benefit patients, should not be of substantial value, and should not be related to physicians' prescribing patterns. In 1993, the CEJM promulgated another opinion on CME, stating that the educational value of the program must be the primary consideration in a physician's decision to attend, that all potential COIs be fully disclosed, and that industry should have no control over program content or speakers.[1]

The CEJA's overall and current guideline on COIs in general is well stated and commendable:

> *"Under no circumstances may physicians place their own financial interests above the welfare of their patients. The primary objective of the medical profession is to render service to humanity; reward or financial gain is a subordinate consideration. For a physician to unnecessarily hospitalize a patient, prescribe a drug, or conduct diagnostic tests for the physician's financial benefit is unethical. If a conflict develops between the physician's financial interest and the physician's responsibilities to the patient, the conflict must be resolved to the patient's benefit."[2]*

It is much easier, however, to issue guidelines and pronouncements of policy than to enforce them, as the last chapter made abundantly clear. Moreover, some of the CEJM's guidelines have left sufficient "wiggle room" to be ineffective. Its position on physician ownership of specialty hospitals is a good example. The CEJM's guideline for COIs involving physician ownership of health facilities is as follows:

> *"There may be situations in which a needed facility would not be built if referring physicians were prohibited from investing in the facility. Physicians may invest in and refer to an outside facility, whether or not they provide direct care or services at the facility, if there is a demonstrated need in the community for the facility and alternative financing is not available. Need might exist when there is no facility of reasonable quality in the community or when use of existing facilities is onerous for patients. Self-referral based on demonstrated need cannot be justified simply if the facility would offer some marginal improvement over the quality of services in the community. The potential benefits of the facility should be substantial."[3]*

One flaw of this policy question is how, and by whom, is "demonstrated need" to be defined.

With regard to the specialty hospital controversy, the AMA opposed efforts to either temporarily or permanently extend the 18-month moratorium on physician referrals to specialty hospitals in which they have an ownership interest. The AMA also supported the efforts of state medical associations to repeal current certificate-of-need statues, and continues to vacillate on the issue.[4]

Some other medical organizations have issued similarly lofty ethical guidelines to address COIs among physicians. Table 9-1 lists provisions regarding professional meetings, consulting fees, and gifts as recently promulgated by the AMA, the Accreditation Council for Continuing Medical Education (ACCME), and the American College of Physicians (ACP).[5,6] Again, however, without mechanisms to codify transgressions and enforce consequences, these pronouncements lack teeth.

The track record of academic medical centers (AMCs) is no better than other professional medical associations when it comes to self-regulation. A study in 2000 found that only 3 of 250 medical schools and research institutions required investigators to disclose their financial COIs to patients before enrolling them in clinical research studies; only 7 percent required their researchers to disclose COIs when submitting their articles to journals.[7] Another report in 2000 revealed that only one of the ten leading medical schools, as ranked by amount of federal research funding, banned their research faculty from doing clinical research on products of companies with which they had significant financial ties.[8] Concerning COIs in AMCs, Professor Sheldon Krinsky, a bioethicist at Tufts University and author of *Science in the Private Interest: Has the Lure of Profits Corrupted Biomedical Research?* sums up the problem this way: "By accepting the premise that conflicts of interest in universities must be subtly managed, rather than prohibited or prevented, nothing less than the public interest function of the American academic enterprise is at stake."[9]

Dr. David Rothman, Professor of Social Medicine and Director of the Center for the Study of Society and Medicine at the Columbia College of Physicians and Surgeons, has called attention to the failure of professional organizations in medicine, with few exceptions, to regulate themselves and discipline their members. As Rothman concludes:

> *"The inadequacies of self-regulation make it clear that an examination of professionalism must go beyond questions of money and managed care. To the extent that self-regulation is the focus, professionalism today has to be invented, not restored."*[10]

Even the professional organizations that make the lofty pronouncements that guide self-regulation are embroiled in COIs. Most of them are beholden to contributions from industry for large parts of their budgets, which they typically defend as essential to carrying out programs in their constituents' best interest. Some professional associations sell their membership lists to

TABLE 9.1

Selected Provisions Of Recent Conflict-Of-Interest Guidelines By Medical Organizations*

Provisions regarding professional meetings (CME, GME, conferences) and informational presentations

AMA[‡]	ACCME[§]	ACP[¶]
Meals must be modest. Conference subsidies should meet the following conditions: •They should be accepted by conference sponsor, not physician attendees •They do not cover travel, lodging, time, or other personal expense of physician attendees who are not faculty • Hospitality subsidies should be limited to modest meals or social events held as part of meeting • Faculty honoraria and reimbursement must be reasonable • Organizers should retain responsibility for and control over selection of content, faculty, educational methods, and materials • Scholarships and special funds for trainees to attend "carefully selected education conferences" are permitted if selection of recipients is controlled by training institution "Legitimate" conferences or meetings are defined as having the following characteristics: • They are primarily dedicated (in time and effort) to objective scientific and educational activities • They are convened to further knowledge on topic presented • They ensure appropriate disclosure of financial support or conflict of interest	Generally, accredited CME providers must be responsible for the content, quality, and scientific integrity of activities. This necessitates eliminating commercial bias for or against any product and maintaining control over planning, program design, faculty selection, educational methods, materials, and evaluations. Specifically, accredited CME providers must do the following: • Accept support only in the form of educational grants • Document grant terms in a signed agreement • Formally report expenditures after CME activity • Refuse support that is conditioned on "advice or services, concerning speakers" or placement of commercial exhibits • Accept subsidies for hospitality only for modest meals or social events held as part of activity • Accept scholarship or special funds to permit trainees to attend only if selection of participants is done by training institution • Control dissemination of information about the activity by commercial supporters • Disclose commercial support in printed materials but do not name specific products • Vet advance copies of commercial presentation • Ensure faculty control content of slides and reference materials • Require that faculty disclose any relationships with commercial entities • Separate commercial exhibits and sales activities from educational activities	Modest hospitality (reception, food, drink) is acceptable if it is connected with a legitimate educational program. CME and GME organizers must do the following: • Follow ACCME guidelines • Avoid focus on a single product or company • Educate trainees on how to evaluate information provided by the pharmaceutical industry • Control access to registrants' mailing addresses • Disclose commercial support • Ban distribution of most promotional materials in educational sessions • Discuss industry support with invited speakers • Accept industry honoraria only for services rendered and reasonable travel costs. Industry-sponsored hospitality should be modest and arranged so that social activities don't compete with educational events • Medical education providers must administer the program budgets. Organizers of medical society activities must do the following: • Ensure that product promotion activities are separated from impartial medical information • Avoid endorsing specific products and services • Develop policies on acceptance and disclosure of industry funding

TABLE 9.1 (continued)
Selected Provisions Of Recent Conflict-Of-Interest Guidelines By Medical Organizations*

Provisions regarding professional meetings (CME, GME, conferences) and informational presentations

AMA[‡]	ACCME[§]	ACP[¶]
	• Ensure that educational events are not eclipsed by commercially supported social events • Avoid trade names where possible • Flag unlabeled uses of any products • Ensure that honoraria and reimbursement for faculty are reasonable • Do not compensate or reimburse non-faculty attendees	

Provisions regarding consulting fees

AMA[‡]	ACCME[§]	ACP[¶]
Payments for consulting services must be limited to reasonable compensation and reimbursement for travel, lodging and meal expenses; must be "genuine" services, not "token".		

Provisions regarding gifts

AMA[‡]	ACCME[§]	ACP[¶]
Physicians may accept gifts from pharmaceutical companies under the following conditions: 1. The gift must be primarily for the benefit of patients and be primarily related to the physician's work 2. The gift must be of insubstantial value and may not be cash 3. The gift must come with no strings attached 4. Drug samples permitted for non-retired physicians; personal and family use of the samples also permitted, provided that it does not interfere with patient access to the samples		To be acceptable, gifts from pharmaceutical companies must be inexpensive and intended for office use, education, or patient care

‡Provisions come from the Opinion of the Council on Ethical and Judicial Affairs of the American Medical Association (AMA)

§Provisions come from the Standards for Commercial Support of Continuing Medical Education of the Accreditation Council for Continuing Medical Education (ACCME).

¶Provisions come from the American College of Physicians (ACP) as outlined in Coyle.

Sources: Coyle S.L. Physician-industry relations. 1. Individual physicians. Ann Intern Med 136:396-402, 2002; and Accreditation Council for Continuing Medical Education. *Standards for commercial support of continuing medical education.* Accessed October 7, 2004, at http://www. accme.org/inconting/17 svstems98 essential.areas.pdf

industry, while some permit companies to decide which presentations at a CME meeting they can sponsor and which CME materials will carry a sponsoring company's logo.[11] At annual meetings of the American College of Physicians (ACP), which attracts about 7,000 members, sponsorship of the ACP official tote bag, given to all attendees at time of registration, is available for $50,000.[12]

To be sure, there have been efforts made by some physicians and a few organizations to resist this tide of commercialism in defense of professionalism and patients' welfare, but these efforts are unfortunately too scattered so far to make a big difference. Here are some examples of these important efforts.

- Academic detailing. Dr. Jerry Avorn, Associate Professor of Medicine at Harvard University and author of *Powerful Medicines: The Benefits, Risks, and Costs of Prescription Drugs*, has pioneered academic detailing as a means to pass along best evidence about drugs to physicians by using industry sales techniques. With funding from the Pennsylvania Department of Aging's drug-assistance program, an 'unsales force' has made contact with physicians about 1,500 times and conducted more than 400 educational meetings over the last three years. In each instance, clinical evidence has been reviewed which negates industry's marketing claims for such drugs as Vioxx, Bextra, and Nexium.[13]

- No-Free-Lunch. This is a not-for-profit organization founded in 1999 by Dr. Bob Goodman, a general internist at Columbia University Medical Center in New York with a mission to encourage health care professionals to practice medicine on the basis of scientific evidence instead of industry promotion. It actively discourages the acceptance of gifts from industry by physicians at all stages of their careers. Reception by medical organizations, however, has been chilly, or ambiguous at best. In 2005, a No-Free-Lunch booth was initially barred from the annual meetings of the American Academy of Family Physicians (AAFP) and ACP, both of which had large Exhibit Halls, filled with gift-laden booths from health-related industries. In first denying No-

Free-Lunch from the AAFP's annual meeting, with an attendance of more than 5,000 physicians, the AAFP's Manager of Sales and Services stated that No-Free-Lunch's position was "not within the character and purpose of the Scientific Assembly" and therefore did not meet the AAFP's "eligibility requirements." At the same time, the AAFP welcomed exhibit booths from such commercial vendors as the Coca-Cola Company, McDonald's Corporation, and the Distilled Spirits Council of the U.S. This position led to negative publicity for both the AAFP and ACP along with outcries from some of their members loud enough to force them to reverse their decisions denying No-Free Lunch exhibit space. At the AAFP's 2005 annual meeting, the No-Free-Lunch booth was well trafficked in its location next to that of the California Table Grape Commission and just opposite that of the Consortium for the Improvement of Erectile Dysfunction.[14,15]

- Public Citizen's Health Research Group. This independent, not-for-profit organization, based in Washington, D.C. and headed by Dr. Sidney Wolfe, works to promote research-based system-wide changes in health policy and provides oversight of drugs, medical devices, physicians and hospitals, and occupational health. Through such publications as *Health Letter* and *Worst Pills Best Pills*, the Health Research Group has often been first to identify dangerous drugs and medical devices. Their crucial work has often paved the way for the withdrawal of these products from the marketplace by manufacturers and the FDA who initially paid little heed to their dangers.[16]

- Kaiser Permanente Medical Group. In recognition of the severity of the COI problem, Kaiser is one of the first major medical organizations to set in place rigorous COI rules. This new policy was adopted in 2005 to apply to interactions between the medical group's 6,000 physicians and the drug industry.[17]

Kaiser physicians cannot:

- "Accept gifts or discounted products from any drug or equipment vendors for themselves or their families;

- Accept compensation, honoraria or gifts from a company that asks them to teach an accredited medical course sponsored by the company; and

- Participate in speakers' bureaus unless they receive prior approval from the medical group, which will grant approval only if it is deemed to be in Kaiser's interest."

Kaiser physicians participating in educational programs are required to sign COI disclosures, and Kaiser will control all funds received from drug companies to support physician training.

- <u>Association of Ethical Spine Surgeons</u>. In the wake of growing public concern over widespread conflicts-of-interest arrangements between spine surgeons and manufacturers of spinal devices, a new small but growing organization has recently been formed, the Association of Ethical Spine Surgeons, including surgeons who have agreed not to invest in companies whose devices they use.[18]

- <u>Academic Medical Centers</u> Stanford, Yale, and the University of Pennsylvania have recently adopted policies which prohibit their physicians from accepting even small gifts from industry, including sponsored meals and free drug samples, while also banning their involvement in journal articles ghost-written by industry contractors.[19] In addition, a rigorous policy proposal has recently been advanced by a group of health professionals representing such groups as the Association of American Medical Colleges (AAMC) and the Institute on Medicine as a Profession. This policy calls upon AMCs to eliminate COIs between physicians and industry by such means as banning all gifting from industry to physicians, excluding physicians with financial ties to drug companies from formulary committees, and prohibiting "no strings" grants or gifts to individual researchers. But without some kind of ability to legally enforce this with penalties, such a remedy will be limited.[20]

- <u>The International Committee of Medical Journal Editors (ICMJE)</u>. As we saw in the last chapter, Editors and the public on occasion have been "burned" by the lack of disclosure by authors and the submission of incomplete data with falsely positive results. The ICMJE is a small working group of editors of leading general medical journals, including *The Journal of the American Medical Association*, *The New England Journal of Medicine*, the *Annals of Internal Medicine*, and *The Lancet*. In response to false representation of research articles submitted for publication, the ICMJE has directly addressed the problem. It began by requiring, as a condition for publication, that clinical trials begun after July 1, 2005 be registered in a public trials registry. In the Committee's words:

> *"Registration is only part of the means to an end; that end is full transparency with respect to performance and reporting of clinical trials. Research sponsors may argue that public registration of clinical trials will result in unnecessary bureaucratic delays and destroy their competitive edge by allowing competitors full access to their research plans. We argue that enhanced public confidence in the research enterprise will compensate for the costs of full disclosure."*[21]

These are excerpts from the ICMJE's current uniform ethical requirements for reporting biomedical research:[22]

- "Conflict of interest exists when an author (or the author's institution), reviewer, or editor has financial or personal relationships that inappropriately influence (bias) his or her actions (such relationships are also known as dual commitments, competing interests, or competing loyalties). These relationships vary from those with negligible potential to those with great potential to influence judgment, and not all relationships represent true conflict of interest. The potential for conflict of interest can exist whether or not an individual believes that the relationship affects his or her scientific judgment. Financial relationships (such as employment, consultancies, stock ownership, honoraria, paid expert testimony) are the most easily identifiable conflicts of interest and the most likely to undermine the credibility of the journal, the authors, and of science itself. However, conflicts can occur for other reasons, such as personal relationships, academic competition, and intellectual passion."

- "Scientists have an ethical obligation to submit creditable research results for publication. Moreover, as the persons directly responsible for their work, researchers should not enter into agreements that interfere with their access to the data and their ability to analyze it independently, to prepare manuscripts, and to publish them. Authors should describe the role of the study sponsor(s), if any, in study design; in the collection, analysis, and interpretation of data; in the writing of the report; and in the decision to submit the report for publication."

- "Editors should consider seriously for publication any carefully done study of an important question, relevant to their readers, whether the results are negative (that is, convincingly allow the null hypothesis to be accepted) or positive (that is, allow the null hypothesis to be rejected). Failure to submit or publish negative studies, in particular, contributes to publication bias."

These are not mere pronouncements without teeth—they can be fully enforced by independent editors and their peer reviewers. But despite these new ethical guidelines, a recent example of undisclosed conflicts of interest involving an editorial writer for *The New England Journal of Medicine* shows that the problem remains even in one of our leading scientific journals. Despite mounting evidence that the drug erythropoietin (EPO) increases the risk of heart failure and the need for dialysis in patients with kidney failure, the *Journal* rejected an editorial critical of its continued use (soon published by *Lancet*) while accepting a less critical editorial by its own deputy editor without disclosure of her COIs. She was the immediate past president of the Massachusetts based chapter of the National Kidney Foundation, which receives more than one-half of its funding from industry and has issued practice guidelines recommending the use of this drug to treat anemia in patients with kidney failure.[23]

SELF-REGULATION BY INDUSTRY

In response to negative publicity about COIs between health care industries and physicians, some industries have also promulgated updated ethical guidelines for these relationships. First to do so was the Pharmaceutical Research and Manufacturers of America (PhRMA), which published its new guidelines in 2002.[24] The Advanced Medical Technology Association (AdvaMed) followed suit two years later.[25] Both are similar in many respects, and largely in harmony with guidance released by the Office of the Inspector General (OIG) in 2003 for the pharmaceutical industry.[26] These new codes of ethics in industry reflect increasing sensitivity to both ethical and legal issues, particularly in the aftermath of the Lupron case discussed in the last chapter.[27]

Noteworthy in these new codes adopted by industry is their shift of ultimate responsibility for planning and content of educational programs to program organizers as neutral intermediaries. In a recent review article on this subject, David Studdert, Associate Professor of Law and Public Health at the Harvard School of Public Health, and his colleagues conclude that these new ethical guidelines are a good start, but also note that they are entirely voluntary and lack mechanisms for enforcement.[28] Table 9-2 lists some typical selected provisions of these codes, as well as OIG's guidance.

REGULATION BY EXTERNAL BODIES

In the absence of effective self-regulation by the medical profession or by industry, regulation by external agencies becomes even more important. But here again, we find the regulatory process compromised by funding constraints, conflicts of interest between regulators and the regulated, and political vulnerability of these agencies to stakeholders resisting regulation of their market-interests. Our two most important regulators, the Food and Drug Agency (FDA) and the Joint Commission on the Accreditation of Healthcare Organizations (JCAHO), illustrate these problems throughout their history.

The FDA, with a budget less than 2 percent of the Department of Agriculture, receives much of its funding through user fees from the industries it is chartered to regulate.[29] COIs between physicians, investigators, regulators, and industry are common at many levels. Unless forced by exposure of these relationships by consumer advocacy groups or investigative reporting, these agencies have tended to accommodate industry's interests over the public interest, as was documented by many examples in Chapter 6. Not only does the FDA lack sufficient resources to become a fully effective regulatory agency, it has not received political support for such obviously needed regulatory tasks as incorporating the use

TABLE 9.2

Selected Provisions Of Recent Conflict-Of-Interest Guidelines By And For Industry

PhRMA[†]	AdvaMED[‡]	OIG[††]
Provisions regarding professional meetings (CME, GME, conferences) and informational presentations		
Payment for meals by pharmaceutical companies should meet the following conditions: •The meal is modest and is associated with valuable scientific or educational activities •The venue is conducive to informational communication • Guests are not included •Takeout meals are excluded • When supporting third-party meetings, pharmaceutical companies should do the following: •Direct support to conference organizers •Cede control over content, faculty, educational methods, materials, and venues to conference organizers •Provide meals only in conformance with organization's guidelines and other meal requirements •Provide no compensation to participants for attendance time • Provide no support for non-faculty attendees * Provide scholarships or educational funds only if they are related to "carefully selected educational conferences" and the selection of recipients is controlled by a training institution	Programs requiring "hands on" training in medical procedures should be held at training facilities, medical institutions, laboratories, or other appropriate facilities. •Members may provide Health Care Professional attendees with hospitality only in the form of modest meals and receptions in connection with these programs. •Members may pay for reasonable travel and modest lodging costs incurred by attending Health Care Professionals. •Members may provide a grant either directly to the conference sponsor to reduce conference costs, or to a training institution or the conference sponsor to allow attendance by medical students, residents, fellows, and others who are Health Care Professionals in training. •Members may make grants to support the genuine medical education of medical students, residents, and fellows participating in fellowship programs.	It is recommended that pharmaceutical manufacturers take the following steps when funding educational activities: •Ensure the activity is sponsored and organized by professional medical organizations •Do not restrict or condition support on sales of the manufacturer's product or specified content of faculty •Separate grant making from sales and marketing functions •Fund only bona fide activities •Avoid payments to physicians for listening to product presentations •Do not compensate "passive" participants for attendance time •Disclosure of industry sponsorship and potential conflicts of interest reduces but does not eliminate the risk.

(continued on next page)

TABLE 9.2 (continued)

Selected Provisions Of Recent Conflict-Of-Interest Guidelines By And For Industry

PhRMA[†]	AdvaMED[‡]	OIG[††]
Provisions regarding consulting fees		

Pharmaceutical companies may provide reasonable compensation and reimbursements to bona fide consultants. The following factors are evidence of a bona fide consulting arrangement:
 	
•A written contract specifies deliverables and basis of payment.
•A need for services is related to consultant's expertise and is clearly identified.
•The number of consultants is appropriate.
•Records are kept of arrangements and use of services.
•The venue and circumstances of meetings with consultants are appropriate.
•Reasonable compensation for speaker training is appropriate under the following conditions:
 	
1. Participants receive training regarding products and FDA requirements
2. Training leads to the provision of valuable services
3. Participants meet criteria for bona fide consultants
	Consulting agreements should be entered into only where a legitimate need and purpose for the services is identified in advance.
	    Selection of consultants should be on the basis of the consultant's qualifications and expertise to address the identified purpose, and should not be on the basis of volume or value of business generated by the consultant.
	    The venue and circumstances for Member meetings with consultants should be appropriate to the subject matter of the consultation.
	    Member-sponsored hospitality that occurs in conjunction with a consultant meeting should be modest in value and should be subordinate in time and focus to the primary purpose of the meeting.
	    When a Member contracts with a consultant for research services, there should be a written research protocol.
		Pharmaceutical companies' payments to physicians for services rendered should be in writing, relate to a legitimate need, reflect bona fide services, actually provided, and provide compensation at fair market value. Suspicious arrangements with consultant physicians include compensation for services related to marketing and sales activities, compensation received by physicians for time spent listening to marketing, and ghostwritten papers or speeches.

Provisions regarding gifts		
Pharmaceutical companies may provide "educational and practice-related items" under the following conditions: The item must be primarily for the benefit of patients and be primarily associated with clinical practice, not personal benefits. The item must be of insubstantial value ($100) and not be cash or cash equivalent	Members occasionally may provide modest gifts to Health Care Professionals, but only if the gifts benefit patients or serve a genuine educational function. Other than the gift of medical textbooks or anatomical models used for educational purposes, any gift from a Member should have a fair market value of less than $100.	Pharmaceutical companies should comply with PhRMA Code with respect to entertainment, recreation, travel, meals, gifts, gratuities and other business courtesies.

[†]Provisions come from the Code on Interactions with Healthcare Professionals of the Pharmaceutical Research and Manufacturers of America (PhRMA).

[‡]Provisions come from Information about AdvaMED guidelines for interactions with health care professionals.

[††]Provisions come from the Office of the Inspector General (OIG) Compliance Program Guidance for Pharmaceutical Manufacturers of the Department of Health and Human Services.

Source: Studdert D.M., Mallo M.M. & Brennan T.A. Financial conflicts of interest in physicians' relationships with pharmaceutical industry-self regulation in the shadow of federal prosecution. *N Engl J Med* 351(18):1891-1900, 2004

of cost-effectiveness as a criterion for drug and medical device approval; or requiring new drug applications to demonstrate benefit over competitor drugs, not just placebo. Moreover, the FDA lacks teeth in not having the authority to subpoena industry records to investigate suspected problems, to levy civil penalties for violations of its regulations, or to mandate drug recalls not done voluntarily by manufacturers.[30]

Industry has lobbied Congress quite effectively over the years to limit the FDA's regulatory reach over industries other than the drug industry. Two examples make the point. The Dietary Supplement Health and Education Act of 1994 minimized requirements for review of dietary supplements.[31] The Medical Device legislation of 2002 exempts many new medical devices from review and still applies a review criterion of whether a new device is equivalent to devices used before 1976.[32]

Oversight of the Medicare program was delegated to the Joint Commission on the Accreditation of Healthcare Organizations (JCAHO) when the program was established in 1965. The non-profit JCAHO, based in Oakbrook Terrace, Illinois, was founded in 1951 and accredits some 15,000 health care facilities across the country, including almost 5,000 hospitals. The JCAHO inspects hospitals every three years, and its approval is a requirement for facilities to receive federal payments. Medicare pays a network of 53 private groups, Quality Improvement Organizations (QIOs) to monitor quality in health care facilities, and also pays state regulators to investigate complaints of poor care and patient injury.[33]

Medicare provides a good example of the extent and limitations of the regulatory process. In 2004, Medicare's budget for policing more than 50,000 facilities, ranging from AMCs to small hospices, was $259 million. While that funding might seem large, it amounts to less than one-third of its expenditures for one day. Funding constraints limit the frequency of inspections. As a result, Medicare has prioritized its inspections into four tiers with nursing homes in the first tier and ambulatory surgicenters (ASCs) in the fourth tier. Scheduled inspections are frequently missed due to lack of funding—ASCs in California, for example, are now receiving inspections on an average of only once in 12 years.[34]

Beyond these funding limitations are other critical restrictions limiting the regulatory capability of the JCAHO. Dennis O'Leary, the president of the JCAHO, readily acknowledges that its role is to help hospitals and other facilities to meet its standards, not to regulate or punish them.[35] The

JCAHO is not authorized to fine or close down a facility. The cooperative ethos between "regulators" and facilities is also marked by COIs in that relationship. The JCAHO itself derives much of its income from its oversight activities (average charge of $26,000 for inspections of large hospitals). Quality Improvement Organizations, which receive almost $300 million a year, are dominated by physicians or health care executives, and conduct their activities in secrecy with little public accountability. Robert Berenson, a former Medicare official in the Clinton administration, has this to say about these organizations: "They've made this huge move from being inspectors to being collaborators. It's a blameless environment."[36]

Tenet's Redding Medical Center in California demonstrates the laxity of the regulatory process. From the early 1990s on, its rate of open-heart surgeries per 1,000 Medicare beneficiaries was more than double the average rate in California. Regulators found evidence of unnecessary surgery in 1999, but no action was taken by Medicare. The situation was unchanged when regulators returned in 2002. Following an FBI raid later that year, litigation ensued, some physicians who had long engaged in unnecessary procedures were dismissed, and the institution's open-heart surgery rate dropped precipitously to approximate the state's average rate.[37]

A federal anti-kickback law was passed in 1972 in an effort to protect the Medicare and Medicaid programs against COIs resulting in inappropriate and unnecessary use of health care services.[38] This law established criminal and civil penalties for "kickback" arrangements between suppliers, institutions and physicians, and was further amended in later years. Since the early 1990s, federal prosecutors have also made use of the False Claims Act, which provides for "whistle-blower, or "qui tam" lawsuits by private citizens on behalf of the government against fraudulent claims and practices.[39] The federal government has taken a more active approach in recent years to prosecuting health care fraud, and now considers four main factors in deciding when payments to physicians represent kickbacks: (1) likelihood that a potential COI arrangement will interfere with objective clinical judgment and decision-making by physicians; (2) likelihood that such an arrangement will increase a physician's use of a company's product; (3) likelihood that costs to federal health care programs will increase as a result of a COI arrangement; and (4) does an arrangement in question adversely affect patient safety or quality of care?[40]

IS EFFECTIVE REGULATION POLITICALLY ACHIEVABLE?

As we've seen, self-regulation by the medical profession of physician COIs has been mired in conflicts of interest by many involved in setting forth regulatory guidelines, such as the AMA and other professional organizations. Self-regulation by industry often comes about only at the threat of negative publicity under pressure by such outside groups as Public Citizen's Health Research Group. Despite lofty pronouncements of intent and guidelines on the part of both the profession and industry, mechanisms and resources are lacking to monitor and enforce these guidelines. Government regulators at both federal and state levels are hindered by limited funding and vulnerability to political interferences, as well as a cooperative, non-regulatory mode with its own entrenched conflicts of interest. And they are also often hindered by the political context in which they attempt to regulate. The question then is whether effective regulation of pervasive COIs in health care is at all realistic politically.

Past Track Record

The track record of regulation to date is indeed depressing. Voluntary self regulation doesn't work or at best has severe limitations, regulators are mired in the very conflicts they are supposed to be regulating, government oversight is under funded and under enforced, while the need for regulation, as discussed in previous chapters, is enormous and increasing. As is well illustrated by passage of the 2003 Medicare bill, described in Chapters 4 and 6, the money culture permeates the health care system as well as the world of legislators and policymakers through permissive campaign finance laws, well-financed lobbying, and a revolving door of leadership between industry and government. Most professional organizations have become dependent on the largesse of industry through unrestricted educational grants and other contributions. When external regulation by government becomes necessary, anti-kickback regulations apply to services reimbursed by federal funds (i.e., Medicare and Medicaid), leaving the rest of the system largely unaccountable. As an example of regulatory gaps, only a state medical board has jurisdiction if a diagnostic imaging center wants to accept only patients with private insurance. The state medical boards, however, tend to focus more on the quality of care and bypass this kind of issue.[41]

Widespread denial of COIs within the profession and its organizations pose a major barrier to regulation and reform. Social science research has shown that small gifts may be as influential as large gifts on behavior of recipients.[42] Yet many physicians still see themselves as beyond influence when their own needs or interests are being advanced by such gifts.[43-45] Similarly, the claims of professional organizations maintaining a "bright line" between their scientific programs and commercial marketing in the Exhibit Halls of their meetings in likewise unpersuasive, given their dependence on industry support.

We can anticipate increasing scrutiny of physician COIs since the stakes of inaction are growing all the time. To the extent that self-regulation of COIs by the profession and industry remains ineffectual, more rigorous regulation by external bodies will become even more necessary to protect the public interest. Disclosure of physician COIs is not sufficient in itself. It is too easy to disclose COIs and still behave as if they aren't there.[46]

Needed Regulatory Reforms

In view of the wide spectrum of COIs throughout our market-based system involving physicians, their professional organizations, industry, and regulators, the list of needed reforms is indeed long. In his excellent book, *On the Take: How Medicine's Complicity with Big Business Can Endanger Your Health*, Dr. Jerome Kassirer, long a leader in academic medicine and former Editor of *The New England Journal of Medicine*, proposes these four principles upon which to base regulatory reforms:[47]

1. "Financial considerations must never be allowed to compromise physicians' decisions about the care of individual patients or the safety of subjects involved in medical research.

2. Because the integrity of scientific knowledge directly affects patient care, physicians' medical information must be free of bias generated by financial entanglements.

3. The profession must be accountable for insuring that undue commercial influence does not make the cost of care so high that it excludes many from receiving it.

4. We must aspire to the ideal of eliminating financial entanglements, but if physicians cannot or will not, we must have clear and

enforceable methods that protect patients and complete disclosure about the conflicts."

Kassirer also suggests this thoughtful and reasonable roadmap for regulatory reform.[48]

"Items for Immediate Implementation:

1. Exclusion of *all* gifts from industry (by law if necessary), even including items that might be considered useful in a doctor's practice or education; elimination of physician participation in company-sponsored speaker's bureaus.
2. Prohibition of consultations with industry for anything except scientific matters, and outlawing of marketing by physicians of drugs or devices in which they have a financial interest.
3. Full disclosure to patients in all doctors' private offices of any and all financial incentives for patient care or clinical research.
4. Elimination of "finder's fees" for identifying patients to drug companies or their intermediates; no "farming out" of patients for clinical research.
5. Permission to conduct clinical research on devices or drugs in which the investigator has a financial interest should be proscribed.
6. The requirement of full accessibility for independent analysis of all data in any published clinical trial in which the investigators had a financial conflict.
7. A requirement of full, detailed disclosure in legible handouts at all teaching events of the type (drugs or devices), dollar amounts, and duration of all financial ties of the lecturer that relate to the subject at hand; full disclosure of the sponsorship of all such events.
8. The selection of journal editors, officers of major professional organizations, and leaders of academic institutions among physicians who have no financial conflicts.
9. A demand for increased scrutiny by medical editors of all financial conflicts of authors, with full disclosure not only of the company relationships but also the specific relevancy of the

conflicts to the subject matter (specific drugs and devices).

10. Pressure for a comprehensive analysis of the problem by the Institute of Medicine that would include drafting principles and guidelines for all types of financial conflicts, not just those associated with research.

Items for further analysis and debate:

1. If CME lectures by individuals with financial conflicts cannot be prohibited, should physicians boycott courses given by financially conflicted lecturers?

2. If clinical-practice-guideline committees cannot be constituted exclusively by non-conflicted individuals, what safeguards can be introduced to reduce the chance of biased recommendations?

3. If ownership of stock in a company that could benefit from a researcher's work and scientific consultations with a company create conflicts, what is the basis for any specific "minimally acceptable" amount that researchers can hold in stock or receive yearly in compensation for consultations?

4. How could a universal Web-based registry of physicians' financial conflicts of interest be implemented?

5. How can the financial arrangements of professional organizations with industry be disclosed, including the amounts, duration, and purposes for which the funds were used?

6. How can the dependence of professional organizations on industry support be reduced?

7. Can industry be convinced that in the long run the harm of physicians' collusion with their marketing practices is more serious than the short-term gain in sales?"

The above directions for reform would go a long way to reduce and make more transparent COIs involving physicians and industry, but are not sufficient in themselves. Here are some additional areas for serious consideration as further ways to reduce opportunities for COIs among providers and stakeholders within the system, to limit exploitation of the public interest, and to bring more accountability to conflicted interests. In some cases, legislation by Congress would likely be required:

1. Limit marketing costs by drug companies to the amounts spent on research and development of new drugs.

2. Disallow for-profit Medical Education and Communication Companies (MECCs) from gaining approval by the Accreditation Council for Continuing Medical Education (ACCME) for CME programs for physicians.

3. Restrict or ban altogether direct-to-consumer advertising (DTCA) by the drug and medical device industries.

4. Require increased oversight and academic rigor of commercially oriented research networks for post-marketing drug trials.

5. Continue the moratorium on specialty hospitals unless they can be demonstrated to provide satisfactory access, costs and quality without jeopardizing the viability of general hospitals.

6. Revisit current federal exemptions from anti-kickback regulations with increased scrutiny and oversight of facilities in which physicians have investment or ownership roles.[49]

7. Expand the mandate and authority of the FDA in these areas:
    - Requiring new drug applications to demonstrate benefit over competitor drugs.
    - Use of cost-effectiveness as a criterion in evaluating new drug and medical device applications.
    - Reviewing dietary supplements for safety.
    - More rigorous review and reporting of post-marketing Phase IV drug studies.
    - Granting the FDA authority to impose civil penalties for violations of its regulations, to subpoena industry records in order to investigate suspicious practices, and to require mandatory recalls of drugs or medical devices when not done voluntarily by manufacturers.

8. Increase funding to regulatory agencies consistent with their expanded roles and responsibilities, starting with the FDA and JACHO, so that these agencies can reduce or eliminate their dependence upon industry funding.

9. Increase the capability of the government to assess new medical

technologies by applying scientific evidence with protection from political and corporate interferences; explore the creation of an independent agency analogous to the Federal Reserve Board[50] for long-term evidence-based technology assessment.

Guarded Optimism for Regulatory Reform

Given the extent to which the deregulated medical marketplace has given rise to widespread COIs throughout the system, is there any hope for positive change? Several factors give us some room for optimism that effective regulatory reforms are achievable.

The failures of regulatory attempts in past years are instructive in themselves. We know that voluntary self-regulation leaves wide latitude for gaming the system, and that underfunded regulatory agencies need independence and protection from corporate and political interference. Future regulatory mechanisms will therefore have to be enforceable and be given higher priority and funding.

We also know that pervasive COIs waste valuable resources, inflate prices, and thereby threaten access, cost containment, and quality of care for much of the population. As health care prices itself beyond the reach of the middle class, pressure for reform and increased accountability will only mount.

The 2006 mid-term elections give further reason to expect that Congress will pay more attention to these problems. The passage by the House of Representatives of a bill to allow Medicare to negotiate drug prices with manufacturers is but one early example of this change. But we are also seeing more bipartisan support for needed reforms, even before the 2006 elections. In 2003, for example, Representatives JoAnn Emerson (R-Missouri) and Tom Allen (D-Maine) introduced a bill that would provide specific funding for comparisons of the cost and effectiveness of prescription drugs.[51] A Congressional investigation of drug companies' "educational" grants was conducted by the Senate Finance Committee in 2004 and 2005 under the leadership of Senators Charles Grassley (R-Iowa) and Max Baucus (D-Montana).[52]

To the extent that physicians are involved or complicit with COIs with corporate interests, the professional integrity of our profession is at risk. As pressure grows for a more transparent and accountable system, it remains to be seen how our profession and organizations will meet this challenge.

CHAPTER 10

HOW HAS THE UNRESTRAINED MEDICAL MARKETPLACE IMPACTED THE PROFESSION?

"Consider what has happened to American medicine over the past thirty years. The physician's relationship to patients has been drastically altered. Medicine's traditional methods of controlling economic competition and making a living have largely been destroyed. Independent, solo, fee-for-service practice is rapidly disappearing. The clinical freedom of the physician has been seriously weakened. Divisions within the profession have intensified. Taken together, these changes have the potential to destroy professionalism in medicine and reduce physicians to the position of technicians."

Eliot Friedson
Professor Emeritus of Sociology,
New York University[1]

"In the end, money is a cruel god, not worthy of devotion. And this is perhaps the clearest way of saying what is troubling about this elusive but all-important interior and motivational dimension of the hegemony of money in medicine: the cruelty lies in the way money overpowers all other values and thereby uproots physicians of the deep rewards of recognizing themselves as part of a healing process. Money (and the considerable list of things it can buy) becomes the chief standard against which doctors judge themselves and seek to be judged. But for professionals the only god worthy of solemn devotion is signified in the etymology of 'profession,' viz., an avowal of service beyond self."

Larry Churchill
Bioethicist, Vanderbilt University[2]

The above two insightful observations speak to the impacts of the sea change of commercialism which has engulfed medicine over the last 30 years, together with the loss of autonomy among physicians and erosion of their influence over directions of the health care system itself. As we have seen in earlier chapters, the traditional professionalism of medicine based on a dominant service ethic has been threatened by the business ethic, which pervades the system. In Chapter 8, we saw how many physicians have been complicit with these changes and have found new ways to serve their self-interest, but many others have been caught up in a new system not of their making. Now it's time to ask what impacts these transformational changes have had on the profession itself.

This chapter attempts to answer this question by addressing two goals: (1) to consider some of the major impacts of the business ethos on medicine as a profession; and (2) to examine some ways in which physicians and their organizations have responded to these changes.

SOME MAJOR IMPACTS
OF THE BUSINESS ETHOS ON MEDICINE

Among the many impacts on the profession of system changes which have converted health care from a human service into a commodity, these stand out as especially important.

Decreased Clinical autonomy, Independence, and Practice Satisfaction

As we saw in Chapter 2, a major power shift has taken place over the last 40 years in health care. Whereas physicians played a dominant role in shaping the directions and content of health care up to the 1960s, they have lost much of their influence over today's corporate-based system. The major players now are the insurers, managed care plans, hospitals, employers, and to a lesser extent, the government through its public programs. Physicians now find themselves salaried more often than not, and are increasingly dependent on economic arrangements set by other organizations. Solo and small group practice have increasingly been replaced by large group and corporate structures. The cottage industry of health care in past years, with physicians as captains of their own practices, has mostly disappeared, and physicians struggle to adapt to an ever-changing environment controlled by third party managers.

Many physicians contract with several managed care organizations (MCOs), whether HMOs or PPOs, whereby they agree to coverage and reimbursement rules established by such plans. Physician judgments of necessary care are often questioned by plan managers (or their clerks). Plan decisions are final unless a successful appeal can be mounted. Drug formularies, which establish which drugs are to be covered by a health plan, are frequently changed so that a physician's choice of drug therapy is another common source of contention between physician and health plan. Physicians also often have to deal with multiple formularies from different insurers and agencies. Primary care physicians caring for older patients with multiple chronic diseases often receive telephone calls from nurses employed by private disease management vendors in distant locations concerning chronic care plans with the intention to better "coordinate" care, even though these nurses have no personal relationship with patients or their physicians. Primary care physicians are often pressured by MCOs to see more patients, limit what they tell their patients and limit referrals.[3]

The transition from independent clinical practice to one or another form of employment structure usually requires major changes for physicians. Some physicians who successfully make these adjustments trade off independence for a more rewarding practice environment and enhanced trust, especially if they retain a participatory role in governance (e.g., Group Health Cooperative and Kaiser Permanente).[4] Other physicians find it difficult to cope with these system changes as their frustration and antagonism builds toward those seeking to limit expenses by second guessing them.

Many studies in recent years have documented declining practice satisfaction among U.S. physicians.[5-7] A 2003 study found that about one in five of generalist and specialist physicians across the country between 1997 and 2001 reported being somewhat or very dissatisfied with their careers in medicine.[8] The Massachusetts Medical Society, which has tracked satisfaction of U.S. physicians since 1992 by a nine-point index, has found that physician satisfaction fell by 15 percent between 1992 and 2002, with most of that decline since 1997.[9]

Erosion of Physician-Patient Relationship

The quality and continuity of the physician-patient relationship have been hit hard by system changes over the past 30 years, especially in primary care. In pursuit of increased efficiency and productivity, managed care organizations have pressured physicians to see more patients in less time. By 1997, primary care physicians were spending an average of only eight minutes talking to each patient, less than one-half the time spent ten years earlier.[10] Not only have shorter office visits been found to result in poorer patient outcomes,[11] but they also contribute to dissatisfaction, burnout, and impaired mental health among physicians.[12] Many other trends have eroded continuity of care with patients, including increasing mobility of both patients and physicians; instability of health plan coverage, with one study showing typical annual turnover rates of patients' insurance coverage of 20 percent often resulting in change of physicians.[13] Another study reported in 2004 found that only one-half of Medicare + Choice patients changing HMOs kept their primary care physicians.[14] More primary care physicians have been withdrawing from inpatient care as the hospitalist movement spreads, and many are opting for urgent care or emergency settings without any continuity of care.[15]

Primary care physicians are placed in conflicting roles as they attempt to balance the constant pressures by managed care plans to contain costs by limiting care. Dr. Marcia Angell, former editor of *The New England Journal of Medicine*, effectively rebuts the premise that physicians should act as "double agents," noting that containment of spiraling health care costs will require coherent reorganization of the health care system itself, and that attempts to contain costs patient by patient cannot succeed in our present unaccountable market-based system.[16] A 1998 report of a study of more than 1,000 primary care physicians in Pennsylvania found that two-thirds of respondents felt that the gatekeeper role places physicians in an adversary position to their patients. More than one-half of physicians in that study also felt that it is difficult to avoid financial conflicts of interest in that role, while two-thirds believe that managed care has a negative effect on choice of specialists, location and length of hospitalization.[17]

Increased Bureaucracy and Hassle Factor

The level of bureaucracy in U.S. health care has grown exponentially over the last 30 years, exceeding by far that of other industrialized nations. A 2003 study found that administrative costs now consume 31 percent of total annual health care spending, and that administrative and clerical workers account for 43 percent of the work force in physicians' offices. Dealing with over 1,300 private insurers is the biggest challenge of all, with each insurer heaving different coverage policies. Clerical and other non-clinical employees now outnumber physicians and other medical workers in U.S. doctors' offices.[18]

Comparisons of health care administration between the U.S. and our Canadian neighbors to the north are stark in their contrasts. Compared to annual costs in Canada, U.S. administrative costs are five times higher for insurance overhead, seven times higher for employers' costs to manage health benefits, and three times higher for administrative costs of physicians. Two leading U.S. insurers, UnitedHealthcare and Cigna, have more than 30 employees for every 10,000 enrollees, about 25 times the number of employees for Canadian plans for that number of enrollees.[19] Figure 10.1 compares the remarkable growth in numbers of administrators compared to physicians in this country since 1970. The reason is simple: in Canada there is only one insurer, the government. Doctors there don't face a multitude of insurers with a wide range of paperwork requirements. Canada's administrative costs are no more than 2 percent of the health care dollar. The only place where the U.S. approaches that level of efficiency in overhead is in the administration of Medicare, which is the part of the system most run by the government, just like in Canada.

Another large part of the "hassle factor" for U.S. physicians is the increased burden of utilization review by third parties in their efforts to contain costs. The average American physician spends 8 hours per week on paper work.[20] Providers and patients are both dissatisfied with the bureaucracy of health care.[21] Figure 10.2 displays marked differences in the intrusiveness of outside cost reviews between U.S. physicians and those in other industrialized countries.[22]

Increased Entrepreneurism Among Physicians

We saw in Chapter 8 how many physicians in recent years have put their financial self-interest above their patients' interests through conflicts of interest with the pharmaceutical and medical device industries, ownership of facilities, and other means. One still has to wonder to what extent physicians in everyday community practice succumb to incentives to increase their own income in our market-based system at the expense of their patients. There has to be great variation from physician to physician and from one medical community to another, but two studies shed some light on this question.

The Community Tracking Study Physician Survey in 2002 to 2003 examined how health plan payment, group ownership, compensation methods, and other practice management tools affected physician perceptions

FIGURE 10.1

Growth of Physicians and Administrators
1970-2002

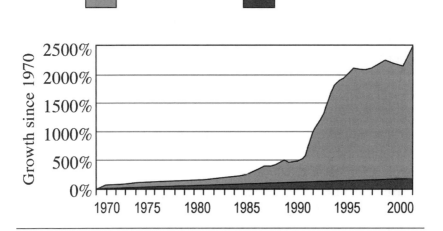

SOURCE: Reprinted with permission from: Woolhandler S. & Himmelstein DU. The National Health Program Slide-show Guide, Center for National Health Program Studies, Cambridge, Mass, 2006.

of whether their financial incentives tilted toward increasing or decreasing services to patients. The study involves more than 12,000 physicians in a nationally representative survey of 12 major health care markets across the country. It was found that practice ownership and variable compensation and bonuses for employed physicians were mostly associated with incentives to increase patients' services. Compensation through capitation (i.e., predetermined contractual payments based on number of enrollees) was associated with fewer services to patients and more concerns about quality of care. The physician survey in 2002-03 confirmed widespread strategies to increase the volume of patient visits and use of ancillary and specialty facilities, as well as strategies to limit care of the underserved and stop accepting new Medicare and Medicaid patients.[23]

A more recent study examined patterns of primary care physician

FIGURE 10.2

U.S. Physicians Face More Intrusive Cost Reviews

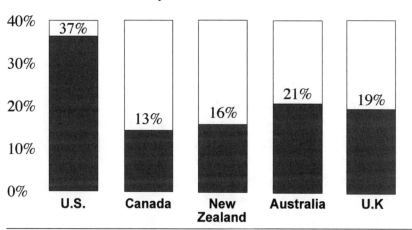

% of Doctors Saying Outside Review to Control Costs Is a Major Problem In Their Practice

Source: Reprinted with permission from: Woolhandler S. & Himmelstein DU. The National Health Program Slide-show Guide, Center for National Health Program Studies, Cambridge, Mass, 2000.

behavior in higher and lower Medicare spending areas across the country. Despite very little variation in illness severity from one region to another, physicians in higher spending areas were more likely to order further evaluation or treatment than physicians faced with the same patients in lower spending areas.[24]

Impact on Physicians' Income

Although physicians have been markedly constrained by system changes in recent decades from setting their own reimbursement levels and are subject to continuing increases in their practice overhead, their compensation nevertheless remains in the top one percent of all professions in the country.[25] Table 10.1 lists practice revenue and total median compensation for U.S. physicians by specialty in 2004, as compiled by a 2005 *Medical Economics* Continuing Survey.[26] These figures are similar to those obtained by income surveys of the Medical Group Management Association (MGMA).

Striking differences in income by specialty are readily apparent in this table, owing largely to a reimbursement system favoring procedures (such as a colonoscopy or surgical procedure) over cognitive services (such as evaluation of chest pain or other complaints). This system dates back to the resource-based relative value scale (RBRVS) established during the 1980s. For this reason surgical specialties have always enjoyed higher practice incomes than their colleagues in primary care and most medical specialties. This pattern has been altered in more recent years as some medical specialties gain new procedures, such as gastroenterologists (various endoscopic procedures) and dermatologists (with improved skin surgery procedures). Figure 10.3 shows marked differences in income between procedure-oriented specialties and their primary care counterparts.[27] These differences might seem understandable, but they open up new ways to distort the system. As we have seen in earlier chapters, areas with higher concentrations of specialists and more specialized services cost more, but have no better patient outcomes, sometimes even worse patient outcomes than less specialized parts of the country.[28] Moreover, areas with larger numbers of primary care physicians per capita have better patient outcomes than areas with a more specialized physician workforce.[29]

The last several years have seen plateauing of physician incomes in many specialties as a result of many factors, including rising practice expenses (especially in malpractice insurance premiums for some specialties), increasing cost sharing with patients (higher co-pays, coinsurance, and deductibles), declining access to care, increased bargaining clout of third party payers, and decreasing reimbursement in public programs (Medicare, Medicaid, SCHIP).[30] According to national surveys of more than 6,000 U.S. physicians, conducted by the Center for Studying Health System Change in 2004, 2005 and earlier years, average physicians' net income, after adjusting for inflation, declined by 7 percent from 1995 to 2003.[31] Reimbursement for many services, especially in public programs, has fallen well below the costs of providing services. The 600 physician-Marshfield Clinic in Wisconsin, for example, found that only 70 percent of the costs of providing care to Medicare patients was reimbursed. That was even before a 5 percent Medicare cut in 2002.[32] Many physicians, however, have responded to plateauing or declines in fees by increasing their frequency of

TABLE 10.1

Who's Chief of Income?

	2004 Practice Revenue[1]	2004 Total Compensation[2]
Cardiologists, invasive	$800,000	$400,000
Neurosurgeons	955,000	400,000
Plastic surgeons	1,000,000	400,000
Gastroenterologists	611,000	340,000
Thoracic surgeons	600,000	323,000
Urologists	750,000	303,000
Orthopedic surgeons	680,000	300,000
Cardiologists, noninvasive	600,000	300,000
Ophthalmologists	680,000	285,000
Dermatologists	560,000	282,000
General surgeons	420,000	233,800
Pulmonologists	437,700	224,000
Allergists/Allergy immunologists	575,000	221,800
Nephrologists	450,000	220,000
Ob/gyns	569,300	215,000
Rheumatologists	500,000	200,000
Infectious disease specialists	294,000	167,800
Endocrinologists	374,000	160,000
Internists	350,000	150,000
Pediatricians	380,000	147,900
FPs	381,800	147,000
Psychiatrists	200,000	145,000
GPs	260,000	120,000
All respondents	**$425,000**	**$180,000**

[1]Practice revenue represents 2004 collections after all adjustments, discounts, and write-offs. [2]Total compensation for unincorporated physicians is earnings after tax-deductible expenses but before income taxes. For physicians in professional corporations, its the sum of salary, bonuses, and retirement/proflt-sharing contributions made on their behalf. All figures are medians. Data apply to Individual office-based MDs and DOs.

SOURCE: Lowes R. Medical Economics 2005 Continuing Survey The earnings freeze: now it's everybody's problem. *Medical Economics, September 16, 2005, p59*

FIGURE 10.3

Specialty Salaries Surged as the Millenium Neared

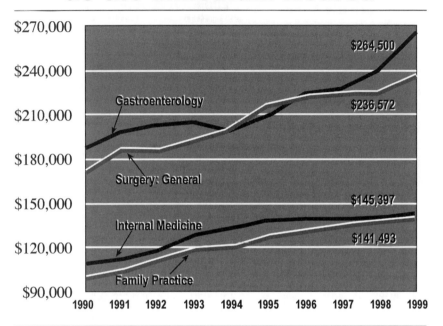

SOURCE: Physician Compensation and Production Survey, Medical Group Management Association, Englewood, Cob, 2000; and Compensation Monitor. *Managed Care Magazine.* Available at: http://www.managedcaremag.com/archives/0103/0103.compinon.html. Accessed on January 11, 2006.

patient visits and/or procedures[33] The Executive Director of the Medicare Payment and Advisory Commission (MedPAC) has recently acknowledged the challenge of controlling increasing volume of physician services for Medicare patients; in 2005, spending on physician services increased by 8.5 percent while the number of beneficiaries in fee-for-service Medicare grew by only 0.3 percent.[34]

Shift in Specialty Choice Away from Primary Care

Market forces do not lead to distribution of physicians either geographically or by specialty according to the health care needs of the population.[35] As we saw in Chapter 3, an "inverse care law" describes a reality that the sickest people in greatest need are the least profitable and worst served when markets control the system.[36] Physicians, especially in the non-primary care specialties, tend to congregate in more highly reimbursed markets. New medical graduates also gravitate to specialties offering higher reimbursement and more attractive lifestyles. All three lower reimbursed primary care fields—family medicine, general internal medicine, and general pediatrics—are in decline in recent years, despite the increasing need for a stronger primary care base of U.S. health care. Only about 10 percent of graduates of U.S. medical schools opt for residency training in one of these primary care specialties.[37] Although substantial numbers of international medical graduates (IMGs) fill many vacant residency training positions in the primary care specialties, especially in internal medicine, the U.S. physician workforce remains skewed toward the non-primary care specialties. The future of primary care is further clouded by the finding by the AMAs *Physician Characteristics and Distribution in the U.S.* that 35 percent of the nation's physicians are over 55 years of age and will likely retire within the next five to ten years.

There are undoubtedly many factors which contribute to the worrisome decline in primary care, including these factors:

- Primary care services are undervalued by all payers within the system and cognitive (non procedural) services have been underreimbursed compared to procedures for over 40 years; the gap between incomes in primary care and non-primary care specialties continues to widen.

- The estimated costs of attending four years of medical school have grown to about $140,000 for public schools and $225,000 for private schools; by 2004, average debts by medical school graduates had increased to $105,000 (public) and $140,000 (private) and only 20 percent of graduates had no debt.[38]

- Many medical graduates understand that the rewards of procedure-oriented non-primary care specialties offer a more attractive lifestyle without the emphasis on productivity and bureaucratic hassles of current primary care practice.

- The Council on Graduate Medical Education (COGME) has

recently projected a physician shortage by 2020, with other forecasts that the demand for specialized services will increase faster than the supply of physicians, which is projected to grow at 5 percent.[39,40]

- The Association of American Medical Colleges (AAMC) echoed this concern calling for an increase in medical school enrollment of 30 percent by 2020, but without any mechanisms for correction of maldistribution by specialty[41]; while this recommendation may respond to future needs, it is unlikely to resolve system problems and seems certain to increase physician-induced demand, together with an increase in the amounts of inappropriate and unnecessary services.

- It appears that large numbers of internists and pediatricians will continue to subspecialize.

The decline in primary care capacity is a serious problem for U.S. health care, still largely avoided by policymakers. Nations with the best performing health care systems all have strong bases of primary care generalists (e.g.,70 percent in the U.K., 50 percent in Canada).[42] Without an adequate primary care base, the system becomes increasingly fragmented, inefficient and overspecialized, with lower quality of care, increased health disparities, and uncontrollable costs. Underserved populations are at special risk without enough primary care physicians, as is already being seen in the nation's network of community health centers.[43] It has become very difficult to recruit and retain primary care physicians, especially family physicians in rural centers.[44]

Adverse Impacts on Academic Medical Centers

Academic medical centers (AMCs) are dedicated to a three-pronged mission—patient care, including care of the underserved; teaching medical students, residents and fellows; and development of new knowledge through clinical research. The challenges of sustaining these missions have been increasing greatly in recent years as the medical marketplace becomes more competitive, third party reimbursement for clinical activities is reduced, and other sources of support become more difficult to obtain. Many medical schools have no more than 10 percent of their budgets covered by state funding. Teaching itself tends to be an unreimbursed activity, and obtaining research funding through the National Institutes of Health (NIH) or other sources remains a formidable undertaking. AMCs are especially vulnerable to market forces as they struggle to care for the underserved as part of their clinical and social mission. Teaching hospitals and their clinics typically serve as safety net facilities for the uninsured and those on public programs such as Medicare, Medicaid and SCHIP, all of which are under-reimbursed.

As a result of budget pressures, AMCs have had to devote more of their faculty's effort to patient care, often with a negative impact on their teaching programs. Some have withdrawn, at least in part, from their safety net role, as illustrated by this letter to the faculty from the University of California Irvine Hospital Chief: "(We can) no longer tolerate patients with complex and expensive-to-treat conditions being encouraged to transfer to our group."[45] Other AMCs have been found by regulators to have gamed the reimbursement system through fraudulent billings; as an example, one of the country's largest health care universities, the University of Medicine and Dentistry of New Jersey, is being prosecuted for "purposeful overbilling" (double-billing) of Medicaid involving at least $4.9 million, even continuing that practice for three years after an initial warning.[46]

SOME RESPONSES BY THE PROFESSION TO THE MARKET-BASED ENVIRONMENT

The above impacts on the medical profession have been gradual but cumulative and profound. These are some of the responses of the profession to the new health care landscape.

Frustration, Demoralization, and Early Retirement

Many primary care physicians feel frustrated by system constraints, which limit their time with patients, as well as the continuity and quality of their relationship with patients. This frustration even goes to the point that they feel unable to practice the kind of medicine for which they were trained. Here is a widespread and typical expression of the problem by William Hueston, chairman of the Department of Family Medicine at the Medical University of South Carolina in Charleston:

"Family physicians are unhappy because the health care environment inhibits us from achieving the goals that first attracted us to the specialty. Changes have eroded the values that were the foundation of family medicine. Even the central value of family medicine (i.e., forming a lasting relationship with a core set of patients) is slowly dissolving. Relationships that had been established and nurtured over decades are severed when employers change health plans and our patients are forced to find new doctors. Primary care has become a commodity that many believe any physician can provide equally well."[47]

In an effort to help their patients obtain the kind of care they feel is indicated, some physicians acknowledge "gaming" the system in various ways, such as exaggerating the severity of a patient's condition to help them avoid early discharge from a hospital. Many physicians now believe that some gaming of the system is necessary in order to provide high quality of care.[48] Caught between the conflicting goals of patients and for-profit health plans, some primary care physicians in managed care plans discourage sicker patients from joining capitated plans even as they encourage healthier patients to do so.[49] A 2003 study found that one-third of physicians elected not to offer useful services to patients because of coverage restrictions.[50] The pressures to serve two masters—the patient and the health plan—has bred cynicism among many physicians and a threat to their own feelings of self-worth. As Larry Churchill observes:

"Physicians have also had a significant portion of their professional independence and autonomy stripped away by corporate managers, and been systematically encouraged to think of their stewardship of money—rather than, or in addition to, their stewardship of patients— as the right way to measure whether they are "good" doctors. In this transition money can become the substitute for the lost sense of professional self-worth. In the past this sense of worth could be derived from developing therapeutic relationships, and a general altruism of purpose. The industrial-managerial model of care makes these sources of reward less available."[51]

A 2006 report examined the reasons for physicians leaving medicine basing its data on the first two rounds of the 9-Year Community Tracking Study (CTS) and interviews with more than 16,000 physicians. It found a strong correlation between physician dissatisfaction and the decision to reduce practice time to less than 20 hours per week or to leave medicine altogether, with higher-paid specialties more likely to retire early. The investigators note the potential impact that physician dissatisfaction can have on adequacy of the future physician workforce and call for close monitoring of this problem.[52]

Search for More Independence

In order to gain an increased measure of practice independence and autonomy, small but growing numbers of physicians are refusing to contract with managed care organizations,[53] instead setting up concierge practices for care of more affluent patients, or exploring options to unionize. The latter two approaches are especially interesting as departures from the traditional culture of medicine.

Concierge practice, otherwise known as boutique or retainer-based medicine, is a new trend started in the 1990s whereby physicians, mostly in primary care, charge retainer fees for more convenient and personalized services. There are three main models of concierge practice—(1) higher retainer fees (e.g., $5,000 to $20,000 a year) and the physician doesn't bill insurance; (2) lower retainer fees (e.g., $65 to $100 a month) and the physician still bills insurance; and (3) the patient pays cash at the time of all services, and insurance may still be billed. Services included in retainer-based medicine vary, but typically include same day, wait-free appointments, after hours availability, unhurried visits, and periodic wellness checkups. While there may be no more than 300 concierge physicians now (mostly on East and West coasts), its advocates see retainer-based medicine as a growing patient-driven movement that meets the needs of patients for more personalized care and of physicians for more a rewarding practice style with fewer patients, less stress, and usually enhanced income. Two new organizations have been established, both in 2003, to advance this approach to practice—the American Society of Concierge Physicians and the Society for Innovative Medical Practice Design.[54-56]

While concierge practice may become much more popular among physicians increasingly stressed by today's practice environment, there are still legal and regulatory concerns that cloud its future. Health plans may have contractual limitations on this type of practice. Medicare has concerns about adverse impacts of concierge practice on access for other Medicare beneficiaries. The Office of Inspector General (OIG) released this Alert on March 31, 2004: "When participating providers request any other (i.e., additional) payment for covered services from Medicare patients they are liable for substantial penalties and exclusion from Medicare and other Federal health care programs."[57] The General Accounting Office (GAO) issued a report in August 2005 stating that concierge practice is permitted if it does not violate any Medicare requirements and that it does not yet present a systemic access problem.[58] However, potential legal and regulatory problems persist, and some practice management consultants are geared up to assist physicians to avoid pitfalls in establishing such practices,[59] while the GAO will monitor this trend closely. From the standpoint of non-affluent patients, of course, concierge practice just adds another barrier to access as a new upper tier within an already tiered system, thereby increasing inequalities of access among patients.

The concept of unionism among physicians is not entirely new, but it has had a checkered history. There have been three waves of interest in physician unions since the early 1970s—the first was in response to federal legislation in the 1960s, the second in the early 1980s in response to the malpractice liability issue, and the third in the 1990s in response to managed care. In each instance, the effort has been to protect physicians' economic interests and increase their bargaining power.[60,61] Physicians' interest in unions has waxed and waned over the years. Of the more than 20 unions established during the 1970s, almost all were disbanded 30 years later.[62] A review article in 2000 on physician unionization in the U.S. identified the major physician specific unions with a collective membership of about 36,000, almost all of whom were physicians paid by salary (Table 10.2).[63] The total number of U.S. physicians in unions today is unclear. Another article in 2000 estimated that number to be as many as 47,000, still a small number compared to the nation's physician workforce of more than 800,000.[64]

Physicians and unions make an ambiguous combination. On the one hand, one can understand that approach as an attempt to regain lost autonomy and negotiating power as professionals now largely accountable to health plan managers. On the other hand, there are legal and ethical constraints to unionism among physicians. The Sherman Antitrust Act outlaws monopolies, so that collective bargaining by physicians can be seen as price fixing.[65] Moreover, physicians are hardly an economically disadvantaged group and they are reluctant to make themselves unavailable to their patients by carrying their bargaining efforts to a strike. Many physicians are addressing their interests in other ways. Physicians employed by such staff model

TABLE 10.2

Major Physician-Specific Unions in the U.S and Their Affiliations

Union/Guild	Origin	Primary Clientele	Affiliation	Membership
Committee on Interns and Residents (CIR)*	1957	Physicians-in-training	SEIU [1]	10,000
United Salaried Physicians and Dentists (USPD)*	1978	Salaried physicians	SEIU	1,000
Union of American Physicians and Dentists (UAPD)	1972	Salaried physicians	AFSCME [2]	6,000
Doctors Council *	1961	Salaried physicians	None	3,400
Federation of Physicians and Dentists	1989	Self-employed physicians	AFSCME	3,000
The National Guild for Medical Providers	1996	Self-employed physicians	OPEIU [3]	13,000

* recently formed an alliance (affiliated with the SEIU) called the National Doctors Alliance
1. Service Employees International Union
2. American Federation of State, County, and Municipal Employees
3. Office and Professional Employees International Union

SOURCE: Hoff TJ. Physician unionization in the United States: Fad or phenomenon? JHHSA, summer 2000:5-23.

HMOs as Kaiser Permanente and Group Health Cooperative, for example, have their own elected governance and participate in decision-making about professional standards and incomes.[66]

SOME RESPONSES BY MEDICAL ORGANIZATIONS

The responses of the major medical organizations to the new practice environment, controlled as it is by a plethora of managers employed by private and public payers, have been largely focused on their economic self-interest. The AMA serves as a good example. We saw in the last chapter how the AMA's Council on Ethical and Judicial Affairs (CEJA), with regard to physician ownership of specialty hospitals, gives enough wiggle room to permit further development of this trend, while also stating its concern about costs, access, and quality of care.[67] AMA policy is likewise permissive on both the concierge practice and union issues as well, again cloaked in rhetoric of public concern.

With regard to concierge practice, the AMA adopted these ethical guidelines in 2003, which are both permissive and unenforceable if its guidance is not followed:

- "Physicians must not abandon their patients, meaning that they must provide their patients with adequate advance notice of the changeover and must help those patients who leave the practice to find new physicians.

- Patients have the freedom to select and supplement insurance for their healthcare on the basis of what appears to be an acceptable tradeoff between quality and cost.

- When entering into a retainer contract, both the physician and patient must understand the terms of the relationship and agree to them. Patients must be able to opt out of a retainer contract without undue inconveniences or financial penalties.

- Physicians must always ensure that they provide medical care only on the basis of scientific evidence, sound medical judgment, relevant professional guidelines, and concern for economic prudence. They shouldn't promote a retainer contract as a promise for more or better diagnostic and therapeutic services.

- Physicians converting their traditional practices into retainer practices must facilitate the transfer of their nonparticipating patients to other physicians, without an extra fee for transmission of their medical records. If other physicians aren't available to care for non-retainer patients in the local community, the physician may be ethically obligated to continue caring for them.

- Physicians who enter into retainer contracts will usually receive reimbursement from their patients' healthcare plans for medical services. Physicians are ethically required to be honest when billing for reimbursement.

- Physicians have a professional obligation to provide care to those in need, particularly to those in need of urgent care. Physicians who engage in retainer practices should seek specific opportunities to fulfill this obligation."[68]

Behind this cloak of ethical concerns, these guidelines in effect facilitate the growth of concierge practice, and are silent on its impact on health of the public.

The AMA has long been opposed to traditional labor unions representing physicians, but now supports the right of all physicians to bargain collectively.[69] The AMA established Physicians for Responsible Negotiation (PRN) to act as a bargaining agent for employed physicians, including non-AMA members, who join the organization.[70] With the same intent, the American College of Physicians (ACP) and the American Society of Internal Medicine (ASIM) have sought waivers of federal antitrust laws to permit collective bargaining.[71] But these efforts have failed to receive political or judicial support. The AMA and other activist physicians promoted the Campbell-Conyers bill in Congress in 1999, which would have authorized independent physicians to take part in collective bargaining. Although the bill was passed by the Republican House, it then died in the Senate without a sponsor.[72] The U.S. Supreme Court weighed in on the issue, rejecting the National Labor Relations' Board's interpretation of the National Labor Relations Act's (NLRA) as permitting physicians and other health professionals to bargain collectively even as a manager or "supervisor."[73]

Although the AMA and other professional groups contend that collective bargaining by physicians can improve the health care system and benefit patients,[74] there remains a widespread perception that physicians are well compensated as elite and entrepreneurial professionals, and their political activities are seen as more in their self-interest than in the public interest.

An extensive 2002 review of the likely effects of physician unions on the health care system concluded that increased unionization would increase costs without improving access or quality of care.[75]

In earlier chapters we have seen a constant tension between the economic and professional concerns of the profession. Pellegrino and Relman offer this important perspective on this matter:

> "The extent to which professional medical associations should attempt to protect the economic interests of their members or represent their members in negotiations with government regulators, insurers, and other third parties is debatable, but some such activity may well be unavoidable. However, associations should be aware of the dangers of focusing too much attention on the economic concerns of their members at the expense of their many—and more important—public and professional responsibilities. A reasonable compromise should be struck between the legitimate economic concerns of a professional facing an increasingly hostile workplace and the ethical obligations of a profession that wishes to be trusted and hopes to continue to hold a privileged place in U.S. society. These latter obligations should prevail. As a practical matter, medical associations should recognize that their power and influence in effecting almost any change in the health care system will increasingly depend on public trust and support, which, in turn, will depend on whether the associations are seen to be working for the public interest."[76]

CONCLUDING COMMENT

In the face of the wave of commercialism which has engulfed the medical profession in a market-based system, it is inevitable that physicians and their organizations need to cope with changing economic and political circumstances. But medicine's professionalism and motivation are being sorely tested today as health care becomes unaffordable and inaccessible for a growing part of the population. The present market-based system, which renders health care as just another commodity, is not sustainable. Health care reform becomes more urgent with each passing day. The medical profession could play an important role in leading the nation toward a more accessible, affordable, cost-effective and just health care system. Its track record to date, however, has been disappointing to poor as much of the profession continues to exploit the current system. The question now before the profession is whether it can be trusted to act strongly in the public interest and become part of the solution, not part of the problem. That question will be our focus in the next and last part of this book.

PART IV

RECLAIMING MEDICINE'S MORAL CREDIBILITY

CHAPTER 11

WHERE ARE WE GOING?
OPTIONS FOR SYSTEM REFORM

"The care of human life and happiness, and not their destruction, is the first and only legitimate object of good government."

Thomas Jefferson, in an address to
The Republican Citizens of Washington County, Maryland, 1809[1]

"Katrina will not go away soon, and she has the power to change America. The cause was political through and through—a matter of values and principles. The progressive-liberal values are America's values, and we need to go back to them. The heart of progressive-liberal values is simple: empathy (caring about and for people) and responsibility (acting responsibly on that empathy). These values translate into a simple principle: Use the common wealth for the common good to better all our lives. In short, promoting the common good is the central role of government."

George Lakoff, 2005[2] Linguist,
University of California Berkeley, and author of
Moral Politics: How Liberals and Conservatives Think, 2002

Health care reform, daunting as it is, is made more confusing because of the smoke and mirrors that accompany many of the proposals being brought forward. Some are based upon flawed ideology, others on wishful thinking, still others on disinformation. Fortunately, however, there is now a rich literature base and science of health policy which can help us sort through the likelihood of any one approach to be effective in achieving the goals claimed by its advocates.

This chapter will attempt to clarify which among a myriad of proposals has any chance of bringing lasting reform to this runaway system. To do so, we will (1) discuss the major alternatives for reform; (2) assess the alternatives based on principles and evidence; (3) offer rebuttals against some common arguments made by stakeholders in our present system against the single-payer model; and (4) describe how single-payer national health insurance can be a win-win for society, business, and the medical profession.

WHAT ARE THE ALTERNATIVES
FOR HEALTH CARE REFORM?

There have been so many reform proposals put forward over the last 30 years for U.S. health care that it is difficult to keep track of them. Most, however, fall into one of three basic categories—(1) those based on employer-based insurance (including employer mandate), (2) on consumer choice (including individual mandate), or (3) single-payer health insurance. There is considerable overlap between the first two (e.g., consumer-directed health care (CDHC) and tax credits may be components in either type), but these basic categories provide a useful framework for discussion. In its 2004 report *Insuring America's Health: Principles and Recommendations,* the Institute of Medicine's (IOMs) Committee on the Consequences of Uninsurance recognized a fourth prototype for health care reform—major public program extension and new tax credit.[3] We will not discuss that prototype here since unprecedented federal budget deficits and foreign debt render such expansion unfeasible, and all current trends point instead to continued contraction of public programs.

Employer-Based Model

Employer-based health insurance has a long history in the U.S., dating back to the 1930s. It saw rapid expansion during World War II, and tax policy exempting employers and individuals from the costs of health insurance has maintained this policy since then. Employer mandates, whereby all employers are required to provide coverage for their employees, also have a considerable history. President Nixon proposed a "play or pay" plan in the early 1970s, which was not enacted into law.[4] The State of Hawaii has a 30-year experience with an employer mandate system, and other states more recently have enacted variations of such mandates (e.g., California, Maryland, Massachusetts, Vermont). Despite this history, however, the employer-based system of health insurance is rapidly deteriorating, with less than two-thirds of employers providing any such coverage and most of them wanting to limit their contributions in the face of relentless growth of health care costs.

The Consumer Choice Model

As we saw in Chapter 5, this approach is currently the most politically popular one, drawing strong support from the Administration, Republicans (and some Democrats) in Congress, and business interests. It drives the recent trend toward CDHC and is based on the concept of "moral hazard," which holds that insured people will overutilize services which they may perceive as "free." CDHC is supported by its advocates on the premise that imprudent choices will be avoided by patients if they are held more financially responsible for their choices through such means as larger co-payments, deductibles, and other cost-sharing restrictions. Several "enabling" strategies are proposed by supporters of this approach, including tax credits and other subsidies to help people to afford premiums, health savings accounts (HSAs), and use of the Federal Employees Health Benefits Program (FEHBP) as a model. Individual mandate legislation, whereby all state residents are required to purchase health insurance (with subsidies if necessary) has recently been enacted in several states (egs., Massachusetts and Vermont), and the AMA recently voted to endorse such mandates.[5] Not surprisingly, America's Health Insurance Plans (AHIP), the national trade group representing the private health insurance industry, issued its new "reform" proposal in November 2006 calling for universal coverage through expansion of Medicaid and SCHIP, increased government subsidies and tax credits to allow lower-income people to purchase private coverage.[6,7] But since this proposal involves increased cost-shifting to individuals and families, perpetuates inefficiencies and waste of a private insurance industry, has no mechanisms for cost containment, and offers no means of funding its proposal, it can only be seen as a self-serving non-starter to health care reform.

Single-Payer Model (Medicare for All)

Of these three models, only the single-payer approach would bring fundamental structural reform to the health care system. Both the employer-based and consumer choice models retain a market-based system with a large private insurance industry. It is ironic and not widely known that most of the nation's health care is already paid for by the government, but without the efficiency and cost-savings of a single-payer system. Thomas Selden, economist at the federal Agency for Healthcare Research and Quality (AHRQ) has recently calculated that government funding accounts for 61 percent of total health care costs, including payments for Medicare, Medicaid and other federal programs, premiums paid for public-sector employees, and tax subsidies for employment-related coverage. Princeton's health economist Uwe Reinhardt adds another 5 percent for the federal mandate that hospitals provide free care for the uninsured, so that government spending totals two-thirds of health care costs. Despite claims by advocates of our market-based system of its alleged efficiencies, and the myth that U.S. health care is predominantly private, private insurance covers about two-thirds of the population while financing only one-third of its costs and profiting handsomely in an open marketplace.[8]

Whether first implemented on a state or national level, the single-payer model covers everyone for all necessary health care in a large single risk pool through a program of social health insurance. The wasteful expense of a fragmented and inefficient private insurance industry would be replaced with a single tax-financed public insurer as is done in most European countries, Canada, and elsewhere. The delivery system would remain private in order to preserve the crucial right of patients to freely choose their physicians, other providers, and hospitals. Although there has been strong public support for such a system for at least 50 years, stakeholders in the present market-based system have managed to defeat all previous attempts to enact a national health insurance program that would assure universal coverage.

Other Reform Proposals

There are a number of other reform proposals which do not fall neatly into any of these three categories. All are incremental strategies claimed by their supporters to remedy or improve one or another aspect of the present system. These are some recent examples.

•   State high-risk pools. These are state-sponsored health insurance plans intended to create a pool of individuals turned down by private insurers in an attempt to provide additional opportunities for the uninsured to gain health care coverage. Premiums are usually 1.5 to 2 times higher than those charged by private insurers. This concept has been promoted by the insurance industry as it also lobbies against states' imposing requirements to guarantee issue and regulate premium rates.[9] These high-risk plans are funded by a combination of state and federal funding; federal legislation in 2006 extended matching funds for this purpose through 2009.[10]

- Association health plans (AHPs). These are being promoted by business interests and conservative legislators as a means to allow small businesses to band together across state lines, to enlarge their risk pool, and to purchase health insurance at more affordable rates, while also exempting them from state regulations.[11]

- Information technology. Proposals in this area include those for wide adoption of electronic health records[12] and use of the Internet for availability of health care information on line.[13]

- Disease management (DM). Effective DM approaches based on a chronic care model have been pioneered by Group Health Cooperative and Kaiser Permanente for years; a new for-profit DM industry of private vendors is now emerging with claims (still undocumented) of improving quality of care while reducing costs. These private vendors sell programs of patient education and self-management for patients with chronic disease to employers and managed care organizations. Some vendors now use claims data to identify patients with selected chronic diseases. Their interventions are usually done by nurses by telephone from distant call centers with little or no involvement with the patients' primary care physicians.[14]

- Pay-for-performance (P4P). Various initiatives are being proposed and planned which would tie reimbursement of hospitals, health systems, and providers to performance benchmarks as incentives to improve the quality of care. Current plans by CMS, for example, call for collaborative quality improvement initiatives within the Medicare program with feedback to providers, technical assistance, and dissemination of best practices.[15]

PRINCIPLES FOR REFORM
AND ASSESSMENT OF ALTERNATIVES

Before assessing the evidence for and against any of these reform alternatives, we need to consider the principles for reform. In 2004, the Institute of Medicine's (IOMs) Committee on the Consequences of Uninsurance identified these principles as an "approach to health insurance that will promote better overall health for individuals, families, communities, and the nation by providing financial access for everyone to necessary, appropriate, and effective health services.[16]

1.   Health care coverage should be universal.

2.   Health care coverage should be continuous.

3.   Health care coverage should be affordable to individuals and families.

4.   The health insurance strategy should be affordable and sustainable for society.

5.   Health care coverage should enhance health and well-being by promoting access to high-quality care that is effective, efficient, safe, timely, patient-centered, and equitable."

In that same report, the IOM assessed our three major reform alternatives—employer mandate, individual mandate, and single-payer as shown in Table 11.1.[17]

Neither the employer mandate nor individual mandate, or combinations thereof, can meet the IOM's principles, based upon their track record to date or a number of recent studies comparing the feasibility of these approaches. Both are incremental approaches which "tweak" the current marketplace system without any chance of real reform. One fatal flaw of both approaches is leaving in place an expensive, wasteful, and inefficient private insurance industry which by avoiding coverage of sicker individuals can never achieve universal coverage without being an untenable strain on the public sector. Ample documentation has been cited in earlier chapters of the declining coverage and reliability of the employer-based system, the growing unaffordability of private insurance and health care, the increasing access and quality of care problems, and the rising number of uninsured and underinsured even as the public safety net further deteriorates.

TABLE 11.1 - Major Reform Alternatives

Principles	Employer Mandate, Premium Subsidy, and Individual Mandate	Individual Mandate and Tax Credit	Single Payer
Coverage should be universal	*Coverage likely to be high; depends on enforcement of mandates*	*Depends on size of tax credit, enforcement, and cost of individual insurance*	*Likely to achieve universal coverage*
Coverage should be continuous	*Brief gaps related to life and job transitions*	*Minimal gaps*	*Continuous until death or age 65*
Coverage should be affordable for individuals and families	*Yes, for workers, assuming adequate employer premium assistance; public program designed to be affordable for all enrollees*	*Subsidy based only on income and family size leaves older, less healthy, and those in expensive areas with less affordable coverage*	*Minimal cost sharing, but could be problem for lowest income*
Strategy should be affordable and sustainable for society	*All participants contribute; package less costly than current employment coverage; revenue from patients in public program; sustainability depends on revenue sources for employers' premium assistance and public program*	*No limit on aggregate health expenditures or on tax expenditure, though federal costs relatively predictable and controllable through size of credit; sustainable through federal income tax base; size of credit depends on political support*	*Nearly all participants contribute; aggregate expenditures controllable, though utilization not directly or centrally controlled; high cost to federal budget; administrative savings; sustainability depends on revenue source and political support*
Coverage should enhance health through high-quality care	*Could design quality incentives in expanded public program and basic benefit package; current employer incentives for quality remain*	*Similar incentives to current private insurance system, consumer could choose quality plans*	*Potentially yes; depends on proper design*

SOURCE: Adapted with permission from: Committee on the Consequences of Uninsurance. *Insuring America's Health: Principles and Recommendations.* Institute of Medicine. Washington, DC: National Academy Press, 2004:150–1

All incremental market-based "reform" attempts have failed to remedy these problems, and recent studies comparing reform alternatives in various states offer no evidence that they can ever achieve universal coverage, contain costs, or lead to a sustainable health care system. In California, for example, the Lewin Group studied nine different alternatives to address the state's high rate of uninsurance (about 24 percent). Six were one or another variant of employer and individual mandates, while three were single-payer plans. The costs and outcomes of each approach were studied by means of microsimulations. None of the employer or individual mandate strategies achieved universal coverage while all *increased* costs; all of the three single-payer plans provided universal coverage while saving the state as much as $7 billion a year.[18] Other states have demonstrated similar results (egs., Maryland[19], Massachusetts,[20] Vermont,[21] Connecticut,[22] and Georgia[23]). The passage of individual mandate legislation in Massachusetts in 2006, though enthusiastically acclaimed by its supporters as the silver bullet for universal coverage, will be just another failure because of several flaws—it does not account for 245,000 uninsured people who could not respond to a phone survey because they had no phone or did not speak English or Spanish, it lacks effective mechanisms to provide adequate coverage at affordable rates, and its longer-term funding is unclear.[24,25]

Tax credits as a strategy to reduce the number of uninsured has been around for many years. Each year the current Administration proposes a $1,000 tax credit to help uninsured low-income people purchase health insurance on the individual market. But the costs of health insurance, if available at all, are much higher than any tax credit.[26] This policy has been compared to "throwing a 10-foot rope to an uninsured person in a 40-foot hole,"[27] and at best the numbers of uninsured might be reduced by only 5 percent.[28] Based upon his studies of alternative tax policies, Jonathan Gruber, Professor of Economics at the Massachusetts Institute of Technology, concludes that tax policies aimed at the private market are much less efficient than policies for expansion of public insurance (public insurance costs the government only $1.17 to $1.33 per dollar of insurance provided vs. $2.36 to $12.85 in the private market).[29]

Health savings accounts (HSAs), as the linchpin of current CDHC policies intended to rein in escalating health care costs, are destined to become still another policy failure. As we saw in Chapter 5, they are intended to be coupled with high deductible health insurance (HDHI) plans. Although hyped by the current Administration, conservative legislators and business interests as an advance that will encourage people to save money in their own tax-free accounts and take more responsibility for their own health care decisions (i.e., seek care more prudently), this concept has been slow to take hold. Although America's Health Insurance Plans (AHIP) claims that 3 million Americans have taken up HSAs,[30] the real number is probably only about 1 million. A 2006 report by the Commonwealth Fund and Employee Benefit Research Institute found that only 1 percent of privately insured adults were enrolled in high-deductible CDHC plans with HSAs, about the same as the previous year, with many enrollees more likely to skip doctors' appointments or delay filling prescriptions.[31]

As an incremental "reform" approach, HSAs and HDHI will fail for all of the reasons noted in Chapter 6. They are much more likely to appeal to healthy and more affluent people, while older and sicker people will find them unaffordable and/or too skimpy in their coverage. A January 2007 report by the Vimo Research Group, a national Web-based portal for comparison shopping for health care products and services, recognizes that consumers' interest in HSAs has been weak, that HSAs are unlikely to contain health care costs, and that their value is really mostly as wealth-building tax-sheltered investment devices.[32]

Five other incremental "reforms" are being put forward by enthusiastic supporters in the hopes of restraining health costs, expanding insurance coverage, or improving quality of care. There is little reason to believe that any of them can effectively meet their claimed objectives.

- <u>State high risk pools.</u> Although high-risk health insurance pools have been adopted by 30 states, they cover only about 180,000 people nationwide, and have many problems which seriously limit their usefulness as an instrument of health policy. Waiting periods of 6 to 12 months are imposed on coverage of pre-existing conditions. Benefits are limited in some states for such services as maternity care or mental health. Premiums are adjusted for age so that people in their 50s or older often find the premiums unaffordable.[33] Demand perenially exceeds the capacity of high-risk pools, which are also constrained by limited state and federal dollars. As a result of these and other problems, very few of those needing insurance can gain it this way. California, with one of the largest high-risk pools in the country, covers only 7,800 of the state's 6 million uninsured in its high-risk pool, a mere 0.0013 percent of the uninsured population.[34]

- Association health plans (AHPs). *Families USA* has recently compiled an analysis of AHPs[35] which shows that AHPs will fail to control costs (administrative costs will be higher than other plans[36], and most small employers will see increased costs)[37]; AHPs may actually increase the number of uninsured[38;] and AHPs will open up new opportunities for fraud and abuse.[39] California's pioneering AHP, PacAdvantage, including Blue Shield, Kaiser and Health Net, failed to control costs and recently announced its dissolution when Blue Shield acknowledged it was losing money.[40]

- Information technology (IT). It is already apparent that electronic health records (EHRs) can improve efficiency and quality of care in some practices. It is unlikely, however, that widespread adoption of EHRs, without other system reforms, can meet their policy goals of reducing health care costs by up to 20 percent a year as expected by the new Office of the National Coordinator for Health Information Technology (ONC), established in 2004.[41] In a recent review of this question, Dr. Jaan Siderov, medical director of Care Coordination of the Geisinger Health Plan, casts doubt on EHRs as a cost containment initiative,[42] including the likelihood that increased billing efficiencies may instead lead to cost increases.[43,44] Further doubt on the potential of EHRs to contain costs was cast in an excellent recent appraisal of the subject, calling particular attention to the unproven assumptions of and wishful thinking of their advocates, some of whom are enthusiastic vendors of IT products (e.g., how can the use of EMRs realistically double patients' compliance with advice to stop smoking or lose weight?).[45] Recent studies by the General Accounting Office have identified other concerns about EHRs as a national strategy to improve health care. Detailed plans, milestones and performance measures have not yet been developed, and more than 40 percent of federal contractors and state Medicaid agencies using EMRs have reported privacy breaches of personal health information.[46,47]

• Disease management (DM). There is little question that shifting to the chronic care model, especially if integrated with primary care, could improve the care of the 125 million Americans with at least one chronic disease. But it does not follow that disease management, especially in the hands of a new for-profit DM industry, will contain costs. Unless closely integrated with primary care physicians, as is the case with Group Health Cooperative and Kaiser Permanente, DM is redundant, inefficient, and unlikely to improve quality of care while potentially adding to the costs of care, as a 2004 report by the Congressional Budget Office (CBO) concluded.[48] A 2005 report by Dr. David Eddy and colleagues had this to say about long-term effects of DM for diabetes:

> *"Even for the most optimistic picture—a 30-year horizon and assuming no turnover (patients stay with the same plan for 30 years)—the net effect on diabetes-related costs would be an increase of about 25 percent."*[49]

• Pay-for-performance (P4P). While P4P initiatives are well intentioned and appear to be reasonable approaches, especially for hospitals and health plans, there are many challenging problems in implementing the concept, including setting of quality standards, development of monitoring and administrative systems, and overcoming resistance of stakeholders. A recent report of the Community Tracking Study found that one or another P4P program has been initiated by health plans in all 12 communities being tracked, but that preferences and resistance of providers, together with local market environments, stand in the way of any consensus or standardization of performance measures.[50] Most experts agree that P4P alone will not significantly improve quality of care without other system changes. Dr. Donald Berwick, founder of the Institute for Healthcare Improvement and a leading champion of health care quality, is deeply skeptical of the value of P4P for individual physicians and nurses:

"I do not think that the way to get better doctoring and better nursing is to put money on the table in front of doctors and nurses. I think that's a fundamental misunderstanding of human motivation. I think people respond to joy and work and love and achievement and learning and appreciation and gratitude—and a sense of a job well done. I think that it feels good to be a good doctor and better to be a better doctor. When we begin to attach dollar amounts to throughputs and to individual pay, we are playing with fire. The first and most important effect of that may be to begin to dissociate people from their work. That's really where we've come to, and we've done it by pay-for-performance in terms of throughput measurements and manipulating payment schemes.[51]

Dr. Don McCanne adds this concern about P4P as a strategy for quality improvement and cost containment:

"Physicians in difficult practice environments, facing chronic under-funding, poverty, poor patient compliance, and impaired access by patients, will have lower scores even though their actual performance may be superior. On the other hand, physicians in well-financed, uptown practices might well benefit from manipulations of their practice managers who develop expertise in making certain that the quality scores are optimal. P4P would shift funds from the former to the latter. Is that sound policy?"[52]

Based upon the foregoing, it seems obvious that a principle-based approach to health care reform leads us inevitably to a single-payer model as the only effective way to bring lasting reform to U.S. health care, whether initially on a statewide basis or nationally. But the powerful opposition of stakeholders in the current market-based system has for many years trumped public opinion and the efforts of progressive reformers. For this reason, we need to apply evidence to the claims and arguments made by opponents of single-payer.

COMMON CONCERNS ABOUT SINGLE-PAYER

Here are some frequent lines of argument against the single-payer model put forth by stakeholders and other supporters of the present market-based system. In some cases these claims have been made so often over the years as to become memes (i.e., part of our language and culture without basis in fact or experience). In other instances, they are advanced as disinformation in an effort to maintain the status quo and protect the stakeholders from reform. Some rebuttals are listed below which refute the misleading claims.

1.   **"The private health care marketplace will address system problems through competition."**

- Three decades of experience have already failed to resolve cost, access, quality and performance problems of our health care system

- The country's 1,300 private insurers compete to cover lower-risk patients by means of experience rating, thereby defeating the purpose of insurance to share risk through broad risk pools.[53] Any financing and insurance system must deal with the fact that 10 percent of patients account for 72 percent of annual health spending, while 5 percent account for 50 percent of that total).[54]

- The nine-year Community Tracking Study in 12 major U.S. markets has found very little competition between health plans.[55]

- One-third of Americans live in areas (including 9 entire states) with populations too small to enable any real competition between hospitals or managed care plans.[56]

2.   **"The private health care market offers more efficiency and value than the public sector"**

- As a single-payer public program serving the elderly and disabled for more than 40 years, traditional Medicare (*not* its privatized plans) operates with an overhead of only about 3 percent compared to an average of 19.9 percent for commercial carriers and 26.5 percent for investor-owned Blue Cross-Blue Shield plans.[57]

- Between 1998 and 2000, Medicare + Choice HMOs (M+C) were paid 13 percent more than traditional Medicare but many still withdrew from the market, abandoning 2.4 million seniors,[58] Medicare Advantage, as the successor to M+C plans, are still subsidized by an average of 12 percent overpayments (some by as much as 19 percent) compared to traditional Medicare and still exclude coverage of sicker Medicare beneficiaries[59] Princeton economist Paul Krugman has labeled the Bush Administration's pursuit of the heavily subsidized Medicare Advantage programs, which are also involved with substandard care compared to quality performance markers of the VA system, as health policy malpractice.[60]

- The fragmented private health insurance industry is filled with inefficiency and duplicative bureaucracy (e.g., a Seattle study of 2,000 patients with depression found that they were covered by 189 different plans with 755 different policies,[61] single-payer Canadian province health plans have less than two employees per 10,000 enrollees compared to 13 to 35 per 10,000 enrollees in U.S. health plans).[62]

3.   "Patients are the main drivers of rising health care costs"

- This claim ignores the many other more significant drivers of health care costs, including technological advances, the increased prevalence of chronic disease in an aging population, wasteful and redundant administrative costs in an inefficient system, corporate profit-taking throughout the system, and high levels of physician-induced demand (e.g., up to one-third of all health care services in the U.S. are considered either unnecessary or of little value[63;] the Commonwealth Fund has found that 25 percent of hysterectomies and 30 percent of cardiac bypass procedures have questionable indications).[64]

- Increased cost sharing, intended by the "moral hazard" theory to force patients to make more prudent and cost-conscious decisions when seeking health care, instead leads to underutilization of essential care and treatments, resulting in worse clinical outcomes without cost containment.[65,66]

- Countries with single-payer systems have been able to contain health care costs much more effectively than the U.S. without using cost-sharing; after 30 years with its single-payer program, Canada has experienced very little overutilization by patients;[67]

and instead has found that their system encourages the use of timely and appropriate care (e.g., better outcomes for cancer survival compared to patients across the border in the U.S., even after accounting for race or poverty factors).[68]

4.   "Single-payer health insurance will lead to socialized medicine."

- Single-payer health insurance, as Medicare is for the elderly and disabled, is a form of social insurance coupled with a private delivery system of physicians, hospitals, and other providers; "socialized medicine" would involve all means of production and delivery of health services being owned by the state[69]

- The Medicare program, with a track record of service for over 40 years, remains the most popular insurance plan in the country,[70] while physicians have benefited immensely from this program (egs., in its first year of operation in 1966, physicians raised their fees by 7.8 percent, more than twice the CPI for that year).[71]

5.   "A single-payer system will stifle innovation."

- The Medicare program has certainly not stifled innovation for the care of the elderly and disabled, which represent the largest population of people with chronic disease.

- The U.S. already brings too many products to market without sufficient evidence of efficacy (e.g., many new drugs are not really advances, but "me too" drugs with a new marketing program;[72] a 1998 report by the Technology Evaluation Committee found that almost one out of three evaluations of drugs, medical devices, or procedures were lacking or uncertain in their effectiveness).[73]

- Despite the prevalence of single-payer health systems in Europe, new drugs are still produced there while drug and medical device manufacturers make reasonable profit margins.[74]

6.   **"A single-payer system would ration care."**

- All health care systems ration health care in one way or another; the market-based system in the U.S. rations care by class and ability to pay, with widespread evidence of impaired access to necessary services due to financial and other barriers.[75]

- Single-payer systems, as monopsonistic purchasers of health care have the opportunity to demand value and efficacy of health care services and to allocate resources based upon medical need as informed by evidence-based clinical science.

7.   **"A single-payer system will result
in longer waiting times for care."**

- Opponents of single-payer bring up Canada's wait lists as evidence that single-payer systems cause long delays; however, their claims are based upon biased data put out by the ultraconservative Vancouver-based Fraser Institute; according to *Statistics Canada*, the Canadian counterpart of the U.S. Census Bureau, the median waiting times across all provinces in 2003 were 4.0 weeks to see a specialist and 4.3 weeks for non-emergency surgery, refuting the Fraser data of 17.8 weeks delay for surgery or specialty care;[76] a 2006 cross-national population-based survey of over 3,000 Canadians and 5,000 Americans found that only 3.5 percent of Canadians had unmet needs because of waiting times.[77]

- Even for privately insured patients in our system with excess capacity in many areas, waiting times increased from 1997 to 2001 (e.g., one-third of patients waited longer than 3 weeks for a checkup and more than 1 week for a sick visit);[78] uninsured patients and those covered by Medicaid are likely to have more difficulty in accessing care around the country.

- Since the U.S. already spends almost twice as much as Canada on its health care system and has excess capacity in many places, it is unlikely that prolonged waits would be a significant problem with a single-payer system in this country.

8.   **<u>"Single-payer health insurance would require a big increase in taxes."</u>**

• As by far the most expensive health care system in the world, there is already plenty of money in the system (over $2 trillion a year) to pay for universal coverage for less money than we are spending now; large savings have already been projected for some states (e.g., California, Massachusetts, and Georgia) as well as at the national level (a 2003 study estimated that $286 billion a year could be saved that year in administrative expenses alone, almost $7,000 for every American without health insurance).[79]

• These large savings are made possible by replacing an enormous profit-driven private health insurance industry with a more efficient publicly-financed system and reducing the administrative burden of health care from its present level of 31 percent of health spending[80] to somewhere less than 15 percent.

9.   **<u>"The government can't do the job."</u>**

• The Veterans Administration's (VA) integrated health care system, serving almost 6 million veterans, is a classic example of how a government-run public program can perform better than any private program; its 154 hospitals and 875 clinics across the country have outperformed private plans by any measure for over six years; the VA system achieved 100 percent electronic medical records in its hospitals in 2004 (20 percent of private hospitals have computerized records), the VAs error rate in drug prescriptions is less than 0.01 percent (vs. 3-8 percent in the private sector), clinical quality markers are consistently higher across the board, drug prices are 46 percent lower, and patient satisfaction surveys are consistently higher for VA patients.[81,82]

10.   **<u>"NHI is not politically feasible."</u>**

• One-half to three-fourths of Americans have favored government-financed NHI in many national surveys since the 1940s.[83,84]

- Public support for NHI crosses party lines (eg., a 2005 survey found that 88 percent of Democrats, 73 percent of Independents, and 55 percent of Republicans wanted the federal government to "guarantee health coverage for all Americans")[85]; another 2005 survey by the Pew Research Center found that 65 percent of Americans support "government health insurance even if taxes increase, with high levels of support among many "conservative" respondents—"populist conservatives" (63 percent) and "conservative Democrats" (73 percent)—only one group ("conservative libertarian Republicans") did not express majority support for government health insurance.[86]

SINGLE-PAYER NHI AS WIN-WIN FOR SOCIETY, BUSINESS AND MEDICINE

As shown earlier in this and preceding chapters, society would gain fundamental reforms throughout U.S. health care by adopting the single-payer model. Access to all necessary care would be extended to all Americans without regard to income, ethic group or class, with new opportunities for better quality of care and cost savings through more prevention and earlier care. Other cost savings could be realized by bulk purchasing of prescription drugs, medical devices and medical supplies by a monopsonistic single-payer purchaser, while still allowing manufacturers and suppliers reasonable profit margins. An accountable system allowing more effective budgeting and cost containment could be put in place with reduction of the considerable fragmentation of today's market-based system. The current fragmentation, inefficiencies and waste of an enormous private insurance industry would be replaced by a more efficient management structure with sharply reduced administrative costs. With better definition of populations and communities being served, monitoring and quality improvement of health care outcomes could be advanced. Further administrative efficiencies could be achieved by folding in all public programs, especially Medicare and Medicaid, into the new Medicare for All program. Current erosion of Medicare's capability and value by heavily subsidized private Medicare plans could be reversed, together with many of the conflicts of interest in relations between traditional Medicare and industry. Perhaps most important, single-payer NHI could lead to better population health for the country as well as an increased sense of social solidarity.

Although most business interests have traditionally opposed the notion of single-payer NHI, that resistance is starting to dissolve as business begins to confront runaway costs of health care. Indeed, business has much to gain from NHI. Dr. Donald Light, a Fellow at the University of Pennsylvania's Center for Bioethics and co-author of *Benchmarks of Fairness for Health Care Reform* (1996) has noted that conservatives in every other industrialized country have supported universal access to necessary health care on the basis of four conservative moral principles—anti-free-riding, personal integrity, equal opportunity, and just sharing. He suggests these guidelines for conservatives to stay true to these principles:

1. "Everyone is covered, and everyone contributes in proportion to his or her income.

2. Decisions about all matters are open and publicly debated. Accountability for costs, quality and value of providers, suppliers, and administrators is public.

3. Contributions do not discriminate by type of illness or ability to pay.

4. Coverage does not discriminate by type of illness or ability to pay.

5. Coverage responds first to medical need and suffering.

6. Nonfinancial barriers by class, language, education, and geography are to be minimized.

7. Providers are paid fairly and equitably, taking into account their local circumstances.

8. Clinical waste is minimized through public health, self-care, prevention, strong primary care, and identification of unnecessary procedures.

9. Financial waste is minimized through simplified administrative arrangements and strong bargaining for good value.

10. Choice is maximized in a common playing field where

90-95 percent of payments go toward necessary and efficient health services and only 5-10 percent to administration."[87]

Business would gain immensely with a single-payer system in several important ways. Employers, who in 2005 were spending an average of $7,089 a year per family for health insurance,[88] would see that responsibility reduced as they shifted their payments to a more efficient government-financed system with a broad risk pool. Employers could expect to pay a modest payroll tax of not more than 7 percent, much better than the 14 percent or more now paid by large employers in the industrial and manufacturing sector.[89] A recent study in California showed that employers who currently offer health insurance would save an average of 16 percent under a single-payer program.[90] Employers could gain a healthier workforce while paying less for health care. They could also become more competitive in a global economy. General Motors, for example, spends about $1,400 for health care for each car sold in the U.S., more than the cost of steel, while foreign manufacturers may spend only about $200 per car into their countries' social insurance program.[91] A growing number of U.S. employers have become very concerned about this problem. The National Association of Manufacturers, a Washington, D.C.-based trade group which represents hundreds of small employers across the country, acknowledges that U.S. companies are at a competitive disadvantage because of the burden of their high health care costs.[92] The vice chairman of Ford Motor Company had this to say in 2004:

[high health care costs have] "created a competitive gap that's driving investment decisions away from the U.S... Right now the country is on an unsustainable track and it won't get any better until we begin—business, labor and government in partnership—to make a pact for reform. A lot of people think a single-payer system is better."[93]

Though organized medicine feared and opposed Medicare as "socialized medicine" before it was enacted in 1965, the profession soon accepted it and profited from the care of a large new population of insured patients. The same change seems certain to occur when single-payer NHI is finally established in the U.S. Here are some of the many ways in which medicine will gain with NHI:

- All patients will have access to care, with free choice of physician and hospital.

- All necessary health care services will be fairly reimbursed, including preventive and mental health care

- Simplified billing will sharply reduce physicians' administrative burden and practice overhead.

- Physicians will have more time available for direct patient care

- Physicians will see a reduction of the "hassle factor" and intrusion into their clinical decision-making by a myriad of private insurer managers.

- Practice incomes would likely increase for presently under-reimbursed fields, such as psychiatry and the primary care specialties.

- Perhaps most important, physicians will regain the public's trust as essential caregivers in a more equitable system, putting to rest the widespread perception of medicine as most concerned with its own self-interest.

Table 11.2 lists likely comparative scenarios for U.S. health care and its primary care base in 2020 with and without NHI.[94]

Other health care professionals likewise would find their administrative burden, especially involving billing, lightened under single-payer NHI. Hospitals and other facilities would negotiate annual global budgets fully covering their costs and stabilizing their financial positions. Many of today's marketing and administrative jobs, especially related to billing, would disappear with single-payer NHI, so that job retraining and placement would become necessary. Many new employment opportunities would become available as a more efficient single-payer system addresses clinical and social needs of an aging population in such areas as long-term care, home care, and mental health.

WHERE TO FROM HERE?

The continuing failure of market-based "reforms" to contain costs and to improve access, quality, and equity of health care in this country raises the stakes and urgency to reasess reform alternatives. These two perspectives

TABLE 11.2

Alternative Scenarios for 2020

	Without NHI	With NHI
Primary Care	Less in demand Marginal system role Less continuity of care Less well distributed Lower career satisfaction Marginal reimbursement High practice overhead No population-based research Weak primary care workforce	More in demand Strengthened system role More continuity of care Broadly distributed Higher career satisfaction Stabilized reimbursement Lower practice overhead Population-based research growing Larger stabilized workforce
Health Care System	Severe access problems in lower tiers Soaring cost inflation Degraded system performance More health disparities Increased public dissatisfaction Increased bureaucracy and fragmentation	Universal access, less tiering Reasonable cost containment Improved system performance Improved health outcomes Increased patient satisfaction Simplified administration and less fragmented

NHI-national health insurance

SOURCE: Adapted with permission from: Geyman JP. Drawing on the legacy of general practice to build the future of family medicine. Fam Med 36(9):631-8, 2004.

aptly summarize where we now find ourselves.

"We've engaged in a massive and failed experiment in market-based medicine in the U.S. Rhetoric about the benefits of competition and profit-driven health care can no longer hide the reality: Our health system is in shambles."[95]

Marcia Angell, MD, Former Editor of *The New England Journal of Medicine* and author of *The Truth About Drug Companies: How They Deceive Us and What We Can Do About It*

"I'm not an opponent of markets. On the contrary, I've spent a lot of my career defending their virtues. But the fact is that the free market doesn't work for health insurance and never did. All we ever had was a patchwork, semiprivate system supported by large government subsidies... The system is now failing. And a rigid belief that markets are always superior to government programs—a belief that ignores basic economics as well as experience—stands in the way of rational thinking about what should replace it."[96]

Paul Krugman
Professor of Economics
Princeton University

After all the incremental attempts to get a handle on this runaway health care train, which now accounts for one-sixth of the national economy, it is now obvious that none have worked and more fundamental reform is required. That raises two questions, what should that be and how can medicine advocate and lead toward it. We will consider both questions in the next chapter.

CHAPTER 12

A NEEDS-BASED AND PROBLEM-ORIENTED ACTION PLAN FOR MEDICINE

"It is my contention that healthcare delivery is one of those 'goods' which by their nature are not and cannot be mere commodities....The quality of life, our capacity to participate in social and economic activities, and very often life itself are at stake in each serious encounter with the medical care system. This is why we expect healthcare delivery to be a competent and a caring response to the broken human condition-to-human vulnerability. To be sure, we expect our physician to earn a good living and our hospital to be economically viable, but... when it comes to... our hip replacement or our child's cancer treatment, we expect them to be professional in the original sense of that term-motivated primarily by patient need, not economic self-interest."

Cardinal Joseph Bernardin, 1995[1]

In order to further discuss how medicine can advocate and lead toward needed health care reform, this chapter has two objectives: (1) to suggest directions toward reformulating the goals of medicine more in line with the needs of patients rather than those of our profession and other stakeholders on the supply side of health care delivery; and (2) propose an action plan which addresses the problems documented in earlier chapters of this book.

TOWARD NEED-BASED GOALS OF MEDICINE

Current trends in the U.S. health care system are not well targeted to the needs of our population. Biomedical progress and the current financing system reward acute care and procedural medicine over chronic care. Continued disregard for cost-effectiveness of health care services has skewed health care toward the interests of corporate stakeholders in the market-based system and away from the common good. Public health, preventive medicine, mental health, care of chronic diseases, long-term and home care continue to play second fiddle to acute medical care, and much of biomedical research targets the high end of technology for the care of individual patients over lower-cost services that could improve the health of populations.[2] With cost containment nowhere on the horizon, uncontrolled costs have become the Achilles heel of the health care system. Already divided into at least three tiers based upon income and access to care, a large and growing part of the population cannot gain access to necessary care.

Daniel Callahan, leading bioethicist and co-founder of the Hastings Center, sees these as the two main issues facing American medicine.

> *"The fundamental one is the tension between the good of the community and the good of the individual, which the field typically has resolved in the direction of the individual. The other deep issue concerns our judgement of the goals and progress of medicine, which has individual and societal implications. Questions of resource allocation are interesting because in one sense they're questions of justice—what's the fair way to distribute health care? But the allocation crisis provokes us to examine a more fundamental issue: if we have to begin making choices and setting some priorities in allocation, what do we want this whole enterprise of medicine doing for us? These questions have been neglected because the tendency to reduce matters to individual or concrete policy choices almost by definition tends to push these questions out of the picture."*[3]

Clearly, the overall goals of medicine need to be revisited if the present disconnect between health care needs of our population and the current market-based system is to be addressed. This has already been done. A landmark study was underaken by the Hastings Center in 1992. Over the course of the next four years, it coordinated a large study of the subject involving 14 countries, ranging from Europe, Scandinavia, the United Kingdom, and the United States, to Chile and China. Multidisciplinary teams were assembled for each country, typically including leaders in medicine, biology, law, philosophy, theology, health policy, administration, politics, and public health. Each working group was asked to address three questions: (1) Where has medicine been?; (2) Where ought it be going?; and (3) what should its future priorities be? As a result of these deliberations, a comprehensive report, *The Goals of Medicine: Setting New Priorities* was published in 1996.[4] One of the difficult issues confronted by participants in this study was how to prioritize curative versus care goals of medicine. The 1996 report framed the issue in these terms:

> *"Although there is no inherent contradiction between care and*

cure, the bias toward the latter has often done harm to the former. The relentless and expensive wars against disease, particularly such lethal conditions as cancer, heart disease, and stroke, have too often obscured the need for care and compassion in the face of mortality. Both the rate of technological innovation and its curative bias have created a medicine that is difficult to sustain, particularly in an equitable way. There is a limit to what can reasonably be paid for, what is politically feasible, and what market competition can sustain without great pain and inequity. The expansive, ambitious, open-ended pursuit of progress—the battles against illness that are never quite won—that has been the mark of medicine over the past fifty years may now have reached the boundaries of perceived affordability in many countries."[5]

After four years of work, the Hastings Center Report agreed upon three goals of medicine (Table 12.1) as representing the core values of medicine. These reformulated goals were seen as helpful in maintaining the integrity of the medical profession in the face of political or social pressures to serve anachronistic or alien purposes.[6] In addition, the 14 Working Groups developed consensus around six aspirations that can best guide the profession's future (Table 12.2).[7]

These basic goals and aspirations are fundamental to any serious re-examination of U.S. medicine and our health care system. Though few in words, they are powerful in content, and could help greatly to re-orient

TABLE 12.1

Goals of Medicine

1. Prevention of Disease and Injury and Promotion and Maintenance of Health

2. Relief of Pain and Suffering Caused by Maladies

3. Care and Cure of Those with a Malady, and the Care of Those Who Cannot Be Cured

SOURCE: Project Report. *The Goals of Medicine: Setting New Priorities:* Special Supplement. Hastings Center Report, November-December, 1996:Executive Summary.

TABLE 12.2

Future Aspirations of Medicine

1. An Honorable Medicine, Directing Its Own Professional Life
2. A Temperate, Prudent Medicine
3. An Affordable, Sustainable Medicine
4. A Socially Sensitive, Pluralistic Medicine
5. A Just and Equitable Medicine
6. A Medicine That Respects Human Choice and Dignity

SOURCE: Project Report. *The Goals of Medicine: Setting New Priorities:* Special Supplement. Hastings Center Report, November-December, 1996: S23-5.

American medicine and our health care system in the public interest. The Working Groups of all 14 countries began with an assumption that necessary health care is a basic human need that should be available to all members of society. Universal access would help immeasurably to decrease disparities and inequities of today's system and improve the health of the population.

We saw in Chapter 3 many examples of how the healthcare marketplace distorts the goals of medicine. Those examples make clear that excess capacity can be harmful and that the problem of physician-induced demand in a freewheeling market-based system is real. The Hastings Center Report on the Goals of Medicine in 1996 foresaw the hazards of the market in these terms.

> *"The most evident is that a reduction of the responsibility of government will endanger government's most important modern functions: a good public health system, guaranteeing a minimal level of decent, basic health care overall, and monitoring quality and professional standards. More broadly, the hazards of the market include the introduction of an alien set of economic values into the institution of medicine, whose inherent ends have historically been philanthropic and altruistic, not commercial; despite market ideology, an actual decrease in patient choice; an increase in the gap between the health care available to the affluent and that available to the poor; the weakening of those parts of the health care system particularly dependent upon government (notably public health); the commercial encouragement of expensive (and thus profitable) forms of high-technology rescue*

medicine rather than less technology-intensive disease prevention and primary care programs: and the encouragement of the public to look to medicine to fulfill needs and desires that may be commercially attractive but which are far from the traditional goals of medicine or the goals proposed here. Everything can be bought and sold, turned into a commodity. But some goods, values, and institutions can too easily be corrupted by commodification. Health is a vital human good, and medicine a basic way of promoting it. Commercializing them, even for the sake of choice and efficiency, runs a potent risk of subverting them. The integrity of medicine itself is at stake. An excessive and unbalanced commercialization and privatization of medicine is a dire threat to the very goals of medicine. "[8]

A PROBLEM-ORIENTED ACTION PLAN FOR MEDICINE

Here is an action plan for steps which our medical profession could usefully take as means toward improving U.S. health care.

1. Reassert, through words and actions, that the raison d'être' of medicine is the health of patients and families, not the welfare of providers or their organizations.

2. Assert our professionalism and independence in deciding which diagnostic, preventive, and therapeutic services to provide, based upon scientific evidence and cost-effectiveness, not on the marketing efforts by industry.

3. Rein in flat-of-the-curve medicine in favor of a broader application of evidence-based medicine.

4. Embrace the chronic care model, with more temperate use of acute interventions when cure is not possible.

5. Deal more directly with patients and their families about treatment options near the end of life, with greater sensitivity to patients' preferences.

6. Be more skeptical of the claims by industry of effectiveness of new treatments and products, and require evidence of efficacy and cost-effectiveness before adopting new technologies.

7.   Expose and root out financial conflicts of interest of physicians and their organizations, including sanctions when necessary.

8.   Confront the profession's pervasive conflicts of interest with industry, and work towards more transparency and their elimination.

9.   Take more responsibility for the shortcomings of the system itself (and the profession's role in these problems).

10. Become more knowledgeable about the problems of the health care system, and advocate for real health care reform.

11. Take greater interest and become more involved in re-balancing the tension between population-based care and the care of individuals.

12. Advocate for policies which achieve universal access to health care for the entire population, with reduction of disparities and incquities.

13. Advocate for mental health parity (a 2006 review effectively dispelled the old notion that this would lead to unaffordable over-utilization of services).[9]

14. Support policies to redress specialty and geographic maldistribution of physicians to best meet needs of the public, with special emphasis on strengthening primary care at the base of the entire system and the care of the underserved in urban and rural areas.

Table 12.3 reminds us of the major problems of U.S. health care which have been discussed in earlier chapters together with concrete and specific directions for advocacy and action. Single payer NHI would go a long way toward providing a stable structure for reform of U.S. health care, particularly in addressing the top 14 problems in Table 12.3. Parallel reforms in other areas would also be required. For example, without effective assessment of new medical technologies or sufficient regulatory capacity to remove ineffective or harmful drugs and medical devices from the market there would still be room for market interests to exploit the public interest.

In 2000, the Institute of the Future projected three possible scenarios for U.S. health care for the year 2010. Figure 12.1 shows the worst of these three forecasts in its comprehensive report *Health and Health Care 2010:*

The Forecast, the Challenges.[10] Even three years before 2010, there are no grounds to believe that the present system is sustainable without major structural reform.

All ten outcomes of the stormy weather scenario in the two columns on the left of Figure 12.1 are already in place, except for large employers, who are decreasing their contributions to employee health benefits and increasingly limiting or eliminating retiree benefits, an even worse outcome than predicted. As a result, all seven outcomes in the two columns on the right are tracking right on schedule for 2010, not just realistic but inevitable, even as federal spending on safety net programs falls behind the growth in numbers of the uninsured[11] (Figure 12.2). We can therefore anticipate not just stormy weather, but a perfect storm with the health care system imploding under its own weight.

The above problems are not insoluble. If they are taken by our profession as opportunities to lead toward urgently needed reforms, medicine can become part of the solution. The public wants and has every reason to expect that our profession will respond to these opportunities, as we will see in the next chapter.

TABLE 12.3
A Problem-Oriented Approach To System Reform

PROBLEM	ACTION
1. Uncontrolled inflation of health care costs and prices	Advocate for single-payer National Health Insurance (NHI), Medicare for All, a publicly financed program of comprehensive health insurance coupled with a private delivery system lower overhead and improved efficienc by risk pooling across our entire population. NHI would consolidate health care programs, simplify administration, and provide the structure for more accountability to th system.
2. Growing crisis in unaffordability of health care now extending to middle class	
3. Decreasing access to care	
4. Rising rates of uninsured and underinsured	
5. Gaps in coverage for essential services	
6. 29-month waiting period for coverage of disabled on Medicare	
7. Lack of mental health parity	
8. Discontinuity and turnover of insurance coverage	
9. Variable, often poor quality of care	
10. High rates of inappropriate and unnecessary care	
11. Increasing health disparities	
12. Administrative complexity, profiteering and waste of 1,300 private insurers	
13. Decreased choice of hospital and physician in managed care programs	
14. Erosion of safety net programs	
15. Lax federal regulation of drug, medical device, and dietary supplement industries	Advocate for expanded authority an resources for FDA and support its independence from political interference.
16. Inadequate national system for assessment of new medical technologies	Support creation of new federal agenc for this purpose, possibly along the lines of the National Transportation Safety Board.
17. Declining primary care base	Support narrowing of reimbursemen gap between procedural and cognitiv health care services, together with othe policies to expand training programs and strengthen the delivery model fo primary care physicians.

FIGURE 12.1

Forecasts for U.S. Health Care in 2010

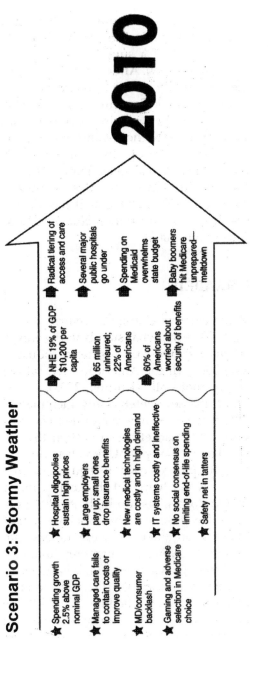

Scenario 3: Stormy Weather

★ Spending growth 2.5% above nominal GDP

★ Managed care fails to contain costs or improve quality

★ MD/consumer backlash

★ Gaming and adverse selection in Medicare choice

★ Hospital oligopolies sustain high prices

★ Large employers pay up; small ones drop insurance benefits

★ New medical technologies are costly and in high demand

★ IT systems costly and ineffective

★ No social consensus on limiting end-of-life spending

★ Safety net in tatters

↑ NHE 19% of GDP $10,200 per capita

↑ 65 million uninsured; 22% of Americans

↑ 60% of Americans worried about security of benefits

↑ Radical tiering of access and care

↑ Several major public hospitals go under

↑ Spending on Medicaid overwhelms state budget

↑ Baby boomers hit Medicare unprepared—meltdown

2010

SOURCE: Adapted with permission from: Institute for the Future. *Health and Health Care 2010: The Forecast, the Challenges*. San Francisco: Jossey-Bass, 2000 :Appendix.

Figure 12.2

Inflation-Adjusted Federal Spending on the Safety Net Has Not Kept Pace with the Growth in the Uninsured, 2001-2004

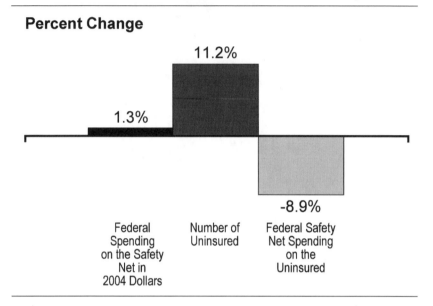

SOURCE: Reprinted with permission from: Hadley et al. Federal Spending on the Health Care Safety Net from 2001-2004: Has Spending Kept Pace with the Growth in the Uninsured? KCMU, November 2005, Publication #7425. This information was reprinted with permission from the Henry J. Kaiser Family Foundation. The Kaiser Family Foundation, based in Menlo Park, California, is a non-profit, private operating foundation focusing on the major health care issues facing the nation and is not associated with Kaiser Permanente or Kaiser Industries.

CHAPTER 13

OUR PATIENTS AS ALLIES:
WHERE THE PUBLIC STANDS

"So it is that contrary to what we have heard rhetorically for a generation now, the individualist, greed-driven, free-market ideology is at odds with our history and with what most Americans really care about. More and more people agree that growing inequality is bad for the country, that corporations have too much power, that money in politics is corrupting democracy and that working families and poor communities need and deserve help when the market system fails to generate shared prosperity. Indeed, the American public is committed to a set of values that almost perfectly contradicts the conservative agenda that has dominated politics for a generation now."

Bill Moyers, "A New Story for America," 2007[1]

Since medicine and the health care system exist (or should only exist) to serve the public, we need to focus on how the general public views the profession and health care. The goals of this chapter are three-fold: (1) to briefly summarize changing public perceptions of medicine in recent decades; (2) to explore public perceptions toward health care as a right, the role of government, and various aspects concerning the system itself; and (3) to examine differences between public perceptions and those held by experts and stakeholders in the market-based system and consider the implications of these differences.

PUBLIC PERCEPTIONS OF MEDICINE

Although physicians in past years were held in high esteem by the public, this is no longer the case. Since physicians play a central role throughout the health care system and order almost all services provided by health care professionals, they naturally bear the brunt of public dissatisfaction with the system. But physicians are also widely perceived as being too money-driven and are closely tied to medical commercialism, high levels of inappropriate and unnecessary care, and frequent conflicts of interest.[2,3] Here are some markers of this transformation of public perceptions over the years.

- According to sequential Harris polls from 1975 to 1999, the percentage of Americans expressing confidence in medical leaders fell from 80 percent to about 40 percent.[4]

- A national survey by the National Coalition on Health Care in 1997 found that four of five respondents agreed that "medical care has become big business that puts profits ahead of people"[5]

- An annual "credibility" study of major social institutions in the U.S., conducted by Yankelovich Partners for *Time* magazine, found that public confidence in physicians and the health care system dropped from over 50 percent to about 22 percent between 1987 and 1999.[6]

- Gallup's annual survey in 2005 on the honesty and ethics of various professionals and occupations showed that nurses led the way, as they had for the three preceding years, with physicians a ways down the list (Table 13.1).[7]

- Many studies have consistently shown a sharp decline in the public's trust of the medical profession in recent decades.[8-11] Three major public surveys over the past 30 to 40 years have quantified the loss of public faith in the authority of the medical profession. The results of the General Social Survey by the National Opinion Research Corporation (NORC), Harris, and Gallup surveys all show marked declines in the public's faith in the authority of the medical profession between 1965 and 1999 (Figure 13.1). Over that period the medical profession changed from one of the most trusted to one of the least trusted social institutions.[12,13] A further public survey of a nationally representative random sample of over 1,500 American adults in the mid-1990s found that among well informed respondents, two-thirds believed that physicians are money driven, 60 percent felt that physicians are not committed to community needs, and one-half believed that physicians should have less political voice. A parallel survey of 150 representatives of provider associations, patient groups, industry and governments, all sophisticated in health policy, found similar findings, with the health policy respondents showing even less trust in the profession's political activities than has been shown

TABLE 13.1

Who Do You Trust Most?

(% rating each "high" or "very high")

Profession	Percentage
Nurses	79%
Grade-school teachers	73
Druggists, pharmacists	72
Military officers	72
Medical doctors	**67**
Policemen	60
Clergy	56
Judges	53
Day care providers	49
Bankers	36
Auto mechanics	26
Local officeholders	26
Nursing home operators	24
State officeholders	24
TV reporters	23
Newspaper reporters	21
Business executives	20
Congressmen	20
Lawyers	18
Advertising practitioners	10
Car salesmen	9

SOURCE: John Q. Public: Nurses are still most trustworthy. *Medical Economics,* February 4, 2005:p 14.

by the public.[14]

The overall decline in public trust of the medical profession in recent decades has been fueled partly by the conflicted roles of physicians in managed care as well as the striking growth of physicians' incomes since the

FIGURE 13.1

Loss of Public Faith in the Authority of the Medical Profession

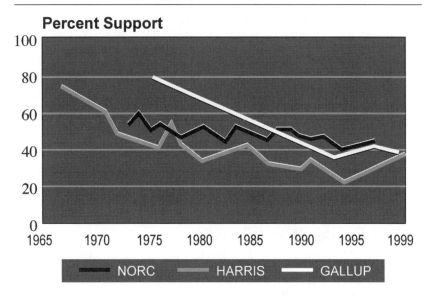

Loss of public faith in the authority of the medical profession. These survey results show the percentage of the American public expressing confidence in medical leaders. For the Harris and NORC results, confidence is the percent responding 'a great deal"; for the Gallup results, it is 'a great deal" and "quite a lot."

SOURCE: Reprinted with permission from: Schlesinger M. A loss of faith: The sources of reduced political legitimacy for the American medical profession. The Milbank Q 80(2):185-235,2002

1960s. Of course, there have been concerns raised in some quarters about the financial self-interest of some physicians for centuries, but it appears that this concern has become more widespread among the public in recent years.[15,16] Flaunting of extravagant lifestyles by some affluent physicians has not helped the public's perception of the profession, especially as many physicians withdraw from the care of uninsured patients and disadvantaged groups.[17-20] Both patients and third party payers have lost trust in the fiduciary ethic of physicians to put patients first and the profession's commitment to manage health care in the public interest. Growing distrust is driven by continuing escalation of health care costs, the relentless growth of medical commercialism, variations in patterns of care, high levels of inappropriate and unnecessary care, pervasive conflicts of interest, and press reports of fraud.[21]

Trust in physicians is an essential requirement of a therapeutic physician-patient relationship. Eric Cassel, internist, bioethicist, and Clinical Professor of Public Health at Cornell University Medical College, reminds us that "sick people are people who are forced to trust."[22] Ethical codes that we reviewed in Chapter 1 have all encouraged physicians to be trustworthy and not exploit patients' vulnerability. The erosion of public trust in the profession's service ethic is therefore a very serious matter for patients and physicians alike.

PUBLIC PERCEPTIONS OF HEALTH CARE

Health Care as a Right

Although health care is recognized as an essential human right in most industrialized nations around the world, as well as by the World Health Organization and the United Nations, this issue still engenders an unresolved and contentious debate in the United States. Conservatives in this country still worry about the "moral hazard" of universal access to health care, that it could lead to excessive and unaffordable utilization of services, and contend that it is up to each individual and family to take responsibility for making sure they have health insurance.

But the general public has been clear on this subject for a long time. A large majority of the public for over 60 years has supported government-financed national health insurance (NHI) to provide universal access to care for everyone. Public support for NHI, also referred to as a single payer system because the government is the sole payer of insurance claims, was 74 percent during the 1940s,[23] and 61 percent of the public supported the single-payer Medicare program when it was established in 1965. Since then, between one-half to two-thirds of Americans have favored government-financed NHI combined with a private delivery system.[24] The National Coalition on Health Care found in 1996 that three of four Americans believe that the federal government should be more active in assuring universal access to care.[25] More recent public surveys continue this consistent trend of public support for guaranteed access to care, as illustrated by these examples:

- "Universal health insurance" was viewed favorably by 75 percent of respondents to a Wall Street Journal/Harris poll in 2005.[26]

- Another 2005 national survey of more than 1,000 adult Americans found that 67 percent support a health care "guarantee" such as provided in Canada and the U.K.[27]

- A 2005 survey of 1,000 Vermont residents found that 86 percent believe that everyone should have access to the same basic coverage.[28]

- A 2005 ballot initiative in Seattle, which stated that health care is a right that Congress should implement, was supported by 69.8 percent of the voting public.[29]

- A 2005 national study by the Pew Research Center of the People and the Press, involving 2,000 interviews and more than 1,000 re-interviews, found that 65 percent of all people interviewed favor government health insurance for all; interestingly, this study showed that Republicans are deeply divided over health care, with 59 percent of social conservatives and 63 percent of pro-government conservatives favoring government-financed NHI, even if taxes increase.[30]

- A 2005 online survey with over 1,400 responses conducted by NBC News' Chief Science and Health Correspondent found that 80 percent supported the statement "Yes. What could be more important than the health of its citizens?"[31]

Health Care Reform: What the Public Wants

The last 30 years in the U.S. have seen many incremental efforts to "reform" the health care system, all ineffective in controlling runaway costs or resolving access and quality problems. A 2002 national Harris poll showed that the perceptions of public citizens are very much in line with other groups polled—physicians, employers, hospital managers, and health plan managers. One-half of all of these groups favored *radical* health care reform; less than 19 percent of any of the five groups believed that only incremental change is needed.[32] A 2004 cross-national study of five countries by the Commonwealth Fund and Harris Interactive found that

Americans led the way in dissatisfaction with their care system; one-third of U.S. respondents felt that "the system needs to be rebuilt completely," more than twice the proportion of respondents in Canada and the U.K. with that view.[33]

Health care reform, of course, is a complicated subject not easily adapted to polling. In addition, many polls are subtly slanted to give misleading answers favoring the polling organization or the sponsors of the poll. For example, the American public has yet to be asked questions that include accurate assumptions of what is possible. A number of studies have already shown that the costs of universal access would be less than what we pay now. It would be Medicare for all; a single-payer system substituted for the unaccountable bureaucracy and waste of a largely profit-driven private health insurance industry.[34-40] A question with that understanding would be along the lines of whether or not they support "a simplified system of national health insurance that would provide universal access to comprehensive benefits of necessary health care at less cost than now being spent on health care."

The experience of "citizen juries" is telling in this regard. Kip Sullivan, health policy expert and activist for universal coverage, was a debate participant in two such juries during the 1990s. Each was a 24-person jury of average Americans convened to examine the question whether the Clinton Health Plan was a good direction to pursue. It was a complex plan which attempted to provide universal coverage through the private insurance industry, supplemented by public programs. The 1,342 page bill, dubbed the "Health Insurance Preservation Act" by critics, ended up dead on arrival in Congress, killed in the crossfire of warring interests.[41] After five days of debate over a range of private and public options, the Clinton Health Plan was voted down, 19 to 5, while informal support was given, 17 to 7, of a single-payer universal access option.[42]

Additional strong public support for single-payer NHI, much stronger than for any other approach to incremental reform, was expressed by a large number of people participating in the federally mandated and funded Citizen's Health Care Working Group. This effort was enacted by the 2003 Medicare legislation (MMA). Over the next two years, many community meetings were held across the country focused upon the problems of the health care system and possible approaches to address them. Overwhelming majorities of participants feel that the health care system is in crisis or constitutes a major problem (96.8 percent), while 94 percent believe that affordable health care should be a part of national public policy. Almost one-half (46 percent) of the more than 800 participants who wanted a "single health care system" wanted a single-payer system. Table 13.2 is busy but conveys important information about the public's views on health care reform. Single-payer NHI was far out in front as the public's leading reform option. Especially striking is the very low public interest in relying on the free market for reforms.[43]

Despite the importance of these findings, however, one has to conclude that this publicly mandated exercise in public participation was no more than political posturing. The recommendations of the Working Group submitted for further public review in mid-2006 did not reflect strong public support for a National Health Program for everyone, instead proposing a system of insurance policies for catastrophic illness with deductibles up to $30,000, a concept not even discussed in community meetings and which generated considerable opposition in online polls.[44]

Even when it comes to the question of increasing taxes in order to achieve universal coverage, the public has shown a willingness to do so. For example, a 2004 study of 4,000 adults by the Commonwealth Fund found that 62 percent of Americans would be willing to forego the entire Bush tax cut in exchange for guaranteed health insurance for everyone. That figure increased to 69 percent if the tax cut was capped at $1,000 per person.[45]

Other Public Perceptions

- Type of Ownership. A major study of public perceptions of not-for-profit versus for-profit ownership of health care facilities and services was carried out by investigators from Yale University and the New York Academy of Medicine in 2002. Based on 5,000 interviews, they found that most Americans expect not-for-profit hospitals and health plans to be more trustworthy, fair, and humane, but lower in quality. For-profit health plans were considered to not provide all necessary tests and procedures (82 percent) and treat you like a number instead of a real person (62 percent). The investigators concluded that the public see investor-owned health plans as a source of untrustworthy practice, and that "for-profit ownership in the managed care industry almost certainly exacerbated public fears and the resultant "backlash"

TABLE 13.2   Public Opinion Concerning Possible Approaches to Health Care Reform

If you believe it is important to ensure access to affordable, high quality health care coverage and services for all Americans, which is most important to you? (SELECT ONE)

Meeting Site	Individual Tax Incentives	Expand Medicaid SCHIP etc.	Rely on Free Market	Expand Medicare/FEHBP	Expand Employer Tax Incentives	Employer Insurance Mandate	Expand Neighborhood Health clinics	Create a National Health Program	Individual Insurance Mandate	Increase State Program Flexibly
Albuquerque, NM	11.1%	2.5%	2.5%	3.7%	2.5%	8.6%	4.9%	56.8%	6.2%	1.2%
Cincinnati, OH	7.8%	11.6%	6.0%	6.6%	3.9%	4.5%	2.4%	39.7%	17.0%	0.6%
Fargo, ND	9.9%	7.7%	7.7%	5.5%	12.1%	4.4%	3.3%	34.1%	9.9%	5.5%
Hartford, CT	0.0%	3.7%	0.0%	3.7%	3.7%	5.6%	5.6%	74.1%	0.0%	0.0%
Las Vegas, NV	5.8%	7.2%	0.0%	8.7%	1.4%	2.9%	2.9%	44.9%	20.3%	5.8%
Lexington, KY	6.3%	5.3%	3.2%	2.1%	2.9%	8.4%	1.1%	54.7%	16.8%	0.0%
Little Rock, AR	11.9%	9.9%	1.0%	11.9%	5.0%	1.0%	5.0%	25.7%	27.7%	1.0%
Los Angeles, CA	6.2%	6.2%	2.6%	7.2%	2.1%	4.1%	6.7%	59.5%	3.6%	1.5%
San Antonio, TX	1.5%	4.9%	4.9%	5.8%	3.9%	1.9%	1.0%	54.4%	19.4%	1.9%
Sioux Falls, SD	7.7%	11.5%	0.0%	15.4%	3.8%	3.8%	0.0%	30.8%	23.1%	3.8%

If you believe it is important to ensure access to affordable, high quality health care coverage and services for all Americans, which of these proposals would you suggest for doing this? (RANKINGS FROM EACH MEETING WHERE QUESTION WAS ASKED THIS WAY)

Meeting Site	Individual Tax Incentives	Expand Medicaid SCHIP etc.	Rely on Free Market	Expand Medicare/FEHBP	Expand Employer Tax Incentives	Employer Insurance Mandate	Expand Neighborhood Health clinics	Create a National Health Program	Individual Insurance Mandate	Increase State Program Flexibly
Billings, MT	8th	6th	10th	3rd	7th	9th	2nd	1st	4th	5th
Charlotte, NC	6th	10th	9th	3rd	4th	8th	2nd	5th	1st	7th
Denver, CO	9th	6th	10th	3rd	7th	7th	2nd	1st	4th	5th
Des Moines, IA	7th	6th	10th	2nd	8th	9th	3rd	1st	5th	4th
Detroit, MI	9th	6th	10th	3rd	8th	4th	2nd	1st	7th	5th
Eugene, OR	9th	6th	10th	5th	8th	7th	3rd	1st	4th	3rd
Indianapolis, IN	5th	6th	10th	9th	4th	8th	2nd	1st	2nd	7th
Jackson, MS	9th	7th	10th	4th	6th	6th	2nd	1st	5th	3rd
Kansas City, MO	7th	4th	NA	3rd	5th	9th	2nd	1st	6th	8th
Memphis, TN	7th	5th	10th	3rd	9th	6th	2nd	1st	4th	8th
Miami, FL	9th	4th	10th	2nd	6th	7th	2nd	1st	5th	8th
New York, NY	9th	4th	10th	3rd	6th	5th	3rd	1st	6th	7th
Philadelphia, PA	7th	9th	10th	5th	8th	5th	2nd	1st	6th	6th
Phoenix, AZ	9th	8th	10th	4th	6th	4th	2nd	1st	3rd	8th
Providence, RI	9th	9th	10th	3rd	7th	6th	2nd	1st	4th	5th
Sacramento, CA	8th	8th	10th	3rd	9th	6th	2nd	3rd	4th	5th
Salt Lake City, UT	8th	7th	9th	5th	8th	10th	2nd	1st	3rd	4th
Seattle, WA	6th	9th	10th	4th	8th	6th	2nd	1st	4th	5th
Tucson, AZ	7th	5th	10th	4th	8th	9th	3rd	2nd	1st	6th

SOURCE: The Health Report to the American People. Report of the Citizens' Health Care Working Group, Appendix B, p 7, July 2006,

against managed care."[46] Another 2002 study, conducted by the Center for Studying Health System Change as part of its Community Tracking Study, found that for-profit HMOs are rated less favorably than not-for-profit HMOs by patients who consider themselves in fair or poor health.[47]

As discussed in Chapter 3, public concerns about for-profit health care services are well founded inasmuch as an extensive literature has found them to have higher costs, higher overhead, higher death rates, and worse quality of care, whether hospitals,[48-53] HMOs,[54,55] dialysis centers,[56] or nursing homes.[57]

- Rising Costs.   Health care is now the leading domestic concern in national polls, surpassing the economy, unemployment, and terrorism, particularly the urgent need to rein in runaway costs of health care.[58] A 2004 national survey by the Kaiser Family Foundation found that 82 percent of respondents are worried about rising health care costs.[59] A *Wall Street Journal* poll in 2005 found that even wealthy Americans are concerned about health care costs—96 percent of millionaires under age 55 were worried that health care costs would affect their retirement.[60] According to a 2006 poll of affluent investors by Citigroup Smith Barney, about one-half are concerned about health care costs, especially the costs of prescription drugs, health insurance, and long-term care.[61] The 2006 Health Confidence Survey, recently reported by the Employee Benefit Research Institute (EBRI), found that public dissatisfaction with U.S. health care has doubled since 1998, mostly due to the rising costs of health care. Almost one in three insured respondents stated they had difficulty paying for basic necessities, such as food, heat, and housing, while one-third reported they have exhausted all or most of their savings.[62]

As we have seen in earlier chapters, the insurance and drug industries account for a very large part of rising health care costs. Administration, overhead and profits of our 1,300 private insurance companies soak up 31 percent of the health care dollar,[63] while the pharmaceutical industry has reigned at or near the top of profits among the Fortune 500 companies for many years.[64] The public sees through the smoke and mirrors of image-building efforts by these industries to recognize this fact, as shown in Figure 13.2.[65]

FIGURE 13.2

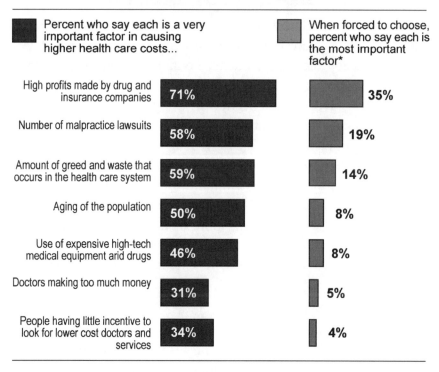

Perceived Reasons for Rising Health Care Costs

Percent who say each is a very important factor in causing higher health care costs...

When forced to choose, percent who say each is the most important factor*

	Very important factor	Most important factor*
High profits made by drug and insurance companies	71%	35%
Number of malpractice lawsuits	58%	19%
Amount of greed and waste that occurs in the health care system	59%	14%
Aging of the population	50%	8%
Use of expensive high-tech medical equipment and drugs	46%	8%
Doctors making too much money	31%	5%
People having little incentive to look for lower cost doctors and services	34%	4%

SOURCE:Reprinted with permission from Kaiser Family Foundation. The public on health care costs: Perceived reasons for rising health care costs. Accessed May 25, 2006 at www.Kff.org/spotlight/healthcosts/index.cfm This information was reprinted with permission from the Henry J. Kaiser Family Foundation. The Kaiser Family Foundation, based in Menlo Park, California, is a non-profit, private operating foundation focusing on the major health care issues facing the nation and is not associated with Kaiser Permanente or Kaiser Industries.

- Pharmaceutical Industry. Although the drug industry used to be favorably viewed by much of the public, its image has plummeted over the last 10 years. An annual Harris poll surveys about 1,000 people concerning their attitudes toward 15 industries. Between 1997 and 2004, the drug industry's favorable ratings dropped from 79 percent to 44 percent. The industry is widely perceived to be price gouging, is distrusted for false or misleading advertising, and seen as buying political power in its own self-interest.[66] A more recent poll in 2005 by the *Wall Street Journal* and *NBC News* found only 3 percent of respondents believing that drug companies work for the public good, with 76 percent viewing them as mostly interested in their own profits.[67] A majority of Americans see the Medicare Prescription Drug, Improvement, and Modernization Act of 2003 as a giveaway to the drug and insurance industries serving private interests much more than the public interest. A 2004 survey by the Kaiser Family Foundation and the Harvard School of Public Health revealed that 80 percent of respondents on Medicare favored the government using the bargaining clout to negotiate lower drug prices, as is done successfully by the Veterans Administration.[68] Three of four Medicare beneficiaries now see that legislation as too complicated and confusing and only one in five feel that the prescription drug benefit will help them personally, according to a 2006 *Wall Street Journal/NBC News* poll.[69] A 2006 Harris survey of more than 2,300 people showed that 82 percent of respondents believed that FDA decisions were influenced to a great extent or some extent by politics instead of medical science.[70]

- Insurance and Managed Care Industries. The insurance and managed care industries have fared even worse than the drug industry in public opinion in recent years. The aforementioned annual Harris surveys of 15 industries found them to have favorable ratings in 2004 at only 36 percent and 30 percent levels, respectively. To put managed care's 30 percent favorable rating in perspective, it tied for last place on the list—with the tobacco industry. Between 1997 and 2004, favorable ratings dropped from

55 percent to 36 percent for the insurance industry and from 51 percent to 30 percent for the managed care industry.[71] According to a 2004 online survey of 5,000 households by Forrester Research, only 21 percent of respondents agreed "My primary health plan is always on my side for any problems or concerns I have."[72] Only 57 percent of insured adults under age 65 feel "well protected" by their insurance plan; more than one-third fear that they will have unmet health care needs; and about three of four Americans have an unfavorable opinion on health savings accounts (HSAs) and similar high-deductible health plans.[73]

Are these surveys biased, somehow lopsided in their findings to magnify dissatisfaction with the current system and desire for one insured by the government? No. A 1997 survey by a public relations firm of almost 600 citations about managed care in newspapers, magazines, and television news programs found five times as many unfavorable stories as favorable ones.[74] Even a 2004 survey conducted by the insurance industry's own trade group, America's Health Insurance Plans (AHIP), involving 800 registered voters in 17 swing states, found that 54 percent of respondents believed that government is better suited to "keep health care affordable."[75]

DISCONNECTS BETWEEN PUBLIC PERCEPTIONS, EXPERTS, AND MARKET STAKEHOLDERS

As we have seen, the general public has been quite clear over many years that health as a basic human need requires a right to care, that the profit-driven market-based system is off track, that not-for-profit health care services are more trustworthy, and that the government should be more active in assuring universal access to care. Although it is reasonable to expect that health policy should be informed, influenced and responsive to public opinion, this is not the case. The perceptions of health care "experts" and stakeholders in preserving our market-based system are in sharp contrast to views of the general public, and so far have been determining the directions of health policy.

Expert Opinion

In his excellent new book, *The Health Care Mess: How We Got Into It and How We'll Get Out of It,* Kip Sullivan compares public perceptions with the views held by health economists and health policy experts regarding the high and soaring costs of health care in the U.S. He reviews the evidence for and against the views of each group, and points out how each side casts blame on different targets for the relentless rise of health care costs. Table 13.3 lists commonly held explanations for health care inflation, together with perceived culprits.[76]

Most health care experts tend to blame patients for overusing the system (moral hazard).[77] The conventional theory of health insurance, established during the 1960s and accepted by most health economists since a landmark article by Mark Pauly in 1968, holds that having insurance encourages over-

TABLE 13.3

Common Perceptions and Perceived Culprits Concerning Health Care Inflation and Waste

Explanation	Culprit
The six common excuses	
(1) Americans get too many medical services	
(a) because doctors order too many services	Doctors
(b) because patients demand too many services	Patients
(2) Americans are older...	Patients
(3) Americans have worse lifestyles	Patients
(4) Americans sue for malpractice too often...................	Patients
(5) Americans are more violent.......................................	Patients, attackers
(6) US quality is superior...	(not applicable)
The four categories of waste	
(1) Administrative waste..	Insurance industry
(2) Excess capacity	Hospitals, doctors
(3) Excessively high fees and prices..............................	Health-care industry
(4) Fraud..	Health-care industry

SOURCE: Sullivan K. *The Health Care Mess: How We Got Into It and How We'll Get Out of It.* Bloomington, In: Author House, 2006, p 201.

utilization, is inefficient, welfare decreasing, and that high prices can reduce moral hazard.[78-80] This theory has been a driving force behind managed care since the early 1980s, and still provides conceptual underpinning for today's emphasis on increasing cost-sharing through consumer-directed health care. Yet it is only recently that this theory has been called into question by a few health economists, despite the growing evidence that underuse of health care services is a larger problem. In his 2004 book *The Theory of Demand for Health Insurance,* Dr. John Nyman, a health economist at the University of Minnesota, persuasively rebuts this theory, arguing that too much cost-sharing is often harmful by restricting access to care, and that insurance is beneficial and welfare-increasing.[81-82]

The Rand Health Insurance Experiment, a large study conducted between 1974 and 1981, examined how health care behaviors and utilization rates are affected by out-of-pocket payments. As a well-known and highly respected research institution since the late 1940s, Rand draws much of its support from industry, foundations, and government. The overall finding of the Health Insurance Experiment that patients with less insurance used less care provided impetus to the moral hazard premise. But the grounds for this conclusion have been challenged by an increasing number of studies, including some by Rand investigators, that find underuse of appropriate and necessary care to be a major problem with cost-sharing.[83-84] To Rand's credit, their studies in recent years have begun to acknowledge the underuse problem for what it is. We still need to recognize, however, that hidden conflicts of interest can still influence the work and findings of a prestigious non-profit research institution, just as we found in Chapter 8 in academic medicine and even the NIH. As one example, a clinical practice guideline for the use of ear tubes in young children with ear infections was developed by a private for-profit company, Value Health Sciences (VHS) that did utilization review for managed care organizations. In its brochure, VHS stated that it saved its clients more than $67 million in treatment denials in 1995. The use of ear tubes has been controversial for years, but two of the four authors of the Rand ear tube study worked for and held stock in VHS.[85-87]

Some employers and health plans are already seeing the economic shortcomings of cost-sharing when employees or enrollees underutilize necessary health care. They are beginning to recognize that motivating patients toward preventive care and most needed medications can delay or prevent major costly illness down the road. These experiments are now underway in an effort to encourage patients to seek necessary care earlier by cutting or eliminating cost-sharing: Marriott has cut copayments for drugs prescribed for heart disease, diabetes, and asthma; Pitney Bowes provides diabetes and asthma drugs free; the University of Michigan has reduced copays for diabetes drugs.[88]

The public has a very different view from the experts about problems of the health care system, pointing instead to administrative waste, high prices and fees, excess capacity, and fraud within the system.[89] Here again, the general public's views are a much more accurate assessment of reality than the experts' views. Earlier chapters have provided extensive documentation of excess capacity, administrative waste, unnecessary and inappropriate care generated by the supply side of the system, as well as pervasive conflicts of interest and profit-driven practices.

Market Stakeholders

As we saw in Chapters 2 and 5, the medical industrial complex is enormous, comprising one-sixth of the nation's GDP and largely driven by a business ethic that places financial bottom lines in top priority. Health services have become just another commodity to be bought and sold in a deregulated medical marketplace.[90,91] As is well documented in earlier chapters, stakeholders on the supply side of the system jealously guard their prerogatives in pricing and resist more accountability or regulation. They typically defend their turf and lobby for continuance of the so-called "free market" by perpetuating these kinds of myths about U.S. health care:

- The U.S. has the best health care system in the world, and free enterprise has made it so.

- The private sector is more efficient and provides more value than a public system.

- Price controls would curtail innovation of new technologies and services.

- Health care costs can be contained by giving consumers more choice and more information to comparison shop.

- More regulation of the system would lead to rationing (with denial that we already ration care by ability to pay).

- The more technology, the better the health care.

All of these claims have been repeated so often by stakeholders in the market-based system as to become memes (self-replicating ideas that are promulgated without regard to their merits). They have been rebutted earlier in this book, and in further detail elsewhere.[92] But they have so far been successful in framing much of what debate has taken place over health care, and since they are largely unfounded, represent a barrier to health care reform.

If public opinion is so clear, as it is about the public's expectations of the health care system, why is reform so elusive? Several explanations immediately come to the fore, including the lobbying and political power of market stakeholders (dollars trump votes); disinformation by the media, engendered by market stakeholders; and flawed theories of health economics which still have many proponents. Kuttner offers a succinct answer to the barriers to reform: *"Only the insurance industry, the drug companies, the Fortune 500, half the American Medical Association, and the Republican Party, that's all."*[93]

WHAT'S NEXT?

The U.S. is facing a serious health care crisis. Care is becoming unaffordable and inaccessible for a growing part of the population; cost containment is nowhere in sight; quality of care is variable, with inequities and disparities increasing as the safety net further deteriorates. The public is increasingly dissatisfied with the system and wants major reform, including a larger role of government. A political stalemate persists, however, as legislators and policymakers continue to hope for this or that incremental change to resolve the crisis. Meanwhile, the stakeholders in the market-based system are thriving as the system falls apart.

Physicians witness and participate every day in the growing crisis that our health care system has become. This gives us a responsibility to advocate for our patients' best interest and a unique opportunity to lead the country past this political gridlock. Will we do so? The next three chapters provide a roadmap for how we can reassert our professional service ethic, and how we can expand beyond narrow concerns of self-interest to once again become champions of the public interest.

CHAPTER 14

RESTORING PROFESSIONALISM AND MEDICAL ETHICS

"What is the future of medicine in the public sphere, as expressed through its professional organizations? Will the profession continue to be just one of many competing interest groups, whose influence will continue to wane? Or is there a basis on which the professional organizations of medicine might assume a new position of moral leadership in American health care?"

Rosemary Stevens, Professor of History and Sociology of Sciences,
University of Pennsylvania[1]

"They [organized doctors] forget perhaps that medicine is for the people, not for the doctors."

James Howard Means [1885-1967][2]

As we saw in the opening chapter, the medical profession has had a long tradition of recognized public service in many societies for centuries. We also saw that this tradition has been challenged by entrepreneurialism and self-interest on many occasions over those years. Later chapters have traced the continued erosion over the last 40 years of the service ethic, loss of public trust, and increasing dominance of a business "ethic" putting profits over service. With all these extraordinary obstacles facing American medicine today, can its professionalism be restored? Or will the business ethos continue to trump a morality-based ethic of service?

This chapter undertakes four goals: (1) to summarize the responsibilities and societal expectations of professions and professionals; (2) to assess the extent of deprofessionalization of the medical profession in recent decades; (3) to briefly discuss how the profession's social contract can be re-negotiated to restore its social and political legitimacy; and (4) to consider what kind of ethical code will best serve the public and profession.

WHAT ARE PROFESSIONS AND PROFESSIONALS?

Professionalism in medicine has become an ambiguous term with different meanings for different people. It has been a subject of interest to many scholars and observers outside of medicine for many years. There is an extensive literature on professionalism in medicine, especially in the sociology and ethics literature. There is less literature within medicine itself, and there has often been little dialogue across disciplines on the subject.

In general usage, professions have a body of special knowledge, practicing within some ethical framework, meeting some societal need, and having a social mandate providing discretionary latitude in setting standards for education and practice. Among professions, some have been regarded as "learned professions" because of their educational breadth and importance of meeting fundamental human needs (e.g., medicine, law and the ministry).[3,4] As we saw in Chapter 1, the medical profession "professes" its dedication to the welfare of those they serve, beyond their own self-interest, through one or another oaths taken by graduates entering the profession as well as by the behavior of its members in daily practice (e.g., "how can I help you today?"). As professionals, physicians have enjoyed special status through their roles as healers. Table 14.1 lists the widely accepted characteristics of professions and professionals.[5]

The sine qua non of professionalism is a moral commitment to service beyond self-interest, acting for the benefit of society. In return for this commitment, professions are granted status, prestige, and sometimes considerable autonomy with the assumption that they will set their own standards and conduct themselves in the public interest.[6,7] As part of this contract with society, such professions as medicine, the law, and architecture have gained far more autonomy than most other professions.[8]

DEPROFESSIONALIZATION:
A MORAL CRISIS FOR MEDICINE

There has been a widespread consensus developing among sociologists, ethicists, and other observers of the medical profession since about 1960 that it has increasingly pursued its own self-interest with little regard for the public interest.[9-12] Many believe that the managed care era has accelerated this perception,[13] and a number of physician leaders in the profession have joined this consensus.[14-16] Rosemary Stevens describes a commonly held criticism of physicians as "self interested individuals who have masqueraded far too long as aloof, scientific altruists, and have behaved, collectively, as a questionable cultural force in the United States."[17] Recent years have seen the Federal Trade Commission looking more closely at the

TABLE 14.1

Characteristics of Professions and Professionals

A profession possesses a discrete body of knowledge and skills over which its members have exclusive control.

The work based on this knowledge is controlled and organized by professional associations that are independent of both state and capital (i.e., the marketplace).

The mandate of these associations is formalized by a variety of written documents, including laws covering licensure and regulations granting authority.

Professional associations are the ultimate authorities on the personal, social, economic, cultural, and political affairs relating to their domains, and they are expected to influence public policy and inform the public within their areas of expertise.

Admission to professions requires prolonged education and training; the professions are responsible for determining the qualifications and (usually) the numbers to be admitted, the substance of training, and the requirements of its completion.

Within the constraints of the law, the professions control admission to practice and the terms, conditions, and goals of the practice.

The professions are responsible for the ethical and technical criteria by which their members are evaluated, and have the exclusive right and duty to discipline unprofessional conduct.

Individual members remain autonomous in their workplaces within the limits of rules and standards laid down by the associations and relevant laws.

Professionals are expected to gain their livelihoods by providing service to the public in the areas of their expertise.

Members are expected to value performance above reward.

Professions and professionals must be moral and are held to higher standards of behavior than are non-professionals.

Professionalism is an ideal to be pursued.

Source: Cruess R., Cruess S. & Johnston S. Renewing professionalism: an opportunity for medicine. Acad Med 74:880, 1999.

business practices of physicians, their associations, and medical schools, while state and federal regulators have found detection and prosecution of fraud a growing challenge. The profession's ethical standards have been called into question,[18,19] with one study of major social institutions in the U.S. finding that public confidence in physicians dropped from 50 percent in 1987 to about 22 percent in 1999.[20] The profession has also lost much of its influence over health policy as both patients and third party payers have lost trust in the fiduciary ethic of physicians to put patients first and the profession's ability to competently manage health care in the public interest. This growing distrust of the profession is understandable in view of uncontrolled escalation of health care costs, the continued growth of medical commercialism, high levels of inappropriate and unnecessary care, and pervasive conflicts of interest among physicians and their organizations.[21]

Many physicians, perhaps even most, are honest, hardworking, and dedicated to the welfare of their patients and feel trapped in a system over which they have little control. There are good examples of professionalism in medicine in many parts of the system, especially in the public sector's safety net. Community health centers, the Indian Health Service, and rural and underserved urban areas attract dedicated physicians motivated by the service ethic. Together, they preserve and extend the profession's noble tradition of service. Likewise, some organizations in medicine have taken a leadership role in reversing the corrosive efforts of commercialism of medicine (e.g., Physicians for Social Responsibility (PSR), Physicians for a National Health Program (PNHP), National Medical Association (NMA), American Medical Women's Association (AMWA), American Medical Students Association (AMSA), American Public Health Association (APHA), and the American Society for Bioethics and Humanities). Other notable achievements by medical organizations include widespread process improvements initiated by the American Society of Anesthesiology, which greatly reduced surgical morbidity and mortality,[22] the addition of performance measurement as part of competency evaluation for physicians certified by the American Board of Internal Medicine,[23] and the leadership of three mental health organizations (the American Psychiatric Association, the American Academy of Child and Adolescent Psychiatry, and the American Academy of Psychiatry and the Law) in reacting to the abuses of the interrogation process at Abu Gharib and at Guantanamo Bay, (which initially directly involved psychologists or psychiatrists in interrogations involving abuse and torture).[24] As a result of their efforts, these organizations and the AMA adopted new ethical guidelines prohibiting such activities by physicians as an unethical violation of their roles as healers.[25]

Notwithstanding these many good examples of medical professionalism, medicine as a collective body deserves much of the criticism that has been directed towards it. The reactions of most of the profession's organizations have been defensive and ineffective, with continued support for the "free marketplace" which generates many of the corrosive practices. Since the status and privileges which society has granted to the medical profession depend on two basic commitments—service above self-interest and effective self-regulation—it is useful to assess its track record with both responsibilities.

The report card for each responsibility leaves much to be desired, as reflected by these examples, which were discussed in detail in earlier chapters.

The Rise of Self-Interest over Service

- Widespread acceptance by physicians of gifts and "consulting" income from industry (especially the pharmaceutical and medical device industries) that influence their use of their products[26-30] with denial of that influence as a conflict of interest.[31]

- Extensive conflicts of interest between physicians and the drug industry in creation of clinical practice guidelines[32] and CME programs.[33-36]

- Pervasive conflicts of interest between academic medical centers (AMCs) and industry, which in many cases influence what research is undertaken, how it is conducted, and whether or how it is reported.[37-42]

- Rapid growth of physician investment in diagnosis, screening, and imaging centers across the country (e.g., endoscopy, bone densitrometry, CT and PET scanning),[43] which generate large volumes of lucrative but often unnecessary or clinically questionable services.[44]

- Widespread acceptance by medical organizations of unrestricted "educational" grants from industry, with no strings attached, including grants to promote off-label usage of drugs.[45]

The Failures of Self-Regulation

- The profession's failure to rein in, or speak effectively against physician-induced demand; it has not taken responsibility for the one-third of health care services estimated to be inappropriate, unnecessary or even contraindicated[46-47] while areas of the country with higher reimbursement rates and excess capacity of specialists and technology produce *lower* quality of care than areas with less capacity.[48,49]

- The profession's silence concerning cost-benefit and cost-effectiveness of new products brought to market by industry (eg., according to a recent survey of U.S. oncologists, 80 percent support spending $70,000 on new cancer drugs to extend a cancer patient's life by two months).[50]

- Growth in physician ownership and investments in health care facilities and services (e.g., opening of more than 100 specialty hospitals which attempt to skirt around anti-kickback laws and permit physicians to "triple dip"[51] while selecting out less sick and better insured patients;[52] overutilization and profiteering in facilities operating as joint ventures with physicians, such as radiation therapy centers[53] and physical therapy facilities).[54]

- Ceding undue influence and control to industry in exchange for funding (e.g., the drug industry funds more than 70 percent of the costs of clinical trials, thereby exerting strong influence over the design, conduct, and publication of this research;[55] in 2003, according to the ACCME, the profession's accrediting body for CME, the drug industry funded 90 percent of the nation's costs for CME in that year,[56] resulting in many conflicts of interest over the content of what practicing physicians are taught and blurring the lines between education and marketing).[57]

- Promulgation by medical organizations of lofty ethical guidelines without teeth to "manage" physicians' financial conflicts of interest (e.g., recent updated guidelines by the AMA, ACP and

ACCME are more exhortative than enforceable, and mechanisms for monitoring and compliance are lacking).[58]

- Lax oversight of conflicts of interest in academic medical centers (AMCs)[59,60] (e.g., a 2000 study revealed that only one of ten leading AMCs barred their investigators from conducting clinical research on products of companies with which they had significant financial ties).[61]

It seems clear from the above shortfalls on the two major requirements of professionalism that the medical profession in this country has come to a crisis in its moral credibility and its professional integrity. It is failing to counter commercialization of medical practice, while medical education and clinical research are enmeshed in pervasive conflicts of interest, and its social contract is in tatters. As we saw in Chapter 13, the public and some policymakers have come to recognize this crisis. Concerning the profession's recent attempts to address conflicts of interest of AMCs with industry, Dr. Jerome Kassirer, former Editor of *The New England Journal of Medicine* and author of the excellent 2005 book *On The Take: How Medicine's Complicity with Big Business Can Endanger Your Health*, has this to say:

> *"Not one powerful medical center has declared war on financial conflicts. None has outlawed faculty participation in speaker's bureaus, participation in consulting arrangements that are thinly veiled marketing efforts, or completely eliminated company-sponsored meals. Many set no limits on stock options or income from patent royalties. Most have no rules about how often their faculty members can be involved with for-profit entities. And the rules that most institutions do invoke are often enforced irregularly. Few institutions have turned their conflict-of-interest issues over to a regulative body that is independent of the parent institution, but that is exactly what they should do."[62]*

Further insight into the present condition of the profession is offered by Dr. David Lotto, a psychoanalytic psychohistorian, in these words:

> *"There are far too many health professionals among us who are willing to bend, contort, and turn inside out, our traditional professional values. Too many are willing to accommodate to the values of the corporate world where protecting the wealth of those who are paying you becomes a legitimate part of your professional function. Making*

this kind of accommodation has its rewards: mainly financial security and a comfortable middle class lifestyle. But like all such Faustian bargains, there is a steep price to pay. The problem is that in order to avoid anxiety and guilt we come to share the moral blind spots of our corporate culture. "[63]

RESTORING PROFESSIONALISM: RENEWAL OF A SOCIAL CONTRACT

Now well into the first decade of the 21st Century, American medicine finds itself in a dilemma—advanced technologically, busy as ever, and still prosperous but in an unsustainable system beset with increasingly unaffordable costs, limited access, variable quality, and near-chaotic bureaucracy. Despite its technical competence, public trust in the profession is declining and it has become a marginal player in the debate over the future of health care. With managed care the current villain being blamed for the failures of the health care system, there is now a widespread consensus that major changes will be required in the financing and delivery of care, but no clear sense of what direction these changes should take.

At this pivotal time of change, the professionalism of medicine is being questioned, as are its political and social relevance. Medicine seems to have lost its way, no longer at the helm of the health care ship, and enmeshed with corporate and business interests. Dr. James Robinson of the School of Public Health at the University of California Berkeley sees this as a fluid time of opportunity for medicine, a time of "creative chaos."[64]

The foregoing has documented the extent to which medical professionalism has eroded in recent decades with abrogation, at least in part, of its traditional social contract of service and ineffective approaches to self-regulation. Many observers of the profession, as friendly critics, are calling for re-negotiation of the profession's social contract. These are some examples:

"Modern American medicine has wedded scientific advance to a small business model of the individual practitioner, defining professionalism as technical understanding. If the profession is to survive, it must draw on older ideals of the learned professions as acting on behalf of the community, and reinvigorate a civic understanding of professional life. It is hard to see how medicine can resolve its crisis

of legitimacy without simultaneously seeking to redefine its identify around a public mission."

William Sullivan, PhD[65]
Professor of Philosophy, LaSalle University
Senior Scholar, the Carnegie Foundation
for the Advancement of Teaching

"The medical profession needs to re-establish its social contract with society. It must stop viewing public officials as the enemy and develop better ways of responding more broadly to the interests of the public."

Julius B. Richmond, MD
Leon Eisenberg, MD[66]

"Today, the dominant influence on professional associations is economic, and the tension between self-interest and ethical principles is greater than ever. This conflict is eroding the moral foundations of all professional associations, not only in medicine, but in law, education, and even the ministry.

Physicians must now choose more definitively than ever whether their professional associations will assert the primacy of ethical commitment or shed any pretense of being moral enterprises and instead, allow economic considerations to dominate their policies. The time is propitious for the medical profession to act responsibly to reaffirm the ethical commitment that grounds physicians' authenticity. Only then can physicians justify the claim to the moral integrity that patients expect. The present dilemma provides an opportunity for professional medical associations to shift the balance from self-interest to the interests of patients, thereby regaining public support and influence. Judging from recent trends, it is an opportunity that may not come again."

Edmund D. Pellegrino, MD
Arnold S. Relman, MD[67]

Two medical organizations have taken initial steps toward clarifying their professional roles. A *Charter on Medical Professionalism* was developed by the Medical Professionalism Project through the joint efforts of the ABIM Foundation, ACP-ASIM Foundation, and the European Federation of Internal Medicine. It identified three fundamental principles which should underpin medical professionalism (Table 14.2). The Physician Charter set forth these ten explicit professional commitments to:

"professional competence; honesty with patients; patient confidentiality; maintaining appropriate relations with patients; improving quality of care; improving access to care; a just distribution of finite resources; scientific knowledge; maintaining trust by managing conflicts of interest; and other professional responsibilities.[68] At about the same time, the AMA adopted its Declaration of Professional Responsibility (Table 14.3).[69]

Worthy and laudable as these professional statements are, however, they are of little consequence if not coupled with action and enforceable policies. What should a new social contract between medicine and society look like? The same criteria for professionalism still hold—service over self-interest and self-regulation—but the profession's track record must match

TABLE 14.2

Fundamental Principles for Medical Professionalism

Principle of primacy of patient welfare. This principle is based on a dedication to serving the interest of the patient. Altruism contributes to the trust that is central to the physician-patient relationship. Market forces, societal pressures, and administrative exigencies must not compromise this principle.

Principle of patient autonomy. Physicians must have respect for patient autonomy. Physicians must be honest with their patients and empower them to make informed decisions about their treatment. Patients' decisions about their care must be paramount, as long as those decisions are in keeping with ethical practice and do not lead to demands for inappropriate care.

Principle of social justice. The medical profession must promote justice in the health care system, including the fair distribution of health care resources. Physicians should work actively to eliminate discrimination in health care, whether based on race, gender, socioeconomic status, ethnicity, religion, or any other social category.

SOURCE: Project of the ABIM Foundation. ACP-ASIM Foundation and European Federation of Internal Medicine. Medical professionalism in the new millennium: A physician charter. Ann Intern Med 136(3):244, 2002.

TABLE 14.3

Declaration of Professional Responsibility: Medicine's Social Contract With Humanity

Preamble: Never in the history of human civilization has the well being of each individual been so inextricably linked to that of every other. Plagues and pandemics respect no national borders in a world of global commerce and travel. Wars and acts of terrorism enlist innocents as combatants and mark civilians as targets. Advances in medical science and genetics, while promising great good, may also be harnessed as agents of evil. The unprecedented scope and immediacy of these universal challenges demand concerted action and response by all.

As physicians, we are bound in our response by a common heritage of caring for the sick and the suffering. Through the centuries, individual physicians have fulfilled this obligation by applying their skills and knowledge competently, selflessly and at times heroically. Today, our profession must reaffirm its historical commitment to combat natural and man-made assaults on the health and well being of humankind. Only by acting together across geographic and ideological divides can we overcome such powerful threats. Humanity is our patient.

Declaration: We, the members of the world community of physicians, solemnly commit ourselves to:

I. Respect human life and the dignity of every individual.

II. Refrain from supporting or committing crimes against humanity and condemn all such acts.

III. Treat the sick and injured with competence and compassion and without prejudice.

IV. Apply our knowledge and skills when needed, though doing so may put us at risk.

V. Protect the privacy and confidentiality of those for whom we care and breach that confidence only when keeping it would seriously threaten their health and safety or that of others.

VI. Work freely with colleagues to discover, develop, and promote advances in medicine and public health that ameliorate suffering and contribute to human well being.

VII. Educate the public and polity about present and future threats to the health of humanity.

VIII. Advocate for social, economic, educational, and political changes that ameliorate suffering and contribute to human well being.

IX. Teach and mentor those who follow us for they are the future of our caring profession.

We make these promises solemnly, freely, and upon our personal and professional honor.

Adopted by the House of Delegates of the American Medical Association in San Francisco, California on December 4, 2001.

Source: Kurlander JE, Wynia MK & Morin K. The social contract model of professionalism: baby or bath water? Am J Bioethics 4(2):33-6, 2004.

its intent. For medicine, this will require recognition that it has to change, that it must ally itself more closely with other health professions, and that it needs to engage the public in new ways. A renewed social contract should recognize that medicine is but one voice, albeit an essential one, in a public discussion over the future of health care. Medicine cannot be a sovereign decision-maker, but has a key leadership rule to play in addressing such big issues as these which now confront the nation's health care system:

- What are the limits to technology, and how do we control its use based upon clinical evidence of efficacy and cost-effectiveness?

- How can we reduce waste and eliminate unnecessary and inappropriate care?

- How can we make necessary health care affordable and the health care system sustainable?

- How can we develop a system which assures access for all to necessary health care?

- How can we achieve social justice in health care and reduce disparities by income, race, and ethnic group?

- How can we implement performance-based professional competence and evidence-based quality improvement throughout the system?

Major change is inevitable in how health care is financed and delivered. Rosemary Stevens suggests these as the fundamental issues for the profession to address regardless of who controls health care:

1. "The ability to treat patients, using high standards of care, without undue concerns about cost and insurance issues as these affect individual patients.

2. Satisfaction in providing continuity of care to patients.

3. Building and maintaining trusting relationships with patients and with the general public.

4. Opportunities to participate creatively in improving the network or system on behalf of patients.

5. Good information systems for more effective patient care and

continuous improvement in clinical and team skills.

6. The ability to exercise professional curiosity (most formally, through clinical research and evaluation).

7. Open and fair communications with other members of the health care organization, including managers.

8. Reasonable working conditions and income levels."[70]

WHICH ETHIC WILL PREVAIL IN 21ST CENTURY MEDICINE?

The medical profession cannot renew its contract with society without clarifying its ethical core and what the profession stands for. We have seen in earlier chapters the ongoing battle for the soul of medicine between the market "ethic" and a professional service ethic. Pellegrino views the current moral challenge to the profession, as compared to the challenge to medicine 150 years ago, in these terms:

> "Today, we face another, but far more complicated, moral crisis. The enormous power of medical technology, coupled with the legitimization of the market ethos in health care, threatens to overshadow both physician and patient. What will our moral response be? What place in that response should and will the moral guideposts of the Hippocratic Oath, and the AMA Code of Ethics play? Should professional codes of ethics be abandoned entirely in an autonomy-obsessed society? Should the traditional medical ethos be replaced entirely by a new code, one modified to suit current economic and political realities? Is a universal code even possible in our multicultural, morally pluralistic, democratic society?"[71]

Deciding between the business "ethic" and a professional ethic of service cannot be done merely by adopting new ethical principles on paper. If medicine is to be serious about rebuilding its service ethic, major course changes are required. For starters, teeth need to be added to all of the lofty ethical guidelines now being promulgated for more professional behavior of physicians, medical educators, researchers, medical organizations, and academic-medical centers. Monitoring and enforcement mechanisms are largely absent and are urgently needed.

Here are a few examples of concrete ethical reforms which medical organizations could take if serious about eliminating financial conflicts of interest within their ranks:

- Ban the drug industry's bizarre of gifts and marketing materials from their professional meetings, replacing them with peer-reviewed scientific exhibits.

- Stop endorsing journal supplements produced with the support of unrestricted educational goals from drug companies, typically written by authors (including ghost authors) with financial conflicts of interest.

- Withdraw ACCME accreditation allowing for-profit Medical Education and Communication Companies (MECCs) to independently produce and conduct CME programs for physicians.

- Prohibit physicians who own, or are invested in health care facilities from adding to their income by referring their patients to such facilities or services (e.g., specialty hospitals, ambulatory surgery centers, clinical laboratories, imaging centers, radiation therapy and physical therapy centers).

- Exclude physicians with financial conflicts of interest from serving on panels creating clinical practice guidelines involving products for which the guidelines are being developed

- Bar faculty members with financial ties to industry from serving on institutional review boards (IRBs) of AMCs when research involving the company's products is being reviewed.

- Apply sanctions to members of their organizations who violate these new ethical standards.

This is obviously much too short a list to address the wide range of ethical problems described in Chapter 8 and elsewhere in this book. In addition, some medical organizations may find these examples naïve, impractical or unacceptable to their constituents. Indeed, such steps as banning drug company exhibits from professional meetings would dramatically reduce the budgets of professional organizations and call for increased support by members themselves. But rigorous steps of this kind could be taken if coupled with political will.

Another important challenge for medicine is how to expand its ethical framework beyond care of the individual patient to the welfare of populations being served through a closer alliance with public health. If we are to improve the performance of our health care system, physicians need to accept more responsibility for its failings and become more involved with population health issues. But that is a major departure from Hippocratic medicine. How can the physician's ethical commitment to the individual patient be reconciled with population-health's utilitarian ethic of the greatest good for the greatest number? This will be a difficult challenge for medicine, since it calls for a definition of the population. Most physicians see populations in terms of their own practices or communities, skewed as they usually are by such factors as income and insurance coverage. For health care to be most effective, a system of universal coverage is an obvious requirement, which will test the profession's commitment to that goal. Dr. Christine Cassell, President of the American Board of Internal Medicine and former Dean of the Oregon Health & Sciences University School of Medicine, offers this important perspective on the subject:

> *"With universal coverage, the concept of community underlying population health goals is much more meaningful. This would be an ideal moral framework in which to construct a benefit structure that would be flexible enough to change with scientific advances and that would reflect the values of both the enrollees and the healthcare providers. The argument is both moral and practical. First, morally, we have ample evidence that being uninsured leads to worse health outcomes; therefore, goals of population health must work from this fact. Second, only universal systems allow coherent health data and geographic descriptions of populations that make epidemiological measurements accurate enough to assess which health issues should be given priority. The transition to a utilitarian ethic will be difficult enough for U.S. physicians to do, and to do well. Lack of a universal commitment to access and to a broad population base will make it much more difficult. Anything in between is simply population rhetoric, not population health."*[72]

CONCLUDING COMMENTS

This chapter has raised more questions than answers. The medical profession in the U.S. is clearly at a crossroads. Its ethical framework has fallen apart, while its social and political relevance is waning. Organized medicine for most of the last century has resisted intrusion upon its sovereignty by government or others external to the profession. In the context of that fight for independence from regulation, it is ironic that the profession has lost much of its past autonomy, and is now beholden to corporate managers in a market-based system.

Medicine can no longer deny the extent to which unbridled self-interest has eroded its professionalism. As documented in earlier chapters, these excesses are pervasive throughout the profession for all to see, involving patient care, education and research as well as academic medical centers and many of the profession's organizations. The extent of deprofessionalization makes clear that the cause extends well beyond a few "bad apples." If medicine is to restore its professionalism, the profession must accept responsibility for letting down the public trust, recommit itself to service over self-interest, and build effective mechanisms of self-regulation which can gain the public's confidence.

Whether medicine will give up its customary defensive mode and respond positively to its moral and professional challenges is an open question. Despite its long struggle to maintain its independence, the profession has lost much of its autonomy as it increasingly serves corporate interests. In a more proactive stance, medicine may recognize a larger role of government as a potential force to support the context within which it can restore its professionalism. Business as usual will not serve the profession or the public well. The profession now has a window of opportunity to expand its vision and lead toward better health care for all Americans. To do so, it must involve itself with rebuilding the capability of public health and with advocacy for real health care reform, which leads us to the last chapters.

CHAPTER 15

BUILDING A NEW PARTNERSHIP WITH PUBLIC HEALTH

"What we need is a unique partnership between public health and medicine. Medicine means treating individuals, one at a time. Public health means working with community institutions like schools and worksites to promote good health and prevent what illness we can. Physicians and other health care providers need to bring more public health into their offices by offering prescriptions to change lifestyles, cease smoking, and increase physical activity. Public health also worries about cultural competency and barriers to access to high-quality health care. These concerns need to be reflected in the offices of physicians as well. Public health informs health care and vice versa; it's a partnership. That partnership is what the universal system of the future will need in order to succeed."

Dr. David Satcher,
former U.S. Surgeon General[1]

As we saw in Chapter 4, medicine has increasingly diverged from public health over the last 90 years. Their relationship has been described today as dysfunctional separation, even as challenges to health of the public have become more diverse and threatening. As the medical profession moves to expand the goals of medicine and to recommit itself to public service, it is only reasonable to expect that it expand its focus beyond the care of individual patients to include needs of populations being served. It is therefore clear that a new partnership is urgently needed between medicine and public health if the nation is to better respond to today's threats to the health of our population.

This chapter asks two questions: (1) what are some recent initiatives which public health has undertaken as it seeks to address the new challenges of the 21st Century?; and (2) what kind of a shared vision could enable medicine and public health to work more closely together toward common goals?

SOME RECENT INITIATIVES IN PUBLIC HEALTH

An important 2005 article by public health leaders around the country called attention to serious problems of public health's infrastructure, including a critical workforce shortage which has declined by about one-half in the last 30 years, chronic underfunding, the need to upgrade professional training programs, and widespread inconsistencies in public health standards and effectiveness due to unclear division of authority among government agencies at federal, state, and local levels. This report laid out a roadmap for rebuilding and sustaining the public health infrastructure, with these priorities for action.[2]

1.　"Assure a sound financial base;

2.　update antiquated public statutes;

3.　accredit public health agencies;

4.　certify the competency of public health professionals;

5.　invest in public health research; and

6.　strengthen public health communications".[3]

With the help of federal and/or foundation funding, the Center for Disease Control and Prevention (CDC) has led the way with these recent initiatives:[4]

- Public Health Training Network for national distance learning capacity.

- National Laboratory Training Network.

- Management Academy for Public health, which has already trained more than 60 managers.

- Centers for Public Health Preparedness, established in 2000 and sponsoring 34 academic sites, including training in responses to bioterrorism.

- National Health Alert Network (HAN) created in 1999 to improve information access, training, and organizational capacity in local health departments.

- National Electronic Disease Surveillance System (NEDSS),

established in 2000 to provide support to states and large metropolitan areas for the purpose of working with HAN to better detect and manage outbreaks that affect more than one local or state jurisdiction.

• A new partnership has been launched between federal agencies, professional public health associations, and academicians to develop schematics for core competencies in bioterrorism and public health emergency preparedneses.[5]

Just as medicine has revisited its ethical framework to better address today's challenges, so too has the public health profession. Together with the Public Health Leadership Society and other professional groups, the American Public Health Association (APHA) in 2002 adopted these principles and values listed in Table 15.1 for the ethical practice of public health.[6] As observed by Dr. James Thomas, director of the Program in Public Health Ethics at the University of North Carolina's School of Public Health and a member of APHAs Ethics Forum:

> *"Public health has significant power. We need to set standards and be held accountable for how that power is used so that we earn and keep the trust of the people we serve. With this code, we are helping to establish a compass for the public health profession."*[7]

TOWARD A NEW PARTNERSHIP BETWEEN MEDICINE AND PUBLIC HEALTH

For such a new partnership to develop, medicine and public health need to embrace a shared goal and vision of how they can work together to more effectively promote health and prevent disease for both individuals and populations at large. Their skills and expertise are complimentary and interdependent. Public health brings to this partnership three critical functions which the medical model does not address (Table 15.2).[8]

A recent seven-year study of cardiovascular risk in almost 60,000 postmenopausal women provides a good illustration of the first function of public health—assessment. Levels of urban air pollution due to fine articulate matter resulting from burning of fossil fuels (gasoline, diesel fuel, and coal) were correlated with risks of dying from cardiovascular disease. It was found that each increase in fine soot levels of 10 micrograms per cubic

TABLE 15.1
Public Health Code Of Ethics

Principles of the Ethical Practice of Public Health

1. Public health should address principally the fundamental causes of disease and requirements for health, aiming to prevent adverse health outcomes.

2. Public health should achieve community health in a way that respects the rights of individuals in the community.

3. Public health policies, programs, and priorities should be developed and evaluated through processes that ensure an opportunity for input from community members.

4. Public health should advocate and work for the empowerment of disenfranchised community members, aiming to ensure that the basic resources and conditions necessary for health are accessible to all.

5. Public health should seek the information needed to implement effective policies and programs that protect and promote health.

6. Public health institutions should provide communities with the information they have that is needed for decisions on policies or programs and should obtain the community's consent for their implementation.

7. Public health institutions should act in a timely manner on the information they have within the resources and the mandate given to them by the public.

8. Public health programs and policies should incorporate a variety of approaches that anticipate and respect diverse values, beliefs, and cultures in the community.

9. Public health programs and policies should be implemented in a manner that most enhances the physical and social environment.

10. Public health institutions should protect the confidentiality of information that can bring harm to an individual or community if made public. Exceptions must be justified on the basis of the high likelihood of significant harm to the individual or others.

11. Public health institutions should ensure the professional competence of their employees.

12. Public health institutions and their employees should engage in collaborations and affiliations in ways that build the public's trust and the institution's effectiveness.

Values and Beliefs Underlying the Code

Health

1. Humans have a right to the resources necessary for health. The public health code of ethics affirms Article 25 of the Universal Declaration of Human Rights, which states in part "Everyone has the right to a standard of living adequate for the health and well-being of himself and his family..."

Public Health Code Of Ethics (continued)

Community

2. Humans are inherently social and interdependent. Humans look to each other for companionship in friendships, families, and community; and rely upon one another for safety and survival. Positive relationships among individuals and positive collaborations among institutions are signs of a healthy community. The rightful concern for the physical individuality of humans and one's right to make decisions for oneself must be balanced against the fact that each person's actions affects other people.

3. The effectiveness of institutions depends heavily on the public's trust. Factors that contribute to trust in an institution include the following actions on the part of the institution: communication; truth telling; transparency (i.e., not concealing information); accountability; reliability; and reciprocity. One critical form of reciprocity and communication is listening to as well as speaking with the community.

4. Collaboration is a key element to public health. The public health infrastructure of a society is composed of a wide variety of agencies and professional disciplines. To be effective, they must work together well. Moreover, new collaborations will be needed to rise to new public health challenges.

5. People and their physical environment are interdependent. People depend upon the resources of their natural and constructed environments for life itself. A damaged or unbalanced natural environment, and a constructed environment of poor design or in poor condition, will have an adverse effect on the health of people. Conversely, people can have a profound effect on their natural environment through consumption of resources and generation of waste.

6. Each person in a community should have an opportunity to contribute to public discourse. Contributions to discourse may occur through a direct or a representative system of government. In the process of developing and evaluating policy, it is important to discern whether all who would like to contribute to the discussion have an opportunity to do so, even though expressing a concern does not mean that it will necessarily be addressed in the final policy.

7. Identifying and promoting the fundamental requirements for health in a community are a primary concern to public health. The way in which a society is structured is reflected in the health of a community. The primary concern of public health is with these underlying structural aspects. While some important public health programs are curative in nature, the field as a while must never lose sight of underlying causes and prevention. Because fundamental social structures affect many aspects of health, addressing the fundamental causes rather than more proximal causes, is more truly preventive.

Source: Principles of the Ethical Practice of Pubic Health. Version 2.2 @2002 Public Health Leadership Society. Available on American Public Health Association's Web site http://www.apha.crg/programs/education/progeduethicalguidelines.htm. Accessed February 2, 2007.

TABLE 15.2

The Three Pillars of Public Health

Assessment

The diagnosis of community health status and needs through
epidemiology, surveillance, research, and evaluation of
information about disease, behavioral, biological, environmental,
and socioeconomic factors.

Policy Development

Planning and priority setting, based on scientific knowledge and
under the leadership of the governmental agency, for the
development of comprehensive public health policies and decision
making.

Evaluation

Assurance

The securing of universal access to a set of essential personal
and community-wide health services through delegation,
regulation, or direct public provision of services.

Reprinted with permission from: The Institute for the Future. Health and Health
Care 2010: The Forecast, the Challenge (2nd Ed). San Francisco: Jossey-Bass,
2003:168.

---

meter is associated with an increased risk of death from heart attack and
stroke of 76 percent. This study also illustrates political obstacles which often
block policy development, the second function of public health. Although
a panel of scientists voted 20-2 in 2006 to recommend lowering the current
standard of 15 micrograms to 13 to 14 micrograms per cubic meter, the
Environmental Protection Agency's (EPA) administrator has refused to adopt
this standard. About one-third of the U.S. population lives in areas above
the EPA's current legal limit, while the World Health Organization (WHO)
recommends that governments drop their long-term limits to 10 micrograms
per cubic meter.[9,10] More than two months after the 2006 mid-term elections,
the White House moved to weaken the authority of regulatory agencies by
asserting expanded review authority through political appointees over many
informal agency dictates known as guidance.[11]

The Institute of Medicine (IOM) issued two companion reports on the future of public health several years ago. Its first report, *The Future of the Public's Health in the 21st Century*, called for a broad-based ecological approach to address the multiple determinants of health ranging from individual behavior to broad social, economic, cultural, health, and environmental conditions.[12,13] Reflecting on this challenge, Dr. Steven Schroeder, general internist and past CEO of the Robert Wood Johnson Foundation, has this to say:

> *"When you look at the determinants of health and what it will take to make our country healthier, we could have an ICU on every block and still not get there. Yet most foundation and government funding is targeted at providing medical care rather than advancing the public's health in more consequential ways."*[14]

The IOM's, second report, *Who Will Keep the Public Healthy? Educating Health Professionals for the 21st Century*, again emphasized the importance of a broad ecological approach to human health and identified eight key content areas in public health education—communication, community-based participatory research, cultural competence, ethics, genomics, global health, informatics, and policy/law.[15] A 2003 study by the Association of Schools of Public Health found that 94 percent of the nation's 33 schools of public health had incorporated that approach into one or more of their activities, and encouraging progress was noted in the new curricular areas.[16] In order to address these wide-ranging needs, schools of public health are being encouraged to forge new partnerships with medical schools, nursing schools, law schools, and urban planning departments,[17] but most public health activities are still underfunded.

For a new relationship between medicine and public health to take root and flourish, both the medical and public health professions need to change. Nicole Lurie, former principal deputy to David Satcher as Surgeon General and Professor at Rand in Arlington, Virginia, calls for redesign of this relationship between medicine and public health:

> *"We cannot run an effective, efficient system without a fundamentally altered set of relationships. While many have tried to do this in the past, the truth is that the systems, in both medicine and public health haven't supported or reinforced the need for interdependency. Simply rebuilding the old system won't change that."*[18]

These are some examples of such changes in each field.

For Medicine

- Recognize the limits of the medical model and embrace the goals of population-health.

- Replace attitudes of competition and distrust toward public health with a spirit of collaboration and mutual interdependence.

- Change medical education to add new emphasis on preventive medicine and public health.

- Encourage much larger numbers of physicians to pursue graduate training in public health; physicians now make up only about 3 percent of the nation's practicing public health workforce[19]; only 23 percent of the almost 2,500 local health agencies around the country are directed by physicians, and only 8 percent of these physicians hold MPH degrees or are fellows in the American College of Preventive Medicine.[20]

- Advocate for national health policies which can assure universal coverage to preventive and necessary health care services, strengthen primary care and the public health infrastructures, and work toward greater accountability for the health care system as a whole.

For Public Health

- Revitalize and expand its state agency workforce, which presently is plagued by high retirement eligibility rates, high vacancy rates, and high annual staff turnover rates; there is a critical workforce shortage for which the largest state budget cuts in 60 years are partly responsible.[21]

- Expand and revise its multidisciplinary educational programs along the lines suggested in the recent IOM reports, including new emphasis on cross-cultural education and approaches to reduce disparities in racial/ethnic disparities in health care.[22]

- Improve communications across agencies, facilities and disciplines in the public and private sectors, and enhance the public health system's capacity to gather, process, and share information.

- Build new alliances with employers, health care organizations, and community organizations to develop and promote community health education programs and conduct research into the effectiveness of health-related interventions.[23]

- Strengthen surveillance activities, including building international networks of public health laboratories, increasing information sharing among national surveillance authorities, and joint training of public health personnel.[24]

CONCLUDING COMMENT

The current U.S. health care system performs poorly compared to most industrialized countries around the world in terms of access to health care, quality of care and indices of population health. Improving the performance of our health care system will require a far more interactive and productive partnership between medicine and public health than we now have. That relationship has deteriorated and become dysfunctional in recent decades. Building a new and effective partnership between the two fields requires redesign to cope with new threats to the health of the public, not just increased funding reallocated within the present system. Medicine and public health worked well together a century ago in advancing the country's health care. The times and needs are now different, and a new kind of partnership must be forged. Can we generate the political will to do so for the common good?

In order for a rejuvenated medicine-public health bond to be effective in improving the health of individuals and our population in this country, another overriding requirement is now necessary—reform of the health care system to assure universal access to all necessary preventive and medical care. That challenge accordingly becomes the subject of the next and last chapter of this book.

CHAPTER 16

MEDICINE'S TWIN CRISES
AS OPPORTUNITIES TO LEAD

"The test of our progress is not whether we add more to the abundance of those who have so much; it is whether we provide enough for those who have too little."

Franklin Delano Roosevelt
Second Inaugural Address (1937)

"Of all the forms of inequality, injustice in health care is the most shocking and inhumane."

Martin Luther King Jr.
Second National Convention for the Medical
Committee for Human Rights, Chicago, 1966[1]

The medical profession in the U.S. is now confronted with two serious crises—a deteriorating and unsustainable health care system and erosion of the profession's public trust, political and social relevance. The profession is engulfed in a commercialized market-based system where the quest for profits by corporate managers regularly trumps the service ethic of the profession. We have seen in earlier chapters how some members of the profession have been complicit with these changes, but for much of the profession, this has resulted in growing frustration and loss of autonomy. The bottom line question is whether medicine will take a leadership role toward addressing both crises or continue its defensive and reactionary posture. In sum, will the profession be part of the solution or part of the problem?

In this final chapter, we ask two questions: (1) what are some of the major new opportunities now arising which favor real health care reform?; and (2) how will the medical profession respond to its twin crises?

A GATHERING STORM:
NEW OPPORTUNITIES FOR REFORM

As we have seen in earlier chapters, the problems of U.S. health care, including runaway costs, decreased affordability and access, variable quality, and increasing inequities, are getting worse despite all incremental efforts to address them. The market was not designed to protect the public interest, and that realization is growing in our society. We are seeing an increasing flurry of attempted incremental "reforms," especially in state legislatures, as the system spins further out of control (Table 16.1).[2] But the refractory problems are inherent in the system itself so that the structure and financing of the system must be changed before significant reform can be achieved.

In response to the crisis in health care, there is now widespread dissatisfaction in the public toward our health care system. The general public now sees the need for radical reform. Business and labor are also becoming increasingly disenchanted with the rising costs of health care, even looking more to the government for help. As all of this pressure builds for reform, the opportunities for structural reform grow. Indeed, we are now seeing new coalitions of unlikely bedfellows forming, such as the current effort of leaders of the Business Roundtable, AARP, and the Service Employees International Union, in a joint effort to tackle the unaffordability of health care issue.[3]

While hope springs eternal among supporters of incremental reforms that costs can be contained and other system problems can be remedied, there is little evidence to support such hopes. Employer mandates have a 30 year history (in Hawaii), with universal coverage still elusive. The individual mandates being tried in many states have no mechanisms for cost containment or assurances of universal coverage. The highly publicized Massachusetts plan is already failing just out of the starting gate. The insurers have quoted costs twice the initial estimate by the state, and have been sent back to the drawing board by the Commonwealth Health Insurance Connector Board, which was charged to implement the new law.[4]

The problems of U.S. health care go back to its basic financing system. The private insurance industry cannot serve the primary function of health insurance—broad pooling of risk. Instead it competes for the "best" medical loss ratio by avoiding coverage of the sick and taking back as much of its premium revenue as possible. Several examples illustrate the point. Wellpoint's Blue Cross of California is now marketing its Tonik plans to healthy younger people with a $5,000 deductible, individual coverage only after medical underwriting, with premiums and coverage subject to change or termination on 30 days' notice. Its stated policy in its enrollment guidelines states that "We believe that the cost of covering someone whose health can

TABLE 16.1
Towards "Health Care for All" in the States

■ = Components of 2007 Proposals

○ = Recent Reforms or Initiatives

State	Cover All Kids/Major Expansion	Adult Expansion	Public/Private Program	Pay or Play/Employer Mandate	Individual Mandate	Reform Commission	Single-Payer	Insurance Market Reforms	Cost Controls	Quality Improvement
CA	■	■	■	■	■		■	■		■
CT				■			■			
IL	○		■			○	■	■	■	■
IN		■	■					■		
MA	○	○	○	○	○			○	○	○
ME		○	○	■		○	■	■	○	○
MN	■	■	○	■		■		■		
NJ						○				
NM		○	○	■		○	■			
NC	■					■		■		
OR	■		■		■	○				
PA	○	■	■	■			■	■	■	■
VT	○	○	○	○			■		○	○
WA	■		■			■		■	■	■
WI	■	○	■	■						

This selection of states that appear likely to make progress in 2007 was prepared by the **Progressive States Network** in collaboration with the **Universal Health Care Action Network.**

SOURCE: Towards "Health Care for All" in the States. *Action for Universal Health Care* 14(1): January 2007

be predicted to require costly care should not be subsidized by someone with minimal health care needs."[5] At the same time, Wellpoint reported a 23 percent increase in fourth-quarter 2006 net income, and assured investors that its premium pricing would continue to outpace costs.[6] Health insurance premiums alone are becoming increasingly unaffordable (for less coverage) as dramatically shown in Figure 16.1 between 2000 and 2006 and in Figure 16.2 from 1996 to 2025. And of course, the cost of health insurance may be much less than the total costs of health care which individuals and their families face.

The crux of the problem of uncontrolled cost increases in health care is not overutilization of care through imprudent choices by patients, as supporters of consumer-directed health care believe. Instead, the unaffordability of health care is leading to underutilization of necessary care as a growing problem. As discussed in earlier chapters, there are many forces driving up health care costs much faster than cost of living and household incomes, including widespread waste throughout the system, the impact of advancing medical technology, escalating prices in a deregulated system, and a substantial amount of unnecessary care in areas of excess capacity. These forces are untouched by incremental reforms which leave the status quo in place.

Princeton's Paul Krugman reminds us that the country is as polarized in the economy and electorate today as in the 1930s, and that bipartisanship in the political middle ground is unlikely to be adequate to resolve our big problems. He notes that Franklin D. Roosevelt faced fierce opposition from many quarters as he advanced and passed Social Security, unemployment insurance, and more progressive taxation to address the nation's wide gap in equality. As F.D.R. acknowledged in 1936: "We had to struggle with the old enemies of peace—business and financial monopoly, speculation, reckless banking, class antagonism, sectionalism, war profiteering. Never before in all our history have these forces been so united against one candidate as they stand today. They are unanimous in their hate for me—and I welcome their hatred."[7] We can expect the increasing inequities in access to even basic health care services to fuel a strong and polarized pressure for real reform.

FIGURE 16.1

Cumulative Changes in Health Insurance Premiums, Overall Inflation, and Workers' Earnings 2000-2006

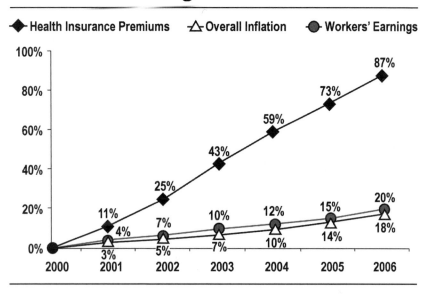

Note: Data on premium increases reflect the cost of health insurance premiums for a family of four. Source: KFF/HRET Survey of Employer-Sponsored Health Benefits, 2001-2006; Bureau of Labor Statistics, Consumer Price Index, U.S. City Average of Annual Inflation (April to April), 2001-2006; Bureau of Labor Statistics, Seasonally Adjusted Data from the Current Employment Statistics Survey (April to April), 2001-2006. This information was reprinted with permission from the Henry J. Kaiser Family Foundation. The Kaiser Family Foundation, based in Menlo Park, California, is a non-profit, private operating foundation focusing on the major health care issues facing the nation and is not associated with Kaiser Permanente or Kaiser Industries.

HOW WILL THE MEDICAL PROFESSION RESPOND TO ITS TWIN CRISES?

In view of the combined energy of the political and market forces described in this book, it may seem unrealistic to think that the medical profession could have been a significant force counteracting our growing health care system problems. Indeed, there have been some strong efforts by a number of organizations in the profession to uphold the professional service ethic and resist commercialization of the marketplace, notably Physicians for Social Responsibility (PSR), Physicians for a National Health

FIGURE 16.2

Annual Health Insurance Premiums And Household Income, 1996-2025

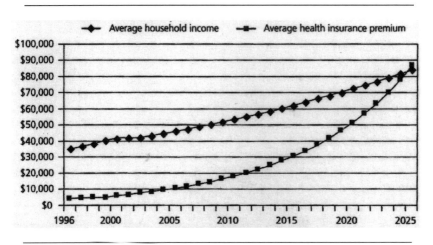

SOURCE: Reprinted with permission from Graham Center One-Pager. *Who will have health insurance in 2025? Am Fam Physician 72(10):1989, 2005*

Program (PNHP), the National Medical Association (NMA), the American Medical Women's Association (AMWA), the American Medical Students Association (AMSA), the American Public Health Association (APHA), the Society for Health and Human Values, the Health Research Group of Public Citizen, and others. But the track record of organized medicine as a whole has not been impressive.

The AMA has consistently opposed any kind of universal coverage in this country since 1917, usually supporting instead such approaches as tax credits or other strategies that will never achieve such coverage. In the intense political debate in the 1960s over Medicare and Medicaid, the AMA strongly opposed both programs.[8] It saw Medicare as "socialized medicine" and saw it as a dangerous first step toward national health insurance. Instead, the AMA proposed Eldercare as a state administered program which would subsidize low-income seniors to buy private health insurance (despite the reality that the private insurance market had already failed the elderly.[9] When the passage of Medicare became inevitable, the AMA shifted gears and lobbied hard for a liberal reimbursement system while voicing serious concerns about a national fee schedule, again viewed as a step toward "socialized medicine."[10] Today, some 40 years later, according to its own Web site, the AMA 'continues to press for adoption of a consumer-driven market-based plan and to expand coverage through tax credits and insurance market reforms."[11]

Incremental efforts to reform the system have failed for more than 30 years. This country is an outlier among all industrialized countries in not having universal coverage through some form of social health insurance. The currently most popular approach toward universal coverage—individual mandate, with CDHC, HSAs, and the private insurance industry marketing plans with higher deductibles and less coverage—offers no solution to access and cost problems. Instead, we are heading for an expansion of ever more inadequate insurance while health care costs go through the roof. The predictable result—growing numbers of uninsured and underinsured people, with health care unaffordable for much of the population.

At this crossroads, American medicine also faces a moral crisis. At its core, does it follow its traditional professional service ethic, conducting itself in the best interests of patients and communities under whatever system it finds itself, or does it turn away from system problems while pursuing its own self-interest?

More than 100 years ago, the AMA provided strong leadership uniting the profession by a common commitment to reform of medical education and reaffirmation of the ethical nature of medical practice. Those efforts welded American medicine together as a profession standing for more than its self-interest.[12] Today, the situation is quite different. The profession has been fragmented into many dozens of specialties and subspecialties, and the AMAs membership has fallen to 232,000, less than 30 percent of the nation's 800,000 plus physicians. Each specialty and subspecialty group has its own political agenda, and there is no longer a unified voice representing the profession. More than that, many have come to view medical organizations as self-interest groups, and their role in shaping health policy has been marginalized as corporate and business interests have come to dominate health care politics.

Medicine has much to offer at this critical juncture in U.S. health care. What other profession is so well placed with the necessary expertise to help answer such pressing questions as to what health care services are necessary and cost-effective and which new technologies should be broadly introduced into everyday health care? Organized medicine has the capacity to make a difference, as illustrated by its strong leadership role in reforming medical education a century ago. The problems today are quite different, but no less demanding. Medicine can regain its moral legacy and credibility by advocating strongly for lasting health care reform, with universal coverage of all necessary health care regardless of income, ethnic group or class.

Drs. Gilbert Welch and Elliott Fisher, who have contributed so much excellent health services research over the years from their base at Dartmouth Medical School, pointed out in 1992 that, although there is no one negotiating table, negotiations between American physicians and society are already well underway. Indeed, organized medicine has had a marginal role in that renegotiation, which is being played out between insurers, employers, government, and others external to the profession. Welch and Fisher reminded us then that as a medical profession our power is not the power to walk away. It is the power derived from our willingness, capacity, and creativity to design solutions to the problems facing society and physicians."[13] Those words are even more important today as the time window narrows for medicine to make a positive difference in health care reform.

It is still an open question whether and how organized medicine will respond to its twin crises. Except for a few progressive professional organizations, its track record in recent decades does not give much reason for optimism. It does no good to posture advocacy for health care reform by calling for ineffective and already discredited approaches, such as individual mandates, tax credits and expansion of public programs already being cut back amidst a sea of red ink. But there are now new opportunities for medicine to lead. As the current market-based system falls apart, physicians see every day the harms and pain being incurred by their patients as they try to navigate an increasingly impersonal and costly system. More than ever before, patients and their families need physicians to be their advocates, not just their care-givers.

The time is overdue for the profession to reassert its professional and moral influence by rededicating itself to service over self-interest. This will require a major change of direction, but by doing so the profession can reclaim its moral legacy which has persevered through the centuries from one society to another. The stakes are high for the profession, the public, and the country. Rosemary Stevens, regarded by many as the country's leading historian of American medicine, leaves us with this challenge and still unanswered question:

> *"At this time of uncertainty and lack of clear direction, the professional organizations of medicine take on enlarged importance. For if not the profession, nor the federal government, who will act us national conscience or mobilizer for tomorrow's medicine?—the American medical profession rose to eminence in the twentieth century through effective national organizations (notably the American Medical Association, the American College of Surgeons, and the specialty certifying boards). In today's very different environment, will national leadership prove powerful again?"*[14]

Appendix

Suggested Reading and Other Resources

Articles

On Professionalism

1. Pellegrino E.D. The commodification of medical and health care: the moral consequences of a paradigm shift from a professional to a market ethic. *J Med Philos* 24(3):243-66, 1999.
2. Cruess R., Cruess S., & Johnston S. Renewing professionalism: an opportunity for medicine. *Acad Med* 74:878-84, 1999.
3. Pellegrino E.D., & Relman A.S. Professional and medical associations: ethical and practical guidelines. JAMA 282(10):985, 1999.
4. Pellegrino E.D. Medical professionalism: can it, should it survive? *J Am Board Fam Pract* 13:147-9, 2000.
5. Angell M. Academic medical centers and conflicts of interest. JAMA 295(24):2848, 2006.

On the Health Care System

1. Relman A.S. The new medical-industrial complex. *N Engl J Med* 303:963-70, 1980.
2. Morgan R. O., Virnig B.A., DeVito C.A. & Persily N.A. The Medicare-HMO revolving door—the healthy go in and the sick go out. *N Engl J Med* 337(3):169-75,1997.
3. Woolhandler S., & Himmelstein D. U. When money is the mission—the high costs of investor-owned care. *N Engl J Med* 341:444-6, 1999.
4. Kuttner R. Must good HMOs go bad? First of two parts: the commercialism of prepaid group health care. *N Engl J Med* 338:1558-63, 1998.
5. Himmelstein D.U., Woolhandler S., Hellander I., & Wolfe S.M. Quality of care in investor-owned versus not-for-profit HMOs. *JAMA* 282:159-63, 1999.
6. Silverman C.E., Skinner J.S., & Fisher E.S. The association between for-profit hospital ownership and increased Medicare spending. *N Engl J Med* 341(6):444-6, 1999.
7. Ferrer R. L. A piece of my mind: within the system of no-system. *JAMA* 286:2513-4, 2001.
8. Harrington C., Woolhandler S., Mullan J., Carrillo H., & Himmelstein. D. U. Does investor ownership of nursing homes compromise quality of care? *Am J Public Health* 91 (9):1452-5, 2001.

9. Devereaux P.J., Schuneman H.J., Ravindran N., Bhandari M., & Garg A.X., et al. Comparison of mortality between private for-profit and private not-for-profit hemodialysis centers: A systematic review and meta-analysis. *JAMA* 288:2449-57, 2002.

10. Katz S, et al. Phantoms in the snow: Canadians' use of health care services in the United States. *Health Aff* (Millwood) 21(3): May/June 2002.

11. Geyman J. P. The corporate transformation of medicine and its impact on costs and access to care. *J Am Board Fam Pract* 16(5):443-54, 2003.

12. Woolhandler S., Campbell T., & Himmelstein D. U. Costs of health care administration in the United States and Canada. *N Engl J Med* 349:768-75, 2003.

13. Himmelstein D. U., Woolhandler S., & Wolk S. M. The cost (of Health Care Administration) to the Nation, the States and the District of Columbia, with state-specific estimates of potential savings. Public Citizen, The Health Research Group, August 20, 2003.

14. Nichols L.M., Ginsburg P.B., Berseson R.A., Christianson J. & Hurley R.C. Are market forces strong enough to deliver efficient health care systems? Confidence is waning. *Health Aff* (Millwood) 23(2):3-21, 2004.

15. Himmelstein D. U. Warren E., Thorne D. & Woolhandler S. Illness and injury as contributors to bankruptcy. *Health Affairs Web Exclusive.* W5-63, 2005.

16. Lesser K.E., Himmelstein D. U., & Woolhandler S. Access to care, health status, and health disparities in the United States and Canada: Results of a cross-national population-based survey. *Am J Public Health* 96(7):1300-7, 2006.

On Health Insurance

1. Bodenheimer T. Underinsurance in America. *N Engl J Med* 327(4):174-8, 1992.

2. Carrasquillo, O, Himmelstein D.U., Woolhandler S. & Bor D.H. A reappraisal of private employers' role in providing health insurance. *N Engl J Med* 340(2):109-114, 1999.

3. Kuttner R. The American health care system—employer-sponsored health coverage. *N Engl J Med* 340:248-52, 1999.

4. Bell H. Life without insurance: true stories of unnecessary illness, death and humiliation. *The New Physician* (AMSA). September 2000.

5. Grumbach K. Insuring the uninsured. Time to end the aura of invisibility. *JAMA* 284(16):2114-6, 2000.

6. Miller J.E. *A Perfect Storm: The Confluence of Forces Affecting Health Care Coverage.* National Coalition on Health Care. November 2001.

7. Fuchs R. What's ahead for health insurance in the United States. *N Engl J Med* 346(23):1822-24, 2002.

8. The Unraveling of Health Insurance. *Consumer Reports*, (July 2002):48-53.
9. Woolhandler S., & Himmelstein D. U. Paying for National Health Insurance—and Not Getting It. *Health Aff* (Millwood) July/August 2002.
10. Priselac T. M. The erosion of health insurance: The unintended consequences of tiered products by health plans. *Health Affairs Web Exclusive*, W3-158-61, March 19, 2003.
11. Geyman J. P. Myths and memes about single-payer health insurance in the United States: A rebuttal to conservative claims. *Int J Health Services* 35(1):63-90, 2005.

On Health Care Reform

1. Himmelstein D.U. & Woolhandler S. A national health program for the United States: A physician's proposal. *N Engl J Med* 320:102-8, 1989.
2. Grumbach K. & Bodenheimer T. Reins or fences: a physician's view of cost containment. *Health Aff* (Millwood) 9(4):120-6, 1990.
3. Navarro V. Why Congress did not enact health care reform. *J Health Polit Policy Law* 20:455-62, 1995.
4. Simon S.R., Pan R.J., Sullivan A.M., et al. Views on managed care—a survey of medical students, residents, faculty, and deans at medical schools in the United States. *N Engl J Med* 340:928-36, 1999.
5. Himmelstein D. U. & Woolhandler S. National health insurance. Liberal benefits, conservative spending. *Arch Intern Med* 162:973-5, 2002.
6. Himmelstein D. U. & Woolhandler S. National health insurance or incremental reform: aim high or at our feet? *Am J Public Health* 93(1):31-4, 2003.
7. Proposal of the Physicians Working Group for single-payer national health insurance. *JAMA* 290:798-305, 2003.
8. Oberlander J. *The Politics of Health Reform: Why Do Bad Things Happen to Good Plans? Health Affairs* Web Exclusive, W3-391, 2003.
9. Families USA. HSAs: Missing the target. Report from Families USA. Washington, D.C., December 2005.
10. Geyman J. P. Moral hazard and consumer-driven health care: A fundamentally flawed concept. *Int J Health Services* 37(2):2007 (in press).

Books

1. Rodwin M.A. *Medicine, Money & Morals: Physicians' Conflicts of Interest.* New York: Oxford University Press, 1993.
2. Eddy D.M. *Clinical Decision Making from Theory to Practice :A Collection of Essays from the Journal of the American Medical Association.* Boston: Jones & Bartlett Publishers, 1996.
3. Kuttner R. *Everything for Sale: The Virtues & Limits of Markets.* Chicago: University of Chicago Press, 1999.
4. Nyman J.A. *The Theory of Demand for Health Insurance.* Stanford, Calif:

Stanford University Press, 2003.

5.   Warren E. & Tyagi A. W. *The Two-Income Trap. Why Middle-Class Mothers and Fathers Are Going Broke.* New York: Basic Books, 50-7, 2003.

6.   Bodenheimer T.S. & Grumbach K. *Understanding Health Policy: A Clinical Approach.* New York: Lange Medical Books/McGraw-Hill, 2004.

7.   Geyman J.P. *The Corporate Transformation of Health Care: Can the Public Interest Still Be Served?* New York: Springer Publishing Company, 2004.

8.   Kassirer J.P. *On the Take: How America's Complicity With Big Business Can Endanger Your Health.* New York: Oxford University Press, 2005.

9.   Deyo R.A. & Patrick D.L. *Hope or Hype: The Obsession with Medical Advances and the High Cost of False Promises.* New York: American Management Association, 2005, p 265.

10. Geyman J.P. *Shredding the Social Contract: The Privatization of Medicare.* Monroe, ME: Common Courage Press, 2006.

Newsletters

1.   PNHP (Physicians for a National Health Program) quarterly newsletter, 20 E. Madison, Suite 602, Chicago, IL 60602.

2.   Health Letter. Public Citizen Health Research Group, 1600 20th Street, NW, Washington, DC 20009 (www.citizen.org/hrg).

1.   Quote of Day. (QoD). Available daily from Don McCanne, MD, retired family physician in Orange County, Calif, and past president, Physicians for a National Health Program (don@mccanne.org).

2.   www.pnhp.org. The newly revised PNHP web site contains a bibliography with many full articles on-line, a section for PNHP press releases and other breaking news ("news and updates"), and links to many state-based campaigns for single payer health care reform.

3.   www.everybodyinnobodyout.org. This web site has information about many state efforts for non-incremental health care reform.

4.   www.kff.org. Kaiser Family Foundation web site.

5.   www.cmwf.org. The Commonwealth Fund web site.

6.   www.consumersunion.org. Detailed analyses of national legislation and trends such as the new Medicare Drug Bill, "consumer-directed" health initiatives, etc.

7.   www.oecd.org. Information on international health systems.

8.   www.healthcarecommission.ca. Final report of the Romanow Commission on Canada.

9.   www.charf.ca. Mythbusters. A series of essays giving the research evidence behind Canadian healthcare debates.

References

Preface

1. Brennan TA. Physicians' professional responsibility to improve the quality of care. *Acad Med* 2002; 77(10):973-80.
2. Rodwin MA. *Medicine, Money & Morals: Physicians' Conflicts of Interest.* New York: Oxford University Press, 1993.
3. Annas GJ. *Some Choice: Law, Medicine, and the Market.* New York: Oxford University Press, 1998.
4. Angell M. *The Truth about the Drug Companies: How They Deceive us and What We Can Do About It.* New York: Random House, 2004.
5. Abramson J. *Overdo$ed America: The Broken Promise of American Medicine.* New York: Harper Collins, 2004.
6. Kassirer JP. *On the Take: How America's Complicity With Big Business Can Endanger Your Health.* New York: Oxford University Press, 2005.
7. Andereck W. Concluding remarks at Symposium on Commercialism in Medicine. California Pacific Medical Center, September 2005.
8. Geyman JP. *Health Care in America: Can Our Ailing System Be Healed?* Woburn, Mass: Butterworth-Heinemann, 2002.
9. Geyman JP. *The Corporate Transformation of Health Care: Can the Public Interest Still Be Served?* New York: Springer Publishing Company, 2004.
10. Geyman JP. *Falling Through the Safety Net: Americans Without Health Insurance.* Monroe, ME: Common Courage Press, 2005.
11. Geyman JP. *Shredding the Social Contract: The Privatization of Medicare.* Monroe, ME: Common Courage Press, 2006.

Chapter 1: Medicine as a Moral Enterprise

1. Pellegrino E.D. The medical profession as a moral community. Bulletin. Bull N Y *Acad Med* 66(3): 222, 1990.
2. Ibid. #1, 226-8.
3. Pellegrino E.D. & Thomasma D.T. *For the Patient's Good: The Restoration of Beneficence in Health Care.* New York: Oxford University Press, 1987.
4. Comfort A. *The Listener*, November 29, 1951.
5. Pellegrino E.D. The Hippocratic Oath and clinical ethics. *J Clin Ethics* 1 (4): 290-1, 1990.
6. Edelstein L. The professional ethics of the Greek physician. In: *Ancient Medicine: Selected Papers of Ludwig Edelstein*, edited by O. Temkin & C.L. Temkin. Baltimore: Johns Hopkins Press, 1967.
7. Galen, as quoted in Faria M.A. Transformation of medical ethics through time (Part II): Medical ethics and organized medicine. *Medical Sentinel* March/April 1998.
8. Osler W. On the Educational Value of the Medical Society. In: *Aequanimitas, With other Addresses to Medical Students, Nurses, and Practitioners of*

   Medicine. 3rd ed. Philadelphia: P. Blakiston's Son & Co., 1932, p 333.

9.   Ibid. # 8, Chauvinism in Medicine, p 268.

10. Stevens R. *Medical Practice in Modern England: The Impact of Specialization and State Medicine.* New Haven, London: Yale University Press, 1966: 13-8.

11. Ibid. #5.

12. Yanofsky C.S. A catalogue of physicians' oaths. www.pneuro.com/publication/oaths/ Accessed January 17, 2006.

13. Edelstein L. The Hippocratic Oath: text, translation and interpretation. In: Temkin O, Temkin CL, eds. *Ancient Medicine: Selected Papers of Ludwig Edelstein.* Baltimore: Johns Hopkins University Press, 1967: 3-64.

14. Pellegrino E.D. Toward a reconstruction of medical morality: the primacy of the act of profession and the fact of illness. *J Med Phil* 4:32-56, 1979.

15. Market H. "I swear by Apollo"—On taking the Hippocratic Oath. *N Engl J Med* 350(20): 2026-8, 2004.

16. Orr R.D., Pang N., Pellegrino E.D., & Siegler M. Use of the Hippocratic Oath: a review of twentieth century practice and a content analysis of oaths administered in medical schools in the U.S. and Canada in 1933. J Clin Ethics 8:377-88, 1993.

17. Brody H. Personal communication, August 6, 2006.

18. Jonsen A.R. *A Short History of Medical Ethics.* New York: Oxford University Press, 2000.

19. Ibid #18, pp 54-5.

20. Ibid #18, pp 115-20.

21. Jonsen A.R. Watching the doctor. *N Engl J Med* 308:1531-35, 1983.

22. McCullough L.B.The physician's virtues and legitimate self-interest in the patient-physician contract. *Mt Sinai J Med* 60(1): 11-14, 1998.

23. Schiedermayer D, McCarty D.J. Altruism, professional decorum, and greed: Perspectives on physician compensation. *Perspect Biol Med* 38(2): 238-53, 1995.

24. Asnes R.S. Physicians' fees: 1856 – 2056. *N Engl J Med* 290:751-2, 1974.

25. Blanton W.B. *Medicine in Virginia in the Seventeenth Century.* New York: Arno Press, 1971, 235-49.

26. Klein R.S. Medical expenses and the poor in Virginia: Roger and Ann May indentured to John Stringer. *J Hist Med Allied Sci* 30:260-7, 1975.

27. Churchill L.R. Commercialism and professionalism in American medicine. Presented at Symposium on Commercialism in Medicine. Program in Medicine & Human Values. California Pacific Medical Center, San Francisco: September 2005. *Cambridge Quarterly of Health Care,* spring 2007.

28. Rodwin M.A. *Medicine, Money & Morals: Physicians' Conflicts of Interest.*

New York: Oxford University Press, 1993: 56.

29. Andereck W. Where does the money come from? Presented at Symposium on Commercialism in Medicine. Program in Medicine & Human Values. California Pacific Medical Center. San Francisco: September 2005. *Cambridge Quarterly of Health Care*, spring 2007.

30. Jonscn A. Opening remarks. Symposium on Commercialism in Medicine. Program in Medicine & Human Values. California Pacific Medical Center, San Francisco: September 2005. *Cambridge Quarterly of Health Care*, spring 2007.

31. Ibid #1, p 221.

32. Engelhard H.T. & Rie M.A. Morality for the medical-industrial complex: a code of ethics for the mass marketing of health care. *N Engl J Med* 319: 1086, 1989.

33. Pellegrino E.D. & Thomasma D.T. *For the Patient's Good: The Restoration of Beneficence in Health Care*. New York: Oxford University Press, 1987.

Chapter 2: The Rise of the Medical Industrial Complex

1. Starr P. *The Social Transformation of American Medicine: The Rise of a Sovereign Profession and the Making of a Vast Industry*. New York: Basic Books, p 448, 1982.

2. Relman A.S. The new medical-industrial complex. *N Engl J Med* 303:963-70, 1980.

3. Gray B.H. (Ed). The new health care for profit: Doctors and hospitals in a competitive environment. Washington, DC: Institute of Medicine. National Academy Press, 1983, 13.

4. Commerce Department—www.census.gov/press-release/www.1999/cb99-178.html and Interstudy.

5. Ibid. #2.

6. Lindorff D. *Marketplace Medicine: The Rise of the For-Profit Hospital Chains*. New York: Bantam Books, 1992:22.

7. U.S. Dept. of Commerce, Bureau of Economic Analysis. The National Income and Product Accounts of the United States, 1929-82: Statistical Tables, September 1986, Table 6.21B. 1990 figures from *Survey of Current Business*, August 1993, Table 6.19C.

8. The global giants: amid market pain, U.S. companies hold greater sway. *Wall Street Journal*, October 14, 2002:R10.

9. Wallach L. & Sforza M. World Trade Organization? Corporate Globalization and the Erosion of Democracy. Washington, D.C., *Public Citizen*, 1999.

10. Waitzkin H. The strange career of managed competition: Military failure to medical success? *J Am Public Health Assoc* 84:482-89, 1994.

11. Thompson T. The impact of the new WTO policies on the Canadian national

health system. PhD thesis, Johns Hopkins University, 2003.

12. Korten D.C. *When Corporations Rule the World*. San Francisco: Berrett-Koehler Publishers, 2001:68:71.

13. Finnegan W. *The Economics of Empire*. Harper's Magazine; May 2003, Vol. 306 (1836), pp 41-60.

14. Robinson J.C. *The Corporate Practice of Medicine: Competition and Innovation in Health Care*. Berkeley, University of California Press, 1999, pp. 1-2.

15. VHA Inc. *Environment assessment: Setting foundations for the millennium*. Irving, Tex, 1998.

16. Gray B.H. (Ed). *For-profit enterprise in health care: Supplementary statement on for-profit enterprise in health care*. Washington, DC: Institute of Medicine, National Academy Press, 1986.

17. Physicians for a National Health Program (PNHP), Chicago, 2002; based on Schram, Blue Cross Conversion, Abell Foundation and CMS.

18. PNHP slide set, 2005, based on Graef Crystal source, October 8, 2004.

19. Hot Topic. Are CEOs worth their weight in gold? *Wall Street Journal*, January 21-22, 2006:A7.

20. Phillips K. Wealth and Democracy. Rich-poor gap, corruption are harbingers of economic decline. *Public Citizen News*. November/December 2002:22(6). 7.

21. Bandler J. & Forelle C. Bad options. How giant insurer decided to oust hugely successful CEO. *New York Times*, December 7, 2006: A1.

22. Maremint M. & Forelle C. Open spigot: Bosses pay. How stock options become part of the problem. *Wall Street Journal*, December 27, 2006: A1.

23. Vaillancourt Rosenau P. & Linder S.H. Two decades of research comparing for-profit and nonprofit health provider performance in the United States. *Social Science Quarterly* 84(2): 219-41, 2003.

24. Vaillancourt Rosenau P. & Linder S.H. A comparison of the performance of for-profit and nonprofit U.S. psychiatric inpatient care providers since 1980. *Psychiatric Services* 54(2):183-7, 2003.

25. Ginsberg C. The patient as profit center: Hospital, Inc. comes to town. *The Nation*, November 18, 1996, 18-22.

26. Benda D. Surgery charges high at RMC. Hospital ranked fifth in U.S. for operating room markups. Redding, Calif: *Record Searchlight*, May 17, 2003.

27. Legnado L. California hospitals open books, showing huge price differences. *Wall Street Journal*, December 27, 2004.

28. Phillips K. Wealth and Democracy. Rich-poor gap, corruption are harbingers of economic decline. *Public Citizen News*. November/December 2002:22(6)77.

29. 1995 GAO study commissioned by Senator Byron Dorgan (D-North

Dakota).

30. Ibid #25 pp 18 and 22.

31. Kuttner R. Columbia/HCA and the resurgence of the for-profit hospital business (second of two parts). *N Engl J Med* 335(6):450-1, 1996.

32. Apple R.D. The medicalization of infant feeding in the United States and New Zealand: Two countries, one experience. *J Hum Lact* 10(1): 31-37, 1994.

33. Manning M. Anti-aging becomes big business. Doctors open medical spas around the country. *Tampa Bay Business Journal*, December 8, 2006: 33.

34. Jensen M.C., Brant-Zawadzki M.N., Obuchowski N., et al. Magnetic resonance imaging of the lumbar spine in people without back pain. *N Engl J Med* 331:69-73, 1994.

35. Kornick J., Trefelner E., McCarthy S, et al. Meniscal abnormalities in the asymptomatic population at MR imaging. *Radiology* 177:463-65, 1990.

36. Schwartz L. M. & Wolosin S. Changing disease definitions: Implications for disease prevalence. Analysis of the Third National Health and Nutrition Examination Survey. *Eff Clin Pract* 2(2):76-35, 1999.

37. Moynihan R. The making of a disease: Female sexual dysfunction. BMJ 326:45, 2003.

38. Higginson G. Political considerations for changing medical screening programs. JAMA 282: 1472-74, 1999.

39. DiGuiseppi C., Atkins D. & Woolf S.H. (eds). *US Preventive Services Task Force Guide to Clinical Preventive Services* (2nd ed). Alexandria, Va: International Medical Publishing, 1996:525.

40. Weisbrod B.A. The nature of technological change: Incentives matter! In: Committee on Technological Innovation in Medicine, Institute of Medicine, Gilijns A.C. & Dawkins H.V. (eds). *Adopting new medical technology: Medical innovation at the crossroads*. Vol. 4 Washington, D.C., National Academy Press, 1994:10.

41. Goldsmith J. Technology and the boundaries of the hospital: Three emerging technologies. *Health Aff* (Millwood) 23(6): 149-56, 2004.

42. U.S. Food and Drug Administration. CDER 2002 *Report to the Nation: Improving Public Health through Human Drugs*. (Washington: FDA 13 May 2003); and FDA, Office of Device Evaluation Annual Report, Fiscal Year 2002. Washington: FDA, 4 December 2002.

43. Thomas L. *The lives of a cell: Notes of a biology watcher*. New York: Bantam Books, 1975.

44. Armstrong D. & Zimmerman A. Drug makers find new way to push pills. *The Wall Street Journal*, June 14, 2002, p B1.

45. Schneiderman, L. The media and the medical market. *Cambridge Quarterly of Health Care*. Spring, 2007

46. Heath I. Promotion of disease and corrosion of medicine. *Can Fam Physician*: 51: 1320-2, October 2005.
47. Cook-Deegan R. M. The physician and technological change. In: *The Physician as Captain of the Ship: A Critical Reappraisal*, King M.P., LR. Churchill & A.W. Cross (eds)., Dordrecht: Reidel, 1988,. 127.
48. Morreim E. H. *Balancing Act: The New Medical Ethics of Medicine's New Economics*. Washington, D.C.: Georgetown University Press, 1995, p 139.
49. Friedson E. L. Professionalism and institutional ethics. In: Baker R.B., Caplan A.L., Emanuel L.L. & Latham, S.R. (eds). *The American Medical Ethics Revolution*. Baltimore: Johns Hopkins University Press, 1999:130-1.
50. Churchill, L.R. Hegemony of money: Commercialism and professionalism in American medicine. *Cambridge Quarterly of Health Care,* Spring, 2007
51. Chicago Tribune, 2005. See http://www.chicagotribune.com/business/chi-0506170079jun17, 1, 2880993. Story? coll = chi-business-hed.
52. Stevens R. A. Public roles for the medical profession in the United States: Beyond theories of decline and fall. *The Milbank Quarterly,* 79 (3):327, 2001.

Chapter 3: Medicine and Markets

1. Annas GL. *Some Choice: Law, Medicine and the Market*. New York: Oxford University Press, 1998, p 46; also citing Relman A.S. Shattack Lecture: The Health Care Industry: Where is it Taking Us? N Engl J Med 325:854-9, 1991; Relman A.S. What Market Values Are Doing to Medicine? *Atlantic Monthly*, March 1992, 999-106.
2. National Center for Policy Analysis. www.Ncpa.org/abo/. Accessed June 28, 2004.
3. Goodman J.C. & Herrick D.M. *Twenty Myths about Single-Payer Health Insurance: International Evidence on the Effects of National Health Insurance in Countries around the World*. National Center for Policy Analysis, Dallas, 2002.
4. Geyman J. P. Myths and memes about single-payer health insurance in the United States: A rebuttal to conservative claims. *Int J Health Serv* 35(1):63-90, 2005.
5. Cogan J.F., Hubbard R.G. & Kessler D.P. Keep government out. *Wall Street Journal* January 13, 2006: A12.
6. Pauly M.V. The economics of moral hazard: Comment. *Am Econ Review* 58, no. 3, 1968.
7. Nyman J.A. *The Theory of Demand for Health Insurance*. Stanford, Calif: Stanford University Press, 2003.
8. Churchill, L.R., Hegemony of money: Commercialism and professionalism

in American medicine. *Cambridge Quarterly of Health Care*, Spring, 2007.

9. Thorpe K.E. Health care cost containment: reflections and future directions. In: Kovner A.R. & Jones S. (eds). *Health Care Delivery in the United States.* New York: Springer Publishing Company, 1999; 439-73.

10. Hart J. T. Health care or health trade? A historic moment of choice. *Int J Health Serv* 34(2).245-54, 2004.

11. Glasser R. J. The doctor is not in: On the managed failure of managed medical care. *Harper's Magazine*, March 1998, pp 35-41.

12. Hart J.T. The Inverse Care Law. *Lancet* 1:405-12, 1971.

13. Physicians for a National Health Program (PNHP). Chicago, Ill: Available at www.pnhp.org, 2002.

14. Schafer A. It's all about values. Centre for Professional and Applied Ethics. University of Manitoba. Ethics Centre. Website, September 19, 2002.

15. Kronick R., Goodman D.C., Weinberg J. & Wagner E. The marketplace in health care reform. The demographic limitations of managed competition. *N Engl J Med* 328:148, 1993.

16. Stein L. Pulling the plug. *Metro.* Silicon's Valley's weekly newspaper, September 20, 2002.

17. Geyman J.P. The corporate transformation of medicine and its impact on costs and access to care. *J Am Board Fam Pract* 16(5):449, 2003.

18. Chen J, et al. Do "America's Best Hospitals" perform better for acute myocardial infarction? *N Engl J Med* 340:286, 1999.

19. Hartz A. J., et al. Hospital characteristics and mortality rates. *N Engl J Med* 321: 1720, 1989.

20. Kover C. & Gergen P. J. Nurse staffing levels and adverse events following surgery in U.S. hospitals. *Image J Nurs Scholarship* 30:315, 1998.

21. Silverman E. M., et al. The association between for-profit hospital ownership and increased Medicare spending. *N Engl J Med* 341:420, 1999.

22. Woolhandler S. & Himmelstein D. U. Costs of care and administration at for-profit and other hospitals in the United States. *N Engl J Med* 36:769, 1997.

23. Yuan Z. The association between hospital type and mortality and length of stay: A study of 16.9 million hospitalized Medicare beneficiaries. *Med Care* 38:231, 2000.

24. Himmelstein D. U., et al. Quality of care in investor-owned vs not-for-profit HMOs. *JAMA* 282:159, 1999.

25. HMO honor roll. *U.S. News & World Report* October 23, 1997, p 62.

26. Kuttner R. The American health care system: Wall Street and health care. *N Engl J Med* 340:664, 1999.

27. Devereaux P.J., et al. Comparison of mortality between private for-profit and private not-for-profit hemodialysis centers: A systematic review and meta-

analysis. *JAMA* 288:2449, 2002.

28. Garg R.P., et al. Effect of the ownership of dialysis facilities on patients' survival and referral for transplantation. *N Engl J Med* 341:1653, 1999.

29. Harrington C., et al. Does investor-ownership of nursing homes compromise the quality of care? *Am J Public Health* 91(9):1, 2001.

30. Wrich J. *Brief Summary of Audit Findings of Managed Behavioral Health Services*. Chicago: J. Wrich & Associates, 1998.

31. Munoz R. How health care insurers avoid treating mental illness. *San Diego Union Tribune*, May 22, 2002.

32. Nichols L.M., et al. Are market forces strong enough to deliver efficient health care systems? Confidence is waning. *Health Aff* (Millwood) 23(2):8-21, 2004.

33. Achman L. & Gold M. *New Analysis Describes 2004 Payment Increases to Medicare Advantage Plans*. Mathematica Policy Research, Washington, D.C., April 2004.

34. Biles B., Nicholas L.H., Cooper B.S., Adrion E., & Gaterman S. The cost of privatization: Extra payments to Medicare Advantage plans, updated and revised. Issue Brief. *The Commonwealth Fund*, November 2006.

35. MedPAC update of Medicare Advantage overpayments. MEDPAC report to Congress. June, 2006. Available at: http://www.house.gov/stark/news/109th press-releases/200606066 MEDPAC, pdf.

36. Pear R. Medicare actuary gives wanted data to Congress. *New York Times*, March 20, 2004:A8.

37. Schearer G. Medicare prescription drugs: Conference Committee agreement asks beneficiaries to pay too high a price for a modest benefit. *Consumers Union*, Washington, D.C., November 25, 2003.

38. Martinez B. Drug price surge may erode savings from Medicare card. *Wall Street Journal*, March 24, 2004:B1.

39. Berenson A. Pfizer and other drug makers report higher profits. *New York Times*, October 20, 2006:C2.

40. Lipton E. Setbacks plague bid to stockpile bioterror drugs. *New York Times*, September 18, 2006:A1.

41. Evans R.G. Going for the gold: The redistributive agenda behind market-based health care reform. *J Health Polit Policy Law*, 22:427, 1997.

42. Whiteis D.G. Unhealthy cities: Corporate medicine, community economics underdevelopment and public health. Int J Health Serv 27(2): 227-42, 1997.

43. Starfield B. New paradigms for quality in primary care. *Br J Gen Pract* 51:303-9, 2001.

44. Starfield B. *Primary Care: Concept, Evaluation and Policy*. Oxford University Press, New York, 1992.

45. Shi L., Starfield B., Kennedy B., & Kawachi I. Income inequality, primary care, and high indicators. *J Fam Pract* 45(4):275-84, 1999.

46. Parchman M. & Culter S. Primary care physicians and avoidable hospitalization. J Fam Pract 39:123-6, 1994.

47. O'Malley A.S., Gerland A.M. Pham H.H., et al. Rising pressure: Hospital emergency departments as barometers of the health care system. Center for Studying Health System Change. Issue Brief No. 101, November 17, 2005.

48. Lesser C.G., Ginsburg P.B., & Felland L.E. Initial findings from HSCs 2005 site visits: Stage set for growing health care cost and access problems. Center for Studying Health SystemChange. Issue Brief No. 97, August, 2005.

49. Borger C., Smith S., Truffer C., Keehan S., & Sisko A., et al. Health spending projections through 2015: changes on the horizon. *Health Affairs* Web Exclusive. February 22, 2006.

50. Smith C., Cowan C., & Heffler S, Catlin A. & the National Health Accounts Team. National health spending in 2004: Recent slowdown led by prescription drug spending. *Health Aff* (Millwood) 25(1):186-96, 2006.

51. Brenner D.J., & Elliston C.D. Estimated radiation risks potentially associated with full-body CT screening. *Radiology* 232(3):735-8, 2004.

52. Lee T.H. & Brennan T.A. Direct-to-consumer marketing of high-technology screening tests. *New Engl J Med* 346:529, 2003.

53. Galvin R. A deficiency of will and ambition: A conversation with Donald Berwick. *Health Aff* Web Exclusive 24 (1):W5-7, 2005.

54. Medicare Rights Center. Asclepios, *Weekly Medicare Consumer Advocacy Update* June 11, 2004, p 4.

55. Eisenberg M.J., Filion K.B., Azoulay A., Brox A.C., Haider S., et al. Outcomes and cost of coronary artery bypass graft surgery in the United States and Canada. *Arch Intern Med* 165(13):1506-13, 2005.

56. World Health Report 2000. Available at: http//www.who.int/whr/2000en/report.htm.

57. White R.D. Tenet continuing resurgence. *Los Angeles Times,* January 5, 2002.

58. Berenson R. A., Bazzoli G. J. & Au M. Do specialty hospitals promote price competition? Center for Studying Health System Change. Issue Brief No. 103, January 2006.

59. Dartmouth Atlas of Healthcare Project Web site. (Accessed October 3, 2003) at http://www.dartmouthatlas.org/annals/fisher03.

60. Wennberg J.B., Fisher E.S. & Skinner J.S. Geography and the debate over Medicare reform. *Health Affairs* Web Exclusive W96-114, February 13, 2002.

61. Geyman J.P. *Shredding the Social Contract: The Privatization of Medicare.*

Monroe, Me: Common Courage Press, 2006, p 206.

62. Fisher E.S. & Welch H.G. Avoiding the unintended consequences of growth in medical care: How might more be worse? JAMA 281:445-53, 1999.

63. Ibid #52.

64. Ibid #51.

65. Schuster M.A., McGlynn E.A. & Brook R. H. How good is the quality of health care in the United States? *Milbank Q* 76(4):517,509, 1998.

66. Commonwealth Fund. *Quality of Health Care in the U.S.* New York: Chartbook, 2002.

67. Lurie J.D., Birkmeyer N. J. & Weinstein J. N. Rates of advanced spinal imaging and spine surgery. *Spine* 28:616-20, 2003.

68. Emanuel E. J., Young-Xu Y., Levinsky N.G., Gazelie G., Saynina O., et al. Chemotherapy use among Medicare beneficiaries at the end of life. *Ann Intern Med* 138:639-43, 2003.

69. Somogyi-Zalud E., Zhong Z., Hamel M.B., Lynn J. The use of life-sustaining treatments in hospitalized persons aged 80 and older. *J Am Geriatr Soc* 50:930-34, 2002.

70. Fisher E.S., Wennberg D.E., Stukel T.A., Gottlieb D. J., Lucas F. L., & Pinder E. L. The implications of regional variations in Medicare spending. Part 1: The content, quality, and accessibility of care. *Ann Intern Med* 138:273-87, 2003.

71. Rabeneck L., Wray N. P., & Petersen N. J. Long-term outcomes of patients receiving percutaneous endoscopic gastrostomy tubes. *J Gen Intern Med* 11:287-93, 1996.

72. Woolhandler S. & Himmelstein D. U. When money is the mission—The high costs of investor-owned care. *N Engl J Med* 341:444-6, 1999.

Chapter 4: Public Health

1. Peng R. The goals of medicine and public health. In: Hanson M. J. & Callahan D. (eds). *The Goals of Medicine: The Forgotten Issue in Health Care Reform.* Washington, D.C.: Georgetown University Press, 1999:174-6.

2. McKinlay J.B., McKinlay S.M. & Beaglehole R. A review of the evidence concerning the impact of medical measures on recent mortality and morbidity in the United States. *Int J Health Serv* 19:181, 1989.

3. Fisher E.S., Wennberg D.E., Stukel T.A., Gottlieb D.J., Lucas F.L., et al. The implications of regional variations in Medicare spending. Part 1: The content, quality, and accessibility of care. *Ann Intern Med* 138:273-87, 2003.

4. Grumbach K. Specialists, technology, and newborns—too much of a good thing. N Engl J Med 346:1574-5, 2002.

5. Bodenheimer T.S., & Grumbach K. *Understanding Health Policy: A Clinical Approach.* (2nd ed). Stamford, CT: Appleton & Lange, 1998:167.

6.   Rose G. Sick individuals and sick populations. *Int J Epidemiol* 14(1):32, 1985.

7.   Terris M. The changing relationships of epidemiology and society. The Robert Cruikshank Lecture. *J Public Health Policy* 6:15, 1985.

8.   Ibid #2.

9.   Winslow CEA. Who killed Cock Robin? *Am J Public Health* 34:658, 1944.

10. Ibid #1.

11. Terris M. Healthy lifestyles: the perspective of epidemiology. *J Public Health Policy* 13:186, 1992.

12. Stamler J. The marked decline in coronary heart disease mortality rates in the United States. 1968-1981:Summary of findings and possible explanations. Cardiology (Karger, Basel) 72:11, 1985.

13. Goldman L., & Cook E.F. The decline in ischemic heart disease mortality rates. *Ann Intern Med* 101:825, 1984.

14. U.S. Department of Health and Human Services. Health United States 1995, 1996.

15. Warner K.E. Smoking and health: A 25-year perspective. *Am J Public Health* 79:141, 1989.

16. The Institute for the Future. *Health and Health Care 2010: The Forecast, the Challenge* (2nd Ed). San Francisco: Jossey-Bass, 2003:167.

17. Ibid #16, p 166.

18. Levinsky N. The doctor's master. *N Engl J Med* 311:1573-75, 1984.

19. Ibid #16, p 179.

20. Ibid #5.

21. Committee for the Study of the Future of Public Health. Institute of Medicine: Washington, D.C.: National Academy Press, 1:1988.

22. Miller B., Rosenbaum S., Stange P.V., Solomon S. L, & Castro K.G. Tuberculosis control in a changing health care system: model contract specifications for managed care organizations. *Clin Infect Dis* 27:677-86, 1998.

23. Committee on Assuring the Health of the Public in the 21st Century. Institute of Medicine. *The Future of the Public's Health in the 21st Century*. Washington, D.C.: National Academy Press, 2002.

24. Ibid #16.

25. Institute of Medicine. *2020 Vision: Health in the 21st Century*. Washington, D.C.: National Academy Press, 1996:19.

26. Baker E.L., Potter M.A., Jones D.L, Mercer S.L, Cioffi J.P., et al. The public health infrastructure and our nation's health. *Annu Rev Public Health* 26:305, 2005.

27. Koplan J.P. & Fleming D.W. Current and future public health challenges.

JAMA 284(13):1696-98, 2000.

28. Frenk J., Gomez-Dantes O. Globalization and the challenges to health systems. *Health Aff* (Millwood) 21(3):160-5, 2002.

29. Institute of Medicine. *America's Vital Interest in Global Health: Protecting Our People, Enhancing Our Economy, and Advancing Our International Interests.* Washington, D.C.: National Academy Press, 1997.

30. Frenk J., Sepulveda J., Gomez-Dantes O., McGuinness M.J. & Knaul F. The new world order and international health. *BMJ* 314(7091): 1404-7, 1997.

31. Ibid. #28.

32. Garrett L. The nightmare of bioterrorism. *Foreign Affairs* 80(1):76-89, 2001.

33. Rhode D., McNeill D.G., Abelson R., & Dewan S. Vulnerable, and doomed in the storm. *New York Times*, September 19, 2005:A1.

34. Klein N. Now the real looting begins: Purging the poor. *The Nation* 281(11): October 10, 2005:15.

35. Krugman P. Miserable by design. Op-ed. *New York Times* October 3, 2005: A25.

36. Lueck S. & Rogers D. Katrina lays bare Medicaid dispute. *Wall Street Journal* September 14, 2005:B4.

37. Addressing the health care impact of Hurricane Katrina. Kaiser Commission on Medicaid and the Uninsured Web site. September 15, 2005. Available at http://www.kff.org/katrina/index.cfm. Accessed September 17, 2005.

38. Hurricanes Katrina and Rita Emergency Information. Louisiana State University Web site. Available at http://www.lsuhsc.edu/hcsd/. Accessed November 11, 2005.

39. Rudowitz R., Rowland D., & Shartzer A. Health care in New Orleans before and after Hurricane Katrina. *Health Affairs* Web Exclusive, August 26, 2006.

40. Iglehart J. K. The pursuit of public health: How serious is society? *Health Aff* (Millwood) 21(6):7, 2002.

41. Gostin L.O. Public health law in an age of terrorism: Rethinking individual rights and common goals. *Health Aff* (Millwood) 21(6):80, 2002.

42. Boufford J.J., & Lee P.R. *Health Policies for the Twenty-first Century: Challenges and Recommendations for the U.S. Department of Health and Human Services.* New York: Milbank Memorial Fund, 2001.

43. CDC internal research, unpublished, 2001.

44. Gerzoff R.B., Brown C.C. & Baker E.L. Full-time employees of U.S. local health departments, 1992-1993. J Public Health Management and Practice 5(3):1-9, 1999.

45. Mullan F. Interview. David Satcher takes stock. *Health Aff* (Millwood) 21(6):160, 2002.

46. Alexander G.C. & Wynia M.K. Ready and willing? Physicians' sense of

preparedness for bioterrorism. *Health Aff* (Millwood) 22(5):189, 2003.

47. American College of Emergency Physicians Safety Net Task Force. *Defending America's Safety Net*, White Paper. Dallas: ACEP, 1999.

48. Lurie N. The public health infrastructure: Rebuild or redesign? *Health Aff* (Millwood) 21(6):28-30, 2002.

49. Nestle M. Food marketing and childhood obesity—A matter of policy. *N Engl J Med* 354(24):2527-9, 2006.

Chapter 5: Inside the Medical Arms Race

1. Kuttner R. *Everything for Sale: The Virtues and Limits of Markets*. Chicago: The University of Chicago Press, 1999, p 158.

2. Soros G. *The Bubble of American Supremacy: Correcting the Misuse of American Power*. New York: Public Affairs, November 2004.

3. Woolhandler S., Campbell T., & Himmelstein, D.U. Costs of health care administration in the United States and Canada. *N Engl J Med* 349:768, 2003.

4. Kleinke J.D. *Oxymorons: The Myths of the U.S. Health Care System*. San Francisco: Jossey-Bass, 2001, p 192.

5. Robertson K. "Are Health Plan Brokers Paid Too Much?" *Sacramento Business Journal*, September 13, 1999. Available at: http://bizjournals. bcentral.com/sacramento/stories/1999/09/13story4.html.

6. Ibid #1.

7. Freudenheim M. Wellpoint's blue period may be over. *New York Times* September 28, 2005:C1.

8. Hallam K. Health benefits may cost 12 percent more. *Hartford Courant* August 16, 2005.

9. Associated Press. Wellpoint's 3Q profit more than doubles. *New York Times* October 26, 2005.

10. McCanne D. Comment on Bradford S.L. Cheapest insurance found out west. SmartMoney.com, December 7, 2004. In: *Quote of the Day* December 10, 2004 (don@mccanne.org).

11. Girion L. Health insurers deny policies in some jobs. Common medications also can be deemed too risky in California. *Los Angeles Times*, January 8, 2007.

12. Terhune C. Side effect—Insurer's tactic: If you get sick, the premium rises— American Medical's practice adds to surge in profits, roils lives of customers. Will rival firms follow suit? *The Wall Street Journal*, April 9, 2002:A1.

13. Fuhrmans V. Unstable condition. After streak of strong profits, health insurers may see decline. *Wall Street Journal*, July 31, 2006:A1.

14. Court J. Insurance: You pay, they bait and switch. *Los Angeles Times*, May 8, 2002; B13.

15. Morrison A.B. & Wolfe S.M. Outrage of the month: None of your business. *Public Citizen's Health Research Group Health* Letter, 2001, p 11.
16. Terhune C. Insurers avoid state regulations by selling via groups elsewhere. *The Wall Street Journal*, April 9, 2002, pA20.
17. Girion L. Hospital sues Blue Cross for payments. *Los Angeles Times*, October 14, 2006.
18. Martinez B. CIGNA to settle suit over cuts in doctor bills. *The Wall Street Journal*, November 27, 2002, p A3.
19. Robinson J. Consumer-directed health insurance: The next generation. An interview with John Rowe *Health Affairs Web Exclusive*, December 13, 2005.
20. AARP offers a plan, but the experts aren't buying it. *Washington Post*, February 11, 2003.
21. Terhune C. Thin cushion. Fast-growing health plan has a catch: $1,000-a-year cap. *The Wall Street Journal*, May 2003, p A1.
22. Chaker A. M. A pinch hit on health coverage. *The Wall Street Journal*, May 7, 2001, p D6.
23. McCanne D. Comment on Kazel R. Insurers post robust profits for the second quarter. *American Medical News* August 25, 2003. In: *Quote of the Day*, August 25, 2003. (*Quote-of-the-day* @mccanne.org).
24. Press release. 13th Annual Knox-Keene report by CMA finds Blue Cross spent 78.9 percent of premium on patients in 2004-05. California Medical Association, August 14, 2006.
25. Benko L. B. Managed care. Shakeup in California. *Modern Healthcare*, May 13, 2002, p 32.
26. Kahn J.G., Kronick R., Kreger M., Gans D.N. The cost of health insurance in California: Estimates for insurers, physicians, and hospitals. *Health Aff* (Millwood) 24(6): 1-11, 2005.
27. Born P. & Geckler C. HMO quality and financial performance: Is there a connection? *J Health Care Finance* 24(2):65-77, 1998.
28. Hellander I. Quality of care lower in for-profit HMOs than in non-profits. PNHP news release. July 12, 1999.
29. Schlesinger M., Quon N., Wynia M., Cummins D., & Gray B. Profit-seeking, corporate control, and the trustworthiness of the health organizations: assessments of health plan performance by their affiliated physicians. *Health Serv Res* 40(3):605-45, 2005.
30. Ibid #28.
31. Court J. & Smith F. *Making a Killing: HMOs and the Threat to Your Health.* Monroe, ME: Common Courage Press, 1999.
32. Morgan R. O., Virnig B.A., DeVito C. A., & Persily N.A. The Medicare-

HMO revolving door—the healthy go in and the sick go out. *N Engl J Med* 337:169-75, 1997.

33. Brody H. Gag rules and trade secrets in managed care contracts. *Arch Intern Med* 157:2037-43, 1997.
34. McCormick D., Himmelstein D.U., Woolhandler S., Wolfe S. M. & Bor D. II. Relationship between low quality-of-care scores and HMOs subsequent public disclosure of quality-of-care scores. *JAMA* 288:1484, 2002.
35. Sparrow M. K. *License to steal: How fraud bleeds America's health care system.* Boulder, CO: Westview Press, 71: 106-7, 2000.
36. Mechanic D. Managed care as a target of distrust. *JAMA* 277:1810-11, 1997.
37. Frieden J. Vital signs. *Family Practice News*, 32(3), 1, 2002.
38. Robinson J. C. *The Corporate Practice of Medicine: Competition and Innovation in Health Care.* Berkeley, CA: University of California Press, 1999.
39. Duff C. Americans tell government to stay out—except in case of health care. *The Wall Street Journal*, June 25, 1998.
40. Ibid #36.
41. Freudenheim M. Some concerns thrive on Medicaid patients. *The New York Times*, February 19, 2003, C1.
42. Bush R. Jury finds HMO bias in signing patients. Amerigroup shunned pregnant women, high-risk patients. *Chicago Tribune*, October 31, 2006.
43. Krasner J. Insurer hits millions of seniors with drug cost hike. *Boston Globe*, December 31, 2006.
44. Geis S. Cheaper across the border: California HMOs send some enrollees to Mexico. *Washington Post* National Weekly Edition 23(4):31, 2006.
45. Rosenbaum S. Managed care and patients' rights. *JAMA* 289:906, 2003.
46. Naik G. Care-gap. Hospital building boom sparks worry cities will be left behind. *Wall Street Journal*, November 22, 2006:A1.
47. VHA Inc. *Environment assessment: Setting foundations for the millennium.* Irving, TX, 1998.
48. Sorkin A. R. Huge buyout of hospital group highlights era of going private. *New York Times* July 25, 2001, p A1.
49. Iglehart J.K. U.S. hospitals: Examining their fraying social contract. *Health Aff* (Millwood) 25(1):8-9, 2006.
50. Berenson R.A., Bodenheimer T., & Pham H.H. Specialty-service lines: Salvos in the medical arms race. *Health Affairs* Web Exclusive, July 25, 2006:W337-43.
51. Dobson A., Da Venzo, J., & Sen N. The cost-shift payment hydraulic: Foundation, history, and implications. *Health Aff* (Millwood) 25(1): 24, 2006.

52. Kahn C. N. Intolerable risk, irreparable harm: The legacy of physician-owned specialty hospitals. *Health Aff* (Millwood) 25(1):130-3, 2006.
53. Miller M.E., Director, Medicare Payment Advisory Commission. "Physician-Owned Specialty Hospitals," testimony before the Subcommittee on Federal Financial Management, Government Information, and International Security, Senate Committee on Homeland Security and Governmental Affairs, May 24, 2005, http://hsgac.senate.gov/_files/MedpacTestimony_Miller_senGovtReform52405_pdf (accessed September 20, 2005).
54. Lueck S. Medicare deals setback to specialty hospitals. *Wall Street Journal*, May 13, 2005:A7.
55. Berenson R.A., Bazzoli G. J. & Au M. Do specialty hospitals promote price competition? Center for Studying Health System Change. Issue Brief No. 103, January 2006.
56. Szabo J. Washington Watch. Medicare law bans some doctor-owned hospitals. *Physicians Financial News* (22(2): February 15, 2004, p 13.
57. Public Citizen Report. April 18, 2002. Full report available at http://www.citizen.org/congressreform/drug_industry/profits/articles.ctm? ID= (416).
58. Families USA. *The Choice: Health Care for People or Drug Industry Profits.* Publication No. 05-104, September 2005, p 4.
59. Lueck S. Drug industry exaggerates R & D costs to justify pricing, consumer groups says. *The Wall Street Journal*, July 24, 2002, p B6.
60. National Institute for Health Care Management Research and Education Foundation. *Changing patterns of pharmaceutical innovation.* Washington, D.C.: NIHCM, 2002.
61. Reinhardt U.E. Perspectives on the pharmaceutical industry. *Health Aff* (Millwood) 20(5):136, 2001.
62. Light D.W. & Lexchin J. Foreign free riders and the high price of U.S. medicines. BMJ 331:958-60, 2005.
63. Public Citizen Press Release. Drug industry employs 675 Washington lobbyists many with a revolving door connection, new report finds. Washington, D.C.: June 23, 2003.
64. Saul S. Drug lobby got a victory in trade pact vote. *New York Times,* July 2, 2005:B1.
65. Saul S. In the newest war of the states, forget red and blue. *New York Times,* January 31, 2006:C1.
66. Wolfe S. M. (ed). Outrage of the Month. The causes of mis-prescribing and over-prescribing. Washington, D.C.: *Health Letter.* Public Citizen's Health Research Group, May 2005:9-12.
67. Rubenstein S. How Lilly influences what prescribers say about Cymbalta. *Wall Street Journal*, August 5, 2005:B1.

68. Wolfe S. M. (ed). Sleight-of-hand. Merck contemplated Vioxx reformulation in 2000 while denying risk. Washington, D.C.: *Health Letter*, Public Citizen Health Research Group, August 2005:1-2.
69. Public Citizen Report, November 9, 2001.
70. Carreyron J. New regimen. Inside Abbot's tactics to protect AIDS drug. *Wall Street Journal*, January 3, 2007:A1.
71. Larkin M. Whose article is it anyway? *Lancet* 354:136, 1999.
72. Lexchin J., Bero L.A., Djulbegovic B. & Clark O. Pharmaceutical industry sponsorship and research outcome and quality: A systematic review. BMJ 326:1167, 2003.
73. Rennie D. M. Thyroid storm. JAMA 277:1242, 1997.
74. Erichacker, P.Q., Natanson C., & Danner, R.L. Surviving sepsis—Practice guidelines, marketing campaigns, and Eli Libby. *N Engl J Med* 355(16):1640-2, 2006.
75. Abboud L. & Zuckerman G. Drug maker draws heat for sharing non-public data with stock analysts. *Wall Street Journal,* October 4, 2005:C1.
76. Saul S. Doctors object as drug makers learn who's prescribing what. *New York Times,* May 4, 2006:A1.
77. Reuters. Glaxo to pay $70 million to settle suits on drug prices. *New York Times*, August 11, 2006:C4.
78. Wilke J.R. Cases, fines soar in fraud probes of drug pricing. *Wall Street Journal*, June 7, 2005:A1.
79. Berenson A. Lilly settles with 18,000 over Zyprexa. *New York Times*, January 5, 2007:C1.
80. Kaiser Daily Health Policy Report. October 24, 2006.
81. Office of Research, Development & Information. *Health care industry market update.* Washington, D.C.: October 10, 2002.
82. Abelson R. Pricing power at risk for orthopedics makers. *New York Times,* June 29, 2006:C3.
83. Feigal D.W., Gardner S.N. & McClellan J. Ensuring safe and effective medical devices. *New Engl J Med* 348:191, 2003.
84. Palast G. *The Best Democracy Money Can Buy.* Sterling, VA: Pluto Press, 2002.
85. Berman D. K., Burton T. M. & Westphal S.P. How Boston Scientific beat J & J. *Wall Street Journal*, January 26, 2006:C1.
86. Meier B. FDA says flaws in heart devices pose high risks. *New York Times*, July 2, 2005:B2.
87. Finz S. Guilty plea in medical fraud—12 patients die; Bay area branch of Guidant fined $92 million over malfunctions. *San Francisco Chronicle*, June 13, 2003, p A1.

88. Meier B. Files show Guidant foresaw some risks. *New York Times,* December 24, 2005:B1.
89. Burton T. M. & Mathews A. W. Guidant sold heart device after flaws. *Wall Street Journal,* June 2, 2005: D3.
90. Harris G. & Feder B. J. FDA warns device maker over safety. *New York Times,* January 29, 2006:C1.
91. Frensenius Medical Care reports third quarter and nine months 2005 results; outlook for 2005 confirmed. www.fmc-na.com, accessed February 13, 2006.
92. Devereaux P. J., Schunemann H. I., Ravindran M., Bhandari M., Garg A. X. & Choi P.T. Comparison of mortality between private for-profit and private not-for-profit hemodialysis centers: A systematic review and meta-analysis. JAMA 288:2449, 2002.
93. Garg R.P., Frick K.D., Diener-West, & Power N.R. Effect of the ownership of dialysis facilities on patients' survival and referral for transplantation. *New Engl J Med* 341:1653, 1999.
94. Himmelstein D. U., Woolhandler S. & Hellander I. *Bleeding the Patient: The Consequences of Corporate Health Care.* Monroe, ME: Common Courage Press, 2001.
95. Press Release, January 19. Settlement with Fresenius Medical Care. Washington, D.C.: U.S. Department of Health and Human Services, Office of Inspector General, 2000.
96. Harrington C., Woolhandler S., Mullen J., Carillo H. & Himmelstein D. U. Does investor-ownership of nursing homes compromise the quality of care? *Am J Public Health* 91:1-5, 2001.
97. Wolfe S. M. (ed). "Neglected to Death": The scandalous condition of American nursing homes. Washington, D.C.: Public Citizen Health Research Group. Health Letter 19(1): 1-4, 2003, as adapted from "Neglected to Death," a series run by the *St. Louis Post Dispatch* in October 2002 and available on its Web site http://www.stltoday.com/nursing homes.
98. *Consumer Reports* analysis, as cited in *Medicare Watch* 9(17): August 15, 2006, p 3.
99. Bogdanich W. Conflict case at hospitals is settled. *New York Times*, January 25, 2007:C1.
100. Walsh M.W. A mission to save money: A record of otherwise. *The New York Times Online*, June 7, 2002.
101. Bogdanich W. Hospital chiefs get pay and perks for advice on selling hospitals. *New York Times*, July 17, 2006:A1.
102. Walsh M.W. Wide U.S. inquiry into purchasing for health care. *New York Times*, August 21, 2004:A1.
103. Business for Social Responsibility Web site, http://www.bsr.org/ accessed

February 14, 2006.

104. Derber C. *Corporation Nation: How Corporations Are Taking Over Our Lives, and What We Can Do About It.* New York: St. Martin's Griffin, 1998, pp 221-42.

105. Friedman M. *Capitalism and Freedom.* Chicago: University of Chicago Press, 1967.

106. Master Settlement Agreement between Settling State Officials and Participating Manufacturers. November 23, 1998, p 19. Available at www.naag.org.tobac/index.html.

107. Chung P.J., Garfield C.F., Rathouz P.J., Lauderdale D.S., Best D.J. & Lantos J. Youth targeting by tobacco manufacturers since the Master Settlement Agreement. *Health Aff* (Millwood) 21(2):254-263, 2002.

108. Carpenter C. M., Wayne G.F., Pauly J. L., Koh, H.K., Connolly G. N. New cigarette brands with flavors that appeal to youth: Tobacco marketing strategies. *Health Aff* (Millwood) 24(6): 1601-10, 2005.

109. Burton B. & Rowell A. Brisith American Tobacco's socially responsive smoke screen. *PR Watch*, 2002, p 6.

110. Schmit J. Drug makers shell out millions to influence California drug discount vote. *USA Today*, August 15, 2005:2B.

111. Anand G. Support system. Through charities, drug makers help people—and themselves. *Wall Street Journal*, December 1, 2005:A1.

112. Berenson A. A cancer drug shows promise, at a price that many can't pay. *New York Times,* February 15, 2006:A1.

113. Reuters. Genentech's profit rises 79 percent, yet shares fall. *New York Times*, July 12, 2006:C3.

114. Hensley S., & Wysockie B. Shots in the dark. As industry profits elsewhere, U.S. lacks vaccines, antibiotics. *Wall Street Journal*, November 8, 2005:A1.

115. Ibid #104, p 110.

116. Wagner L. Outsourcing making inroads in medicine. *Physicians Financial News* 22(6):14-15, June 15, 2004.

117. Elliott S. G.E. to spend $100 million promoting itself as innovative. *The New York Times*, January 16, 2003, p C1.

118. Naisbitt J. *Global Paradox.* New York: William Morrow, 1994.

119. Kent A. Breaking down the barriers. *Nation*, June 8, 1998, p 29.

120. Schroeder M. States' efforts to curb outsourcing stymied. *Wall Street Journal*, April 16, 2004:A4.

121. Barbaro M. State mandate for Wal-Mart on health care. *New York Times,* January 13, 2006:A1.

122. Hudson K. Campaign tactics: Behind the scenes. PR firm remakes Wal-Mart's image; political veterans at Edelman tackle woes of 'Candidate' but sometimes

stumble; holding 79 news conferences. *Wall Street Journal*, December 7, 2006:A1.

123. Press release. Washington, DC: Families USA, July 17, 2002.
124. *Families USA*. The Choice: Health Care for People or Drug Industry Profits. Washington, DC: *Families USA*, September 2005, p 7.
125. Ibid #104, p 241.
126. Kuttner R. Taking Care of Business, *The American Prospect*, July-August (6-8) 1996, p7.

Chapter 6: Market Tiers and Patients' Tears

1. Hayek F.A. *The American Economic Review,* 1946.
2. Smith C., Cowan C., Heffler S., Catlin A., et al. National health spending in 2004. *Health Aff* (Millwood) January/February 2006:186-96.
3. Pear R. Growth of national health spending slows along with drug sales. *New York Times* January 10, 2006:A15.
4. Calmes J. Elephant in the room. Budget wish lists come and go, but 'entitlements' outweigh all. *Wall Street Journal*, February 3, 2006:A1.
5. Andrews E.L. Brighter '06 deficit outlook, but long term looks grim. *New York Times*, August 18, 2006:A12.
6. Solomon D. Public pensions press state budgets. *Wall Street Journal*, February 23, 2006:A2.
7. Stolberg S.G. House approves budget cutbacks of $39.5 billion. *New York Times* February 2, 2006: A1.
8. Woolhandler S., Campbell T., & Himmelstein D.U. Costs of health care administration in the United States and Canada. *New Engl J Med* 349:768, 2003.
9. Skinner J.S. & Fisher E.S. Regional disparities in Medicare expenditures: an opportunity for reform. *National Tax Journal* 50:413-25, 1997.
10. Schuster M., McGlynn E.A, & Brook R.H. How good is the quality of health care in the United States? *Milbank Q* 76(4):517-63, 1998.
11. Fisher E.S., Wennberg D.E., Stukel T.A., Gottlieb D.J., et al. The implications of regional variations in Medicare spending. Part 1: The content, quality, and accessibility of care. *Ann Intern Med* 138(4):273-87, 2003.
12. Fisher E.S., Wennberg D.E., Stukel T.A., et al. The implications of regional variations in Medicare spending. Part 2: Health outcomes and satisfaction with care. *Ann Intern Med* 138(4):288-98, 2003.
13. Walsh M.W. Many companies ending promises of retirement. *New York Times*, January 9, 2006:A1.
14. Wessel D., Schultz E.E., & McGinley L. Engine overhaul. Pressured GM slashes pay benefits. *Wall Street Journal*, February 8, 2006:A1.
15. Himmelstein D.U., Warren E., Thorne D. & Woolhandler S. Illness and injury

as contributors to bankruptcy. *Health Affairs Web Exclusive*. W5-63, 2005.

16. Wolfson B. 'Vicious cycle' of care. *The Orange County Register*. March 30, 2005.

17. Lueck S. Health check: Benefits are added to HSAs. *Wall Street Journal*, December 9-10, 2006:B4.

18. Rubenstein S. Is an HSA right for you? *Wall Street Journal*, February 2, 2006: D1.

19. Families USA. HSAs: Missing the target. Report from *Families USA*. Washington, D.C., December 2005.

20. *Why the Working Poor Pay More*. Washington: SEIU, March 2003.

21. Davis K. *Will Consumer-Directed Health Care Improve System Performance?* Washington: The Commonwealth Fund, August 2004.

22. Blumberg L. & Burman L. *Most Households' Medical Expenses Exceed HSA Deductibles*. Washington: Tax Policy Center, August 2004.

23. Kaiser Family Foundation Survey, June 5, 2002.

24. GAO. Federal Employees Benefit Program. First-year experience with high-deductible health plans and health savings accounts. Washington, D.C.: General Accounting Office, January 2006.

25. Francis T. & Schultz E.E. Health accounts have benefits for employers. *Wall Street Journal*, February 3, 2006:B1.

26. Robinson J. Consumer-directed health insurance: The next generation. An interview with John Rowe, *Health Affairs Web Exclusive,* December 13, 2005.

27. Terhune C. Thin cushion. Fast-growing health plan has a catch: $1,000-a-year cap. *The Wall Street Journal,* May 2003, pA1.

28. Chaker A. M. A pinch hit on health coverage. *The Wall Street Journal*, May 7, 2001, pD6.

29. Robinson J.C. Hospital tiers in health insurance: Balancing consumer choice with financial incentives. *Health Affairs Web Exclusive* W-135-46, March 13, 2003.

30. Rosenthal M.R. et al. Managed care and market power: Physician organizations in four markets. Health Aff (Millwood) 20 (5):187-93, Sep/Oct 2001.

31. Kahn C.N. Intolerable risk, irreparable harm: The legacy of physician-owned specialty hospitals. *Health Aff* (Millwood) 25(1): 130-3, 2006.

32. Brennan T.A. Luxury primary care—market innovation or threat to access? *N Engl J Med* 346:1165-8, 2002.

33. Mays G.P., Hurley R.E. & Grossman J.M. Consumers face higher costs as health plans seek to control drug spending. Washington, D.C. Center for Studying Health System Change. Issue Brief No. 45, November, 2001.

34. Priselac T. M. The erosion of health insurance: The unintended consequences

of tiered products by health plans. *Health Affairs Web Exclusive*, W3-158-61, March 19, 2003.

35. Ibid #29.
36. Yegian J.M. Tiered hospital networks. *Health Affairs Web Exclusive.* W3-152, March 19, 2003.
37. Ibid #23
38. Henderson N. Greenspan's mixed legacy: America prospered during the Fed chief's tenure, but built up massive debt. *Washington Post National Weekly Edition.* January 30-February 5, 2006, p 6.
39. Kaiser Commission on Medicaid and the Uninsured. Health Insurance Coverage in America: 2000 Data Update. February 2002:9.
40. May J. H. & Cunningham P. J. *Issue Brief #85.* Center for Studying Health System Change, Washington, D.C.: 2004.
41. Hanson K.W., et al. Uncovering the health challenges facing people with disabilities: The role of health insurance. *Health Aff Web Exclusive*, November 19, 2003, W3-553.
42. Duboy L., Holahan J., & Cook A. The uninsured and the affordability of health insurance coverage. *Health Affairs* Web Exclusive. November 30, 2006.
43. Robbins J. The health costs of wealth inequity. *Common Dreams News Center*, October 1, 2006 (CommonDreams.org accessed October 3, 2006).
44. Krugman P. Wages, wealth and politics. *New York Times,* August 18, 2006: A19.
45. Phillips W. Wealth and Democracy. Rich-poor gap, corruption are harbingers of economic decline. *Public Citizen News.* November/December 2002;22(6):7.
46. Warren E. & Tyagi A.W. *The Two-Income Trap: Why Middle-Class Mothers and Fathers Are Going Broke.* New York: Basic Books, 2003:50-57.
47. Lueck S. & McKinnon J.D. Ranks of the poor, uninsured grew last year in U.S. *Wall Street Journal*, August 27, 2004: A2.
48. Kuttner R. & Marshall W. Come together. *The American Prospect* 6(15):28, 2004.
49. Henderson N. Greenspan's mixed legacy: America prospered during the Fed chief's tenure, but built up massive debt. *Washington Post National Weekly Edition.* January 30-February 5, 2006, p 6.
50. Greider W. A warning bell. *The Nation* 282(7), February 20, 2006, p 7.
51. Roubideaux Y. Beyond Red Lake—The persistent crisis in American Indian health care. *N Engl J Med* 353(18):1882, 2005.
52. Pear R. Governors' group proposes Medicaid curbs. *New York Times,* June 16, 2005:A17.
53. Press E. Ruling class warriors. *The Nation*, 282(2), January 23, 2006:p5.
54. Solomon D. Wrestling with Medicaid cuts. *Wall Street Journal*, February 16,

2006:A4.
55. Pear R. *New York Times,* January 19, 2005.
56. Kleffman S. Cuts to Medi-Cal threaten program's future. *Contra Costa Times,* January 3, 2006.
57. Pear R. Budget to hurt poor people on Medicaid, report says. *New York Times,* January 30, 2006:A14.
58. Ibid #53.
59. National Association of Community Health Centers. With new census figures, community health centers brace for more uninsured patients: Health centers already struggling with more patients, less resources. Available from: URL: http://www.nachc.com/press/newcensus.asp.2003.
60. Schiff G. & Fegan C. Community health centers and the underserved: Eliminating disparities or increasing despair. *J Health Policy* 24(3/4):45-7, 2004.
61. Weber E. J., et al. The ED and the uninsured. *JAMA* 293:39-40, 2005.
62. Barrett K. & Greene R. (eds). Pew Center on the States. Special Report on Medicaid, A19, 2006.
63. Artiga S. & O'Malley M. Increasing premiums and cost sharing in Medicaid and SCHIP: Recent state experiences. Issue Paper. Kaiser Commission on Medicaid and the Uninsured, Kaiser Family Foundation, May 2005, p2.
64. California HealthCare Foundation. Health insurance: Can Californians afford it? May 3, 2005.
65. Nyman J.A. *The Theory of Demand for Health Insurance.* Stanford, Calif: Stanford University Press, 2003.
66. Tamblyn R., Laprise R., Hanley J.A., Abrahamowitz M, Scott S, et al. Adverse events associated with prescription drug cost-sharing among poor and elderly persons. JAMA 285:421-9, 2001.
67. Goldman D. P., Joyce G.F., Escarce J.E., et al. Pharmacy benefits and the use of drugs by the chronically ill. *JAMA* 291:2344-50, 2004.
68. Hadley J., & Cunningham P. J. Perception, reality and health insurance: Uninsured as likely as insured to perceive need for care but half as likely to get care. Washington, D.C.: Center for Studying Health System Change, Issue Brief #100. October 2005.
69. Asplin B. R., Rhodes K.V., Levy H., et al. Insurance status and access to urgent ambulatory care follow-up appointments. *JAMA* 294(10):1248-54, 2005.
70. Neuman P. Testimony to the Committee on Ways and Means Subcommittee on Health. U.S. House of Representatives, Washington, D.C.: May 1, 2003. Available at: http://waysandmeans.house.gov/hearings.asp?formmode=_view&id+338.

71. Committee on the Consequences of Uninsurance. Institute of Medicine. *Care Without Coverage: Too Little, Too Late*. Washington, D.C.: National Academy Press, 2002:1-2.

72. Committee on the Consequences of Uninsurance: *Hidden costs, value lost: Uninsurance in America*. Institute of Medicine. Washington, D.C.: National Academy Press, 2003.

73. Kaufman M. & Stein R. What's ailing us? Health care costs rise to a record 16 percent of nation's economic output. *Washington Post National Weekly Edition*, January 16-22, 2006: p21.

74. Davis B. Lagging behind the wealthy, many use debt to catch up. *Wall Street Journal*, May 17, 2005:A1.

75. Ibid #15.

76. Commonwealth Fund. Only one-fourth of workers would keep health coverage through COBRA if they lost their jobs. Press release. August 29, 2002.

77. Dranove D, & Millenson M.L. Medical bankruptcy: Myth versus fact. *Health Affairs Web Exclusive*, February 28, 2005: W74-83.

78. Himmelstein D. U., Woolhandler S., Thorne D., & Warren E. Discounting the debtors will not make medical bankruptcy disappear. *Health Affairs Web Exclusive,* February 28, 2005, W84-88.

79. Ibid #63, p 3.

80. Ibid #62, p A5.

Chapter 7: Where are Market Forces Taking Us?

1. Lapham L. H. Notebook, The simple life. *Harper's Magazine* 311(1867), December 2005, p 9.

2. Norquist G, as quoted on NPR's *Morning Edition* in May 2001.

3. Bigelow G. Let there be markets: the evangelical roots of markets. *Harpers's Magazine*, May 2005, pp 33-38.

4. Carey A. *Taking the Risk Out of Democracy: Corporate Propaganda versus Freedom and Liberty*. Chicago: University of Illinois Press, 1995:91-3.

5. National Center for Policy Analysis. www.ncpa.org/abo/; accessed March 4, 2004.

6. King M. & Schlesinger M. (editors*). Final Report of the Study Panel on Medicare and Markets—The Role of Private Health Plans in Medicare: Lessons from the Past, Looking to the Future*, p 28. Washington, D.C.: National Academy of Social Insurance, September 2003.

7. *Commonwealth Fund*. MedPAC votes to urge billions in cuts to private plans in Medicare. *Health Policy Week*, April 25, 2005.

8. Closed-door deal makes $22 billion difference. *Washington Post*, January 24, 2005.

9. Hensley S. & Wysockie B. Shots in the dark. As industry profits elsewhere,

U.S. lacks vaccines, antibiotics. *Wall Street Journal*, November 8, 2005: A1.

10. Wysocki B.J., Lueck S. Margin of safety: Just-in-time inventories make U.S. vulnerable in a pandemic. *Wall Street Journal*, January 12, 2006:A1.

11. Korten C. D. *When Corporations Rule the World.* San Francisco: Berrett-Koehler Publishers, Inc., 2001.

12. *The Wall Street Journal*. Global Giants: Amid Market Pain, U.S. Companies Hold Greater Sway. October 14, 2002, p R10.

13. Hartmann T. *Unequal protection: The rise of corporate dominance and the theft of human rights*. Emmaus, PA: Rodale Press, 2002, p 37.

14. Lewis C. & The Center for Public Integrity. *The buying of the congress: How special interests have stolen your right to life, liberty and the pursuit of happiness*. New York: Avon Books, 1998, p 142.

15. FY 2004 Justification of Estimates for Appropriations Committees. Promoting public health through patient, food, and consumer safety. Rockville, Md: Food and Drug Administration, 2003. Accessed December 30, 2004, at http://www.fda.gov/oc/oms/ofm/budget/2004/bib1.htm.

16. Slater E. Today's FDA. *New Engl J Med* 352(30): 293-97, 2005.

17. Ibid #14.

18. Barrett S. How the Dietary Supplement Health and Education Act of 1998 weakened the FDA. Retrieved May 13, from www.quackwatch.org/02 ConsumerProtection, dshea.html.

19. Merrill R. A. Modernizing the FDA: An incremental revolution. *Health Affairs* (Millwood) 18:96, 1999.

20. Public Citizen. Public Citizen decries conflict of interest created by new law regulating safety of medical devices. Press release. Washington, D.C.: October 18, 2002.

21. Pear R. FDA seeks quicker approval of new drugs. *The New York Times*, December 12, 2002, p A16.

22. Public Citizen Health Research Group. Unsafe drugs: Congressional silence is deadly (Part 2). *Health Letter*, 8(11): 1, 2002.

23. Sigelman D. Unsafe drugs: Congressional silence is deadly. *Public Citizen Research Group Health Letter*, 18, 1:2002.

24. Mundy A. Risk management. *Harper's Magazine*, September 2004, p. 83-4.

25. Harris G. Report details. FDA rejection of next-day pill. *New York Times*, November 15, 2005:A1.

26. Harris G. & Berenson A. 10 advisors voting on pain pills' sale have industry ties. *New York Times*, February 25, 2005:A1.

27. Lurie P., Almeida C.M., Stine N., Stine A.R., & Wolfe S.M. Financial conflict of interest and voting patterns at Food and Drug Administration Drug Advisory Committee meetings. JAMA 295(16):1921-8, 2006.

28. General Accounting Office. GAO report backs link between drug user fees and higher rate of drug withdrawals. *Health Letter*, 18:11, 2002.

29. Ives N. Advertising. After a pitcher's death, marketers of dietary supplements try to dodge the taint of ephedra. *The New York Times*, May 17, 2003, pC9.

30. Wolfe S. M. The FDA finally bans ephedra. Worst Pills Best Pills. Health Research Group, *Public Citizen*, 2004, pp 9-10.

31. Matthews A.W. & Burton T. M. After Medtronic lobbying push, the FDA had change of heart. *Wall Street Journal*, July 9, 2004:A1.

32. Gahart M. T., Duhamel L. M., Dievler A. & Price R. Examining the FDA's oversight of direct-to-consumer advertising. *Health Affairs* February 26, 2003, W3, 120.

33. Schmit J. A winded FDA races to keep up with drug ads that go too far. *USA Today*, May 31, 2005:1A.

34. Harris G. Top Democrat finds efforts by the FDA have plunged. *New York Times*, June 27, 2006:A15.

35. Matthews A. W. FDA issues new rules for drug labels. *Wall Street Journal*, January 19, 2006:D1.

36. Ibid #23.

37. Wolfe S. M. (Ed). Sleight-of-hand. Merck contemplated Vioxx reformulation in 2000 while denying risk. Washington, D.C.: *Health Letter,* Public Citizen Health Research Group, August 2005:1-2.

38. Burton T. M. & Mathews A. W. Guidant sold heart device after flaws. *Wall Street Journal*, June 2, 2005:D3.

39. Rennie D. M. Thyroid storm. *JAMA* 277:1242, 1997.

40. Larkin M. Whose article is it anyway? *Lancet* 354:136, 1999.

41. Groopman J. Medical dispatch: Hormones for men. *The New Yorke*r, July 29, 2002, pp 34-38.

42. Deyo R.A., Psaty B. M., Simon G., Wagner E. H. & Omenn G.S. The messenger under attack: Intimidation of researchers by special interest groups. *New Engl J Med* 336:1176, 1997.

43. Crime pays, CEOs who cook the books earn more. PNHP Slide Set, 2005, Chicago, IL, based on data from United for a Fair Economy, August 26, 2002.

44. Bandler J. & Forelle C. Embattled CEO to step down at United Health. *Wall Street Journal*, October 16, 2006:A1.

45. Sparrow M. K. *License to steal: How fraud bleeds America's health care system.* Boulder, CO: Westview Press, 2000, p 74-75.

46. Bowe C. & Chaffin J. Convictions for U.S. healthcare fraud up by 22 percent. Financial Times, August 13, 2003. Retrieved from www.ft.com/healthcare

47. Tenet Healthcare paying $54 million in fraud settlement. *New York Times*,

August 7, 2003.

48. Norris F. In U. S. eyes, a fraud particularly bold. *The New York Times*, March 20, 2003, p C1.

49. Finz S. Guilty plea in medical fraud—12 patients die: Bay area branch of Guidant fined $92 million over malfunctions. *San Francisco Chronicle*, June 13, 2003, p A1.

50. Callahan P. Health industry sees a surge in fraud fines. *The Wall Street Journal*, August 18, 2003, p B1.

51. Wilke J.R. Cases, fines soar in fraud probes of drug pricing. *Wall Street Journal*, June 7, 2005:A1.

52. Ibid #12.

53. Ibid #13, p 131.

54. 1995 GAO study commissioned by Senator Byron Dorgan (D-North Dakota).

55. Murray A. Broadcasters get a pass on campaign reform. *The Wall Street Journal*, September 29, 1997, p A1.

56. Action Alert. FAIR Fairness & Accuracy in Reporting, New York City. NBC slams universal health care. November 12, 2002.

57. McQuaid K. The Roundtable. Getting Results in Washington. May/June, 1981, p 114.

58. Green M. & Buchsbaum A. The corporate lobbies: Political profiles of the business roundtable and the chamber of commerce. Washington, D.C.: Public Citizen Gale Research, 1980.

59. Young Q. Right-wing 'think' tanks and health policy. Chicago, Ill: Physicians for a National Health Program. PNHP Newsletter, Summer 2005, pp 38-9.

60. Marmor T. & Sullivan K. Canada's burning! Media myths about universal health coverage. *Washington Monthly*, 2000, July/August, p 15.

61. Ibid #13.

62. Mullins B. U.S. lobbying tab hits a record. *Wall Street Journal*, February 14, 2006:A6.

63. Mullins B. Growing role for lawmakers: Raising funds for lawmakers. *Wall Street Journal*, January 27, 2006: A1.

64. Krugman P. First, do less harm. *New York Times*, Op Ed, January 5, 2007: A17.

65. Pear R. Medicare law prompts a rush for lobbyists. *New York Times*, August 23, 2005: A1.

66. Ismail M. A. Prescribing influence: How the pharmaceutical industry gets its way in Washington. *The Public I*: Investigative Journalism in the Public Interests 11(4): July 2005, p 5.

67. Birnbaum J. H. Lobbying's cost-benefit ratio. *Washington Post*, National

Weekly Edition, 23(18), February 20-26, 2006:p 12.
68. Ibid #66, p 2.
69. Knott A. Lobbyists double spending in six years. Washington, D.C.: The Center for Public Integrity. *The Public I* 11(2), April 2005, p 1.
70. Mulkern A. When advocates become regulators. *Denver Post*, May 23, 2004.
71. Guldin B. How to earn millions after Congress: Become a lobbyist and cash in. *Public Citizen News* July/August 2005, p 7.
72. Birnbaum J. The road to riches. *Washington Post* National Weekly Edition, June 27-July 10, 2005, 22(36, 37): p 16.
73. Lueck S. Tauzin is named top lobbyist for pharmaceuticals industry. *Wall Street Journal*, December 16, 2004: A4.
74. PNHP Newsletter. Data Update. Government-corporate revolving door. Physicians for a National Health Program. Chicago: Spring, 2004, p 9, citing *Washington Post*, December 3, 2003.
75. Pear R. Corporate-government revolving door. *New York Times*, August 19, 2005, as cited in PNHP Newsletter, Spring 2006, 1.
76. Drinkard J. AARP accused of conflict of interest. *USA Today*, November 21, 2003, p 11A.
77. Klein E. Drug beneficiary. *The American Prospect* 16(12), December 2005, p 8.
78. Smith D.G. *Entitlement Politics: Medicare and Medicaid* 1995-2001. New York: Aldine de Gruyter, 2002:71, citing *Congressional Quarterly Almanac*, 1995, p 7-13.
79. *Congressional Quarterly Almanac*, 1995, p 7-11.
80. Williams P. J. Money, money, money. *The Nation*, January 5, 2004:10.
81. Kuttner R. *Everything for Sale: The Virtues and Limits of Markets*. Chicago: University of Chicago Press, 1999, p 158.

Chapter 8: Doctors on the Take

1. Ayres A. (ed). *The Wit and Wisdom of Mark Twain*. New York: Meridian Books, 1987, p 31.
2. Richmond J.B. & Fein R. *The Health Care Mess: How We Got Into It and What It Will Take to Get Out*. Cambridge, MA: Harvard University Press, 2005, p 220.
3. Reiling J. (ed). *JAMA* 100 years ago. Business methods and professional morals. March 10, 1906, reprinted in *JAMA* 295(10):1196, 2006.
4. Reinhardt U.E. An information infrastructure for the pharmaceutical market. Health Aff (Millwood) 23(1):107-12, 2004.
5. Wazana A. Physicians and the pharmaceutical industry; is a gift ever just a gift? *JAMA* 283:373-80, 2000.

6. Darves B. Too close for comfort? How some physicians are reexamining their dealings with drug detailers. *ACP Observer.* July-August 2003; 1. Philadelphia: American College of Physicians.

7. Ibid. #4.

8. National survey of physicians. Part 2. Doctors and prescription drugs. Washington, D.C.: Kaiser Family Foundation, March 2002.

9. Blumenthal D. Doctors and drug companies. *N Engl J Med* 351(18): 1885-90, 2004.

10. Dana J. & Lowenstein G. A social science perspective on gifts to physicians from industry. *JAMA* 290:752-5, 2003.

11. Katz D, Caplan A.L. & Merz JF. All gifts large and small: toward an understanding of the ethics of pharmaceutical industry gift giving. *Am J Bioeth* 3(3):39-46, 2003.

12. Sandberg W.S., Carlos R., Sandberg E.H. & Roizen M.F. The effect of educational gifts from pharmaceutical firms on medical students' recall of company names of products. *Acad Med* 72:916-8, 1997.

13. Brotzman G.L.& Mark D.H. Policies regulating the activities of pharmaceutical representatives in residency programs. *J Fam Pract* 34:54-57, 1992.

14. Cleary J.D. Impact of pharmaceutical sales representatives on physician antibiotic prescribing. *J Pharm Technol* 8:27-29, 1992.

15. Lurie H., Rich E.C., & Simpson D.E, et al. Pharmaceutical representatives in academic medical centers. *J Gen Intern Med* 5:240-43, 1990.

16. Ibid. #5.

17. Orlowski J.P. & Wateska L. The effects of pharmaceutical firm enticements on physician prescribing patterns: there's no such thing as a free lunch. *Chest* 102:270-73, 1992.

18. Chren M. M. & Landefeld C.S. Physicians' behavior and their interactions with drug companies. A controlled study of physicians who requested additions to a hospital drug formulary. *JAMA* 271:684-89, 1994.

19. Ferguson J. My $100,000 sideline. *Medical Economics,* November 19, 2004, pp 28-9.

20. Choudry N.K., Stelfox H.T., & Detsky A.S. Relationships between authors of clinical practice guidelines and the pharmaceutical industry. *JAMA* 287(5): 612-7, 2002.

21. Torry E.F. The going rate on shrinks: Big PhRMA and the buying of psychiatry. *American Prospect* July 15, 2002, p 26.

22. Torry E.F. Big PhRMA buys psychiatry: An aura of scandal. *Health Letter* 18(7), 2002, p 1.

23. Callahan P. Health industry sees a surge in fraud fines. *The Wall Street Journal,* August 18, 2003:pB1.

24. United States v. TAP Pharmaceuticals, sentencing memorandum of the United States. Criminal Action No. 01-CR-10354-WGY, Dec. 24, 2001.
25. Groopman J. Medical dispatch: Hormones for men. *The New Yorker*, July 29, 2002: pp 34-38.
26. Peterson M. Court papers suggest sale of drug's use. *The New York Times,* May 30, 2003: p C1.
27. Harris G. Pfizer to pay $430 million over promoting drug to doctors. *New York Times*, May 14, 2004:C1.
28. ACCME annual report data 2003. Chicago: Accreditation Council for Continuing Medical Education, 2003.
29. The Pharmaceutical Research and Manufacturers of America (PhRMA). HHS OIG compliance program guidance for the pharmaceutical industry: key insights from regulators and compliance experts. In: PhRMA Congress Conference, Spring 2003: June 8-9, 2003, Washington, D.C.
30. Relman A.S. Separating continuing medical education from pharmaceutical marketing. *JAMA* 285(15):2009-12, 2001.
31. Harris G. Drug makers scrutinized over grants. *New York Times*, January 11, 2005:C1.
32. Moynihan E. Who pays for the pizza? Redefining the relationships between doctors and drug companies, 2. Entanglements. *BMJ* 326:1189-92, 2003.
33. Borfitz D. Can "phase IV" trials work for you? *Medical Economics*, June 6, 2003, pp 58-67.
34. Vogel J. R. Maximizing the benefits of SMOs. *Applied Clinical Trials* 8(11):56, 1999.
35. Pear R. FDA seeks quicker approval of new drugs. *The New York Times*, December 12, 2002, p A16.
36. Physicians for a National Health Program (PNHP). Chicago, Ill: Data Update. *PNHP Newsletter*, May 2001:8.
37. Abboud L. Medical device industry faces more scrutiny by U.S. officials. *Wall Street Journal*, February 25,2005:A2.
38. Armstrong D. Delicate operation. How a famed hospital invests in device it uses and promotes. *Wall Street Journal*, December 12,2005:A1.
39. Armstrong D. Cleveland Clinic to tighten its disclosure policies. *Wall Street Journal*, February 9, 2006:A3.
40. Armstrong D. Medical centers cut AtriCure ties; stock drops 22 percent. *Wall Street Journal*, February 18, 2006:A3.
41. Abelson R. Whistle-blower suit says device maker generously rewards doctors. *New York Times*, January 24, 2006:C1.
42. Abelson R. Medtronic will settle accusations of kickbacks. *New York Times*, July 19, 2006:C4.

43. Burton T. M. Guidant draws fire for doctor survey payments. *Wall* Street Journal, September 27, 2005:B5.
44. Abelson R. Hospitals see possible conflict on medical devices for doctors. *New York Times*, September 22, 2005:A1.
45. Meier B. A race to train implant doctors creates concern. *New York Times*, August 1, 2006:A1.
46. Rose J. Focus on practice. Why hospitals love you. *Medical Economics*, November 15, 2004: 17.
47. Rundle R. Recruiting trouble. As hospitals battle for patients, a prosecutor alleges bribery. *Wall Street Journal*, June 1, 2004:A1.
48. Kahn C. N. Intolerable risk; irreparable harm: The legacy of physician-owned specialty hospitals. Health Aff (Millwood) 25(1):130-3, 2006.
49. Medicare Payment Advisory Commission, Report to the Congress: Physician-Owned Specialty Hospitals (Washington: MedPAC, March 8, 2005.)
50. Guterman S. Specialty hospitals: A problem or a symptom? Health Aff (Millwood) 25(1):95-105, 2006.
51. Leavitt M. O. *Study of Physician-Owned Specialty Hospitals Required in Section 507*(c) (2) *of the Medicare Prescription Drug, Improvement, and Modernization Act* of 2003, May 2005, http://www.cms.hhs.gov/media/press/files/052005/RTC-Study of PhysOwnedSpecHosp.pdf (accessed 6 October 2005); and Thomas Gustafson, deputy director, CMS Center for Medicare Management. "Physician-Owned Specialty Hospitals," testimony before the House Ways and Means Subcommittee on Health, 8 March 2005.
52. Ibid. #48.
53. Foster J., president and CEO, St. David's HealthCare partnership, testimony before the House Ways and Means Subcommittee on Health, March 8, 2005. http://www.fah.org/issues/testimony/2005/Jon%20Foster%20 testimony%20Ways%20and%20Means%203-8-05.pdf (accessed 23 November 2005).
54. Armstrong D. Skillful operation. A surgeon earns riches, enmity by plucking profitable patients. *Wall Street Journal*, August 8, 2005: A1.
55. Web site for Federated Ambulatory Surgery Association, www.fasa.org/, accessed March 28, 2006.
56. Luxenberg S. Invest in a surgicenter? *Medical Economics* December 5, 2003, pp 60-5.
57. Armstrong D. Lucrative operation. How some doctors turn a $90 profit from a $17 test. *Wall Street Journal*, September 30, 2005:A1.
58. Pham H.H., Devers J. J., May J. H. & Berenson R. Financial pressures spur physician entrepreneurialism. *Health Aff* (Millwood) 23(2):70-81, 2004.
59. Pennachio D. L. Full-body scans—or scams? *Medical Economics*, August 9, 2002; 62-71.

60. Armstrong D. Medical center is investigated for scan deals. *Wall Street Journal*, July 28, 2005:B1.
61. Armstrong D. Own image. MRI and CT centers offer doctors way to profit on scans. *Wall Street Journal*, May 2, 2005:A1.
62. Hillman B. J., Joseph C.A., Mabry M.R., Sunshine J. H., Kennedy S.D. & Noether M. Frequency and costs of diagnostic imaging in office practice—a comparison of self-referring and radiologist-referring physicians. *N Engl J Med* 323(23):1604-8, 1990.
63. Mitchell J. M. & Sunshine J. H. Consequences of physician ownership of health care facilities—joint ventures in radiation therapy. *N Engl J Med* 327:1497-501, 1992.
64. Mitchell J. M. & Sass T.R. Physician ownership of ancillary services: Indirect demand inducement or quality assurance? *J Health Econ* 14:263-89, 1995.
65. Bok D. *Universities in the Marketplace: The Commercialization of Higher Education.* Princeton & Oxford: Princeton University Press, 2003:x.
66. Bayh-Dole Act. Public Law No. 96-517, 35USC, 1980.
67. Ibid. #65, p 12.
68. Moses H., Dorsey E.R., Mathesen D.H.M., & Thiery S.C. Financial anatomy of biomedical research. *JAMA* 294(11):1333-42, 2005.
69. Bowie N. University-Business Partnerships: An Assessment. Lanham, MD: Rowan & Littlefield Publishers, Inc., 1994.
70. Campbell E.G., Louis K.S. & Blumenthal D. Looking a gift horse in the mouth: Corporate gifts that support life sciences research. JAMA 279 (13):995-9, 1998.
71. Bray M. J. & Lee J. N. University revenues for technology transfer. Licensing fees vs. equity positions. *J Business Venturing* 15:385-92, 2000.
72. Thursby J. G. & Thursby M.C. Who is selling the ivory tower? Sources of growth in university licensing. *Management Science* 48:90-104, 2002.
73. Campbell E.G., Moy B., Feibelmann S., Weisman J.S. & Blumenthal D. Institutional academic industry relationship: Results of interviews with university leaders. *Accountability in Research* 11:103-18, 2004.
74. Campbell E.G., Weismann J.S., Clarridge B., Yucal R., Causino N, et al. Characteristics of medical school faculty members serving on institutional review boards: Results of a national survey. *Acad Med* 78 (8):831-6, 2003.
75. Associated Press. Report urges review of researchers' ties. *New York Times*, December 27, 2001. http://www.nytimes.com/2001/12/27/national/27RESE.html.
76. Silverstein F.E., Faich G., Goldstein J.L., et al. Gastrointestinal toxicity with celecoxib vs. nonsteroidal anti-inflammatory drugs for osteoarthritis and rheumatoid arthritis: The CLASS study: a randomized controlled trial. JAMA

284:1274-55, 2000.

77. Bombardier C., Laine L., Reicin A., Shapiro D., Burgos-Vargar R., et al. Comparison of upper gastrointestinal toxicity of rofecobix and naproxen in patients with rheumatoid arthritis. The VIGOR study group. *N Engl J Med* 343:1520-8, 2000.

78. Steinbrook R. Gag clauses in clinical-trial agreements. *N Engl J Med* 352:2160-2, 2005.

79. Zimmerman R. & Tomsho R. Medical editor turns activist on drug trials. *Wall Street Journal*, May 26, 2005:B1.

80. Baird P., Downie J. & Thompson J. Clinical trials and industry. *Science*, 297:2211, 2002.

81. Rennie D. M. Thyroid storm. *JAMA* 277:1242, 1997.

82. Bekelman J.E., Li Y., & Gross C. P. Scope and impact of financial conflict of interest in biomedical research: a systematic review. *JAMA* 289:454, 2003.

83. Lexchin J., Bero L.A., Djulbegovic B., & Clark O. Pharmaceutical industry sponsorship and research outcome and quality: A systematic review. *BMJ* 326:1167, 2003.

84. Rennie D. & Flanagin A. Authorship! Authorship! Guests, ghosts, grafters, and the two-sided coin. *JAMA* 271:469, 1994.

85. Mathews A. W. Ghost story. At medical journals, writers paid by industry play big role. *Wall Street Journal*, December 13, 2005:A1.

86. Stolberg S. G. Scientists often mum about ties to industry. *New York Times*, April 25, 2001.

87. Grundy S. M., Cleeman J. I. & Merz C. N., et al. Implications of recent clinical trials for the National Cholesterol Education Program Adult Treatment Panel III guidelines. *Circulation* 110:227-39, 2004.

88. National Cholesterol Education Program. Third Report of the Expert Panel on Detection, Evaluation, and Treatment of High Blood Cholesterol in Adults (Adult Treatment Panel III). Available from: http://www.nhlbi.nih.gov/ guidelines/cholesterol/atp3upd04_disclose.htm accessed 6/14/05. Bethesda, Md: National Heart, Lung, and Blood Institute, 2004.

89. Willman D. The National Institutes of Health: public servant or private marketer? *Los Angeles Times*, December 22, 2004:1.

90. Bodenheimer T. Uneasy alliance-clinical investigators and the pharmaceutical industry. *N Engl J Med* 342:1539-44, 2000.

91. The House of Commons Health Committee. The Influence of Pharmaceutical Industry, Volume 1. April 5, 2005, p 55. Available from: http://www.parliament. the-stationeryu-office.co.uk/pa/cm200405/cmselect/cmhealth/42/42.pdf, accessed 6/08/05.

92. Peterson M. Madison Ave. has growing role in the business of drug research.

New York Times, November 22, 2002.
93. Topol E. J. & Blumenthal D. Physicians and the investment industry. JAMA 293(21):2654-7, 2005.
94. Gerson Lehrman Group. Interview with Mark Gerson, January 24, 2005. Available at: http://www.gigroup.com. Accessed April 28, 2005.
95. Gottleib S. Wall Street seeks doctors' medical advice on stocks. *American Medical News*, May 27, 2002. Available at: http://www.ama-assn.org/amednews/2002/05/27/bith0-527.htm. Accessed April 28, 2005.
96. Bodow S. It's not what they know, but whom. *New York Times*, December 23, 2001:sect 3-8.
97. Leerink Swann & Co. Interview with Daniel Dubin, January 24, 2005. Available at: http://www.leerink.com. Accessed April 28, 2005.
98. Anand G. & Smith R. Trial heat: biotech analysts strive to peek inside clinical tests of drugs. *Wall Street Journal*, August 8, 2002:A1.
99. Saul S. & Anderson J. Doctors links with investors raise concerns. *New York Times,* August 16, 2005:A1.
100. Kaiser Policy Report, August 9, 2005.
101. Heath P. & Timmerman L. Drug researchers leak secrets to Wall Street. *Seattle Times*, August 7, 2005:A1.
102. Pellegrino E.D. Medical professionalism: Can it, should it survive? J Am Board Fam Pract 13(2):147-9, 2000.

Chapter 9: Where are the Regulators?

1. Tenery R. M. Interactions between physicians and the health care technology industry. *JAMA* 283(3):391-3, 2000.
2. American Medical Association E-8.03. Conflicts of Interest: Guidelines. Available at http://www.ama-assn.org/apps/pf_new/pf_online, accessed March 1, 2006.
3. American Medical Association E-8.032. Conflicts of Interest: Health Facility Ownership by a Physician. Available at: http://www.ama-assn.org/apps/pf_new/pf_online accessed March 1, 2006.
4. American Medical Association D-215.995. Specialty Hospitals and Impact on Health Care. Available at: http://www.ama-assn.org/apps/pf_new/pf_online, accessed March 1, 2006.
5. Coyle S. L. Physician-industry relations. 1. Individual physicians. *Ann Intern Med* 136:396-402, 2002.
6. Accreditation Council for Continuing Medical Education. Standards for commercial support of continuing medical education. Accessed October 7, 2004, at http://www.accme.org/inconting/17_systems98_essential_areas.pdf.
7. McCrary S.V., Anderson C.B., Jakovljevic J., Khant T., McCullough L.B., et al. A national survey of policies on disclosure of conflicts of interest in

biomedical research. *N Engl J Med* 343(22): 1621-6, 2000.

8. Lo B., Wolf L.E. & Berkeley A. Conflict-of-interest policies for investigators in clinical trials. *N Engl J Med* 343:1616, 2000.

9. Krimsky S. *Science in the Private Interest: Has the Lure of Profits Corrupted Biomedical Research?* New York: Rowman & Littlefield Publishers, Inc., 2003; p 230.

10. Rothman D. J. Medical professionalism-focusing on the real issues. *N Engl J Med* 342(17):1284-6, 2000.

11. Kassirer J. P. *On the Take: How America's Complicity with Big Business Can Endanger Your Health.* Oxford: New York: Oxford University Press, 2005:p 61.

12. Press release. No-Free-Lunch. The American College of Physicians says yes to No Free Lunch, and just about everything else. March 26, 2006.

13. Hensley S. Negative advertising. As drug bill soars, some doctors get an 'unsales' pitch. *Wall Street Journal*, March 13, 2006:A1.

14. Ibid #12.

15. Press releases. No-Free-Lunch. The American Academy of Family Physicians says Yes to McDonald's, Yes to Free Lunch, No to "No Free Lunch." September 14, 2005; mind, says yes to No-Free-Lunch, September 21, 2005.

16. Health Research Group. Public Citizen. www.citizen.org/hrg/. Accessed April 4, 2006.

17. California Healthline. Permanente Medical Group adopts new conflict-of-interest policy. California Healthcare Foundation, April 22, 2005.

18. Abelson R. The spine as profit center. Surgeons invest in makers of hardware. *New York Times*, December 30, 2006. B1.

19. Pollack A. Stanford to ban drug makers' gifts to doctors, even pens. *New York Times*, September 12, 2006: C2.

20. Brennan T.A., Rothman D.J., Blank L., Blumenthal D., & Chimones S.C., et al.
Health industry practices that create conflicts of interest: a policy proposal for academic medical centers. JAMA 295(4):429-33, 2006.

21. DeAngelis C.D., Drazen J. M., Frizelle F.A., Haug C., Hoey J., et al. Clinical trial registration: A statement from the International Committee of Medical Journal Editors. JAMA 292(11):1363-4, 2004.

22. *Uniform Requirements for Manuscripts Submitted to Biomedical Journals: Writing and Editing for Biomedical Publication.* Updated February, 2006. Available at www.icmje.org/, accessed April 4, 2006.

23. Armstrong D. Medical journal spikes article on industry ties of kidney group. *Wall Street Journal*, December 26, 2006:B1.

24. Pharmaceutical Research and Manufacturers of America. Code on interactions

with healthcare professionals. Accessed October 7, 2004, at http://www.phrma.org/publications/policy/2004-01-19.391.pdf.

25. AdvaMED. Information about new AdvaMED guidelines for interactions with health care professionals, 2003. Available at www.advamed.org/publicdocs/coe.html, accessed on April 4, 2006.

26. Department of Health and Human Services, Office of Inspector General. OIG compliance program guidance for pharmaceutical manufacturers. Fed Regist 2003; 68(86): 23731-43. Also available at: http:/oig.hhs.gov/authorities/docs/03/050503FRCPGPharmac.pdf.

27. United States v. TAP Pharmaceuticals, sentencing memorandum of the United States. Criminal Action No. 01-CR-10354-WGY, Dec. 24, 2001.

28. Studdert D. M., Mallo M. M. & Brennan T.A. Financial conflicts of interest in physicians' relationships with the pharmaceutical industry—Self-regulation in the shadow of federal prosecution. *N Engl J Med* 351(18):1891-1900, 2004.

29. Slater E. Today's FDA. *New Engl J Med* 352(30):293-97, 2005.

30. Sigelman D. Unsafe drugs: Congressional silence is deadly. *Public Citizen Research Group Health Letter*, 18, 1:2002.

31. Barrett S. How the Dietary Supplement Health and Education Act of 1998 weakened the FDA. Retrieved May 13, from www.quackwatch.org/02.

32. Deyo R.A. & Patrick D.L. *Hope or Hype: The Obsession with Medical Advances and the High Cost of False Promises*. New York: American Management Association, 2005, p 265.

33. Gaul G. M. Medicare's oversight gap: Accreditors are blamed for overlooking problems, and for conflicts of interest. *Washington Post Weekly Edition*, April 8-14, 2005:8-9.

34. Gaul G. M. Which gets inspected more often: hospital or taco truck? Washington Post Weekly Edition, April 8-14, 2005:9.

35. Ibid. # 33.

36. Gaul G. M. Regulators as partners: Medicare pays private groups of doctors and hospital executives to assure quality. *Washington Post Weekly Edition*. April 15-21, 2005:10-11.

37. Ibid. #36.

38. 42 U.S.C.1320-7a (2004).

39. Rabecs R. N. Kickbacks as false claims: the use of the civil False Claims Act to prosecute violations of the federal health care program's anti-kickback statute. *Mich State Law Rev* 2001; Spring:1-84.

40. Ibid. #27.

41. Ibid. #38.

42. Perlstein S. Referrals appear to be ethical conflict. MD-owned imaging centers

raise questions. *Fam Pract News* April 15, 2004:102.
43. Katz D., Caplan A.L., Merz J.F. All gifts large and small: toward an understanding of the ethics of pharmaceutical industry gift giving. *Am J Bioeth* 3(3):39-46, 2003.
44. Chren M. Interactions between physicians and drug company representatives. *Am J Med* 107:182-3, 1999.
45. Dana J., Loewenstein G. A social science perspective on gifts to physicians from industry. *JAMA* 290:252-5, 2003.
46. Brett A.S., Burr W. Are gifts from pharmaceutical companies ethically problematic? A survey of physicians. *Arch Intern Med* 163:2213-8, 2003.
47. Ibid #11, pp 192-3.
48. Ibid. #11, pp 211-2.
49. Pham H. H., Devers K. J., May J. H. & Berenson R. Financial pressures spur physician entrepreneurialism. *Health Aff* (Millwood) 23(2):70-81, 2004.
50. Ibid. #32, p 271.
51. Editorial. Let drugs duke it out. *Los Angeles Times*, September 7, 2003, p M4.
52. Harris G. Drug makers scrutinized over grants. *New York Times*, January 11, 2005: C1.

Chapter 10: The Unrestrained Medical Market Place & Medicine

1. Friedson E. L. Professionalism and institutional ethics. In: Baker R.B., Caplan A.L., Emanuel L. L. & Latham S. R. (eds). *The American Medical Ethics Revolution.* Baltimore: Johns Hopkins University Press, 1999:130-1.
2. Churchill, L.R. Hegemony of money: Commercialism and professionalism in American medicine. *Cambridge Quarterly of Health Care,* Spring, 2007
3. Grumbach K., Osmond D., Vranizan K., Jaffe D., & Bindman A.B. Primary care physicians' experience of financial incentives in managed-care systems. *N Engl J Med* 339:1516-21, 1998.
4. Schultz D.V. Physicians and organizations: For whom the bell tolls. *Front Health Serv Manage* 14(3):46-48; discussion: 49-50, 1998.
5. Burdi M.D. & Baker L.C. Physicians' perceptions of autonomy and satisfaction in California: *Health Aff* (Millwood) 18(4):134-145, 1999.
6. Pennachio D. L. Are you sorry you went into primary care? *Med Econ* 79(18):31-32, 2002.
7. Landon B.E., Aseltine R. Jr., Shaul J.A., Miller Y., Auerbach B.A. & Cleary P.D. Evolving dissatisfaction among primary care physicians. *Am J Manag Care* 8(10):890-901, 2002.
8. Landon B.E., Reschovsky J., & Blumenthal D. Changes in career satisfaction among primary care and specialist physicians, 1997-2001. *JAMA* 289:442-449,2003.

9. Practice Beat. Doctor's misery index continues to worsen. *Medical Economics,* June 7, 2002:22.
10. Goldberg R. M. What's happened to the healing process? *Wall Street Journal,* June 18, 1997, p. A22.
11. Davidoff F. Time. *Ann Intern Med* 127:483-85, 1997.
12. Linzer M.A. The Physician Worklife Study: The Results Are In. *Society of General Internal Medicine Forum,* October 1998, pp. 2,9.
13. Franks P., Cameron C., Bertakis K.D. On being new to an insurance plan: health care use associated with the first years in a health plan. *Ann Fam Med* 1:156-61, 2003.
14. Chernew M.E., Wodchis W.P., Scanlon D. P. & McLaughlin C.G. Overlap in HMO physician networks. *Health Aff* (Millwood) 23(2):91-101, 2004.
15. Geyman J. P. Drawing on the legacy of general practice to build the future of family medicine. Fam Med 36(9):631-8, 2004.
16. Angell M. The doctor as double agent. *Kennedy Institute of Ethics Journal* 3(3):279-286, 1993.
17. Feldman D. S., Novack D. I. & Gracely E. Effects of managed care on physician-patient relationships, quality of care, and the ethical practice of medicine. *Arch Intern Med* 158:1626-32, 2004.
18. Wessel D., Wysocki J.B., & Martinez B. Spending bypass. As health middlemen thrive, employers try to tame them. *Wall Street Journal,* December 29, 2006: A1.
19. Woolhandler S., Campbell T. & Himmelstein D. U. Costs of health care administration in the United States and Canada. *N Engl J Med* 349(8):768-75, 2003.
20. Remler D. K., Gray B. M. & Newhouse J. P. Does managed care mean more hassle for physicians? *Inquiry* 37:304-16, 2000.
21. Harris Poll. Attitudes toward the United States health care system: long-term trends—views of the public, employers, physicians, health plan managers are closer now than at any times in the past. *Harris Interactive* 2(17), 2002.
22. Blendon R.J., Schoen C., Donelan K., Osborn R., DesRoches C. M., et al. Physicians' views on quality of care: A five-country comparison. *Health Aff* (Millwood) 20(3):233-43, 2001.
23. Pham H.H., Devers K.J., May J. H. & Berenson R. Financial pressures spur physician entrepreneurialism. *Health Aff* (Millwood) 23(2):70-81, 2004.
24. Sirovitch B. E., Gottlieb D. J., Welch H.G. & Fisher E.S. Variation in the tendency of primary care physicians to intervene. *Arch Intern Med* 165(1):2252-6, 2005.
25. Romano M. Holding steady. *Modern Healthcare* 35(29):51, 2005.
26. Lowes R. The earnings freeze: now it's everybody's problem. *Medical*

Economics September 16, 2005, 59.

27. Compensation Monitor. *Managed Care Magazine*. Available at: http://www. managedcaremag.com/archives/0103/0103.compinon.html. Accessed on January 11, 2006.
28. Welch H.G. Avoiding the unintended consequences of growth in medical care: How might more be worse? *JAMA* 281:446-53, 1999.
29. The impending collapse of primary care medicine and its implications for the state of the nation's health care. Washington, D.C.: Accessed August 10, 2006, at http://www.acponline.org/hpp/statehc06_1.pdf.
30. Ibid #26.
31. Abelson R. Doctors' average pay fell 7 percent in 8 years, report says. *New York Times*, June 22, 2006:C3.
32. Wagner L. Citing national losses of $2.2 billion, physicians closing doors to seniors. *Physicians Financial News* May 15, 2002, 20(7):1,24.
33. Ibid #31.
34. Miller M.E. Medicare payment to physicians. Testimony before Subcommittee on Health, Committee on Energy and Commerce, U.S. House of Representatives, July 25, 2006.
35. Goodman D.C. Twenty-year trends in regional variations in the U.S. physician workforce. *Health Aff* (Millwood) (suppl Web exclusive):var90-97, 2004.
36. Hart J.T. The Inverse Care Law. Lancet 1:405-12, 1971.
37. Pugno P.A., Schmittling G.T., Fetter G.T., & Kahn N. B. Results of the 2005 National Resident Matching Program: Family Medicine. *Fam Med* 37(8):555-64, 2005.
38. Morrison G. Mortgaging our future—the cost of medical education. *N Engl J Med* 352(2):117-9, 2005.
39. *Summary of Sixteenth Report: Physician Workforce Policy Guidelines for the United States, 2000-2020*. Washington, D.C.: Council on Graduate Medical Education, 2005.
40. Cooper R.A., Getzen T.E., McKee H. J. & Laud P. Economic and demographic trends signal an impending physician shortage. *Health Aff* (Millwood) 21:140-54, 2002.
41. Press release. ASMA endorses new physician workforce position. American Medical Student Association, July 28, 2006.
42. Starfield B. Is primary care essential? *Lancet* 344:1129-33, 1994.
43. Forrest C.B. Strengthening primary care to bolster the health care safety net. *JAMA* 295(9):1062-4, 2006.
44. Rosenblatt R.A., Andrilla C.H., Curtin T. & Hart L.G. Shortages of medical personnel at community health centers: implications for planned expansion. *JAMA* 295:1042-49, 2006.

45. PNHP. Slide set of Physicians for a National Health Program. Chicago: with excerpt of letter published in *Modern Healthcare*. September 21, 1995, p 172.

46. Kocieniewski D. U.S. to monitor medical school in New Jersey. *New York Times* December 30, 2005:A1.

47. Houston W. J. Rekindling the fire of family medicine. *Fam Pract News* January 15, 2006.

48. Wynia M.K., Cummins D.S., Van Geest J.B. & Wilson I.B. Physician manipulation of reimbursement rules for patients. *JAMA* 283(14):1858-65, 2005.

49. Wynia M.K., Zucker D., Supran S., & Selker H. P. Patient protection and risk selection. Do primary care physicians encourage their patients to join or avoid capitated health plans according to the patients' health status? *J Gen Intern Med* 17:40-7, 2002.

50. Wynia M.K., Van Geest J.B., Cummins D.S. & Wilson I.B. Do physicians not offer useful services because of coverage restrictions? *Health Aff* (Millwood) 22(4):190-7, 2003.

51. Ibid #2.

52. Landon B.E., Reschovsky J.D., Pham H.H. & Blumenthal D. Leaving medicine: the consequences of physician dissatisfaction. *Med Care* 44(3):234-42, 2006.

53. O'Malley A.S., Reschovsky J.D. No exodus: Physicians and managed care networks. Tracking Report #14. Center for Studying Health System Change, May 2006.

54. Fleck C. Want your doctor to pamper you? Pay extra. *AARP Bulletin* 45(9): 32-3, 2004.

55. Guadagnino C. Forming a national society of concierge physicians. *Physicians' News Digest*, April 2004.

56. Web site of *Society for Innovative Medical Practice Design* (SIMPD) accessed May 14, 2006.

57. Geraci J.V. The steady creep towards concierge medicine. November 14, 2005; available from jgeraci@mailbmc.com.

58. GAO. Physician Services: Concierge Care Characteristics and Considerations for Medicare. GAO-05-929, August 12, 2005.

59. Ibid #56.

60. Scherer R. A. Physicians' unions: a growing power. *Psychiatric Times* 16(5): May 1999.

61. Budrys G. When doctors join unions. Ithaca, NY: Cornell University Press, 1997.

62. Ibid #61.

63. Hoff T. J. Physician unionization in the United States: Fad or phenomenon? JHHSA summer 2000: 5-23.
64. Albart T. More doctors following trend to unionize. *American Medical News*, November 27, 2000:1.
65. Appleby C. Labor unions for physicians: an idea whose time is coming? *Managed Care Magazine*, 1996. Available at: www.managecaremag.com, accessed May 15, 2006.
66. Ibid #65.
67. American Medical Association E-8.032. Conflicts of Interest: Health Facility Ownership by a Physician. Available at: http://www.ama-assn.org/apps/pf_new/pf_online accessed March 1, 2006.
68. SIMPD. Explore an affordable alternative to boutique medicine. *Private Practice Success*. February 2005. Available on Society for Innovative Medical Practice Design's Web site. Accessed May 15, 2006 and based on AMA's policy 8.055 on Retainer Practices (accessed May 21, 2006, at www.ama.assn.org/ama/pub/categorg/11967.html.
69. Gianelli D. Delegates say AMA must do more to foster collective bargaining. *American Medical News*, January 4, 1999.
70. Collective bargaining: AMA-created unit files NLRB petition seeking representation of HMO doctors. BNA Health Law Rep 9:171, 2000.
71. Ginsburg J. Physicians and joint negotiations. *Ann Intern Med* 134:787-92, 2001.
72. Ibid #64.
73. NLRB v Kentucky River Community Care, 121 S Ct, 1861 (2001), as cited in Kinderman K. Unionization of health care professionals. Medical-legal highlights. *J Med Pract Manage*, November-December, 162-5:2002.
74. American Medical Association (AMA). 2001a AMA: Antitrust Relief Needed for Physicians. Available on-line at www.ama-assn.org/ama/pub/article/40303979. html (accessed May 4, 2001).
75. Brewbaker W.S. Will physician union improve health system performance? *J Health Polit Policy Law* 27(4):575-604, 2002.
76. Pellegrino E.D., & Relman A.S. Professional and medical associations: ethical and practical guidelines. *JAMA* 282(10):985, 1999.

Chapter 11: Where Are We Going?

1. Jefferson T. Statement made to the Republican Citizens of Washington County, MD. March 31, 1809.
2. Lakoff G. The post-Katrina era. *The Huffington Post*, September 8, 2005.
3. Committee on the Consequences of Uninsurance. *Insuring America's Health: Principles and Recommendations*. Institute of Medicine. Washington, D.C.: National Academy Press, 2004: 150-1.

4. Kuttner R. *Everything for Sale: The Virtues and Limits of Markets*. Chicago: University of Chicago Press, 1997, p 114.
5. AMA. Reference Committee Highlights. 2006 Annual Meeting of the House of Delegates.
6. Pear R. Health insurance industry urges expansion of coverage. *New York Times*, November 14, 2006:A14.
7. HealthCast video of AHIP's release of the proposal is available at http://www.kaisernetwork.org/health_cast/hcast_index.cfm?display+detail&hc=1974.
8. Gross D. National health care? We're halfway there. *New York Times*, December 3, 2006.
9. CAHI issues: High-risk pools. Web site of Council for Affordable Health Insurance, Alexandria, VA: accessed January 5, 2007. www.cahi.org/.
10. Abbe B. Overview—State high-risk health insurance pools today. www.selfemployedcountry. org, accessed January 5, 2007.
11. Friedan J. Vital signs. *Family Practice News*, 32(3):1, 2002.
12. Brailer D. Healthcare information and management systems society (HIMSS). Keynote, 2005.
13. Freudenheim M. Web MD wants to go beyond information. *New York Times*, February 23, 2006:C1.
14. Villagra V. Strategies to control costs and quality: a focus on outcomes research for disease management. *Med Care* 42(4 Suppl) 1124-30, 2004.
15. Straube B. The CMS quality roadmap: Quality plus efficiency. *Health Affairs* Web Exclusive W5-555-57, 2005.
16. Ibid. #3, p 152.
17. Ibid #3, pp 150-1.
18. California Health Care Options project; full drafts of each proposal are available at   http://www.health-access.org/doc/FINAL%20PAPER%20Lewin—041002.DOC
19. Sheils J.F. & Haught R.A. Analysis of the costs and impact of universal health care models for the state of Maryland: the single-payer and multi-payer models. Fairfax, VA: The Lewin Group, 2000.
20. Brand R., Ford D., Sager A., & Socolar D. Universal comprehensive coverage: a report to the Massachusetts Medical Society. Waltham, MA: The Massachusetts Medical Society, 1998.
21. Smith R.F. Universal health insurance makes business sense. *Rutland Herald*, November 2, 2001.
22. Policy Brief. Health care in Connecticut: Sounding the alarm. Economic and Social Research Institute (ERSI), June 22, 2006.
23. Miller A. 'Single-payer' Georgia health plan pushed. *Atlanta Journal Constitution*, June 22, 2004.
24. Barry P. Coverage for all. *AARP Bulletin*. 47(7):8-9, 2006.

25. Woolhandler S. & Himmelstein D. U. Massachusetts' health bill failed before, will again. *Atlanta Journal Constitution*, April 7, 2006.
26. *Families USA*. Too little, too late: Why a $1,000 tax credit won't help the uninsured. Washington, D.C.: December 2005.
27. *Families USA*. Abstracted in Med Benefits November 15, 2001:10-11.
28. Gruber J. Written testimony at Hearing on Health Insurance Credits before the House Ways and Means Subcommittee on Health. February 13, 2002.
29. Gruber J. Tax policy for health insurance. National Bureau of Economic Research, December 2004.
30. Pearlstein S. Pearlstein Live. Washingtonpost.com. February 8, 2006.
31. Fronstein P., & Collins S.R. The 2nd Annual EBRI/Commonwealth Fund Consumerism in Health Care Survey, 2006: Early experience with high-deductible and consumer-driven health plans. The Commonwealth Fund, December 2006.
32. Cochrane T. HSA funding. Are health care consumers leaving money on the table? Vimo Research Group Report, January 4, 2007.
33. American Diabetes Association. High-risk pools. Health Insurance Resource Manual. Alexandria, VA, 2006.
34. Girion L. Healthy? Insurers don't buy it. Minor ailments can thwart applicants for individual policies. *Los Angeles Times*, December 31, 2006.
35. *Families USA*. AHPs: Bad medicine for small employers. *Washington*, D.C.: December 2005.
36. Mercer W. *Association Health Plan Legislation: Impact on Health Plan Administrative Costs for Small Businesses*. Human Resources Consulting: March 1999.
37. Baumgardner J. & Hagen S. *Increasing Small Firm Health Insurance Coverage Through Association Health Plans and Health Marts*. Washington, D.C.: Congressional Budget Office, January 2000.
38. Fritchen B. & Bender K. *Impact of Association Health Plans on Premiums and Coverage for Small Employers*. Washington,D.C.: Mercer Risk, Finance & Insurance, June 2003.
39. *Private Health Insurance: Employers and Individuals Are Vulnerable*. Washington, D.C.: Government Accountability Office, February 2004.
40. Chan G. Insurance-pool plug pulled. *Sacramento Bee*, August 12, 2006.
41. U.S. Department of Health and Human Services. Office of the National Coordinator for Health Information Technology. May 23, 2005, http://www.hhs.gov/healthit/valueHIT.html. (accessed April 27, 2006.)
42. Sidorov J. It ain't necessarily so: The electronic health record and the unlikely prospect of reducing health care costs. *Health Aff* (Millwood) 25:4, 1179-85, 2006.

43. Miller R.H., West C., Brown T.M., Sim I. & Ganchoff C. The value of electronic health records in solo or small group practices. *Health Aff* (Millwood) 24(5):1127-37, 2005.

44. Wang S.J., Middleton B., Prosser L.A., Bardon C.G., Sparr C.D., et al A cost-benefit analysis of electronic medical records in primary care. *Am J Med* 114(5):397-403, 2003.

45. Himmelstein D.U. & Woolhandler S. Hope and hype: predicting the impact of electronic medical records. *Health Aff* (Millwood) 24(5):1121-3,2005.

46. GAO (U.S. Government Accountability Office). Statement of David A. Powner. Testimony Before the Subcommittee on Federal Workforce and Agency Organization, Committee on Government Reform, House of Representatives Health Information Technology. HHS is Continuing Efforts to Define Its National Strategy, September 1, 2006.

47. GAO. Report to Congressional Committee on Domestic and Offshore Outsourcing of Personal Information in Medicare, Medicaid, and TRICARE, September 2006.

48. Holtz-Eakin P. CBO Director, testimony to Congress. October 13, 2004.

49. Eddy D.M., Schlessinger L. & Kahn R. Clinical outcomes and cost-effectiveness of strategies for managing people at high risk for diabetes. Ann Intern Med 143:251-64, 2005.

50. Trude S., Au M. & Christianson J.B. Health plan pay-for-performance strategies. *Am J Manag Care* 12(9):537-42, 2006.

51. Galvin R. Interview. 'A deficiency of will and ambition': A conversation with Donald Berwick. *Health Affairs* Web Exclusive W55, 2006.

52. McCanne D. Comment on Remes D. Exploring the nexus of quality and cost. Premier, August 31, 2006. In: "Quote of the Day," September 5, 2006 (Quote of the Day@mccanne.org).

53. Morrison A.B. & Wolfe S.M. Outrage of the month. None of your business. Public Citizen's Health Research Group. *Health Letter*, February 2001:11.

54. Stoll K. & Denker P. What's wrong with tax-free savings accounts for health care? Issue Brief. *Families USA*. Washington, D.C.: November 2003.

55. Nichols L.M., Ginsburg P.B., Berseson R.A., Christianson J. & Hurley R.C. Are market forces strong enough to delivery efficient health care systems? Confidence is waning. *Health Aff* (Millwood) 23(2):8-21, 2004.

56. Kronick R., Goodman D.C., Weinberg J. & Wagner E. The marketplace in health care reform. The demographic limitations of managed competition. *N Engl J Med* 328:148, 1993.

57. Himmelstein D. U. The National Health Program Slide-show Guide. Center for National Health Program Studies. Cambridge, Mass: 2000.

58. Achman L. & Gold M. *New Analysis Describes 2004 Payment Increases to*

Medicare Advantage Plans. Mathematica Policy Research, Washington, D.C.: April 2004.

59. MEDAC. Report of the Medicare Payment Advisory Commission on government subsidies of private Medicare Advantage Plans, 2007.

60. Krugman P. Health policy malpractice. *New York Times*, Op Ed, September 4, 2006:A19.

61. Grembowski D.F., et al. Measuring the "managedness" and covered benefits of health plans. *Health Serv Res* 35(3):707-34, 2000.

62. Woolhandler S., Campbell T., & Himmelstein D. U. Costs of health care administration in the United States and Canada. *N Engl J Med* 349:768, 2003.

63. Fisher E.S., Wennberg D.E., Stukel T.A., et al. The implications of regional variations in Medicare spending. Part 2: Health outcomes and satisfaction with care. *Ann Intern Med* 138(4):288-98, 2003.

64. Commonwealth Fund. Quality of Health Care in the U.S. Chartbook, New York: 2002.

65. Newhouse J.P. Consumer-directed health plans and the RAND health insurance experiment. *Health Aff* (Millwood) 23(6):107-13, 2004.

66. Soumerai S.B., Ross-Degnan D., Avorn J., McLaughlin T. J. & Choodnovskkiy I. Effects of Medicaid drug-payment limits on admission to hospitals and nursing homes. *N Engl J Med* 325:1072-77, 2004.

67. Greg L. & Stoddart G.L., et al. *Why Not User Charges? The Real Issues,* a discussion paper prepared for the [Ontario] Premier's Council on Health, Well-being and Social Justice. September 1993, pp. 5-6.

68. Gorey K.M., Holoway E.J., Febinger G., Laukkann E., Moskowitz E.A., et al. An international comparison of cancer survival. Toronto and Detroit, Michigan metropolitan areas. *Am J Public Health* 87:1156-63, 1997.

69. Drum K. Political animal. *Washington Monthly,* June 11, 2006.

70. Davis K. Medicare vs. private insurance: rhetoric and reality. *Health Aff* Web exclusive. October 9, 2003, W311-23.

71. Marmor T.R. *The Politics of Medicare.* New York: Aldine Publishing Company, 1970, p 86.

72. Wolfe S. Selling 'new' drugs using smoke and mirror (images). *Health Letter,* p 2., March 2003.

73. Blue Cross and Blue Shield. Technology Evaluation Committee Reports, No. 1-28. Chicago: 1999.

74. National Institute for Health Care Management Research and Educational Foundation. *Changing patterns of pharmaceutical innovations.* Washington, D.C.: 2002.

75. Blendon R.J., Schoen C. & DesRoches, C.M.,et al. Inequities in health care:

A five-country survey. *Health Aff* (Millwood) 21(3):186, 2002.
76. Canadian Health Services Research Foundation Newsletter. Vol. 1 No. 4, available at www.chsrf.ca.
77. Lasser K.E., Himmelstein D.U., & Woolhandler S. Access to care, health status, and health disparities in the United States and Canada: Results of a cross-national population-based survey. *Am J Public Health* 46(7):1-8, 2006.
78. Center for Studying Health System Change (CSHSC). Sept. 5, 2002, Washington, D.C.
79. Himmelstein D.U., et al. *Administrative Waste in the U.S. Health Care System in 2003: The Cost to the Nation, the States and the District of Columbia, with State-Specific Estimates of Potential Savings*. Public Citizen Health Research Group, Washington, D.C.: August 20, 2003.
80. Ibid. #62.
81. Gaul G.M. Back in the pink: The VA health care system outperforms Medicare and most private plans. *Washington Post* National Weekly Edition, August 29-September 4, 2005:29.
82. Arnst C. The best medical care in the U.S.: How Veterans Affairs transformed itself—and what it means for the rest of us. *Business Week*, July 17, 2006.
83. Steinmo S. & Watts J. It's the institutions, stupid? Why comprehensive national health insurance always fails in *America. J Health Polit Policy Law* 20:329, 1995.
84. Blendon R.J. & Benson J. M. Americans' views on health policy: a fifty-year historical perspective. *Health Aff* (Millwood) 20(2):33, 2001.
85. Peter D. Hart Research Associations. Labor Day: 2005, the State of Working America, August 2005.
86. Pew Research Center. Beyond Red vs. Blue. Survey Report, May 10, 2005.
87. Light D.W. A conservative call for universal access to health care. *Penn Bioethics* 9(4):4-6, 2002.
88. Mercer Human Resource. Consulting health benefit cost slows for a third year, rising just 6.1 percent in 2005. November 21, 2005.
89. Russell E. An equitable way to pay for Universal coverage. *Int J Health Serv* 29(1):179-88, 1999.
90. http://www.healthcareforall.org/lewin.pdf#search=%22lewin%20group%20california%20study%22
91. Ha Kim D. GM says costs for retiree care tops $60 billion. *New York Times*, March 12, 2004.
92. Andrews E.L. Small business: Health care heights. *New York Times*, February 24, 2004.
93. Downey K. A heftier dose to swallow. *Washington Post*, March 6, 2004.
94. Geyman J.P. Drawing on the legacy of general practice to build the future of

family medicine. *Fam Med* 36(9):631-8, 2004.
95. Angell M. Sweeping health care reform proposed by nations' top physicians. Press Release. Physicians for a National Health Program, Chicago: 2001.
96. Krugman P. Health economics 101. Op Ed. *New York Times*, November 14, 2005:A21.

Chapter 12: An Action Plan for Medicine

1. Making the Case for Not-for-Profit Health Care, excerpts from a speech by Cardinal Joseph Bernardin. The Harvard Business School Club of Chicago, January 12, 1995.
2. Christensen C.M., Bohmer R., & Knagy J. Will disruptive innovations cure health care? *Harvard Business Review*, 103-111, 2000.
3. Callahan D. Beyond individualism: Bioethics and the common good. In: *Second Opinion* 9, 59:1998.
4. Callahan D. Preface to Report, *The Goals of Medicine: Setting New Priorities*. Hastings Center Report, November-December 1996.
5. Project Report. *The Goals of Medicine: Setting New Priorities*: Special Supplement. Hastings Center Report, November-December, 1996: S4.
6. Ibid. #5, Executive summary.
7. Ibid. #5, p S-23-5.
8. Ibid. #5, S20-1.
9.. Barry C.L., Frank R.G., & McGuire T.G. The costs of mental health parity: still an impediment? Health Aff (Millwood) 25(3):623-34, 2006.
10. Institute for the Future. *Health and Health Care 2010: The Forecast, the Challenges*. San Francisco: Jossey-Bass Publishers, 2000: 123-37.
11. Hadley et al. Federal Spending on the Health Care Safety Net from 2001-2004: Has Spending Kept Pace with the Growth in the Uninsured? KCMU, November 2005, Publication #7425.

Chapter 13: Our Patients as Allies

1. Moyers B. A new story for America. *The Nation* 284(3): 17, 2007.
2. Gray B. *The Profit Motive and Patient Care: The Changing Accountability of Doctors and Hospitals*. Cambridge: Harvard University Press, 1991.
3. James C. "Hope" series returns with darker view of doctors. *New York Times*, September 23, 1999: B1, B9.
4. Schlesinger M. A loss of faith: The sources of reduced political legitimacy for the American medical profession. The Milbank Q 80(2):185-235, 2002.
5. National Coalition on Healthcare. A report of a national survey. *J Health Care Finance* 23:12, 1997.
6. Mycek S. We're not in Kansas anymore. *Trustee*, September 1999:52:22.
7. John Q. Public: Nurses are still most trustworthy. *Medical Economics*,

February 4, 2005: p14.

8.   Blendon R. J., Hyams T.S. & Benson J. M. Bridging the gap between expert and public views on health care reform. *JAMA* 269 (19):2573-8, 1993.

9.   Jacobs L. R. & Shapiro R. Y. Public opinion's tilt against private enterprise. Health Aff (Millwood) 12(1): 285-98, 1994.

10. Pescasolido B.A., Tuch S.A. & Martin J.A. The profession of medicine and the public: examining America's changing confidence in physician authority from the beginning of the "Health Care Crisis" to the era of health care reform. *J Health & Soc Behavior* 42(1):1-16, 2001.

11. Mechanic D. Public perceptions of medicine. *N Engl J Med* 312:181-3, 1985.

12. Ibid #4.

13. Ibid #10.

14. Wolfe S.M. (editor). The people have spoken: the drug industry doesn't serve us well. Health Letter, Public Citizen's Health Research Group. Washington, D.C. 20(8):1,2, 2004.

15. Mechanic D. Changing medical organization and the erosion of trust. *MilbankQ* 74:171,89, 1996.

16. Gray B. H. Trust and trustworthy care in the managed care era. *Health Aff* (Millwood) 16(1):34-49, 1997.

17. Reinhardt U.E. Resource allocation in health care: the allocation of lifestyles to providers. *MilbankQ* 65:153-76, 1987.

18. Cauthen D. B. Luxurious cars: should physicians flaunt their wealth?

19. Rodwin M. A. *Medicine, Money and Morals: Physicians' Conflicts of Interest.* New York: Oxford University Press, 1993.

20. Ibid #3.

21. Gray B. *The Profit Motive and Patient Care: The Changing Accountability of Doctors and Hospitals.* Cambridge: Harvard University Press, 1991.

22. Cassell E. *The Changing Concept of the Ideal Physician.* Daedalus, Spring 202, 1986.

23. Steinmo S. & Watts J. It's the institutions, stupid? Why comprehensive national health insurance always fails in America. *J Health Polit Policy Law* 20:329, 1995.

24. Blendon R. J. & Benson J. M. Americans' views on health policy: a fifty-year historical perspective. *Health Aff* (Millwood) 20(2):33, 2001.

25. Ibid #5.

26. *Wall Street Journal*/Harris Poll. October 20, 2005.

27. How access and affordability are shaping views. Civil Society Institute: September 15, 2004.

28. Health care in Vermont: support for universal coverage. AARP, October 2005;

Channel 3 News Poll, May 4-7, 2005.

29. King B. Seattle votes for a right to health care. *Washington Free Press* January-February, 2006, p 5.

30. Beyond Red vs. Blue. Report of the Pew Research Center of the People and the Press, Washington, D.C.: May 10, 2005.

31. Bagell R. Bubba blew it. But can U.S. health care be fixed? MSNBC, May 9, 2006.

32. Harris Poll. Attitudes toward the United States health care system: Long-term trends—views of the public, employers, physicians, health plan managers are closer now than at any times in the past. *Harris Interactive* 2(17), 2002.

33. Schoen C., Osborn R., Huynh P.T., Doty M. & Davis K, et al. Primary care and health system performance: Adults' experiences in five countries. *Health Affairs* Web Exclusive W487-503, 2004.

34. U.S. Government Accounting Office. Canadian health insurance: lessons for the United States. Washington, D.C.: Government Accounting Office (GAO/HRD-91-90), 1991.

35. Himmelstein D. U., Woolhandler S., Wolfe S. M. Administrative waste in the U.S. health care system in 2003. The cost to the Nation, the States and the District of Columbia, with state-specific estimates of potential savings. *Int J Health Serv* 34(1):79, 2004.

36. National Coalition on Health Care. Press release. New projections from nation's largest healthcare coalition show health care reform would produce huge savings. Washington, D.C., May 23, 2005.

37. California Health Care Options Project. http://www.healthcareoptions.ca.gov/doclib.asp.

38. Brand R., Frod D., Sager A. & Socolar D. Universal comprehensive coverage: A report to the Massachusetts Medical Society. Waltham, Mass: The Massachusetts Medical Society, 1998.

39. Sheils J.F. & Haught R.A. Analysis of the costs and impact of universal health care models for the state of Maryland: the single-payer and multi-payer models. Fairfax, VA: The Lewin Group, 2000.

40. Smith R.F. Universal health insurance makes business sense. *Rutland Herald*, November 2, 2001.

41. Gordon C. *The Clinton Health Care Plan: Dead on Arrival*. Westfield, NJ: Open Magazine Pamphlet Series, 1995.

42. E-mail communication between Kip Sullivan and Don McCanne, president of Physicians for a National Health Program, July 19, 2002.

43. The Health Report to the American People. Report of the Citizens' Health Care Working Group, Appendix B, July 2006, available at http://www.citizenshealthcare.gov/recommendations/appendix_b.pdf.

44. Listen up! *Asclepios.* Your Weekly Medicare Consumer Advocacy Update. 6(32): August 10, 2006, p 1.
45. Press release. Commonwealth Fund. New York: March 29, 2004.
46. Schlesinger M., Mitchell S., & Gray B. H. Public expectations of nonprofit and for-profit ownership in American medicine: clarification and implications. *Health Aff* (Millwood) 23(6):181-91, 2004.
47. Tu H.T., & Reschovsky J.D. Assessments of medical care by enrollees in for-profit and non-profit health maintenance organizations. *N Engl J Med* 346:1288-93, 2002.
48. Hartz A. J., Krakauer H., & Kuhn E. M., et al. Hospital characteristics and mortality rates. *N Engl J Med* 321:1720-5, 1989.
49. Woolhandler S. & Himmelstein D. U. Costs of care and administration at for-profit and other hospitals in the United States. *N Engl J Med* 366:769-74, 1997.
50. Kovner C. & Gergen P. J. Nurse staffing levels and adverse events following surgery in U.S. hospitals. *Image J Nurs Sch* 30:315-21, 1998.
51. Chen J., Radford M.J., & Wang Y, et al. Do 'America's best hospitals' perform better for acute myocardial infarction? N Engl J Med 340:286-92, 1999.
52. Silverman E. M., Skinner J.S. & Fisher E.S. The association between for-profit hospital ownership and increased Medicare spending. *N Engl J Med* 1999; 341:420-6.
53. Yuan Z., Cooper G.S., Einstadter D., Cebul R.D. & Rimm A.A. The association between hospital type and mortality and length of stay: a study of 16.9 million hospitalized Medicare beneficiaries. *Med Care* 38:231-45, 2000.
54. The HMO Honor Roll. *U.S. News and World Report,* Oct 23, 1997 p 62.
55. Himmelstein D.U., Woolhandler S., Hellander I. & Wolfe S.M. Quality of care in investor-owned vs. not-for-profit HMOs. *JAMA* 282(2):159-63, 1999.
56. Garg P.P., Frick K.D., Diener-West M., & Powe N.R. Effect of ownership of dialysis facilities on patients' survival and referral for transplantation. *N Engl J Med* 341:653-60, 1999.
57. Harrington C., Woolhandler S., Mullen J., Carrillo H., & Himmelstein D.U. Does investor-ownership of nursing homes compromise the quality of care? *Am J Public Health* 91(9):1, 2001.
58. Dunham R.S. Health care reform is in the air, but—*Business Week* February 5, 2007, p 34.
59. Kaiser Family Foundation, May 11, 2004.
60. Chu. *Wall Street Journal,* February 3, 2005, as cited in PNHP Newsletter. Chicago: summer, 2005.
61. Citigroup Smith Barney. Affluent Investor Poll, May 17, 2006.
62. Helman R., Greenwald M. & Fronstin P. *2006 Health Confidence Survey:*

Dissatisfaction with Health Care System Doubles Since 1998. Employee Benefit Research Institute (EBRI) November 2006.

63. Ibid #35.
64. Public Citizen Report. April 18, 2002. Full report available at http://www. citizen.org/congressreform/drug_industry/profits/articles.ctm? ID=(416).
65. Kaiser Family Foundation. The public on health care costs: Perceived reasons for rising health care costs. Accessed May 25, 2006 at http://www.Kff.org/spotlight/healthcosts/index.cfm.
66. Ibid #14.
67. Abboud L. Stung by public distrust, drug makers seek to heal image. *Wall Street Journal*, August 26, 2005:B1.
68. Kaiser Family Foundation/Harvard School of Public Health. Views of the new Medicare drug law: A survey of people on Medicare. June 16 to July 21, 2004.
69. Lueck S. Drug benefit in play: Which party wins? *Wall Street Journal*, February 24, 2006:A4.
70. Poll: People understand systemic problems at FDA. *Health Letter* 22(6):June 2006:pp 5-6.
71. Ibid #14.
72. Rubenstein S. Insurers offer consumer-friendly health statements. *Wall Street Journal*, January 10, 2006:D4.
73. Kaiser Health Poll Report. September/October, 2004.
74. Kertesz L. Survey confirms HMOs' bad press. *Modern Healthcare*. November 4, 1006:10.
75. Public Opinion Strategies. April 12, 2004, as cited in PNHP Newsletter. Chicago: fall, 2004.
76. Sullivan K. *The Health Care Mess: How We Got Into It and How We'll Get Out of It.* Bloomington, In: Author House, 2006.
77. Ibid #76.
78. Pauly M.V. The Economics of Moral Hazard: Comment. *Am Econ Review* 58, no. 3, 1968.
79. Crew M. Coinsurance and the Welfare Economics of Medical Care. *Am Econ Review* 59 (5) 906-8, 1969.
80. Pauly M.V. When does curbing health costs really help the economy? *Health Aff* (Millwood) 14(2):68-82, 1993.
81. Nyman J.A. *The Theory of Demand for Health Insurance.* Stanford, Calif: Stanford University Press, 2003.
82. Nyman J.A. Is 'moral hazard' inefficient? The policy implications of a new theory. *Health Aff* (Millwood) 23(5):194-99, 2004.
83. Su A. L. Inappropriate use of hospitals in a randomized trial of health insurance

plans. *N Engl J Med* 315:1259, 1986.

84. Kravitz R. L. & Laouri M. Measuring and averting underuse of necessary cardiac procedures: A summary of results and future directions. *Jt Comm J Qual Improv* 23:286-76, 1997.

85. Lawrence C. & Kleinman, et al. The medical appropriateness of tympanostomy tubes proposed for children younger than 16 years in the United States. *JAMA* 271:1250-55, 1994.

86. Lowes R. Straightforward UR—or a 'machine of denial'? *Medical Economics*, May 8, 2000, 180-206.

87. Ibid #76, p 72.

88. Furmans, V. New tack on copays: cutting them. *Wall Street Journal* May 8, 2007: D1

89. Ibid #76, p 213.

90. Relman A. S. The new medical-industrial complex. *N Engl J Med* 303:963-70, 1980.

91. Kuttner R. *Everything for Sale: The Virtues and Limits of Markets.* Chicago: The University of Chicago Press, 1999, p. 158.

92. Geyman J. P. Myths and memes about single-layer health insurance in the United States: A rebuttal to conservative claims. Int J Health Serv 35(1):63-90, 2005.

93. Kuttner R. Face it: We're rationing health. *Boston Globe Online.* June 11, 2003.

Chapter 14: Restoring Professionalism and Medical Ethics

1. Stevens R.A. Public roles for the medical profession in the United States: Beyond theories of decline and fall. *Milbank Q* 79(3):327, 2001.

2. Means J. H. *Daedalus* 92:701, 1963.

3. Pellegrino E.D. Professionalism, profession and the virtues of the good physician. *Mt Sinai J Med* 69(6):378-84, 2002.

4. Freidson E. Profession of medicine: a study of the sociology of applied knowledge. Chicago: University of Chicago Press, 1988.

5. Cruess R., Cruess S., & Johnston S. Renewing professionalism: an opportunity for medicine. *Acad Med* 74:878-84, 1999.

6. Kultgen J. *Ethics and Professionalism.* Philadelphia: University of Pennsylvania Press, 1988.

7. Goode W. Jr. The theoretical limits of professionalism. In: Etzioni A (ed). *The Semiprofessions and their Organization.* New York: Free Press, 266-313, 1969.

8. Ibid. #5.

9. Freidson E. *Professional Dominance: The Social Structure of Medical Care.* Chicago: Aldine, 1970.

10. Haug M. Deprofessionalization: an alternate hypothesis for the future. Soc Rev Monograph 20:195-211, 1973.
11. Starr P. *The Social Transformation of American Medicine*. New York: Basic Books, 1984.
12. Mechanic D. Changing medical organization and the erosion of trust. *Milbank Q* 74:171-89, 1996.
13. Stevens R.A. Themes in the history of medical professionalism. *Mt Sinai J Med* 69(6):357-62, 2002.
14. Relman A.S. The new medical-industrial complex. N Engl J Med 303:963-70, 1980.
15. Cruess R. & Cruess S. Teaching medicine as a profession in the service of healing. *Acad Med* 72:941-52, 1997.
16. Kassirer J. Our endangered integrity—it can only get worse. *N Engl J Med* 336:1666-7, 1997.
17. Ibid #13, p. 358.
18. Mechanic D. Public perceptions of medicine. *N Engl J Med* 312:181-3, 1985.
19. Pescasolido B.A., Tuch S.A. & Martin J.A. The profession of medicine and the public: examining America's changing confidence in physician authority from the beginning of the "Health Care Crisis" to the era of health care reform. *J Health & Soc Behavior* 42(1):1-16, 2001.
20. Mycek S. We're not in Kansas anymore. Trustee 52:22, 1999.
21. Gray B. *The Profit Motive and Patient Care: The Changing Accountability of Doctors and Hospitals*. Cambridge: Harvard University Press, 1991.
22. Pierce E.C. Jr. The development of anesthesia guidelines and standards. *Q Rev Bull* 16(2):61-4, 1990.
23. Wasserman S.I., Kimball H.R. & Duffy F.D. Recertification in internal medicine: a program of continuous professional development. *Ann Int Med* 133(3):202-8, 2000.
24. Marks J.H. The silence of the doctors: medical professionals have colluded in coercive interrogation. Why aren't they pariahs in the field? *The Nation* 281(22):25-32, 2005.
25. Press release. Psychiatry applauds American Medical Association's new policy against physicians participating in interrogation. Statement of the American Psychiatric Association, the American Academy of Child and Adolescent Psychiatry, and the American Academy of Psychiatry and the Law. June 12, 2006.
26. Lurie H., Rich E.C. & Simpson D.E., et al. Pharmaceutical representatives in academic medical centers. *J Gen Intern Med* 5:240-43, 1990.
27. Orlowski J.P. & Wateska L. The effects of pharmaceutical firm enticements

on physician prescribing patterns: there's no such thing as a free lunch. *Chest* 102:270-73, 1992.

28. Chren M. M. & Landefeld C.S. Physicians' behavior and their interactions with drug companies. A controlled study of physicians who requested additions to a hospital drug formulary. *JAMA* 271:684-89, 1994.

29. Abelson R. Whistle-blower suit says device maker generously rewards doctors. *New York Times*, January 24, 2005:C1.

30. Abelson R. Hospitals see possible conflict on medical devices for doctors. *New York Times*, September 22, 2005:A1.

31. Dana J. & Lowenstein G. A social science perspective on gifts to physicians from industry. *JAMA* 290:752-5, 2003.

32. Choudry N.K., Stelfox H.T. & Detsky A.S. Relationships between authors of clinical practice guidelines and the pharmaceutical industry. *JAMA* 287(5):612-7, 2002.

33. Torry E.F. Big PhRMA buys psychiatry: An aura of scandal. *Health Letter* 18(7):1, 2002.

34. ACCME annual report data 2003. Chicago: Accreditation Council for Continuing Medical Education, 2003.

35. The Pharmaceutical Research and Manufacturers of America (PhRMA). HHS OIG compliance program guidance for the pharmaceutical industry: key insights from regulators and compliance experts. In: PhRMA Congress Conference, spring 2003, June 8-9, 2003, Washington, D.C.

36. Relman A.S. Separating continuing medical education from pharmaceutical marketing. JAMA 285(15):2009-12, 2001.

37. Campbell E.G., Weismann J.S., Clarridge B., Yucal R. & Causino N, et al. Characteristics of medical school faculty members serving on institutional review boards: results of a national survey. *Acad Med* 78(8):831-6, 2003.

38. Steinbrook R. Gag clauses in clinical-trial agreements. *N Engl J Med* 352:2160-2, 2005.

39. Baird P., Downie J. & Thompson J. Clinical trials and industry. *Science* 297:2211, 2002.

40. Bekelman J.E., Li Y., & Gross C.P. Scope and impact of financial conflict of interest in biomedical research: a systematic review. *JAMA* 289:454, 2003.

41. Lexchin J., Bero L.A., Djulbegovic B., & Clark O. Pharmaceutical industry sponsorship and research outcome and quality: A systematic review. *BMJ* 326:1167, 2003.

42. Rennie D. & Flanagin A. Authorship! Authorship! Guests, ghosts, grafters, and the two-sided coin. *JAMA* 271:469, 1994.

43. Pham H.H., Devers J.J., May J. H. & Berenson R. Financial pressures spur physician entrepreneurialism. *Health Aff* (Millwood) 23(2):70-81, 2004.

44. Pennachio D. L. Full-body scans—or scams? *Medical Economics*, August 9,

2002:62-71.
45. Moynihan E. Who pays for the Pizza? Redefining the relationships between doctors and drug companies, 2. Entanglements. *BMJ* 326:1189-92, 2003.
46. Schuster M., McGlynn E.A., & Brook R.H. How good is the quality of health care in the United States? *Milbank Q* 76(4):517-63, 1998.
47. Skinner J.S. & Fisher E.S. Regional disparities in Medicare expenditures: an opportunity for reform. *National Tax Journal* 50:413-25, 1997.
48. Fisher E.S., Wennberg D.E., Stukel T.A., Gottlieb D.J., et al. The implications of regional variations in Medicare spending. Part 1: The content, quality, and accessibility of care. *Ann Intern Med* 138(4):273-87, 2003.
49. Fisher E.S., Wennberg D.E., Stukel T.A., et al. The implications of regional variations in Medicare spending. Part 2: Health outcomes and satisfaction with care. *Ann Intern Med* 138(4):288-98, 2003.
50. Nadler E., Eckert B., & Neumann P. Do oncologists believe new cancer drugs offer good value? *The Oncologist* 11:90-5, 2006.
51. Medicare Payment Advisory Commission. Report to the Congress: Physician-Owned Specialty Hospitals. Washington, D.C.: MedPAC, March 8, 2005.
52. Guterman S. Specialty hospitals: a problem or a symptom? *Health Aff* (Millwood) 25(1):95-105, 2006.
53. Mitchell J. M. & Sunshine J. H. Consequences of physician ownership of health care facilities—joint ventures in radiation therapy. *N Engl J Med* 327:1497-501, 1992.
54. Mitchell J. M. & Sass T. R. Physician ownership of ancillary services: indirect demand inducement or quality assurance? J Health Econ 14:2631-89, 1995.
55. Bodenheimer T. Uneasy alliance: clinical investigators and the pharmaceutical industry. *N Engl J Med* 342:1539-44, 2000.
56. Ibid. #34.
57. Ibid. #36.
58. Studdert D. M., Mallo M. M. & Brennan T.A. Financial conflicts of interest in physicians' relationships with the pharmaceutical industry—self regulation in the shadow of federal prosecution. *N Engl J Med* 351(18):1891-1900, 2004.
59. Ibid. #37.
60. Steinbrook R. Gag clauses in clinical-trial agreements. *N Engl J Med* 352:2160-2, 2005.
61. Lo B., Wolf L.E. & Berkeley A. Conflict-of-interest policies for investigators in clinical trials. *N Engl J Med* 343:1616-, 2000.
62. Kassirer J. P. *On The Take: How Medicine's Complicity with Big Business Can Endanger Your Health.* New York: Oxford University Press, 207:2005.
63. Lotto D. L. The corporate takeover of the soul of healthcare. *J Psychohistory* 26(2):603-9, 1998.
64. Robinson J.C. *The Corporate Practice of Medicine: Competition and*

Innovation in Health Care. Berkeley: University of California Press, 1999.
65. Sullivan W. What is left of professionalism after managed care? The Hastings Center Report 29:7, 13, 1999.
66. Richmond J. B. & Eisenberg L. Correspondence. Medical professionalism in society. *N Engl J Med* 342(17):1288, 2000.
67. Pellegrino E.D., & Relman A.S. Professional medical associations: ethical and practical guidelines. *JAMA* 282(10):984, 1999.
68. Project of the ABIM Foundation. ACP-ASIM Foundation and European Federation of Internal Medicine. Medical professionalism in the new millennium: A physician charter. *Ann Intern Med* 136(3):243-46, 2002.
69. Kurlander J.E., Wynia M.K., & Morin K. The social contract model of professionalism: baby or bath water? *Am J Bioethics* 4(2):33-6, 2004.
70. Ibid. #13, p 361.
71. Pellegrino E.D. One hundred fifty years later. The moral status and relevance of the AMA code of ethics. In: Baker R.B., Caplan A.L., Emanuel L.L., & Lathan S.R. (eds). *The American Medical Ethics Revolution: How the AMAs Code of Ethics Has Transformed Physician's Relationships to Patients, Professionals, and Society*. Baltimore: Johns Hopkins Press, 1999: 107-8.
72. Cassel C.K. The challenge of serving both patient and populous. In: Baker R.B., Caplan A.L., Emanuel L.L. & Lathan S. R. (eds*). The American Medical Ethics Revolution: How the AMAs Code of Ethics Has Transformed Physician's Relationships to Patients, Professionals, and Society*. Baltimore: Johns Hopkins Press, 1999:250.

Chapter 15: Building a New Partnership with Public Health

1. Mullan F. Interview. David Satcher takes stock. *Health Aff* (Millwood) 21(6):161, 2002.
2. Baker E.L., Potter M.A., Jones D.L., Mercer S.L., et al. The public health infrastructure and our nation's health. *Annu Rev Public Health* 26:303-18, 2005.
3. Ibid #2, p. 314.
4. Ibid #2, pp 312-14.
5. Gebbie K., & Merrill J. Public health worker competencies for emergency response. *J Public Health Manage Pract* 8(3):73-81, 2002.
6. Public Health Code of Ethics. *Principles of the Ethical Practice of Public Health*, Version 2.2 @ 2002 Public Health Leadership Society. http://www.apha.org/programs/education/progeduethicalguidelines.htm.   Accessed February 2, 2007.
7. Thomas J.C., as cited in e-mail from Brown P. American Public Health Association, August 16, 2006.
8. The Institute for the Future. *Health and Health Care 2010: The Forecast, the*

Challenge (2nd ed). San Francisco: Jossey-Bass, 2003:168.

9. Weinstein K.J. Increased heart risk linked to air pollution. *Wall Street Journal*, February 1, 2007:D1.

10. Miller K.A., Siskovick D.S., Sheppard L. & Shepherd M.S., Sullivan J.H., et al. Long-term exposure to air pollution and incidence of cardiovascular events in women. *N Engl J Med* 356(5):447-58, 2007.

11. McKinnon J.D. White House order tightens grip on policy, stirs debate on controls. *Wall Street Journal*, January 31, 2005, A6.

12. Committee on Assuring the Health of the Public in the 21st Century. Institute of Medicine. *The Future of the Public's Health in the 21st Century*. Washington, D.C.: National Academy Press, 2002.

13. Shortell S.M., Weist E.M., Sow M.K., Foster A. & Tahir R. Implementing the Institute of Medicine's recommended curriculum content in Schools of Public Health: A baseline assessment. *Am J Public Health* 94(10):1671, 2004.

14. Iglehart J. Addressing both health and health care: An interview with Steven A. Schroeder. *Health Aff* (Millwood) 21(6):245, 2002.

15. Committee on Educating Public Health Professionals for the 21st Century. Institute of Medicine. *Who Will Keep the Public Healthy? Educating Health Professionals for the 21st Century.* Washington, D.C.: National Academy Press, 2003.

16. Ibid #13, 1671-4.

17. News and Notes – IOM: Overhaul of public health education needed. *Public Health Reports* 118:74, 2003.

18. Lurie N. The public health infrastructure: Rebuild or redesign? *Health Aff* (Millwood) 21(6):28-30, 2002.

19. Gebbie K., Merrill J. & Tilson H.H. The public health workforce. *Health Aff* (Millwood) 21(6):57-67, 2002.

20. Kahn L. H. A prescription for change: The need for qualified physician leadership in public health. *Health Aff* (Millwood) 22(4):241-7, 2003.

21. Assoc. State Territ. Health Off. *State Public Health Employee Worker Shortage Report: A Civil Service Recruitment and Retention Crisis*. Washington, D.C.: Assoc. State Terrir. Health Off, 2004.

22. Betancourt J.R., & King R.K. Guest editorial. Unequal treatment: The Institute of Medicine Report and its public health implications. *Public Health Reports* 118:287-92, 2003.

23. News and Notes. IOM: Overhaul of Government public health infrastructure, new partners needed. *Public Health Reports* 118:118-9, 2003.

24. Frenk J., Sepulveda J., Gomez-Dantes O., McGuinness M.J. & Knaul F. The new world order and international health. *BMJ* 314(7091): 1404-7, 1997.

Chapter 16: Medicine's Twin Crises as Opportunities to Lead

1. King M.L., Jr. Second National Convention for the Medical Committee for Human Rights, Chicago, IL, March 25, 1966, as cited in its Volunteer Manual, available at *http://www.crmvet.org/docs/mchr.htm*, accessed January 16, 2007.
2. Towards "Health Care for All" in the States. *Action for Universal Health Care* 14(1):January 2007.
3. Solomon D. & Maher K. Health care galvanizes key groups. *Wall Street Journal*, January 17, 2007:A10.
4. Dembner A. Sticker shock for state care plan. *The Boston Globe*, January 20, 2007.
5. Blue Cross of California. Tonik plans. Benefit summary list (T755). Enrollment guidelines. Available at *http://www.tonikplans.com/thrill_seeker_CA*,pdf. Accessed January 25, 2007.
6. Brin D.W. Wellpoint's costs rise, but 2007 targets stand. *Wall Street Journal*, January 25, 2007:C8.
7. Krugman P. On being partisan. *New York Times*, January 26, 2007:A19.
8. Campion F.D. The AMA and U.S. Health policy since 1940. Chicago: *Chicago Review Press*, 1984.
9. Marmor T.R. *The Politics of Medicare.* New York: Aldine Publishing Company, 1970, p 27-31.
10. Gordon C. *Dead on Arrival: The Politics of Health Care in Twentieth Century America.* Princeton: Princeton University Press, 2003, 25-28.
11. AMA Web site, *www.ama-assn.org*, accessed March 6, 2006.
12. Pellegrino E.D. One hundred fifty years later. The moral status and relevance of the AMA Code of Ethics, p 120. Presented at Symposium on Commercialism in Medicine. Program in Medicine & Human Values. San Francisco: California Pacific Medical Center, September 2005.
13. Welch H.G. & Fisher E.S. Let's make a deal: Negotiating a settlement between physicians and society. *N Engl J Med* 327(18):1315, 1992.
14. Stevens R. *American Medicine and the Public Interest: A History of Specialization.* Berkeley, CA: University of California Press, 1998, xxvi.

Credits for Tables and Figures

Table 2.1 Source: The global giants: amid market pain, U.S. companies hold greater sway. *Wall Street Journal*, October 14, 2002:R10.

Table 2.2 Reprinted with permission from: Gray B.E. (ed). *For-profit enterprise in health care: Supplementary statement on for-profit enterprise in health care.* Washington, D.C.: National Academy Press, 1986.

Table 2.3 Sources: Graef Crystal October 8, 2004 and Physicians for a National

Health Care Program, Chicago, IL.

Figure 3.1 Reprinted with permission from: Commonwealth Fund, Quality of health Care in the U.S. Chartbook, 2002.

Figure 3.2 Reprinted with permission from: Fisher E.S. & Welch H.G. Avoiding the unintended consequences of growth in medical care: How might more be worse? JAMA 281:466-53, 1999.

Table 4.1 Reprinted with permission from: The Institute for the Future, *Health and Health Care 2010: The Forecast, the Challenge* (2nd ed). San Francisco: Jossey-Bass, 2003:167

Table 4.2 Reprinted with permission from: The Institute for the Future. *Health and Health Care 2010: The Forecast, the Challenge* (2nd ed). San Francisco: Jossey-Bass, 2003:166.

Figure 4.1 Reprinted with permission from: The Institute for the Future. *Health and Health Care 2010: The Forecast, the Challenge* (2nd ed). San Francisco: Jossey-Bass, 2003:167.

Table 4.3 Reprinted with permission from: Institute of Medicine. *2020 Vision: Health in the 21st Century*. Washington, D.C.: National Academy Press, 1996:19.

Figure 5.1 Reprinted with permission from: Woolhandler S. & Himmelstein D.U. The National Health Program Slide-show Guide, Center for National Health Program Studies, Cambridge, Mass, 2000.

Figure 5.2 Reprinted with permission from: Born P. & Geckler C. HMO quality and Financial performance: Is there a connection? *J Health Care Finance* 24(2):69, 1998.

Figure 5.3 Reprinted with permission from: Dobson A., Da Venzo J. & Sen N. The cost-shift payment hydraulic: Foundation, history, and implications. *Health Aff* (Millwood) 25(1):24, 2006.

Figure 6.1 Reprinted with permission from: Henderson N. Greenspan's mixed legacy: America prospered during the Fed chief's tenure, but built up massive dept. *Washington Post National Weekly Edition*. January 30-February 5, 2006, p 6.

Figure 6.2 Reprinted with permission from: Roubideaux Y. Beyond Red Lake-The persistent crisis in American Indian health care. *N Engl J Med* 353(18):1882, 2005.

Figure 6.3 Reprinted with permission from: Kaufman M. & Stein R. What's ailing us? Health care costs rise to a record 16 percent of nation's economic output. *Washington Post National Weekly Edition*, January 16-22, 2006:p21.

Figure 7.1 Reprinted with permission from: Guldin B. How to earn millions after Congress: Become a lobbyist and cash in. *Public Citizen News* July/August 2005, p 7.

Figure 8.1 Reprinted with permission from: Bekelman J.E., et al. Scope and impact of financial conflict of interest in biomedical research. JAMA 289:459, 2003.

Table 9.1 Sources: Coyle S.L. Physician-industry relations. 1. Individual physicians. Ann Intern Med 136:396-402, 2002; and Accreditation Council for Continuing Medical Education. *Standards for commercial support of continuing medical education.* Accessed October 7, 2004, at http://www.accme.org/inconting/17_systems98_essential.areas. pdf.

Table 9.2 Source: Studdert D.M., Mallo M.M. & Brennan T.A. Financial conflicts of interest in physicians' relationships with the pharmaceutical industry-self regulation in the shadow of federal prosecution. *N Engl J Med* 351(18):1891-1900, 2004.

Figure 10.1 Reprinted with permission from Grumbach K., Osmond D., Vranizan K., Jaffe D. & Bindman A.B. Primary care physicians' experience of financial incentives in managed care systems. *N Engl J Med* 339:1516-21, 1998.

Figure 10.2 Reprinted with permission from: Woolhandler S. & Himmelstein D. U. The National Health Program Slide-show Guide, Center for National Health Program Studies, Cambridge, Mass, 2000.

Table 10.1 Source: Lowes R. Medical Economics 2005 Continuing Survey. The earnings freeze: now it's everybody's problem. *Medical Economics*, September 16, 2005, 59.

Figure 10.3 Sources: Physician compensation and production Survey, Medical Group Management Association, Englewood, Colo, 2000; and compensation Monitor. *Managed Care Magazine.* Available at http://www.managedcaremag.com/archives/0103/0103. compinon.html. Accessed on January 11, 2006.

Table 10.2 Source: Hoff T.J. Physician unionization in the United States: Fad or phenomenon? JHHSA, summer, 2000:5-23.

Table 11.1 Adapted with permission from: Committee on the Consequences of Uninsurance. *Insuring America's Health: Principles and Recommendations.* Institute of Medicine. Washington, D.C.: National Academy Press, 2004:152.

Table 11.2 Adapted with permission from: Geyman J. P. Drawing on the legacy of general practice to build the future of family medicine. *Fam Med* 36(9):631-8, 2004.

Table 12.1 Source: Project Report. *The Goals of Medicine: Setting New Priorities: Special Supplement.* Hastings Center Report, November-December, 1996: S23-5.

Table 12.2 Source: Project Report. *The Goals of Medicine: Setting New Priorities*: Special Supplement. Hastings Center Report, November-December, 1996: S23-5.

Figure 12.1 Reprinted with permission from: Hadley et al. Federal Sending on the Health Care Safety Net from 2001-1004: Has Spending Kept Pace with the Growth in the Uninsured? KCMU, November 2005, Publication #7425.

This information was reprinted with permission from Henry J. Kaiser Family Foundation. The Kaiser Family Foundation, based in Menlo Park, California, is a nonprofit, private operating foundation focusing on the major health care issues facing the nation and is not associated with Kaiser Permanente or Kaiser Industries.

Figure 12.2 Adapted with permission from: Institute for the Future. *Health and Health Care 2010: The Forecast, the Challenges.* San Francisco: Jossey-Bass, 2000: Appendix.

Figure 13.1 Reprinted with permission from: Schlesinger M. A loss of faith: The sources of reduced political legitimacy for the American medical profession. *The Milbank Q* 80(2):185-235. 2002.

Figure 13.2 Source: Reprinted with permission from Kaiser Family Foundation. The public on health care costs: Perceived reasons for rising health care costs. Accessed May 25, 2006 at www.Kff.org/spotlight/heal hcosts/index.cfm. This information was reprinted with permission from the Henry J. Kaiser Family Foundation. The Kaiser Family Foundation, based in Menlo Park, California, is a non-profit, private operating foundation focusing on the major health care issues facing the nation and is not associated with Kaiser Permanente or Kaiser Industries.

Table 14.1 Source: Cruess R., Cruess S. & Johnston S. Renewing professionalism: an opportunity for medicine. Acad Med 74:880, 1999.

Table 14.2 Source: Project of the ABIM Foundation. ACP-ASIM Foundation and European Federation of Internal Medicine. Medical professionalism in the new millennium: A physician charter. Ann Intern Med 136(3):244, 2002

Table 14.3 Source: Kurlander J.E., Wynia M.K. & Morin K. The social contract model of professionalism: baby or bath water? Am J Bioethics 4(2):33-6, 2004.

Table 15.2 Reprinted with permission from: The Institute for the Future. *Health and Health Care 2010: The Forecast, the Challenge* (2nd ed). San Francisco: Jossey-Bass, 2003:168.

Table 16.1 Source: Towards "Health Care for All" in the States. Action for Universa Health Care 14(1): January 2007.

Figure 16.1 Sources: *Employer Health Benefits 2006 Annual Survey – Chartpack* (#7561). The Henry J. Kaiser Family Foundation and Health Research & Educational Trust, September 2006. This information was reprinted with permission from the Henry J. Kaiser Family Foundation. The Kaiser Family Foundation, based in Menlo Park, California, is a non-profit, private operating foundation focusing on the major health care issues facing the nation and is not associated with kaiser Permanente or Kaiser Industries.

Figure 16.2 Reprinted with permission from: Graham Center One-Pager. Who will have health insurance in 2025? Am Fam Physician 72(10:1989, 2005.

Index

About the Author

John Geyman, MD is Professor Emeritus of Family Medicine at the University of Washington School of Medicine in Seattle, where he served as Chairman of the Department of Family Medicine from 1976 to 1990. As a family physician with over 25 years in academic medicine, he has also practiced in rural communities for 13 years. He was the founding editor of *The Journal of Family Practice* (1973 to 1990) and the editor of *The Journal of the American Board of Family Practice* from 1990 to 2003. His most recent books are *Health Care in America: Can Our Ailing System Be Healed?* (Butterworth-Heinemann, 2002), *The Corporate Transformation of Health Care: Can the Public Interest Still Be Served?* (Springer Publishing Company, 2004), *Falling Through the Safety Net: Americans Without Health Insurance* (Common Courage Press, 2005) and *Shredding the Social Contract: The Privatization of Medicare* (Common Courage Press, 2006). Dr. Geyman served as President of Physicians for a National Health Program from 2005 to 2007 and is a member of the Institute of Medicine.

Also from Common Courage Press

Falling Through the Safety Net

Americans Without Health Insurance

John Geyman, M.D.

This is a most important book by one of America's leading experts. We are paying dearly in health system inefficiency and unnecessary pain and suffering because of the cracks in our safety net. Without attention to this issue as illustrated in this text, we will never eliminate disparities in health among different racial and ethnic groups in this nation.

—David Satcher, 16th U. S. Surgeon General,
Director, National Center for Primary Care at Morehouse School of Medicine

A compelling description of our dysfunctional health care system, a reasoned analysis of its problems, and a persuasive argument for a single-payer insurance plan as the best solution—written by someone with real understanding and first-hand experience. A much-needed lesson that ought to change a lot of minds. I recommend it strongly.

—Marcia Angell, M. D.,
Senior Lecturer in Social Medicine, Harvard Medical School,
Former Editor-in-Chief, *New England Journal of Medicine*

Once again, the legendary master of family medicine addresses with clinical compassion the widespread concerns about "unsurance" and uncovered medical costs. Geyman's well-researched recommendations should be read by everyone.

—Donald Light, Professor of Comparative
Health Care Systems, Princeton University

224 pages, $18.95, ISBN 1-56751-254-2
Publication date 2005

Common Courage Press
PO Box 702
Monroe, ME 04951
1-800-497-3207   fax 207-525-3068

www.commoncouragepress.com

Shredding the Social Contract

The Privatization of Medicare

John Geyman, M.D.

"Dr. Geyman is a modern-day Paul Revere. He warns America—with a stirring mixture of evidence and passion—of the wrecking ball the apostles of greed are taking to Medicare, national treasure under attack."

—Robert Hayes
President, Medicare Rights Center

The largest safety net for both seniors and disabled Americans is about to be further "privatized" which, Dr. John Geyman reveals, will be its destruction, unless we act now. " John Geyman has written a trenchant and timely contribution to the important debate on the future of Medicare—a debate that should engage families as well as policymakers."

—Christine K. Cassel, M.D.
President, American Board of Internal Medicine

"The Medicare program is in trouble. The problem is how to fix it. Many politicians advocate further privatization. John Geyman comprehensively and persuasively reviews the evidence, including both published research and the experiences of many of Medicare's beneficiaries, to show that this is the wrong solution. We need a renewed commitment to the original vision of social insurance on which the program was based."

—Timothy Stoltzfus Jost,
Professor, Washington and Lee University Law School

"A valuable counterweight to claptrap about 'modernizing Medicare' when undermining its traditional character is the aim. Historically informed, passionately argued, and valuable to everyone."

—Ted Marmor, author of *The Politics of Medicare*

322 pages, $16.95, ISBN 1-56751-376-x
Publication date 2006

Common Courage Press
PO Box 702
Monroe, ME 04951
1-800-497-3207   fax 207-525-3068
www.commoncouragepress.com